The System of

the Laws of the Moral and

Physical World.

(Volume II)

baron d' Paul Henri Thiry Holbach

Alpha Editions

This edition published in 2024

ISBN : 9789366382067

Design and Setting By
Alpha Editions
www.alphaedis.com
Email - info@alphaedis.com

As per information held with us this book is in Public Domain.
This book is a reproduction of an important historical work. Alpha Editions uses the best technology to reproduce historical work in the same manner it was first published to preserve its original nature. Any marks or number seen are left intentionally to preserve its true form.

Contents

PART II..- 1 -

ON THE DIVINITY:—PROOFS OF
HIS EXISTENCE:—OF HIS
ATTRIBUTES: OF HIS INFLUENCE
OVER THE HAPPINESS OF MAN. ....- 1 -

CHAP. I...- 3 -

The Origin of Man's Ideas upon the
Divinity. ....- 3 -

CHAP. II. ....- 23 -

Of Mythology, and Theology. ....- 23 -

CHAP. III. ....- 41 -

Of the confused and contradictory
Ideas of Theology. ....- 41 -

CHAP. IV..- 61 -

CHAP. V. ....- 91 -

CHAP. VI..- 113 -

Of Pantheism; or of the Natural Ideas
of the Divinity. ....- 113 -

CHAP. VII. ....- 129 -

Of Theism.—Of the System of
Optimism.—Of final Causes..- 129 -

CHAP. VIII. ....- 151 -

CHAP. IX. ....- 173 -

CHAP. X. ....- 191 -

CHAP. XI. ....- 207 -

CHAP. XII. ....- 219 -

Is what is termed Atheism compatible
with Morality?...- 219 -

CHAP. XIII. ....- 233 -

CHAP. XIV. ....- 260 -

A Summary of the Code of Nature. ....- 260 -

[TRANSLATOR'S APPENDIX].......................................- 272 -

PART II.

ON THE DIVINITY:—PROOFS OF HIS EXISTENCE:—OF HIS ATTRIBUTES: OF HIS INFLUENCE OVER THE HAPPINESS OF MAN.

CHAP. I.

The Origin of Man's Ideas upon the Divinity.

If man possessed the courage, if he had the requisite industry to recur to the source of those opinions which are most deeply engraven on his brain; if he rendered to himself a faithful account of the reasons which make him hold these opinions as sacred; if he coolly examined the basis of his hopes, the foundation of his fears, he would find that it very frequently happens, those objects, or those ideas which move him most powerfully, either have no real existence, or are words devoid of meaning, which terror has conjured up to explain some sudden disaster; that they are often phantoms engendered by a disordered imagination, modified by ignorance; the effect of an ardent mind distracted by contending passions, which prevent him from either reasoning justly, or consulting experience in his judgment; that this mind often labours with a precipitancy that throws his intellectual faculties into confusion; that bewilders his ideas; that consequently he gives a substance and a form to chimeras, to airy nothings, which he afterwards idolizes from sloth, reverences from prejudice.

A sensible being placed in a nature where every part is in motion, has various feelings, in consequence of either the agreeable or disagreeable effects which he is obliged to experience from this continued action and re-action; in consequence he either finds himself happy or miserable; according to the quality of the sensations excited in him, he will love or fear, seek after or fly from, the real or supposed causes of such marked effects operated on his machine. But if he is ignorant of nature, if he is destitute of experience, he will frequently deceive himself as to these causes; for want of either capability or inclination to recur back to them, he will neither have a true knowledge of their energy, nor a clear idea of their mode of acting: thus until reiterated experience shall have formed his ideas, until the mirror of truth shall have shewn him the judgment he ought to make, he will be involved in trouble, a prey to incertitude, a victim to credulity.

Man is a being who brings with him nothing into the world save an aptitude to feeling in a manner more or less lively according to his individual organization: he has no innate knowledge of any of the causes that act upon him: by degrees his faculty of feeling discovers to him their various qualities; he learns to judge of them; time familiarizes him with their properties; he attaches ideas to them, according to the manner in which they have affected him; these ideas are correct or otherwise, in a ratio to the soundness of his organic structure: his judgment is faulty or not, as these organs are either well or ill-constituted; in proportion as they are competent to afford him sure and reiterated experience.

The first moments of man are marked by his wants; that is to say, the first impulse he receives is to conserve his existence; this he would not be able to maintain without the concurrence of many analogous causes: these wants in a sensible being, manifest themselves by a general languor, a sinking, a confusion in his machine, which gives him the consciousness of a painful sensation: this derangement subsists, is even augmented, until the cause suitable to remove it re-establishes the harmony so necessary to the existence of the human frame. Want, therefore, is the first evil man experiences; nevertheless it is requisite to the maintenance of his existence. Was it not for this derangement of his body, which obliges him to furnish its remedy, he would not be warned of the necessity of preserving the existence he has received. Without wants man would be an insensible machine, similar to a vegetable; like that he would be incapable of preserving himself; he would not be competent to using the means required to conserve his being. To his wants are to be ascribed his passions; his desires; the exercise of his corporeal functions; the play of his intellectual faculties: they are his wants that oblige him to think; that determine his will, that induce him to act; it is to satisfy them or rather to put an end to the painful sensations excited by their presence, that according to his capacity, to the natural sensibility of his soul, to the energies which are peculiar to himself, he gives play to his faculties, exerts the activity of his bodily strength, or displays the extensive powers of his mind. His wants being perpetual, he is obliged to labour without relaxation, to procure objects competent to satisfy them. In a word, it is owing to his multiplied wants that man's energy is kept in a state of continual activity: as soon as he ceases to have wants, he falls into inaction—becomes listless—declines into apathy—sinks into a languor that is incommodious to his feelings or prejudicial to his existence: this lethargic state of weariness lasts until new wants, by giving him fresh activity, rouse his dormant faculties—throw off his stupor—re-animate his vigour, and destroy the sluggishness to which he had become a prey.

From hence it will be obvious that evil is necessary to man; without it he would neither be in a condition to know that which injures him; to avoid its presence; or to seek his own welfare: without this stimulus, he would differ in nothing from insensible, unorganized beings: if those evanescent evils which he calls *wants*, did not oblige him to call forth his faculties, to set his energies in motion, to cull experience, to compare objects, to discriminate them, to separate those which have the capabilities to injure him, from those which possess the means to benefit him, he would be insensible to happiness—inadequate to enjoyment. In short, *without evil man would be ignorant of good*; he would be continually exposed to perish like the leaf on a tree. He would resemble an infant, who, destitute of experience, runs the risque of meeting his destruction at every step he takes, unguarded by his nurse. What the nurse is to the child, experience is to the adult; when either are wanting, these children of different lustres generally go astray: frequently encounter disaster. Without evil he would be unable to judge of any thing; he would have no preference; his will would be without volition, he would be destitute of passions; desire would find no place in his heart; he would not revolt at the most disgusting objects; he would not strive to put them away; he would neither have stimuli to love, nor motives to fear any thing; he would be an insensible automaton; he would no longer be a man.

If no evil had existed in this world, man would never have dreamt of those numerous divinities, to whom he has rendered such various modes of worship. If nature had permitted him easily to satisfy all his regenerating wants, if she had given him none but agreeable sensations, his days would have uninterruptedly rolled on in one perpetual uniformity; he would never have discovered his own nakedness; he would never have had motives to search after the unknown causes of things—to meditate in pain. Therefore man, always contented, would only have occupied himself with satisfying his wants; with enjoying the present, with feeling the influence of objects, that would unceasingly warn him of his existence in a mode that he must necessarily approve; nothing would alarm his heart; every thing would be analogous to his existence: he would neither know fear, experience distrust, nor have inquietude for the future: these feelings can only be the consequence of some troublesome sensation, which must have anteriorly affected him, or which by disturbing the harmony of his machine, has interrupted the course of his happiness; which has shewn him he is naked.

Independent of those wants which in man renew themselves every instant; which he frequently finds it impossible to satisfy; every individual experiences a multiplicity of evils—he suffers from the inclemency of the seasons—he pines in penury—he is infected with plague—he is scourged by war—he is the victim of famine—he is afflicted with disease—he is the sport of a thousand accidents, &c. This is the reason why all men are fearful; why the whole human race are diffident. The knowledge he has of pain alarms him upon all unknown causes, that is to say, upon all those of which he has not yet experienced the effect; this experience made with precipitation, or if it be preferred, by instinct, places him on his guard against all those objects from the operation of which he is ignorant what consequences may result to himself.

His inquietude is in proportion; his fears keep pace with the extent of the disorder which these objects produce in him; they are measured by their rarity, that is to say, by the inexperience he has of them; by the natural sensibility of the soul; and by the ardour of his imagination. The wore ignorant man is, the less experience he has, the more he is susceptible of fear; solitude, the obscurity of a forest, silence, and the darkness of night, desolate ruins, the roaring of the wind, sudden, confused noises, are objects of terror to all who are unaccustomed to these things. The uninformed man is a child whom every thing astonishes; who trembles at every thing he encounters: his alarms disappear, his fears diminish, his mind becomes calm, in proportion as experience familiarizes him, more or less, with natural effects; his fears cease entirely, as soon as he understands, or believes he understands, the causes that act; or when he knows how to avoid their effects. But if he cannot penetrate the causes which disturb him, if he cannot discover the agents by whom he suffers, if he cannot find to what account to place the confusion he experiences, his inquietude augments; his fears redouble; his imagination leads him astray; it exaggerates his evil; paints in a disorderly manner these unknown objects of his terror; magnifies their powers; then making an analogy between them and those terrific objects, with whom he is already acquainted, he suggests to himself the means he usually takes to mitigate their anger; to conciliate their kindness; he employs similar measures to soften the anger, to disarm the power, to avert the effects of the concealed cause which gives birth to his inquietudes, which fills him with anxiety, which alarms his fears. It is thus his weakness, aided by ignorance, renders him superstitious.

There are very few men, even in our own day, who have sufficiently studied nature, who are fully apprised of physical causes, or with the effects they must necessarily produce. This ignorance, without doubt, was much greater in the more remote ages of the world, when the human mind, yet in its infancy, had not collected that experience, taken that expansion, made those strides towards improvement, which distinguishes the present from the past. Savages dispersed, erratic, thinly scattered up and down, knew the course of nature either very imperfectly or not at all; society alone perfects human knowledge: it requires not only multiplied but combined efforts to unravel the secrets of nature. This granted, all natural causes were mysteries to our wandering ancestors; the entire of nature was an enigma to them; all its phenomena was marvellous, every event inspired terror to beings who were destitute of experience; almost every thing, they saw must have appeared to them strange, unusual, contrary to their idea of the order of things.

It cannot then furnish matter for surprise, if we behold men in the present day trembling at the sight of those objects which have formerly filled their fathers with dismay. *Eclipse, comets, meteors*, were, in ancient days, subjects of alarm to all the people of the earth: these effects, so natural in the eyes of the sound philosopher, who has by degrees fathomed their true causes, have yet the right, possess the power, to alarm the most numerous, to excite the fears of the least instructed part of modern nations. The people of the present day, as well as their ignorant ancestors, find something marvellous, believe there is a supernatural agency in all those objects to which their eyes are unaccustomed; they consider all those unknown causes as wonderful, that act with a force of which their mind has no idea it is possible the known agents are capable. The ignorant see wonders *prodigies, miracles*, in all those striking effects of which they are unable to render themselves a satisfactory account; all the causes which produce them they think *supernatural*; this, however, really implies nothing more than that they are not familiar to them, or that they have not hitherto witnessed natural agents, whose energy was equal to the production of effects so rare, so astonishing, as those with which their sight has been appalled.

Besides the ordinary phenomena to which nations were witnesses without being competent to unravel the causes, they have in times very remote from ours, experienced calamities, whether general or local, which filled them with the most cruel inquietude; which plunged them into an abyss of consternation. The traditions of all people, the annals of all nations, recal, even at this day, melancholy events, physical disasters, dreadful catastrophes, which had the effect of spreading universal terror among our forefathers, But when history should be silent on these stupendous revolutions, would not our own reflection on what passes under our eyes be sufficient to convince us, that all parts of our globe have been, and following the course of things, will necessarily be again violently agitated, overturned, changed, overflowed, in a state of conflagration? Vast continents have been inundated, seas breaking their limits have usurped the dominion of the earth; at length retiring, these waters have left striking, proofs of their presence, by the marine vestiges of shells, skeletons of sea fish, &c. which the attentive observer meets with at every step, in the bowels of those fertile countries we now inhabit—subterraneous fires have opened to themselves the most frightful volcanoes, whose craters frequently issue destruction on every side. In short, the elements unloosed, have at various times, disputed among themselves the empire of our globe; this exhibits evidence of the fact, by those vast heaps of wreck, those stupendous ruins spread over its surface. What, then, must have been the fears of mankind, who in those countries believed he beheld the entire of nature armed against his peace, menacing with destruction his very abode? What must have been the inquietude of a people taken thus unprovided, who fancied they saw nature cruelly labouring to their annihilation? Who beheld a world ready to be dashed into atoms; who witnessed the earth suddenly rent asunder; whose yawning chasm was the grave of large cities, whole provinces, entire nations? What ideas must mortals, thus overwhelmed with terror, form to themselves of the irresistible cause that could produce such extended effects? Without doubt they did not attribute these wide spreading calamities to nature; neither did they conceive they were mere physical causes; they could not suspect she was the author, the accomplice of the confusion she herself experienced; they did not see that these tremendous revolutions, these overpowering disorders, were the necessary result of her immutable laws; that they contributed to the general order by which she subsists; that, in point of fact, there was nothing more surprising in the inundation of large portions of the earth, in the swallowing up an entire nation, in a volcanic conflagration spreading destruction over whole provinces, than there is in a stone falling to the earth, or the death of a fly; that each equally has its spring in the necessity of things.

It was under these astounding circumstances, that nations, bathed in the most bitter tears, perplexed with the most frightful visions, electrified with terror, not believing there existed on this mundane ball, causes sufficiently powerful to operate the gigantic phenomena that filled their minds with dismay, carried their streaming eyes towards heaven, where their tremulous fears led them to suppose these unknown agents, whose unprovoked enmity destroyed, their earthly felicity, could alone reside.

It was in the lap of ignorance, in the season of alarm, in the bosom of calamity, that mankind ever formed his first notions of the *Divinity*. From hence it is obvious that his ideas on this subject are to be suspected, that his notions are in a great measure false, that they are always afflicting. Indeed, upon whatever part of our sphere we cast our eyes, whether it be upon the frozen climates of the north, upon the parching regions of the south, or under the more temperate zones, we every where behold the people when assailed by misfortunes, have either made to themselves national gods, or else have adopted those which have been given them by their conquerors; before these beings, either of their own creation or adoption, they have tremblingly prostrated themselves in the hour of calamity, soliciting relief; have ignorantly attributed to blocks of stone, or to men like themselves, those natural effects which were above their comprehension; the inhabitants of many nations, not contented with the national gods, made each to himself one or more gods, which he supposed presided exclusively over his own household, from whom he supposed he derived his own peculiar happiness, to whom he attributed all his domestic misfortunes. The idea of these powerful agents, these supposed distributors of good and evil, was always associated with that of terror; their name was never pronounced without recalling to man's wind either his own particular calamities or those of his fathers. In many places man trembles at this day, because his progenitors have trembled for thousands of years past. The thought of his gods always awakened in man the most afflicting ideas. If he recurred to the source of his actual fears, to the commencement of those melancholy impressions that stamp themselves in his mind when their name is announced, he would find it in the conflagrations, in the revolutions, in those extended disasters, that have at various times destroyed large portions of the human race; that overwhelmed with dismay those miserable beings who escaped the destruction of the earth; these in transmitting to posterity, the tradition of such afflicting events, have also transmitted to him their fears; have delivered down to their successors, those gloomy ideas which their bewildered imaginations, coupled with their barbarous ignorance of natural causes, had formed to them of the anger of their irritated gods, to which their alarm falsely attributed these sweeping disasters.

If the gods of nations had their birth in the bosom of alarm, it was again in that of despair that each individual formed the unknown power that he made exclusively for himself. Ignorant of physical causes, unpractised in their mode of action, unaccustomed to their effects, whenever he experienced any serious misfortune, whenever he was afflicted with any grievous sensation, he was at a loss how to account for it; he therefore attributed it to his household gods, to whom he made an immediate supplication for assistance, or rather for forbearance of further affliction: this disposition in man has been finely pourtrayed by Aesop in his fable of "the Waggoner and Hercules." The motion which in despight of himself was excited in his machine, his diseases, his troubles, his passions, his inquietude, the painful alterations his frame underwent, without his being able to fathom the true causes; at length death, of which the aspect in so formidable to a being strongly attached to existence, were effects he looked upon either as supernatural, or else he conceived they were repugnant to his actual nature; he attributed them to some mighty cause, which maugre all his efforts, disposed of him at each, moment. Thus palsied with alarm, benumbed with terror, he pensively meditated upon his sorrows; agitated with fear, he sought for means to avert the calamities that threatened him with destruction; his imagination, thus rendered desperate by his endurance of evils which he found inevitable, formed to him those phantoms which he called gods; before whom he trembled from a consciousness of his own weakness; thus disposed, he endeavoured by prostration, by sacrifices, by prayers, to disarm the anger of these imaginary beings to which his trepidation had given birth; whom he ignorantly imagined to be the cause of his misery, whom his fancy painted to him as endowed with the power of alleviating his sufferings: it was thus in the extremity of his grief, in the exacerbation of his mind, weighed down with misfortune, that unhappy man fashioned those chimeras which filled him with the most gloomy ideas, which he transmitted to his posterity, as the surest means of avoiding the evils to which he had been himself subjected.

Man never judges of those objects of which he is ignorant, but through the medium of those which come within his knowledge: thus man, taking himself for the model, ascribed will, intelligence, design, projects, passions; in a word, qualities analogous to his own, to all those unknown causes of which he experienced the action. As soon as a visible or supposed cause affects him in an agreeable manner, or in a mode favourable to his existence, he concludes it to be good, to be well intentioned towards him: on the contrary, he judges all those to be bad in their nature, evilly disposed, to have the intention of injuring him, which cause him any painful sensations. He attributes views, plans, a system of conduct like his own, to every thing which to his limited ideas appears of itself to produce connected effects; to act with regularity; to constantly operate in the same manner; that uniformly produces the same sensations in his own person. According to these notions, which he always borrows from himself, from his own peculiar mode of action, he either loves or fears those objects which have affected him; he in consequence approaches them with confidence or timidity; seeks after them or flies from them in proportion as the feelings they have excited are either pleasant or painful. Having travelled thus far, he presently addresses them; he invokes their aid; prays to them for succour; conjures them to cease his afflictions; to forbear tormenting him; as he finds himself sensible to presents, pleased with submission, he tries to win them to his interests by humiliation, by sacrifices; he exercises towards them the hospitality he himself loves; he gives them an asylum; he builds them a dwelling; he furnishes them with costly raiment; he makes their altars smoke with delicious food; he proffers to their acceptance the earliest flowers of spring; the finest fruits of autumn; the rich grain of summer; in short he sets before them all those things which he thinks will please them the most, because he himself places the highest value on them. These dispositions enable us to account for the formation of tutelary gods, of lares, of larvae, which every man makes to himself in savage and unpolished nations. Thus we perceive that weak superstitious mortals, ignorant of truth, devoid of experience, regard as the arbiters of their fate, as the dispensers of good and evil, animals, stones, unformed inanimate substances, which the effort of their heated imaginations transform into gods, whom they invest with intelligence, whom they clothe with desires, to whom they give volition.

Another disposition which serves to deceive the savage man, which will equally deceive those whom reason shall not enlighten on these subjects, is his attachment to omens; or the fortuitous concurrence of certain effects, with causes which have not produced them; the co-existence of these effects with certain causes, which have not the slightest connection with them, has frequently led astray very intelligent beings; nations who considered themselves very enlightened; who have either been disinclined or unable to disentangle the one from the other: thus the savage attributes bounty or the will to render him service, to any object whether animate or inanimate, such as a stone of a certain form, a rock, a mountain, a tree, a serpent, an owl, &c. if every time he encounters these objects in a certain position, it should so happen that he is more than ordinarily successful in hunting, that he should take an unusual quantity of fish, that he should be victorious in war, or that he should compass any enterprize whatever that he may at that moment undertake: the same savage will be quite as gratuitous in attaching malice, wickedness, the determination to injure him, to either the same object in a different position, or any others in a given posture, which way have met his eyes on those days when he shall have suffered some grievous accident, have been very unsuccessful in his undertakings, unfortunate in the chace, disappointed in his draught of fish: incapable of reasoning he connects these effects with causes, that reflection would convince him have nothing in common with each other; that are entirely due to physical causes, to necessary circumstances, over which neither himself nor his omens have the least controul: nevertheless he finds it much easier to attribute them to these imaginary causes; he therefore *deifies* them; looks upon them as either his guardian angels, or else as his most inveterate enemies. Having invested them with supernatural powers, he becomes anxious to explain to himself their mode of action; his self-love prevents his seeking elsewhere for the model: thus he assigns them all those motives that actuate himself; he endows them with passions; he gives them design—intelligence—will—imagines they can either injure him or benefit him, as he may render them propitious or otherwise to his views: he ends with worshipping them; with paying them divine honours; he appoints them priests; or at least always consults them before he undertakes any object of moment: such is their influence, that if they put on the evil position, he will lay aside the most important undertaking. The savage in this is never more than an infant, that is angry with the object that displeases him; just like the dog who gnaws the stone by which he has been wounded, without recurring to the hand by which it was thrown.

Such is the foundation of man's faith, in either happy or unhappy omens: devoid of experience, unaccustomed to reason with precision, fearing to call in the evidence of truth, he looks upon them either as gods themselves, or else as warnings given him by his other gods, to whom he attributes the faculties of sagacity and foresight, of which he is himself miserably deficient. Ignorance, when involved in disaster, when immersed in trouble, believes a stone, a reptile, a bird, much better instructed than himself. The slender observation of the ignorant only serves to render him more superstitious; he sees certain birds announce by their flight, by their cries, certain changes in the weather, such as cold, heat, rain, storms; he beholds at certain periods, vapours arise from the bottom of some particular caverns? there needs nothing further to impress upon him the belief, that these beings possess the knowledge of future events; enjoy the gifts of prophecy: he looks upon them as supernatural agents, employed by his gods: it is thus he becomes the dupe to his own credulity.

If by degrees the truth flashing occasionally on his mind, experience and reflection arrive at undeceiving him, with respect to the power, the intelligence, the virtues actually residing in these objects; he at least supposes them put in activity by some secret, some hidden cause; that they are the instruments, employed by some invisible agent, who is either friendly or inimical to his welfare. To this concealed agent, therefore, he addresses himself; pays him his vows; emplores his assistance; deprecates his wrath; seeks to propitiate him to his interests; is willing to soften his anger; for this purpose he employs the same means, of which he avails himself, either to appease or gain over the beings of his own species.

Societies in their origin, seeing themselves frequently afflicted by nature, supposed either the elements, or the concealed powers who regulated them, possessed a will, views, wants, desires, similar to their own. From hence, the sacrifices imagined to nourish them; the libations poured out to them; the steams, the incense to gratify their olfactory nerves. Their superstition led them to believe these elements or their irritated movers were to be appeased like irritated man, by prayers, by humiliation, by presents. Their imagination was ransacked to discover the presents that would be most acceptable in their eyes; to ascertain the oblations that would be most agreeable, the sacrifices that would most surely propitiate their kindness: as these did not make known their inclinations, man differed with his fellow on those most suitable; each followed his own disposition; or rather each offered what was most estimable in his own eyes; hence arose differences never to be reconciled the bitterest animosities; the most unconquerable aversions; the most, destructive jealousies! Thus some brought the fruits of the earth, others offered sheaves of corn: some strewed flowers over their fanes; some decorated them with the most costly jewels; some served them with meats; others sacrificed lambs, heifers, bulls; at length such was their delirium, such the wildness of their imaginations, that they stained their altars with human gore, made oblations of young children immolated virgins, to appease the anger of these supposed deities.

The old men, as having the most experience, were usually charged with the conduct of these peace-offerings, from whence, the name PRIEST; [Greek letters], *presbos*, in the Greek meaning an old man. These accompanied them with ceremonies, instituted rites, used precautions by consulting omens; adopted formalities, retraced to their fellow citizens the notions transmitted to them by their forefathers; collected the observations made by their ancestors; repeated the fables they had received; added commentaries of their own; subjoined supplications to the idols at whose shrine they were sacrificing. It is thus the sacerdotal order was established; thus that public worship was established; by degrees each community formed a body of tenets to be observed by the citizens; these were transmitted from race to race; held sacred out of reverence for their fathers; at length it was deemed sacrilege to doubt these pandects in any one particular; even the errors, that had crept into them with time, were beheld with reverential awe; he that ventured to reason upon them, was looked upon as an enemy to the commonwealth; as one whose impiety drew down upon them the vengeance of these adored beings, to which alone imagination had given birth; not contented with adopting the rituals, with following the ceremonies invented by themselves, one community waged war against another, to oblige it to receive their particular creeds; which the old men who regulated them, declared would infallibly win them the favor of their tutelary deities: thus very often to conciliate their favor, the victorious party immolated on the altars of their gods, the bodies of their unhappy captives; frequently they carried their savage barbarity the length of exterminating whole nations, who happened to worship gods different from their own: thus it frequently happened, that the friends of the serpent, when victorious, covered his altars with the mangled carcases of the worshippers of the stone, whom the fortune of war had placed in their hands: such were the unformed, the precarious elements of which rude nations every where availed themselves to compose their superstitions: they were always a system of conduct invented by imagination: conceived in ignorance, organized in misfortune, to render the unknown powers, to whom they believed nature was submitted, either favorable to their views, or to, induce them to cease those afflictions, which natural causes, for the wisest purposes, were continually heaping upon them; thus some irascible, at the same time placable being, was always chosen for the basis of the adopted superstition; it was upon these puerile tenets, upon these absurd notions, that the old men or the priests rested their doctrines; founded their rights; established their authority: it was to render these fanciful beings friendly to the race of man, that they erected, temples, raised altars, loaded them with wealth; in short, it was from such rude foundations, that arose the magnificent structure of superstition; under which man trembled for thousands of years: which governed the condition of society, which determined the actions of the people, gave the tone to the character, deluged the earth with blood, for such a long series of ages. But although these superstitions were originally invented by savages, they still have the power of regulating the fate of many civilized nations, who are not less tenacious of their chimeras, than their rude progenitors. These systems, so ruinous in their principles, have been variously modified by the human mind, of which it is the essence, to labour incessantly on unknown objects; it always, commences by attaching to these, a very first-rate importance, which it afterwards never dares coolly to examine.

Such was the course of man's imagination, in the successive ideas which he either formed to himself, or which he received from his fathers, upon the divinity. The first theology of man was grounded on fear, modelled by ignorance: either afflicted or benefitted by the elements, he adored these elements themselves; by a parity of reasoning, if reasoning it can be called, he extended his reverence to every material, coarse object; he afterwards rendered his homage to the agents he supposed presiding over these elements; to powerful genii; to inferior genii; to heroes; to men endowed with either great or striking qualities. Time, aided by reflection, with here and there a slight corruscation of truth, induced him in some places to relinquish his original ideas; he believed he simplified the thing by lessening the number of his gods, but he achieved nothing by this towards attaining to the truth; in recurring from cause to cause man finished by losing sight of every thing; in this obscurity, in this dark abyss, his mind still laboured, he formed new chimeras, he made new gods, or rather he formed a very complex machinery; still, as before, whenever he could not account for any phenomenon that struck his sight, he was unwilling to ascribe it to physical causes; and the name of his Divinity, whatever that might happen to be, was always brought in to supply his own ignorance of natural causes.

If a faithful account was rendered of man's ideas upon the Divinity, he would be obliged to acknowledge, that for the most part the word *Gods* has been used to express the concealed, remote, unknown causes of the effects he witnessed; that he applies this term when the spring of natural, the source of known causes ceases to be visible: as soon as he loses the thread of these causes, or as soon as his mind can no longer follow the chain, he solves the difficulty, terminates his research, by ascribing it to his gods; thus giving a vague definition to an unknown cause, at which either his idleness, or his limited knowledge, obliges him to stop. When, therefore, he ascribes to his gods the production of some phenomenon, the novelty or the extent of which strikes him with wonder, but of which his ignorance precludes him from unravelling the true cause, or which he believes the natural powers with which he is acquainted are inadequate to bring forth; does he, in fact, do any thing more than substitute for the darkness of his own mind, a sound to which he has been accustomed to listen with reverential awe? Ignorance may be said to be the inheritance of the generality of men; these attribute to their gods not only those uncommon effects that burst upon their senses with an astounding force, but also the most simple events, the causes of which are the most easy to be known to whoever shall be willing to meditate upon them. In short, man has always respected those unknown causes, those surprising effects which his ignorance prevented him from fathoming.

But does this afford us one single, correct idea of the *Divinity*? Can it be possible we are acting rationally, thus eternally to make him the agent of our stupidity, of our sloth, of our want of information on natural causes? Do we, in fact, pay any kind of adoration to this being, by thus bringing him forth on every trifling occasion, to solve the difficulties ignorance throws in our way? Of whatever nature this great cause of causes may be, it is evident to the slightest reflection that he has been sedulous to conceal himself from our view; that he has rendered it impossible for us to have the least acquaintance with him, except through the medium of nature, which he has unquestionably rendered competent to every thing: this is the rich banquet spread before man; he is invited to partake, with a welcome he has no right to dispute; to enjoy therefore is to obey; to be happy is to render that worship which must make him most acceptable; *to be happy himself is to make others happy; to make others happy is to be virtuous; to be virtuous he must revere truth: to know what truth is, he must examine with caution, scrutinize with severity, every opinion he adopts:* this granted, is it at all consistent with the majesty of the Divinity, is it not insulting to such a being to clothe him with our wayward passions; to ascribe to him designs similar to our narrow view of things; to give him our filthy desires; to suppose he can be guided by our finite conceptions; to bring him on a level with frail humanity, by investing him with our qualities, however much we may exaggerate them; to indulge an opinion that he can either act or think as we do; to imagine he can in any manner resemble such a feeble play-thing, as is the greatest, the most distinguished man? No! it is to degrade him in the eye of reason; to violate every regard for truth; to set moral decency at defiance; to fall back into the depth of cimmerian darkness. Let man therefore sit down cheerfully to the feast; let him contentedly partake of what he finds; but let him not worry the Divinity with his useless prayers, with his shallow-sighted requests, to solicit at his hands that which, if granted, would in all probability be the most injurious for himself; these supplications are, in fact, at once to say, that with our limited experience, with our slender knowledge, we better understand what is suitable to our condition, what is convenient to our welfare, than the mighty *Cause of all causes* who has left us in the hands of nature: it is to be presumptuous in the highest degree of presumption; it is impiously to endeavour to lift up a veil which it is evidently forbidden man to touch; that even his most strenuous efforts attempt in vain.

It remains, then, to inquire, if man can reasonably flatter himself with obtaining a perfect knowledge of the power of nature; of the properties of the beings she contains; of the effects which may result from their various combinations? Do we know why the magnet attracts iron? Are we better acquainted with the cause of polar attraction? Are we in a condition to explain the phenomena of light, electricity, elasticity? Do we understand the mechanism by which that modification of our brain, which we tall volition, puts our arm or our legs into motion? Can we render to ourselves an account of the manner in which our eyes behold objects, in which our ears receive sounds, in which our mind conceives ideas? All we know upon these subjects is, that they are so. If then we are incapable of accounting for the most ordinary phenomena, which nature daily exhibits to us, by what chain of reasoning do we refuse to her the power of producing other effects equally incomprehensible to us? Shall we be more instructed, when every time we behold an effect of which we are not in a capacity to develope the cause, we may idly say, this effect is produced by the power, by the will of God? Undoubtedly it is the great *Cause of causes* must have produced every thing; but is it not lessening the true dignity of the Divinity, to introduce him as interfering in every operation of nature; nay, in every action of so insignificant a creature as man? As a mere agent executing his own eternal, immutable laws; when experience, when reflection, when the evidence of all we contemplate, warrants the idea, that this ineffable being has rendered nature competent to every effect, by giving her those irrevocable laws, that eternal, unchangeable system, according to which all the beings she contains must eternally act? Is it not more worthy the exalted mind of the GREAT PARENT OF PARENTS, *ens entium*, more consistent with truth, to suppose that his wisdom in giving these immutable, these eternal laws to the macrocosm, foresaw every thing that could possibly be requisite for the happiness of the beings contained in it; that therefore he left it to the invariable operation of a system, which never can produce any effect that is not the best possible that circumstances however viewed will admit: that consequently the natural activity of the human mind, which is itself the result of this eternal action, was purposely given to man, that he might endeavour to fathom, that he might strive to unravel, that he might seek out the concatenation of these laws, in order to furnish remedies against the evils produced by ignorance. How many discoveries in the great science of natural philosophy has mankind progressively made, which the ignorant prejudices of our forefathers on their first announcement considered as impious, as displeasing to the Divinity, as heretical profanations, which could only be expiated by the sacrifice of the enquiring individuals; to whose labour their posterity owes such an infinity of gratitude? Even in modern days we have seen a SOCRATES destroyed, a GALLILEO condemned, whilst multitudes of other benefactors to mankind have been held in contempt by their uninformed cotemporaries, for those very researches into nature which the present generation hold in the highest veneration. *Whenever ignorant priests are permitted to guide the opinions of nations, science can make but a very slender progress:* natural discoveries will be always held inimical to the interest of bigotted superstitious men. It may, to the minds of infatuated mortals, to the shallow comprehension of prejudiced beings, appear very pious to reply on every occasion our gods do this, our gods do that; but to the contemplative philosopher, to the man of reason, to the real adorers of the great *Cause of causes*, it will never be convincing, that a sound, a mere word, can attach the reason of things; can have more than a fixed sense; can suffice to explain problems. The word GOD is for the most part used to denote the impenetrable cause of those effects which astonish mankind; which man is not competent to explain. But is not this wilful idleness? Is it not inconsistent with our nature? Is it not being truly impious, to sit down with those fine faculties we have received, and give the answer of a child to every thing we do not understand; or rather which our own sloth, or our own want of industry has prevented us from knowing? Ought we not rather to redouble our efforts to penetrate the cause of those phenomena which strike our mind? Is not this, in fact, the duty we owe to the great, the universal Parent? When we have given this answer, what have we said? nothing but what every one knows. Could the great *Cause of causes* make the whole, without also making its part? But does it of necessity follow that he executes every trifling operation, when he has so noble an agent as his own nature, whose laws he has rendered unchangeable, whose scale of operations can never deviate from the eternal routine he has marked out for her and all the beings she embraces? Whose secrets, if sought out, contain the true balsam of life—the sovereign remedy for all the diseases of man.

When we shall be ingenuous with ourselves, we shall be obliged to agree that it was uniformly the ignorance in which our ancestors were involved, their want of knowledge of natural causes, their unenlightened ideas on the powers of nature, which gave birth to the gods they worshipped; that it is, again, the impossibility which the greater part of mankind find to withdraw, themselves out of this ignorance, the difficulty they consequently find to form to themselves simple ideas of the formation of things, the labour that is required to discover the true sources of those events, which they either admire or fear, that makes them believe these ideas are necessary to enable them to render an account of those phenomena, to which their own sluggishness renders them incompetent to recur. Here, without doubt, is the reason they treat all those as irrational who do not see the necessity of admitting an unknown agent, or some secret energy, which for want of being acquainted with Nature, they have placed out of herself.

The phenomena of nature necessarily breed various sentiments in man: some he thinks favorable to him, some prejudicial, while the whole is only what it can be. Some excite his love, his admiration, his gratitude; others fill him with trouble, cause aversion, drive him to despair. According to the various sensations he experiences, he either loves or fears the causes to which he attributes the effects, which produce in him these different passions: these sentiments are commensurate with the effects he experiences; his admiration is enhanced, his fears are augmented, in the same ratio as the phenomena which strikes his senses are more or less extensive, more or less irresistible or interesting to him. Man necessarily makes himself the centre of nature; indeed he can only judge of things, as he is himself affected by them; he can only love that which he thinks favorable to his being; he hates, he fears every thing which causes him to suffer: in short, as we have seen in the former volume, he calls confusion every thing that deranges the economy of his machine; he believes all is in order, as soon as he experiences nothing but what is suitable to his peculiar mode of existence. By a necessary consequence of these ideas, man firmly believes that the entire of nature was made for him alone; that it was only himself which she had in view in all her works; or rather that the powerful cause to which this nature was subordinate, had only for object man and his convenience, in all the stupendous effects which are produced in the universe.

If there existed on this earth other thinking beings besides man, they would fall exactly into similar prejudices with himself; it is a sentiment founded upon that predilection which each individual necessarily has for himself; a predilection that will subsist until reason, aided by experience, in pointing out the truth, shall have rectified his errors.

Thus, whenever man is contented, whenever every thing is in order with respect to himself, he either admires or loves the causes to which he believes he is indebted for his welfare; when he becomes discontented with his mode of existence, he either fears or hates the cause which he supposes has produced these afflicting effects. But his welfare confounds itself with his existence; it ceases to make itself felt when it has become habitual, when it has been of long continuance; he then thinks it is inherent to his essence; he concludes from it that he is formed to be always happy; he finds it natural that every thing should concur to the maintenance of his being. It is by no means the same when he experiences a mode of existence that is displeasing to himself: the man who suffers is quite astonished at the change which his taken place in his machine; he judges it to be contrary to the entire of nature, because it is incommodious to his own particular nature; he, imagines those events by which he is wounded, to be contrary to the order of things; he believes that nature is deranged every time she does not procure for him that mode of feeling which is suitable to his ideas: he concludes from these suppositions that nature, or rather that the agent who moves her; is irritated against him.

It is thus that man, almost insensible to good, feels evil in a very lively manner; the first he believes natural, the other he thinks opposed to nature. He is either ignorant, or forgets, that he constitutes part of a whole, formed by the assemblage of substances, of which some are analogous, others heterogeneous; that the various beings of which nature is composed, are endowed with a variety of properties, by virtue of which they act diversely on the bodies who find themselves within the sphere of their action; that some have an aptitude to attraction, whilst it is of the essence of others to repel; that even those bodies that attract at one distance, repel at another; that the peculiar attractions and repulsions of the particles of bodies perpetually oppose, invariably counteract the general ones of the masses of matter: he does not perceive that these beings, as destitute of goodness, as devoid of malice, act only according to their respective essences; follow the laws their properties impose upon them; without being in capacity to act otherwise than they do. It is, therefore, for want of being acquainted with these things, that he looks upon the great Author of nature, the great *Cause of causes*, as the immediate cause of those evils to which he is submitted; that he judges erroneously when he imagines that the Divinity is exasperated against him.

The fact is, man believes that his welfare is a debt due to him from nature; that when he suffers evil she does him an injustice; fully persuaded that this nature was made solely for himself, he cannot conceive she would make him, who is her lord paramount, suffer, if she was not moved thereto by a power who is inimical to his happiness; who has reasons with which he is unacquainted for afflicting, who has motives which he wishes to discover, for punishing him. From hence it will be obvious, that evil, much more than good, is the true motive of those researches which man has made concerning the Divinity—of those ideas which he has formed to himself—of the conduct he has held towards him. The admiration of the works of nature, or the acknowledgement of its goodness, seem never alone to have determined the human species to recur painfully by thought to the source of these things; familiarized at once with all those effects which are favourable to his existence, he does not by any means give himself the same trouble to seek the causes, that he does to discover those which disquiet him, or by which he is afflicted. Thus, in reflecting upon the Divinity, it was generally upon the cause of his evils that man meditated; his meditations were fruitless, because the evil he experiences, as well as the good he partakes, are equally necessary effects of natural causes, to which his mind ought rather to have bent its force, than to have invented fictitious causes of which he never could form to himself any but false ideas; seeing that he always borrowed them, from his own peculiar mariner of existing, acting, and feeling. Obstinately refusing to see any thing, but himself, he never became acquainted with that universal nature of which he constitutes such a very feeble part.

The slightest reflection, however, would have been sufficient to undeceive him on these erroneous ideas. Everything tends to prove that good and evil are modes of existence that depend upon causes by which a man is moved; that a sensible being is obliged to experience them. In a nature composed of a multitude of beings infinitely varied, the shock occasioned by the collision of discordant matter must necessarily disturb the order, derange the mode of existence of those beings who have no analogy with them: these act in every thing they do after certain laws, which are in themselves immutable; the good or evil, therefore, which man experiences, are necessary consequences of the qualities inherent to the beings, within whose sphere of action he is found. Our birth, which we call a benefit, is an effect as necessary as our death, which we contemplate as an injustice of fate: it is of the nature of all analogous beings to unite themselves to form a whole: it is of the nature of all compound beings to be destroyed, or to dissolve themselves; some maintain their union for a longer period than others; some disperse very quickly, as the ephemeron; some endure for ages, as the planets; every being in dissolving itself gives birth to new beings; these are destroyed in their turn; to execute the eternal, the immutable laws of a nature that only exists by the continual changes that all its parts undergo. Thus nature cannot be accused of malice, since every thing that takes place in it is necessary—is produced by an invariable system, to which every other being, as well as herself, is eternally subjected. The same igneous matter that in man is the principle of life, frequently becomes the principle of his destruction, either by the conflagration of a city, the explosion of a volcano, or his mad passion for war. The aqueous fluid that circulates through his machine, so essentially necessary to his actual existence, frequently becomes too abundant, and terminates him by suffocation; is the cause of those inundations which sometimes swallow up both the earth and its inhabitants. The air, without which he is not able to respire, is the cause of those hurricanes, of those tempests, which frequently render useless the labour of mortals. These elements are obliged to burst their bonds, when they are combined in a certain manner; their necessary but fatal consequences are those ravages, those contagions, those famines, those diseases, those various scourges, against which man, with streaming eyes and violent emotions, vainly implores the aid of those powers who are deaf to his cries: his prayers are never granted; but the same necessity which afflicted him, the same immutable laws which overwhelmed him with trouble, replaces things in the order he finds suitable to his species: a relative order of things which was, is, and always will be the only standard of his judgment.

Man, however, made no such simple reflections: he either did not or would not perceive that every thing in nature acted by invariable laws; he continued stedfast in contemplating the good of which he was partaker, as a favor; in considering the evil he experienced, as a sign of anger in this nature, which he supposed to be animated by the same passions as himself or at least that it was governed by secret agents, who acted after his own manner, who obliged it to execute their will, that was sometimes favourable, sometimes inimical to the human species. It was to these supposed agents, with whom in the sunshine of his prosperity he was but little occupied, that in the bosom of his calamity he addressed his prayers; he thanked them, however, for their favours, fearing lest their ingratitude might farther provoke their fury: thus when assailed by disaster, when afflicted with disease, he invoked them with fervor: he required them to change in his favor the mode of acting which was the very essence of beings; he was willing that to make the slightest evil he experienced cease, that the eternal chain of things might be broken; and the unerring, undeviating course of nature might he arrested.

It was upon such ridiculous pretensions, that were founded those supplications, those fervent prayers, which mortals, almost always discontented with their fate, never in accord in their respective desires, addressed to their gods. They were unceasingly upon their knees before the altars, were ever prostrate before the power of the beings, whom they judged had the right of commanding nature; who they supposed to have sufficient energy to divert her course; who they considered to possess the means to make her subservient to their particular views; thus each hoped by presents, by humiliation, to induce them to oblige this nature, to satisfy the discordant desires of their race. The sick man, expiring in his bed, asks that the humours accumulated in his body should in an instant lose those properties which renders them injurious to his existence; that by an act of their puissance, his gods should renew or recreate the springs of a machine worn out by infirmities. The cultivator of a low swampy country, makes complaint of the abundance of rain with which his fields are inundated; whilst the inhabitant of the hill, raises his thanks for the favors he receives, solicits a continuance of that which causes the despair of his neighbour. In this, each is willing to have a god for himself, and asks according to his momentary caprices, to his fluctuating wants, that the invariable essence of things, should be continually changed in his favour.

From this it must be obvious, that man every moment asks a *miracle* to be wrought in his support. It is not, therefore, at all surprising that he displayed such ready credulity, that he adopted with such facility the relation of the marvellous deeds which were universally announced to him as the acts of the power, or the effects of the benevolence, of the various gods which presided over the nations of the earth: these wonderful tales, which were offered to his acceptance, as the most indubitable proofs of the empire of these gods over nature, which man always found deaf to his entreaties, were readily accredited by him; in the expectation, that if he could gain them over to his interest, this nature, which he found so sullen, so little disposed to lend herself to his views, would then be controuled in his own favor.

By a necessary consequence of these ideas, nature was despoiled of all power; she was contemplated only as a passive instrument, who acted at the will, under the influence of the numerous, all-powerful agents to whom the various superstitions had rendered her subordinate. It was thus for want of contemplating nature under her true point of view, that man has mistaken her entirely, that he believed her incapable of producing any thing by herself; that he ascribed the honor of all those productions, whether advantageous or disadvantageous to the human species, to fictitious powers, whom he always clothed with his own peculiar dispositions, only he aggrandized their force. In short, it was upon the ruins of nature, that man erected the imaginary colossus of superstition, that he reared the *altars of a Jupiter, the temples of an Apollo.*

If the ignorance of nature gave birth to such a variety of gods, the knowledge of this nature is calculated to destroy them. As soon as man becomes enlightened, his powers augment, his resources increase in a ratio with his knowledge; the sciences, the protecting arts, industrious application, furnish him assistance; experience encourages his progress, truth procures for him the means of resisting the efforts of many causes, which cease to alarm him as soon as he obtains a correct knowledge of them. In a word, his terrors dissipate in proportion as his mind becomes enlightened, because his trepidation is ever commensurate with his ignorance, and furnishes this great lesson, that *man, instructed by truth, ceases to be superstitious.*

CHAP. II.

Of Mythology, and Theology.

The elements of nature were, as we have shewn, the first divinities of man; he has generally commenced with adoring material beings; each individual, as we have already said, as may be still seen in savage nations, made to himself a particular god, of some physical object, which he supposed to be the cause of those events, in which he was himself interested; he never wandered to seek out of visible nature, the source either of what happened to himself, or of those phenomena to which he was a witness. As he every where saw only material effects, he attributed them to causes of the same genus; incapable in his infancy of those profound reveries, of those subtle speculations, which are the fruit of time, the result of leisure, he did not imagine any cause distinguished from the objects that met his sight, nor of any essence totally different from every thing he beheld.

The observation of nature was the first study of those who had leisure to meditate: they could not avoid being struck with the phenomena of the visible world. The rising and setting of the sun, the periodical return of the seasons, the variations of the atmosphere, the fertility and sterility of the earth, the advantages of irrigation, the damage caused by floods, the useful effects of fire, the terrible consequences of conflagration, were proper and suitable objects to occupy their thoughts. It was natural for them to believe that those beings they saw move of themselves, acted by their own peculiar energies; according as their influence over the inhabitants of the earth was either favorable or otherwise, they concluded them to have either the power to injure them, or the disposition to confer benefits. Those who first acquired the knowledge of gaining an ascendancy over man, then savage, wandering, unpolished, or dispersed in woods, with but little attachment to the soil, of which he had not yet learned to reap the advantage, were always more practised observers—individuals more instructed in the ways of nature, than the people, or rather the scattered hordes, whom they found ignorant and destitute of experience: their superior knowledge placed them in a capacity to render these services—to discover to them useful inventions, which attracted the confidence of the unhappy beings to whom they came to offer an assisting hand; savages who were naked, half famished, exposed to the injuries of the weather, obnoxious to the attacks of ferocious beasts, dispersed in caverns, scattered in forests, occupied with hunting, painfully labouring to procure themselves a very precarious subsistence, had not sufficient leisure to make discoveries calculated to facilitate their labour, or to render it less incessant. These discoveries are generally the fruit of society: isolated beings, detached families, hardly ever make any discoveries—scarcely ever think of making any. The savage is a being who lives in a perpetual state of infancy, who never reaches maturity unless some one comes to draw him out of his misery. At first repulsive, unsociable, intractable, he by degrees familiarizes himself with those who render him service; once gained by their kindness, he readily lends them his confidence; in the end he goes the length of sacrificing to them his liberty.

It was commonly from the bosom of civilized nations that have issued those personages who have carried sociability, agriculture, art, laws, gods, superstition, forms of worship, to those families or hordes as yet scattered; who united them either to the body of some other nations, or formed them into new nations, of which they themselves became the leaders, sometimes the king, frequently the high priest, and often their god. These softened their manners—gathered them together—taught them to reap the advantages of their own powers—to render each other reciprocal assistance—to satisfy their wants with greater facility. In thus rendering their existence more comfortable, thus augmenting their happiness, they attracted their love; obtained their veneration, acquired the right of prescribing opinions to them, made them adopt such as they had either invented themselves, or else drawn up in the civilized countries from whence they came. History points out to us the most famous legislators as men, who, enriched with useful knowledge they had gleaned in the bosom of polished nations, carried to savages without industry, needing assistance, those arts, of which, until then, these rude people were ignorant: such were the Bacchus's, the Orpheus's, the Triptolemus's, the Numa's, the Zamolixis's; in short, all those who first gave to nations their gods—their worship—the rudiments of agriculture, of science, of superstition, of jurisprudence, of religion, &c.

It will perhaps be enquired, If those nations which at the present day we see assembled, were all originally dispersed? We reply, that this dispersion may have been produced at various times, by those terrible revolutions, of which it has before been remarked our globe has more than once been the theatre; in times so remote, that history has not been able to transmit us the detail. Perhaps the approach of more than one comet may have produced on our earth several universal ravages, which have at each time annihilated the greater portion of the human species.

These hypotheses will unquestionably appear bold to those who have not sufficiently meditated on nature, but to the philosophic enquirer they are by no means inconsistent. There may not only have been one general deluge, but even a great number since the existence of our planet; this globe itself may have been a new production in nature; it may not always have occupied the place it does at present. Whatever idea may be adopted on this subject, if it is very certain that, independent of those exterior causes, which are competent to totally change its face, as the impulse of a comet may do, this globe contains within itself, a cause adequate to alter it entirely, since, besides the diurnal and sensible motion of the earth, it has one extremely slow, almost imperceptible, by which every thing must eventually be changed in it: this is the motion from whence depends the *precession* of the *equinoctial points*, observed by *Hipparchus* and other mathematicians, now well understood by astronomers; by this motion, the earth must at the end of several thousand years change totally: this motion will at length cause the ocean to occupy that space which at present forms the lands or continents. From this it will be obvious that our globe, as well as all the beings in nature, has a continual disposition to change. This motion was known to the ancients, and was what gave rise to what they called their great year, which the Egyptians fixed at thirty-six thousand five hundred and twenty-five years: the Sabines at thirty-six thousand four hundred and twenty-five, whilst others have extended it to one hundred thousand, some even to seven hundred and fifty-three thousand years. Again, to those general revolutions which our planet has at different times experienced, way he added those that have been partial, such as inundations of the sea, earthquakes, subterraneous conflagrations, which have sometimes had the effect of dispersing particular nations, and to make them forget all those sciences with which they were, before acquainted. It is also probable that the first volcanic fires, having had no previous vent, were more central, and greater in quantity, before they burst the crust of earth; as the sea washed the whole, it must have rapidly sunk down into every opening, where, falling on the boiling lava, it was instantly expanded into steam, producing irresistible explosion: whence it is reasonable to conclude, that the primaeval earthquakes wore more widely extended, and of much greater force, than those which occur in our days. Other vapours may be produced by intense heat, possessing a much greater elasticity, from substances that evaporate, such as mercury, diamonds, &c.; the expansive force of these vapours would be much greater than the steam of water, even at red hot heat consequently they, way have had sufficient energy to raise islands, continents, or even to have detached the moon from the earth; if the moon, as has been supposed by some philosophers, was thrown out of the great cavity which now contains the South Sea; the immense quantity of water flowing in from the original ocean, and which then covered the earth, would much contribute to leave the continents and islands, which might be raised at the same time, above the surface of the water. In later days we have accounts of huge stones falling, from the firmament, which may have been thrown by explosion from some distant earthquake, without having been impelled with a force sufficient to cause them to circulate round the earth, and thus produce numerous small moons or satellites.

Those who were able to escape from the ruin of the world, filled with consternation, plunged in misery, were but little conditioned to preserve to their posterity a knowledge, effaced by those misfortunes, of which they had been both the victims and the witnesses: overwhelmed with dismay, trembling with fear, they were not able to hand down the history of their frightful adventures, except by obscure traditions; much less to transmit to us the opinions, the systems, the arts, the sciences, anterior to these petrifying revolutions of our sphere. There have been perhaps men upon the earth from all eternity; but at different periods they may have been nearly annihilated, together with their monuments, their sciences, and their arts; those who outlived these periodical revolutions, each time formed a new race of men, who by dint of time, labour, and experience, have by degrees withdrawn from oblivion the inventions of the primitive races. It is, perhaps, to these periodical revolutions of the human species, that is to be ascribed the profound ignorance in which we see man yet plunged, upon those objects that are the most interesting to him. This is, perhaps, the true source of the imperfection of his knowledge—of the vices of his political institutions—of the defect in his religion—of the growth of superstition, over which terror has always presided; here, in all probability, is the cause of that puerile inexperience, of those jejune prejudices, which almost every where keep man in a state of infancy, and which render him so little capable of either listening to reason or of consulting truth. To judge by the slowness of his progress, by the feebleness of his advance, in a number of respects, we should be inclined to say, the human race has either just quitted its cradle, or that he was never destined to attain the age of virility—to corroborate his reason.

However it may be with these conjectures, whether the human race may always have existed upon the earth, whether it may have been a recent production of nature, whether the larger animals we now behold were originally derived from the smallest microscopic ones, who have increased in bulk with the progression of time, or whether, as the Egyptian philosophers thought, mankind were originally hermaphrodites, who like the *aphis* produced the sexual distinction after some generations, which was also the opinion of Plato, and seems to have been that of Moses, who was educated amongst these Egyptians, as may be gathered from the 27th and 28th verses of the first chapter of GENESIS: "So God created man in his own image, in the image of God created he him; male and female created he them—And GOD blessed them, and GOD said unto them, be fruitful, and multiply, and replenish the earth, and subdue it: and have dominion over the fish of the sea, and over the fowl of the air, and over every living thing that moveth upon the earth:" it is not therefore presuming too much to suppose, as the Egyptians were a nation very fond of explaining their opinions by hieroglyphics, that that part which describes Eve as taken out of Adam's rib, was an hieroglyphic emblem: showing that mankind was in the primitive state of both sexes, united, who was afterwards divided into males and females. However, I say, this may be, it is extremely easy to recur to the origin of many existing nations: we shall find them always in the savage state; that is, to say, dispersed; composed of families detached from each other; of wandering, hordes; these were collected together, approximated at the voice of some missionary or legislator, from whom they received great benefits, who gave them gods, opinions, and laws. These personages, of whom the people newly congregated readily acknowledged the superiority, fixed the national gods, leaving to each individual, those which he had formed to himself, according to his own peculiar ideas, or else substituting others brought from those regions, from whence they themselves had emigrated.

The better to imprint their lessons on the minds of their new subjects, these men became the guides, the priests, the sovereigns, the masters of these infant societies; they formed discourses by which they spoke to the imagination of their willing auditors. POETRY seem best adapted to strike the mind of these rude people, to engrave on their memory those ideas with which they were willing to imbue them: its images, its fictions, its numbers, its rhyme its harmony, all conspired to please their fancy, to render permanent the impressions it made: thus, the entire of nature, as well as all its parts, was personified, by its beautiful allegories: at its soothing voice, trees, stones, rocks, earth, air, fire, water, by imagination took intelligence, held conversation with man, and with themselves; the elements were deified by its songs, every thing was figuratively detailed in harmonious lays. The sky, which according to the then philosophy, was an arched concave, spreading over the earth, which was supposed to be a level plain; (for the doctrine of *antipodes* is of rather modern date) was itself made a god; was considered a more suitable residence, as making a greater distinction for these imaginary deities than the earth on which man himself resided. Thus the firmament was filled with deities.

Time, under the name of Saturn, was pictured as the son of heaven; or Coelus by earth, called Terra, or Thea; he was represented as an inexorable divinity—naturally artful, who devoured his own children—who revenged the anger of his mother upon his father; for which purpose she armed him with a scythe, formed of metals drawn from her own bowels, with which he struck Coelus, in the act of uniting himself to Thea, and so mutilated him, that he was ever after incapacitated to increase the number of his children: he was said to have divided the throne with Janus king of Italy, his reign seems to have been so mild, so beneficent, that it was called the *golden age*; human victims were sacrificed on his altars, until abolished by Hercules, who substituted small images of clay. Festivals in honor of this god, called Saturnalia, were instituted long antecedent to the foundation of Rome they were celebrated about the middle of December, either on the 16th, 17th, or 18th; they lasted in latter times several days, originally but one. Universal liberty prevailed at the celebration, slaves were permitted to ridicule their masters—to speak freely on every subject—no criminals were executed—war never declared; the priests made their human offerings with their heads uncovered; a circumstance peculiar to the Saturnalia, not adopted at other festivals.

The igneous matter, the etherial electric fluid, that invisible fire which vivifies nature, that penetrates all beings, that fertilizes the earth, which is the great principle of motion, the source of heat, was deified under the name of Jupiter: his combination with every being in nature was expressed by his metamorphoses—by the frequent adulteries imputed to him. He was armed with thunder, to indicate he produced meteors, to typify the electric fluid that is called lightning. He married the winds, which were designated under the name of Juno, therefore called the Goddess of the Winds, their nuptials were celebrated with great solemnity; all the gods, the entire brute creation, the whole of mankind attended, except one young woman named Chelone, who laughed at the ceremonies, for which impiety she was changed by Mercury into a tortoise, and condemned to perpetual silence. He was the most powerful of all the gods, and considered as the king and father both of gods and men: his worship was very extended, performed with greater solemnity, than that of any other god. Upon his altars smoked goats, sheep, and white bulls, in which he is said to have particularly delighted; the oak was rendered sacred to him, because he taught mankind to live upon acorns; he had many oracles where his precepts were delivered, the most celebrated of these were at Dodona and Ammon in Lybia; he was supposed to be invisible to the inhabitants of the earth; the Lacedemonians erected his statue with four heads, thereby indicating, that he listened readily to the solicitations of every quarter of the earth. Minerva is represented as having no mother, but to have come completely armed from his brains, when his head was opened by Vulcan; by which it is meant to infer that wisdom is the result of this ethereal fluid. Thus, following the same fictions, the sun, that beneficent star which has such a marked influence over the earth, became an Osiris, a Belus, a Mithras, an Adonis, an Apollo. Nature, rendered sorrowful by his periodical absence, was an Isis, an Astarte, a Venus, a Cybele. Astarte had a magnificent temple at Hieropolis served by three hundred priests, who were always employed in offering sacrifices. The priests of Cybele, called Corybantes, also Galli, were not admitted to their sacred functions without previous mutilation. In the celebration of their festivals these priests used all kinds of indecent expressions, beat drums, cymbals, and behaved just like madmen: his worship extended all over Phrygia, and was established in Greece under the name of *Eleusinian mysteries*. In short, every thing was personified: the sea was under the empire of Neptune; fire was adored by the Egyptians under the name of Serapis; by the Persians, under that of Ormus or Oromaze; and by the Romans, under that of Vesta and Vulcan.

Such was the origin of mythology: it may be said to be the daughter of natural philosophy, embellished by poetry; only destined to describe nature and its parts. If antiquity is consulted, it will be perceived without much trouble, that these famous sages, those legislators, those priests, those conquerors, who were the instructors of infant nations, themselves adored active nature, or the great whole considered relatively to its different operations or qualities; that this was what they caused the ignorant savages whom they had gathered together to adore. It was the great whole they deified; it was its various parts which they made their inferior gods; it was from the necessity of her laws they made fate. The Greeks called it Nature, a divinity who had a thousand names. Varro says, "I believe that God is the soul of the universe, and that the universe is God." Cicero says "that in the mysteries of Samothracia, of Lemnos, of Eleusis, it was nature much more than the gods, they explained to the initiated." Pliny says, "we must believe that the world, or that which is contained under the vast extent of the heavens, is the Divinity; even eternal, infinite, without beginning or end." It was these different modes of considering nature that gave birth to Polytheism, to idolatry. Allegory masqued its mode of action: it was at length parts of this great whole, that idolatry represented by statues and symbols.

To complete the proofs of what has been said; to shew distinctly that it was the great whole, the universe, the nature of things, which was the real object of the worship of Pagan antiquity, hardly any thing can be more decisive than the beginning of the hymn of Orpheus addressed to the god Pan.

"O Pan! I invoke thee, O powerful god! O universal nature! the heavens, the sea, the earth, who nourish all, and the eternal fire, because these are thy members, O all powerful Pan," &c. Nothing can be more suitable to confirm these ideas, than the ingenious explanation which is given of the fable of Pan, as well as of the figure under which he is represented. It is said, "Pan, according to the signification of his name, is the emblem by which the ancients have designated the great assemblage of things or beings: he represents the universe; and, in the mind of the wisest philosophers of antiquity, he passed for the greatest and most ancient of the gods. The features under which he is delineated form the portrait of nature, and of the savage state in which she was found in the beginning. The spotted skin of the leopard, which serves him for a mantle, imagined the heavens filled with stars and constellations. His person was compounded of parts, some of which were suitable to a reasonable animal, that is to say, to man; and others to the animal destitute of reason, such as the goat. It is thus," says he, "that the universe is composed of an intelligence that governs the whole, and of the prolific, fruitful elements of fire, water, earth, air. Pan, loved to drink and to follow the nymphs; this announces the occasion nature has for humidity in all her productions, and that this god, like nature, is strongly inclined to propagation. According to the Egyptians, and the most ancient Grecian philosophers, Pan had neither father nor mother; he came out of Demogorgon at the same moment with the Destinies, his fatal sisters; a fine method of expressing that the universe was the work of an unknown power, and that it was formed after the invariable relations, the eternal laws of necessity; but his most significant symbol, that most suitable to express the harmony of the universe, is his mysterious pipe, composed of seven unequal tubes, but calculated to produce the nicest, the most perfect concord. The orbs which compose the seven planets of our solar system, are of different diameters; being bodies of unequal mass, they describe their revolutions round the sun in various periods; nevertheless it is from the order of their motion that results the harmony of the spheres," &c.

Here then is the great macrocosm, the mighty whole, the assemblage of things adored and deified by the philosophers of antiquity; whilst the uninformed stopped at the emblem under which this nature was depicted; at the symbols under which its various parts, its numerous functions were personified; his narrow mind, his barbarous ignorance, never permitted him to mount higher; they alone were deemed worthy of being, initiated into the mysteries, who knew the realities masqued under these emblems. Indeed, it is not to be doubted for an instant, that the wisest among the Pagans adored nature; which ethnic theology designated under a great variety of nomenclature, under an immense number of different emblems. Apuleius, although a decided Platonist, accustomed to the mysterious, unintelligible notions of his master, calls "Nature the parent of all; the mother of the elements, the first offspring of the world;" again, "the mother of the stars, the parent of the seasons, and the governess of the whole world."—She was worshipped by many under the appellation of the *mother of the gods*. Indeed, the first institutors of nations, and their immediate successors in authority, only spoke to the people by fables, allegories, enigmas, of which they reserved to themselves the right of giving an explanation: this, in fact, constituted the mysteries of the various worship paid to the Pagan divinities. This mysterious tone they considered necessary, whether it was to mask their own ignorance, or whether it was to preserve their power over the uninformed, who for the most part only respect that which is above their comprehension. Their explications were generally dictated either by interest, or by a delirious imagination, frequently by imposture; thus from age to age, they did no more than render nature and its parts, which they had originally depicted, more unknown, until they completely lost sight of the primitive ideas; these were replaced by a multitude of fictitious personages, under whose features this nature had primarily been represented to them. The people, either unaccustomed to think, or deeply steeped in ignorance, adored these personages, without penetrating into the true sense of the emblematical fables recounted to them. These ideal beings, with material figures, in whom they believed there resided a mysterious virtue, a divine power, were the objects of their worship, the source of their fears, the fountain of their hopes. The wonderful, the incredible actions ascribed to these fancied divinities, were an inexhaustible fund of admiration, which gave perpetual play to the fancy; which delighted not only the people of those days, but even the children of latter ages. Thus were transmitted from age to age, those marvellous accounts, which, although necessary to the existence of the power usurped by the ministers of these gods, did, in fact, nothing more than confirm the blindness of the ignorant: these never supposed that it was nature, its various operations, its numerous component parts—that it was the passions of man and his diverse faculties that lay buried under an heap of allegories; they did not perceive that the passions and faculties of human nature were used as emblems, because man was ignorant of the true cause of the phenomena he beheld. As strong passions seemed to hurry man along, in despite of himself, they either attributed these passions to a god, or deified them; frequently they did both: it was thus love became a deity; that eloquence, poetry, industry, were transformed into gods, under the names of Hermes, Mercury, Apollo; the stings of conscience were called the Furies: the people, bowed down in stupid ignorance, had no eyes but for these emblematical persons, under which nature was masked: they attributed to their influence the good, to their displeasure the evil, which they experienced: they entered into every kind of folly, into the most delirious acts of madness, to render them propitious to their views; thus, for want of being acquainted with the reality of things, their worship frequently degenerated into the most cruel extravagance, into the most ridiculous folly.

Thus it is obvious, that every thing proves nature and its various parts to have every where been the first divinities of man. Natural philosophers studied these deities, either superficially or profoundly,—explained some of their properties, detailed some of their modes of action. Poets painted them to the imagination of mortals, either in the most fascinating colours, or under the most hideous deformities; embodied them—furnished them with reasoning faculties—recounted their exploits—recorded their will. The statuary executed sometimes with the most enrapturing art, the ideas of the poets,—gave substance to their shadows—form to their airy nothings. The priest decorated these united works with a thousand marvellous qualities—with the most terrible passions—with the most inconceivable attributes; gave them, "a local habitation and a name." The people adored them; prostrated themselves before these gods, who were neither susceptible of love or hatred, goodness, or malice; they became persecuting, malevolent, cruel, unjust, in order to render themselves acceptable to powers generally described to them under the most odious features.

By dint of reasoning upon these emblems, by meditating upon nature, thus decorated, or rather disfigured, subsequent speculators no longer recollected the source from whence their predecessors had drawn their gods, nor the fantastic ornaments with which they had embellished them. Natural philosophers and poets were transformed by leisure into metaphysicians and theologians; tired with contemplating what they could have understood, they believed they had made an important discovery by subtilly distinguishing nature from herself—from her own peculiar energies—from her faculty of action. By degrees they made an incomprehensible being of this energy, which as before they personified, this they called the mover of nature, divided it into two, one congenial to man's happiness, the other inimical to his welfare; these they deified in the same manner as they had before done nature with her various parts. These abstract, metaphysical beings, became the sole object of their thoughts; were the subject of their continual contemplation; they looked upon them as realities of the highest importance: thus nature quite disappeared; she was despoiled of her rights; she was considered as nothing more than an unwieldy mass, destitute of power; devoid of energy, as an heap of ignoble matter purely passive: who, incapable of acting by herself, was not competent to any of the operations they beheld, without the direct, the immediate agency of the moving powers they had associated with her: which they had made the fulcrum necessary to the action of the lever. They either did not or would not perceive, that the *great Cause of causes, ens entium, Parent of parents*, had, in unravelling chaotic matter, with a wisdom for which man can never be sufficiently grateful, with a sagacity which he can never sufficiently admire, foreseen every thing that could contribute not only to his own individual happiness, but also to that of all the beings in nature; that he had given this nature immutable laws, according to which she is for ever regulated; after which she is obliged invariably to act; that he has described for her an eternal course, from which it is not permitted her to deviate, even for an instant; that she is therefore, rendered competent to the production of every phenomena, not only that he beholds, but of an infinity that he has never yet contemplated; that she needs not any exterior energy for this purpose, having received her powers from a hand far superior to any the feeble weak imagination of man is able to form; that when this nature appears to afflict him, it is only from the contraction of his own views, from the narrowness of his own ideas, that he judges; that, in fact, what he considers the evils of nature, are the greatest possible benefits he can receive, if he was but in a condition to be acquainted with previous causes, with subsequent effects. That the evils resulting to him from his own vices, have equally their remedies in this nature, which it is his duty to study; which if he does he will find, that the same omnipotent goodness, who gave her irrefragable laws, also planted in her bosom, balsams for all his maladies, whether physical or moral: but that it is not given him to know what this great, this universal cause is, for purposes of which he ought not to dispute the wisdom, when he contemplates the mighty wonders that surround him.

Thus man ever preferred an unknown power, to that of which he was enabled to have some knowledge, if he had only deigned to consult his experience; but he presently ceases to respect that which he understands; to estimate those objects which are familiar to him: he figures to himself something marvellous in every thing he does not comprehend; his mind, above all, labours to seize upon that which appears to escape his consideration; in default of experience, he no longer consults any thing, but his imagination, which feeds him with chimeras. In consequence, those speculators who have subtilly distinguished nature from her own powers, have successively laboured to clothe the powers thus separated with, a thousand incomprehensible qualities: as they did not see this power, which is only a mode, they made it a spirit—an intelligence—an incorporeal being; that is to say, of a substance totally different from every thing of which we have a knowledge. They never perceived that all their inventions, that all the words which they imagined, only served to mask their real ignorance; that all their pretended science was limited to saying, in what manner nature acted, by a thousand subterfuges which they themselves found it impossible to comprehend. Man always deceives himself for want of studying nature; he leads himself astray, every time he is disposed to go out of it; he is always quickly necessitated to return; he is even in error when he substitutes words which he does not himself understand, for things which he would much better comprehend if he was willing to look at them without prejudice.

Can a theologian ingenuously believe himself more enlightened, for having substituted the vague words spirit, incorporeal substance, &c. to the more intelligible terms nature, matter, mobility, necessity? However this may be, these obscure words once imagined, it was necessary to attach ideas to them; in doing this, he has not been able to draw them from any other source than the beings of this despised nature, which are ever the only beings of which he is enabled to have any knowledge. Man, consequently, drew them up in himself; his own soul served for the model of the universal soul, of which indeed according to some it only formed a portion; his own mind was the standard of the mind that regulated nature; his own passions, his own desires, were the prototypes of those by which he actuated this being; his own intelligence was that from which he formed that of the mover of nature; that which was suitable to himself, he called the order of nature; this pretended order was the scale by which he measured the wisdom of this being; in short, those qualities which he calls perfections in himself, were the archetypes in miniature, of the perfections of the being, he thus gratuitously supposed to be the agent, who operated the phenomena of nature. It was thus, that in despite of all their efforts, the theologians were, perhaps always will be, true Anthropomorphites. A sect of this denomination appeared in 359, in Egypt, they held the doctrine that their god had a bodily shape. Indeed it is very difficult, if not impossible to prevent man from making himself the sole model of his divinity. Montaigne says "man is not able to be other than he is, nor imagine but after his capacity; let him take what pains he may, he will never have a knowledge of any soul but his own." Xenophanes said, "if the ox or the elephant understood either sculpture or painting, they would not fail to represent the divinity under their own peculiar figure that in this, they would have as much reason as Polyclitus or Phidias, who gave him the human form." It was said to a very celebrated man that "God made man after his own image;" "man has returned the compliment," replied the philosopher. Indeed, man generally sees in his God, nothing but a man. Let him subtilize as he will, let him extend his own powers as he may, let him swell his own perfections to the utmost, he will have done nothing more than make a gigantic, exaggerated man, whom he will render illusory by dint of heaping together incompatible qualities. He will never see in such a god, but a being of the human species, in whom he will strive to aggrandize the proportions, until he has formed a being totally inconceivable. It is according to these dispositions that he attributes intelligence, wisdom, goodness, justice, science, power, to his divinity, because he is himself intelligent; because he has the idea of wisdom in some beings of his own species; because he loves to find in them ideas favourable to himself: because he esteems those who display equity; because he has a knowledge, which he holds more extensive in some individuals than himself; in short, because he enjoys certain faculties which depend on his own organization. He presently extends or exaggerates all these qualities in forming his god; the sight of the phenomena of nature, which he feels he is himself incapable of either producing or imitating, obliges him to make this difference between the being he pourtrays and himself; but he knows not at what point to stop; he fears lest he should deceive himself, if he should see any limits to the qualities he assigns, the word infinite, therefore, is the abstract, the vague term which he uses to characterize them. He says that his power is infinite, which signifies that when he beholds those stupendous effects which nature produces, he has no conception at what point his power can rest; that his goodness, his wisdom, his knowledge are infinite: this announces that he is ignorant how far these perfections ma be carried in a being whose power so much surpasses his own; that he is of infinite duration, because he is not capable of conceiving he could have had a beginning or can ever cease to be; because of this he considers a defect in those transitory beings of whom he beholds the dissolution, whom he sees are subjected to death. He presumes the cause of those effects to which he is a witness, of those striking phenomena that assail his sight, is immutable, permanent, not subjected to change, like all the evanescent beings whom he knows are submitted to dissolution, to destruction, to change of form. This mover of nature being always invisible to man, his mode of action being, impenetrable, he believes that, like his soul or the concealed principle which animates his own body, which he calls spiritual, a spirit, is the moving power of the universe; in consequence he makes a spirit the soul, the life, the principle of motion in nature. Thus when by dint of subtilizing, he has arrived at believing the principle by which his body is moved is a spiritual, immaterial substance, he makes the spirit of the universe immaterial in like manner: he makes it immense, although without extent; immoveable, although capable of moving nature: immutable, although he supposes him to be the author of all the changes, operated in the universe.

The idea of the unity of God, which cost Socrates his life, because the Athenians considered those Atheists who believed but in one, was the tardy fruit of human meditation. Plato himself did not dare to break entirely the doctrine of *Polytheism*; he preserved Venus, an all-powerful Jupiter, and a Pallas, who was the goddess of the country. The sight of those opposite, frequently contradictory effects, which man saw take place in the world, had a tendency to persuade him there must be a number of distinct powers or causes independent of each other. He was unable to conceive that the various phenomena he beheld, sprung from a single, from an unique cause; he therefore admitted many causes or gods, acting upon different principles; some of which he considered friendly, others as inimical to his race. Such is the origin of that doctrine, so ancient, so universal, which supposed two principles in nature, or two powers of opposite interests, who were perpetually at war with each other; by the assistance of which he explained, that constant mixture of good and evil, that blending of prosperity with misfortune, in a word, those eternal vicissitudes to which in this world the human being, is subjected. This is the source of those combats which all antiquity has supposed to exist between good and wicked gods, between an Osiris and a Typhoeus; between an Orosmadis and an

Arimanis; between a Jupiter and the Titanes; in these rencounters man for his own peculiar interest always gave the palm of victory to the beneficent deity; this, according to all the traditions handed down, ever remained in possession of the field of battle; it was so far right, as it is evidently for the benefit of mankind that the good should prevail over the wicked.

When, however, man acknowledged only one God, he generally supposed the different departments of nature were confided to powers subordinate to his supreme orders, under whom the sovereign of the gods discharged his care in the administration of the world. These subaltern gods were prodigiously multiplied; each man, each town, each country, had their local, their tutelary gods; every event, whether fortunate or unfortunate, had a divine cause; was the consequence of a sovereign decree; each natural effect, every operation of nature, each passion, depended upon a divinity, which a theological imagination, disposed to see gods every where, mistaking nature, either embellished or disfigured. Poetry tuned its harmonious lays, on these occasions, exaggerated the details, animated its pictures; credulous ignorance received the portraits with eagerness—heard the doctrines with submission.

Such is the origin of Polytheism: indeed the Greek word *Theos*, [Greek letters], is derived from *Theaomai*, [Greek letters], which implies to contemplate, or take a view of secret or hidden things. Such are the foundations, such the titles of the hierarchy, which man established between himself and his gods, because he generally believed he was incapable of the exalted privilege of immediately addressing himself to the incomprehensible Being whom he had acknowledged for the only sovereign of nature, without even having any distinct idea on the subject: such is the true genealogy of those inferior gods whom the uninformed place as, a proportional means between themselves and the first of all other causes. In consequence, among the Greeks and the Romans, we see the deities divided into two classes, the one were called great gods, because the whole world were nearly in accord in deifying the most striking parts of nature, such as the sun, fire; the sea, time, &c. these formed a kind of aristocratic order, who were distinguished from the minor gods, or from the multitude of ethnic divinities, who were entirely local; that is to say, were reverenced only in particular countries, or by individuals; as in Rome, where every citizen had his familiar spirit, called lares; and household god, called penates. Nevertheless, the first rank of these Pagan divinities, like the latter, were submitted to Fate, that is, to destiny, which obviously is nothing more than nature acting by immutable, rigorous, necessary laws; this destiny was looked upon as the god of gods; it is evident, that this was nothing more than necessity personified; that therefore it was a weakness in the heathens to fatigue with their sacrifices, to solicit with their prayers, those divinities whom they themselves believed were submitted to the decrees of an inexorable destiny, of which it was never possible for them to alter the mandates. *But man*, generally, *ceases to reason, whenever his theological notions are either brought into question, or are the subject of his inquiry.*

What has been already said, serves to show the common source of that multitude of intermediate powers, subordinate to the gods, but superior to man, with which he filled the universe: they were venerated under the names of nymphs, demi-gods, angels, daemons, good and evil genii, spirits, heroes, saints, &c. Among the Romans they were called *Dei medioxumi*, intermediate angels; they were looked upon as intercessors, as mediators, as powers whom it was necessary to reverence, in order either to obtain their favour, appease their anger, or divert their malignant intentions; these constitute different classes of intermediate divinities, who became either the foundation of their hopes, the object of their fears, the means of consolation, or the source of dread to those very mortals who only invented them when they found it impossible to form to themselves distinct, perspicuous ideas of the incomprehensible Being who governed the world in chief; or when they despaired of being able to hold communication with him directly.

Meditation and reflection diminished the number of those deities which composed the ethnic polytheism: some who gave the subject more consideration than others, reduced the whole to one all-powerful Jupiter; but still they painted this being in the most hideous colours, gave him the most revolting features, because they were still obstinately bent on making man, his action and his passions, the model: this folly led them into continual perplexities, because it heaped together contradictory, incompatible, extravagant qualities; it was quite natural it should do so: the limited views, the superficial knowledge, the irregular desires of frail, feeble mortals, were but little calculated to typify the mind of the real Divinity; of that great *Cause of causes*, that *Parent of parents*, from whom every thing must have emanated. Although they persuaded themselves it was sinning to give him rivals, yet they described him as a jealous monarch who could not bear a division of empire; thus taking the vanity of earthly princes for their emblem, as if it was possible such a being could have a competitor like a terrestrial monarch. Not having contemplated the immutable laws with which he has invested nature, to which every thing it contains is subjected, which are the result of the most perfect wisdom, they were puzzled to account for the contrariety of those effects which their weak minds led them to suppose as evils; seeing that sometimes those who fulfilled in the most faithful manner their duties in this life, were involved in the same ruin with the boldest, the most inconsiderate violaters: thus in making him the immediate agent, instead of the first author, the executive instead of the formative power, they caused him to appear capricious, as unreasonably vindictive against his creatures, when they ought to have known that his wisdom was unlimited, his kindness without bounds, when he infused into nature that power which produces these apparently contradictory effects; which, although they seem injurious to man's interests, are, if he was but capacitated to judge fairly, the most beneficial advantages that he can possibly derive. Thus they made the Divinity appear improvident, by continually employing him to destroy the work of his own hands: they, in fact, taxed him with impotence, by the perpetual non-performance of those projects of which their own imbecillity, their own erring judgment, had vainly supposed him to be the contriver.

To solve these difficulties, man created enemies to the Divinity, who although subordinate to the supreme God, were nevertheless competent to disturb his empire, to frustrate his views. Can any thing be worse conceived, can any thing be more truly derogatory to the great *Parent of parents*, than thus to make him resemble a king, who is surrounded with adversaries, willing to dispute with him his diadem? Such, however, is the origin of the *Fable of the Titanes*, or of the *rebellious angels*, whose presumption caused them to be plunged into the abyss of misery—who were changed into *demons*, or into evil genii: these according to their mythology, had no other functions, than to render abortive the projects of the Divinity; to seduce, to raise to rebellion, those who were his subjects. Miserable invention, feeble subterfuge, for the vices of mankind, although decorated with all the beauty of language. Can then sublimity of versification, the harmony of numbers, reconcile man to the idea that the puny offspring of natural causes is adequate for a single instant to dispute the commands, to thwart the desires, to render nugatory the decrees of a Being whose wisdom is of the most polished perfection; whose goodness is boundless; whose power must be more capacious than the human mind can possibly conceive?

In consequence of this *Fable of the Titanes*, the monarch of nature was represented as perpetually in a scuffle with the enemies he had himself created; as unwilling totally to subdue those with whom these fabulists have described him as dividing his authority—partaking his supreme power. This again was borrowed from the conduct of earthly monarchs, who, when they find a potent enemy, make a treaty with him; but this was quite unnecessary for the great *Cause of causes*; and only shows that man is utterly incapable of forming any other ideas than those which he derives from the situation of those of his own race, or of the beings by whom he is surrounded. According to this fable the subjects of the universal Monarch were never properly submitted to his authority; like an earthly king, he was in a continual state of hostility, and punished those who had the misfortune to enter into the conspiracies of the enemies of his glory: seeing that human legislators put forth laws, issued decrees, they established similar institutions for the Divinity; established oracles; his ministers pretended, through these mysterious mediums, to convey to the people his heavenly mandates, to unveil his concealed intentions: the ignorant multitude received these without examination, they did not perceive that it was man, and not the Divinity, who thus spoke to them; they did not feel that it must be impossible for weak creatures to act contrary to the will of God.

The *Fable of the Titanes, or rebellious angels*, is extremely ancient; very generally diffused over the world; it serves for the foundation of the theology of the Brachmins of Hindostan: according to these, all living bodies are animated by *fallen angels*, who under these forms expiate their rebellion. These contradictory notions were the basis of nearly all the superstitions of the world; by these means they imagined they accounted for the origin of evil—demonstrated the cause why the human species experience misery. In short, the conduct of the most arbitrary tyrants of the earth was but too frequently brought forth, too often acted upon, in forming the character of the Divinity, held forth to the worship of man: their imperfect jurisprudence was the source from whence they drew that which they ascribed to their god. Pagan theology was remarkable for displaying in the character of their divinities the most dissolute vices; for making them vindictive; for causing them to punish with extreme rigour those, crimes which the oracles predicted; to doom to the most lasting torments those who sinned without knowing their transgression; to hurl vengeance on those who were ignorant of their obscure will, delivered in language which set comprehension at defiance; unless it was by the priest who both made and fulminated it. It was upon these unreasonable notions, that the theologians founded the worship which man ought to render to the Divinity. Do not then let us be at all surprised if the superstitious man was in a state of continual alarm: if he experienced trances—if his mind was ever in the most tormenting dread; the idea of his gods recalled to him unceasingly, that of a pitiless tyrant who sported with the miseries of his subjects; who, without being conscious of their own wrong, might at each moment incur his displeasure: he could not avoid feeling that although they had formed the universe entirely for man, yet justice did not regulate the actions of these powerful beings, or rather those of the priests; but he also believed that their elevated rank placed them infinitely above the human species, that therefore they might afflict him at their pleasure.

It is then for want of considering good and evil as equally necessary; it is for want of attributing them to their true causes, that man has created to himself fictitious powers, malicious divinities, respecting whom it is found so difficult to undeceive him. Nevertheless, in contemplating nature, he would have been able to have perceived, that *physical evil* is a necessary consequence of the peculiar properties of some beings; he would have acknowledged that plague, contagion, disease, are due to physical causes under particular circumstances; to combinations, which, although extremely natural, are fatal to his species; he would have sought—in the bosom of nature herself the remedies suitable to diminish these evils, or to have caused the cessation of those effects under which he suffered: he would have seen in like manner that *moral evil* was the necessary consequence of defective institutions; that it was not to the Divinity, but to the injustice of his fellows he ought to ascribe those wars, that poverty, those famines, those reverses of fortune, those multitudinous calamities, those vices, those crimes, under which he so frequently groans. Thus to rid himself of these evils he would not have uselessly extended his trembling hands towards shadows incapable of relieving him; towards beings who were not the authors of his sorrows; he would have sought remedies for these misfortunes in a more rational administration of justice—in more equitable laws—in more I reasonable institutions—in a greater degree of benevolence towards his fellow man—in a more punctual performance of his own duties.

As these gods were generally depicted to man as implacable to his frailties as they denounced nothing but the most dreadful punishments against those who involuntarily offended, it is not at all surprising that the sentiment of fear prevailed over that of love: the gloomy ideas presented to his mind were calculated to make him tremble, without making him better; an attention to this truth will serve to explain the foundation of that fantastical, irrational, frequently cruel worship, which was paid to these divinities; he often committed the most cruel extravagancies against his own person, the most hideous crimes against the person of others, under the idea that in so doing, he disarmed the anger, appeased the justice, recalled the clemency, deserved the mercy of his gods.

In general, the superstitious systems of man, his human and other sacrifices, his prayers, his ceremonies, his customs; have had only for their object either to divert the fury of his gods, whom he believed he had offended; to render them propitious to his own selfish views; or to excite in them that good disposition towards himself, which his own perverse mode of thinking made him imagine they bestowed exclusively on others: on the other hand, the efforts, the subtilties of theology, have seldom had any other end, than to reconcile in the divinities it has pourtrayed, those discordant ideas which its own dogmas has raised in the minds of mortals. From what has preceded, it may fairly be concluded that ethnic theology undermined itself by its own inconsistencies; that the art of composing chimeras may therefore with great justice be defined to be that of combining those qualities which are impossible to be reconciled with each other.

CHAP. III.

Of the confused and contradictory Ideas of Theology.

Every thing that has been said, proves pretty clearly, that, in despite of all his efforts, man has never been able to prevent himself from drawing together from his own peculiar nature, the qualities he has assigned to the Being who governs the universe. The contradictions necessarily resulting from the incompatible assemblage of these human qualities, which cannot become suitable to the same subject, seeing that the existence of one destroys the existence of the other, have been shewn:—the theologians themselves have felt the insurmountable difficulties which their divinities presented to reason: they were so substantive, that as they felt the impossibility of withdrawing themselves out of the dilemma, they endeavoured to prevent man from reasoning, by throwing his mind into confusion—by continually augmenting the perplexity of those ideas, already so discordant, which they offered him of the gods. By these means they enveloped them in mystery, covered them with dense clouds, rendered them inaccessible to mankind: thus they themselves became the interpreters, the masters of explaining, according either to their fancy or their interest, the ways of those enigmatical beings they made him adore. For this purpose they exaggerated them more and more—neither time nor space, nor the entire of nature could contain their immensity—every thing became an impenetrable mystery. Although man has originally borrowed from himself the traits, the colours, the primitive lineaments of which he composed his gods; although he has made them jealous, powerful, vindictive monarchs, yet his theology, by force of dreaming, entirely lost sight of human nature. In order to render his divinities still more different from their creatures, it assigned them, over and above the usual qualities of man, properties so marvellous, so uncommon, so far removed from every thing of which his mind could form a conception, that he lost sight of them himself. From thence he persuaded himself these qualities were divine, because he could no longer comprehend them; he believed them worthy of his gods, because no man could figure to himself any one distinct idea of them. Thus theology obtained the point of persuading man he must believe that which he could not conceive; that he must receive with submission improbable systems; that he must adopt, with pious deference, conjectures contrary to his reason; that this reason itself was the most agreeable sacrifice he could make on the altars of his gods, who were unwilling he should use the gift they had bestowed upon him. In short, it had made mortals implicitly believe that they were not formed to comprehend the thing of all others the most important to themselves. Thus it is evident that superstition founded its basis upon the absurd principle that man is obliged to accredit firmly that which he is in the most complete impossibility of comprehending. On the other hand, man persuaded himself that the gigantic, the truly incomprehensible attributes which were assigned to these celestial monarchs, placed between them and their slaves a distance so immense, that these could not be by any means offended with the comparison; that these distinctions rendered them still greater; made them more powerful, more marvellous, more inaccessible to observation. Man always entertains the idea, that what he is not in a condition to conceive, is much more noble, much wore respectable, than that which he has the capacity to comprehend. The more a thing is removed from his reach, the more valuable it always appears.

These prejudices in man for the marvellous, appear to have been the source that gave birth to those wonderful, unintelligible qualities with which superstition clothed these divinities. The invincible ignorance of the human mind, whose fears reduced him to despair, engendered those obscure, vague notions, with which mythology decorated its gods. He believed he could never displease them, provided he rendered them incommensurable; impossible to be compared with any thing, of which he had a knowledge; either with that which was most sublime, or that which possessed the greatest magnitude, From hence the multitude of negative attributes with which ingenious dreamers have successively embellished their phantoms, to the end that they might more surely form a being distinguished from all others, or which possessed nothing in common with that which the human mind had the faculty of being acquainted with: they did not perceive that after all their endeavours, it was nothing wore than exaggerated human qualities, which they thus heaped together, with no more skill than a painter would display who should delineate all the members of the body of the same size, taking a giant for dimension.

The theological attributes with which metaphysicians decorated these divinities, were in fact nothing but pure negations of the qualities found in man, or in those beings of which he has a knowledge; by these attributes their gods were supposed exempted from every thing which they considered weakness or imperfection in him, or in the beings by whom he is surrounded: they called every quality infinite, which has been shewn is only to affirm, that unlike man, or the beings with whom he is acquainted, it is not circumscribed by the limits of space; this, however, is what he can never in any manner comprehend, because he is himself finite. Hobbes in his *Leviathan*, says, "whatsoever we imagine is finite. Therefore there is no idea, or conception of any thing we call infinite. No man can have in his mind an image of infinite magnitude, nor conceive infinite swiftness, infinite time, infinite force, or infinite power. When we say any thing is infinite, we signify only, that we are not able to conceive the ends and bound of the thing named, having no conception of the thing, but of our own inability." Sherlock says, "the word infinite is only a negation, which signifies that which has neither end, nor limits, nor extent, and, consequently, that which has no positive and determinate nature, and is therefore nothing;" he adds, "that nothing but custom has caused this word to be adopted, which without that, would appear devoid of sense, and a contradiction."

When it is said these gods are eternal, it signifies they have not had, like man or like every thing that exists, a beginning, and that they will never have an end: to say they are immutable, is to say, that unlike himself or every thing which he sees, they are not subject to change: to say they are immaterial, is to advance, that their substance or essence is of a nature not conceivable by himself, but which must from that very circumstance be totally different from every thing of which he has cognizance.

It is from the confused collection of these negative qualities, that has resulted the theological gods; those metaphysical wholes of which it is impossible for man to form to himself any correct idea. In these abstract beings every thing is infinity,—immensity,— spirituality,—omniscience,— order,—wisdom,—intelligence,— omnipotence. In combining these vague terms, or these modifications, the ethnic priests believed they formed something, they extended these qualities by thought, and they imagined they made gods, whilst they only composed chimeras. They imagined that these perfections or these qualities must be suitable to their gods, because they were not suitable to any thing of which they had a knowledge; they believed that incomprehensible beings must have inconceivable qualities. These were the materials of which theology availed itself to compose those inexplicable shadows before which they commanded the human race to bend the knee.

Nevertheless, experience soon proved that beings so vague, so impossible to be conceived, so incapable of definition, so far removed from every thing of which man could have any knowledge, were but little calculated to fix his restless views; his mind requires to be arrested by qualities which he is capacitated to ascertain; of which he is in a condition to form a judgment. Thus after it had subtilized these metaphysical gods, after it had rendered them so different in idea, from every thing that acts upon the senses, theology found itself under the necessity of again assimilating them to man, from whom it had so far removed them: it therefore again made them human by the moral qualities which it assigned them; it felt that without this it would not be able to persuade mankind there could possibly exist any relation between him and such vague, ethereal, fugitive, incommensurable beings; that it would never be competent to secure for them his adoration.

It began to perceive that these marvellous gods were only calculated to exercise the imagination of some few thinkers, whose minds were accustomed to labour upon chimerical subjects, or to take words for realities; in short it found, that for the greater number of the material children of the earth it was necessary to have gods more analogous to themselves, more sensible, more known to them. In consequence these divinities were re-clothed with human qualities; theology never felt the incompatibility of these qualities with beings it had made essentially different from man, who consequently could neither have his properties, nor be modified like himself. It did not see that gods who were immaterial, destitute of corporeal organs, were neither able to think nor to act as material beings, whose peculiar organizations render them susceptible of the qualities, the feelings the will, the virtues, that are found in them. The necessity it felt to assimilate the gods to their worshippers, to make an affinity between them, made it pass over without consideration these palpable contradictions—this want of keeping in their portrait: thus ethnic theology obstinately continued to unite those incompatible qualities, that discrepancy of character, which the human mind attempted in vain either to conceive or to reconcile: according to it, pure spirits were the movers of the material world; immense beings were enabled to occupy space, without however excluding nature; immutable deities were the causes of those continual changes operated in the world: omnipotent beings did not prevent those evils which were displeasing to them; the sources of order submitted to confusion: in short, the wonderful properties of these theological beings every moment contradicted themselves.

There is not less discrepancy, less incompatibility, less discordance in the human perfections, less contradiction in the moral qualities attributed to them, to the end that man might be enabled to form to himself some idea of these beings. These were all said to be *eminently* possessed by the gods, although they every moment contradicted each other: by this means they formed a kind of patch-work character, heterogeneous beings, discrepant phenomena, entirely inconceivable to man, because nature had never constructed any thing like them, whereby he was enabled to form a judgment. Man was assured they were eminently good—that it was visible in all their actions. Now goodness is a known quality, recognizable in some beings of the human species; this is, above every other, a property he is desirous to find in all those upon whom he is in a state of dependence; but he is unable to bestow the title of good on any among his fellows, except their actions produce on him those effects which he approves—that he finds in unison with his existence—in conformity with his own peculiar modes of thinking. It was evident, according to this reasoning, these ethnic gods did not impress him with this idea; they were said to be equally the authors of his pleasures, as of his pains, which were to be either secured or averted by sacrifices: thus when man suffered by contagion, when he was the victim of shipwreck, when his country was desolated by war, when he saw whole nations devoured by rapacious earthquakes, when he was a prey to the keenest sorrows, he at least was unable to conceive the bounty of those beings. How could he perceive the beautiful order which they had introduced into the world, while he groaned under such a multitude of calamities? How was he able to discern the beneficence of men whom he beheld sporting as it were with his species? How could he conceive the consistency of those who destroyed that which he was assured they had taken such pains to establish, solely for his own peculiar happiness? But had his mind been properly enlightened, had he been taught to know, that nature, acting by unerring laws, produces all the phenomena he beholds as a necessary consequence of her primitive impulse—that like the rest of nature he was himself subjected to the general operation—that no peculiar exemption had been made in his behalf—that sacrifices were useless—that the great *Parent of parents*, equally mindful of all his creatures, had set in action with the most consummate wisdom an invariable system, the apparent, casual evils of which were ever counterbalanced by the resulting good; that without repining, it was his duty, his interest, to submit; at the same time to examine with sedulity, to search with earnestness, into the recesses of this nature for remedies to the sorrows he endured. If he had been thus instructed, we should never behold him arraigning either the kindness, the wisdom, or the consistency of the gods; he would neither have ascribed his sufferings to the malicious interference of inferior deities, so derogatory to the divine majesty of the *Great Cause of causes*, nor would he have taxed with either inconsistency or unkindness, that nature which cannot act otherwise than she does. Perhaps of all the ideas that can be infused into the mind of man, none is more really subversive of his true happiness, none more incompatible with the reality of things, than that which persuades him he is himself a privileged being, the king of a nature where every thing is submitted to laws, the extent of which his finite mind cannot possibly conceive. Even admitting it should ultimately turn out to be a fact, he has yet no one positive evidence to justify the assumption; experience, which after all must always prove the best criterion for his judgment, daily proves, that in every thing he is subjected, like every other part of nature, to those invariable decrees from which nothing that he beholds is exempted.

Feeble monarch! of whom a grain of sand, some atoms of bile, some misplaced humours, destroy at once the existence and the reign: yet thou pretendest every thing was made for thee! Thou desirest that the entire of nature should be thy domain, and thou canst not even defend thyself from the slightest of her shocks! Thou makest to thyself a god for thyself alone; thou supposest that he unceasingly occupieth himself only for thy peculiar happiness; thou imaginest every thing was made solely for thy pleasure; and, following up thy presumptuous ideas, thou hast the audacity to call nature good or bad as thy weak intellect inclines: thou darest to think that the kindness exhibited towards thee, in common with other beings, is contradicted by the evil genii thy fancy has created! Dost thou not see that those beasts which thou supposest submitted to thine empire, frequently devour thy fellow-creatures; that fire consumeth them; that the ocean swalloweth them up; that those elements of which thou sometimes admirest the order, which sometimes thou accusest of confusion, frequently sweep them off the face of the earth; dost thou not see that all this is necessarily what it must be; that thou art not in any manner consulted in any of this phenomena? Indeed, according to thine own ideas, if thou wast to examine them with care, dost thou not admit that thy gods are the universal cause of all; that they maintain the whole by the destruction of its parts. Are they not then according to thyself, the gods of nature—of the ocean—of rivers—of mountains—of the earth, in which they occupiest, so very small a space—of all those other globes that thou seest roll in the regions of space—of those orbs that revolve round the sun that enlighteneth thee?—Cease, then, obstinately to persist in beholding nothing but thy sickly self in nature; do not flatter thyself that the human race, which reneweth itself, which disappeareth like the leaves on the trees, can absorb all the care, can ingross all the tenderness of that universal being, who, according to thyself, properly understood, ruleth the destiny of all things. Submit thyself in silence to mandates which thy unavailing prayers; can never change; to a wisdom which thy imbecility cannot fathom; to the unerring shafts of a fate, which nothing but thine own vanity, aided by thy perverse ignorance, could ever question, being the best possible good that can befall thee! which if thou couldst alter, thou wouldst with thy defective judgment render worse! What is the human race compared to the earth? What is this earth compared to the sun? What is our sun compared to those myriads of suns which at immense distances occupy the regions of space? not for the purpose of diverting thy weak eyes; not with a view to excite thy stupid admiration, as thou vainly imaginest; since multitudes of them are placed out of the range of thy visual organs: but to occupy the place which necessity hath assigned them. Mortal, feeble and vain! restore thyself to thy proper sphere; acknowledge every where the effect of necessity; recognize in thy benefits, behold in thy sorrows, the different modes of action of those various beings endowed with such a variety of properties, which surround thee; of which the macrocosm is the assemblage; and do not any longer suppose that this nature, much less its great cause, can possess such incompatible qualities as would be the result of human views or of visionary ideas, which have no existence but in thyself.

As long as theologians shall continue obstinately bent to make man the model of their gods; as long ask they shall pertinaciously undertake to explain the nature of these gods, which they will never be able to do, but after human ideas, although they may associate the most heterogeneous properties, the most discrepant functions; so long, I say, experience will contradict at every moment the beneficent views they, attach to their divinities; it will be in vain that they call them good: man, reasoning thus, will never be able to find good but in those objects which impel him in a manner favourable to his actual mode of existence; he always finds confusion in that which fills him with grievous sensations; he calls evil every thing that painfully affects him, even cursorily; those beings that produce in him two modes of feeling, so very opposite to each other, he will naturally conclude are sometimes favourable, sometimes unfavourable to him; at least, if he will not allow that they act necessarily, consequently are neither one nor the other, he will say that a world where he experiences so much evil cannot be submitted to men who are perfectly good; on the other hand, he will also assume that a world in which man receives so many benefits, cannot be governed by those who are without kindness. Thus he is obliged to admit of two principles equally powerful, who are in hostility with each other; or rather, he must agree that the same persons are alternately kind and unkind; this after all is nothing more than avowing they cannot be otherwise than they are; in this case it would be useless to sacrifice to them—to make solicitation; seeing it would be nothing but *destiny*—the necessity of things submitted invariable rules.

In order to justify these beings, constructed upon mortal principles, from injustice, in consequence of the evils the human species experience, the theologian is reduced to the necessity of calling them punishments inflicted for the transgressions of man. But then these general calamities include all men. Some, at least, may be supposed not to have offended. Thus he involves contradictions he finds it difficult to reconcile; to effectuate this he makes his *anthropomorphites* immaterial—incorporeal; that is, he says they are the negation of every thing of which he has a knowledge; consequently, beings who can have no relation with corporeal beings: and this avails him no better, as will be evident by reasoning on the subject. To offend any one, is to diminish the sum of his happiness; it is to afflict him, to deprive him of something, to make him experience a painful sensation. How is it possible man can operate on such beings; how can the physical actions of a material substance have any influence over an immaterial substance, devoid of parts, having no point of contact. How can a corporeal being make an incorporeal being experience incommodious sensations? On the other hand, *justice*, according to the only ideas man can ever form of it, supposes, a permanent disposition to render to each what is due to him; the theologian will not admit that the beings he has jumbled together owe any thing to man; he insists that the benefits they bestow are all the gratuitous effects of their own goodness; that they have the right to dispose of the work of their hands according to their own pleasure; to plunge it if they please into the abyss of misery; in short, that their volition is the only guide of their conduct. It is easy to see, that according to man's idea of justice, this does not even contain the shadow of it; that it is, in fact, the mode of action adopted by what he calls the most frightful tyrants. How then can he be induced to call men just who act after this manner? Indeed, while he sees innocence suffering, virtue in tears, crime triumphant, vice recompensed, and at the same time, is told the beings whom theology has invented are the authors, he will never be able to acknowledge them to have *justice*. But he will find no such contradictory qualities in nature, where every thing is the result of immutable laws: he will at once perceive that these transient evils produce more permanent good; that they are necessary to the conservation of the whole, or else result from modifications of matter, which it is competent for him to change, by altering his own mode of action; a lesson that nature herself teaches him when he is willing to receive her instructions. But to form gods with human passions, is to make them appear unjust; to say that such beings chastise their friends for their own I good, is at once to upset all the ideas he has either of kindness or unkindness: thus the incompatible human qualities ascribed to these beings, do in fact destroy their existence. If it be insisted they have the knowledge and power of man, only that they are more extended, then it becomes a very natural reply, to say, since they know every thing, they ought at least to restrain mischief; because this would be the observation of man upon the action of his fellows;—if it be urged these qualities are similar to the same qualities possessed by man, then it may be fairly asked in what do they differ? To this, if any answer be given, be what it may, it will still be only changing the language: it will be invariably another method of expressing the same thing; seeing that man with all his ingenuity, will never be able to describe properties but after himself or those of the beings by whom he is surrounded.

Where is the man filled with kindness, endowed with humanity, who does not desire with all his heart to render his fellow creatures happy? If these beings, as the theologians assert, really have man's qualities augmented, would they not, by the same reasoning, exercise their infinite power to render them all happy? Nevertheless, in despite of these theologists, we scarcely find any one who is perfectly satisfied with his condition on earth: for one mortal that enjoys, we behold a thousand who suffer; for one rich man who lives in the midst of abundance, there are thousands of poor who want common necessaries: whole nations groan in indigence, to satisfy the passions of some avaricious princes, of some few nobles, who are not thereby rendered more contented—who do not acknowledge themselves more fortunate on that account. In short, under the dominion of these beings, the earth is drenched with the tears of the miserable. What must be the inference from all this? That they are either negligent of, or incompetent to, his happiness. But the mythologists will tell you coolly, that the judgments of his gods are impenetrable! How do we understand this term? Not to be taught—not to be informed—impervious—not to be pierced: in this case it would be an unreasonable question to inquire by what authority do you reason upon them? How do you become acquainted with these impenetrable mysteries? Upon what foundation do you attribute virtues which you cannot penetrate? What idea do you form to yourself of a justice that never resembles that of man? Or is it a truth that you yourself are not a man, but one of those impenetrable beings whom you say you represent?

To withdraw themselves from this, they will affirm that the justice of these idols are tempered with mercy, with compassion, with goodness: these again are human qualities: what, therefore, shall we understand by them? What idea do we attach to mercy? Is it not a derogation from the severe rules of an exact, a rigorous justice, which causes a remission of some part of a merited punishment? Here hinges the great incompatibility, the incongruity of those qualities, especially when augmented by the word *omni*; which shews how little suitable human properties are to the formation of divinities. In a prince, clemency is either a violation of justice, or the exemption from a too severe law: nevertheless, man approves of clemency in a sovereign, when its too great facility does not become prejudicial to society; he esteems it, because it announces humanity, mildness, a compassionate, noble soul; qualities he prefers in his governors to rigour, cruelty, inflexibility: besides, human laws are defective; they are frequently too severe; they are not competent to foresee all the circumstances of every case: the punishments they decree are not always commensurate with the offence: he therefore does not always think them just: but he feels very well, he understands distinctly, that when the sovereign extends his mercy, he relaxes from his justice—that if mercy he merited, the punishment ought not to take place—that then its exercise is no longer clemency, but justice: thus he feels, that in his fellow creatures these two qualities cannot exist at the same moment. How then is he to form his judgment of beings who are represented to possess both in the extremest degree? Is it not, in fact, announcing these beings to be men like ourselves, who act with our imperfections on an enlarged scale?

They then say, well, but in the next world these idols will reward you for all the evils you suffer in this: this, indeed, is something to look to, if it could be contemplated alone; unmixed with all they have formerly asserted: if we could also find that there was an unison of thinking on this point—if there was a reasonable comprehensible view of it held forth: but alas! here again human pleasures, human feelings, are the basis on which these rewards are rested; only they are promised in a way we cannot comprehend them; houris, or females who are to remain for ever virgins, notwithstanding the knowledge of man, are so opposed to all human comprehension, so opposite to all experience, are such mystic assertions, that the human mind cannot possibly embrace an idea of them: besides this is only promised by one class of these beings; others affirm it will be altogether different: in short, the number of modes in which this hereafter reward is promised to him, obliges man to ask himself one plain question, Which is the real history of these blissful abodes? At this question he staggers—he seeks for advice: each assures him that the other is in error— that his peculiar mode is that which will really have place; that to believe the other is a crime. How is he to judge now? Take what course he will, he runs the chance of being wrong; he has no standard whereby to measure the correctness of these contradictory assurances; his mind is held suspended; he feels the impossibility of the whole being right; he knows not that which he ought to elect! Again, they have positively asserted these beings owe nothing to man: how then is he to expect in a future life, a more real happiness than he enjoys in the present? This they parry, by assuring him it is founded upon their promises, contained in their revealed oracles. Granted: but is he quite certain these oracles have emanated from themselves? If they are so different in their detail, may there not be reasonable ground for suspecting some of them are not authentic? If there is, which are the spurious, which are the genuine? By what rule is he to guide himself in the choice; how, with his frail methods of judging, is he to scrutinize oracles delivered by such powerful beings—to discriminate the true from the false? The ministers of each will give you an infallible method, one that, is according to their own asseveration, cannot err; that is, by an implicit belief in the particular doctrine each promulgates.

Thus will be perceived the multitude of contradictions, the extravagant hypotheses which these human attributes, with which theology clothes its divinities, must necessarily produce. Beings embracing at one time so many discordant qualities will always be undefinable—can only present a train of ideas calculated to displace each other; they will consequently ever remain beings of the imagination. These beings, say their ministers, created the heavens, the earth, the creatures who inhabit it, to manifest their own peculiar glory; they have neither rivals, nor equals in nature; nothing which can be compared with them. Glory is, again, a human passion: it is in man the desire of giving his fellow-creatures an high opinion of him; this, passion is laudable when it stimulates him to undertake great projects—when it determines him to perform useful actions—but it is very frequently a weakness attached to his nature; it is nothing more than a desire to be distinguished from those beings with whom he compares himself, without exciting him to one noble, one generous act. It is easy to perceive that beings who are so much elevated above men, cannot be actuated by such a defective passion. They say these beings are jealous of their prerogatives. Jealousy is another human passion, not always of the most respectable kind: but it is rather difficult to conceive the existence of jealousy with profound wisdom, unlimited power, and the perfection of justice. Thus the theologians by dint of heaping quality on quality, aggrandizing each as is added, seem to have reduced themselves to the situation of a painter, who spreading all his colours upon his canvas together, after thus blending them into an unique mass, loses sight of the whole in the composition.

They will, nevertheless, reply to these difficulties, that goodness, wisdom, justice, are in these beings qualities so pre-eminent, so distinct, have so little affinity with these same qualities in man, that they are totally dissimilar—have not the least relation. Admit this to be the case, How then can he form to himself any idea of these perfections, seeing they are totally unlike those with which he is acquainted? They surely cannot mean to insinuate that they are the reverse of every thing he understands; because that would, in effect, bring them to a precise point which would not need any explanation; it is therefore a matter of certainty this cannot be the case: then if these qualities, when exercised by the beings they have described, are only human actions so obscured, so hidden, as not to be recognizable by man, How can weak mortals pretend to announce them, to have a knowledge of them, to explain them to others? Does then theology impart to the mind the ineffable boon of enabling it to conceive that which no man is competent to understand? Does it procure for its agents the marvellous faculty of having distinct ideas of beings composed of so many contradictory properties? Does it, in fact, make the theologian himself one of these incomprehensible beings.

They will impose silence, by saying the oracles have spoken; that through these mystical means they have made themselves known to mortals. The next question would naturally be, When, where, or to whom have these oracles spoken? Where are these oracles? An hundred voices raise themselves in the same moment; hands of Briaraeus are immediately stretched forth to shew them in a number of discordant collections, which each maintains, with an equal degree of vehemence, is the true code—the only doctrine man ought to believe: he runs them over, finds they scarcely agree in any one particular; but that in all the heaviest penalties are denounced against those who doubt the smallest part of any one of them. These beings of consummate wisdom are made to speak an obscure, irrational language; some of them, although their goodness is proclaimed, have been cruel and sanguinary; others, although their justice is held forth, have been partial, unjust, capricious; some, who are represented as all merciful, destine to the most hideous punishments the unhappy victims to their wrath: examine any one of them more closely, he will find that they have never in any two countries held literally the same language: that although they are said to have spoken in many places, that they have always spoken variously: What is the necessary result? The human mind, incapable of reconciling such manifest contradictions, unable to obtain from their ministers any corroborative evidence, that is not disputed by the others, falls into the strangest perplexity; is involved in doubts, entangled in a labyrinth to which no clue is to be found.

Thus the relations, which are supposed to exist between man and these theological idols, can only be founded on the moral qualities of these beings: if these are not known to him, if he cannot in any manner comprehend them, they cannot by any ingenuity of argument serve him for models. In order that they may be imitated, it is needful that these qualities were cognizable by the being who is to imitate them. How can he imitate that goodness, that justice, that mercy, which does not resemble either his own, or any thing he can conceive? If these beings partake in nothing of that which forms man—if the properties they do possess, although different, are not within the reach of his comprehension—if, he cannot embrace the most distant idea of them, which the theologian assures him he cannot, How is it possible he can set about imitating them? How follow a conduct suitable to please them—to render himself acceptable in their sight? What can in effect be the motive of that worship, of that homage, of that obedience, which these beings are said to exact—which he is informed he should offer at their altars, if he does not establish it upon their goodness—their veracity—their justice: in short, upon qualities which he is competent to understand? How can he have clear, distinct ideas of those qualities, if they are no longer of the same nature as those which he has learned to reverence in the beings of his own species?

To this they will reply, because none of them ever admit the least doubt of the rectitude of their own individual creed, that there can be no proportion between these idols and mortals, who are the work of their hands; that it is not permitted to the clay to demand of the potter who has formed it, "why ye have fashioned me thus;"—but if there can be no common measure between the workman and his work—if there can be no analogy between them, because the one is immaterial, the other corporeal, How do they reciprocally act upon each other? How can the gross organs of the one, comprehend the subtile quality of the other? Reasoning in the only way he is capable, and it surely will never be seriously argued that he is not to reason, will he not perceive that the earthen vase could only have received the form which it pleased the potter to give; that if it is formed badly, if it is rendered inadequate to the use for which it was designed, the vase is not in this instance to be blamed; the potter certainly has the power to break it; the vase cannot prevent him; it will neither have motives nor means to soften his anger; it will be obliged to submit to its destiny; but he will not be able to prevent his mind from thinking the potter harsh in thus punishing the vase, rather than by forming it anew, by giving it another figure, render it competent to the purposes he intended.

According to these notions the relations between man and these theological beings have no existence, they owe nothing to him, are dispensed from shewing him either goodness or justice; that man, on the contrary, owes them every thing: but contradictions appear at every step. If these have promised by their oracles any thing to man, it is rather difficult for him to believe, that what is so solemnly promised does not belong to him if he fulfils the condition of the promise. The difference a theologian may choose to find in these relations will hardly be convincing to a reasonable mind. The duties of man towards these beings can, according to their own shewing, have no other foundation than the happiness he expects from them: thus the relation has a reciprocity, it is founded upon their goodness, upon their justice, it demands obedience on his part, a conduct suitable to the benefits he receives. Thus, in whatever manner the theological system is viewed, it destroys itself. Will theology never feel that the more it endeavours to exaggerate the human qualities, the less it exalts the beings it pictures; the more incomprehensible it renders them, the more it contributes to swell its own ocean of contradictions; that to take human passions, mortal faculties at all, is perhaps the worst means it can pursue to form a perfect being; but that if it must persist in this method, then the further they remove them from man, the more they debase him, the more they weaken the relations subsisting between them: that in thus aggregating human properties, it should carefully abstain from associating in these pictures those qualities which man finds detestable in his fellows. Thus, despotism in man is looked upon as an unjust, unreasonable power; if it introduces such a quality into its portraits, it cannot rationally suppose them suitable to cultivate the esteem, to attract the voluntary homage of the human race: if, however, the canvas be examined, we shall frequently be struck, with perceiving this the leading feature; we shall equally find a want of keeping through the whole; that shadows are introduced, where lights ought to prevail; that the colouring is incongruous—the design without harmony.

The discrepancy of conduct which theology imputes to these idols, is not less remarkable than the contrariety of qualities it ascribes to them, or the inconsistency of the passions with which it invests them; sometimes, according to this, they are the friends to reason, desirous of the happiness of society; sometimes they are inimical to virtue; interdict the use of reason; flattered with seeing society disturbed, they sometimes afflict man without his being able to guess the cause of their displeasure; sometimes they are favourable to mankind—at others, indisposed towards the human species: sometimes they are represented as permitting crimes for the pleasure of punishing them—at others, they exert all their power to arrest crime in its birth; sometimes they elect a small number to receive eternal happiness, predestinating the rest to perpetual misery—to everlasting torments; at others, they throw open the gates of mercy to all who choose to enter them; sometimes they are pourtrayed as destroying the universe—at others, as establishing the most beautiful order in the planet we inhabit; sometimes they are held forth as countenancing deception—at others, as having the highest reverence for truth—as holding deceit in abomination. This, again, is the necessary result of the human faculties, the mortal passions, the frail qualities of which they compose the beings they hold forth to the admiration, to the worship, to the homage of the world.

Perhaps the most fatal consequences have arisen from founding the moral character of these divinities upon that of man. Those who first had the confidence to tell man that in these matters it was not permitted him to consult his reason, that the interests of society demanded its sacrifice, evidently proposed to themselves to make him the sport of their own wantonness—to make him the blind instrument of their own unworthiness. It is from this radical error that has sprung all those extravagances which the various superstitions have introduced upon the earth: from hence has flowed that sacred fury which has frequently deluged it with blood: here is the cause of those inhuman persecutions which have so often desolated nations: in short, all those horrid tragedies which have been acted on the vast theatre of the world, by command of the different ministers of the various systems, whose gods they have said ordained these shocking spectacles.

The theologians themselves have thus been the means, of calumniating the gods they pretended to serve, under the pretext of exalting their name—of covering them with glory; in this they may have been said to be true atheists, since they seem only to have been anxious to destroy the idols they themselves had raised, by the actions they have attributed to them—which has debased them in the eye of reason—rendered their existence more than doubtful to the man of humanity. Indeed, it would require more than human credulity to accredit the assertion that these beings ever could order the atrocities committed in their name. Every time they have been willing to disturb the harmony of mankind—whenever they have been desirous to render him unsociable, they have cried out that their gods ordained that he should be so. Thus they render mortals uncertain, make the ethical system fluctuate by founding it upon changeable, capricious idols, whom they represent much more frequently cruel and unjust, than filled with bounty and benevolence.

However it may be, admitting if they will for a moment that their idols possess all the human virtues in an infinite degree of perfection, we shall quickly be obliged to acknowledge that they cannot connect them with those metaphysical, theological, negative attributes, of which we have already spoken. If these beings are spirits that are immaterial, how can they be able to act like man, who is a corporeal being? Pure spirits, according to the only idea man can form of them, having no organs, no parts, cannot see any thing; can neither hear our prayers, attend to our solicitations, nor have compassion for our miseries. They cannot be immutable, if their dispositions can suffer change: they cannot be infinite, if the totality of nature, without being them, can exist conjointly with them: they cannot be omnipotent, if they either permit or do not prevent evil: they cannot be omnipresent, if they are not every where: they must therefore be in the evil as well as in the good. Thus in whatever manner they are contemplated, under whatever point of view they are considered, the human qualities which are assigned to them, necessarily destroy each other; neither can these same properties in any possible manner combine themselves with the supernatural attributes given to them by theology.

With respect to the revealed will of these idols, by means of their oracles, far from being a proof of their good will, of their commisseration for man, it would rather seem evidence of their ill-will. It supposes them capable of leaving mankind for a considerable season unacquainted with truths highly important to their interests; these oracles communicated to a small number of chosen men, are indicative of partiality, of predilections, that are but little compatible with the common Father of the human race. These oracles were ill imagined, since they tend to injure the immutability ascribed to these idols, by supposing that they permitted man to be ignorant at one time of their will, whilst at another time they were willing he should be instructed on the subject. Moreover, these oracles frequently predicted offences for which afterwards severe punishments were inflicted on those who did no more than fulfil them. This, according to the reasoning of man, would be unjust. The ambiguous language in which they were delivered, the almost impossibility of comprehending them, the inexplicable mysteries they contained, seemed to render them doubtful; at least they are not consistent with the ideas man is capable of forming of infinite perfection: but the fact clearly is, they were thus rendered capable of application to the contingency of events—could be made to suit almost any circumstances: this would render it not a very improbable conjecture, that these oracles were solely delivered by the priests themselves. It these were tried by the only test of which he has any knowledge—HIS REASON, it would naturally occur to the mind of man, that mystery could never, on any occasion, be used in the promulgation of substantive decrees meant to operate on the obedience, to actuate the moral conduct of man: it is quite usual with most legislators to render their laws as explicit as possible, to adapt them to the meanest understanding; in short, it would be reckoned want of good faith in a government, to throw a thick, mysterious veil over the announcement of that conduct which it wished its citizens to adopt; they would be apt to think such a procedure was either meant to cover its own peculiar ignorance, or else to entrap them into a snare; at best, it would be considered as furnishing a never-failing source of dispute, which a wise government would endeavour to avoid.

It will thus be obvious, that the ideas which theology has at various times, under various systems, held forth to man, have for the most part been confused, discordant, incompatible, and have had a general tendency to disturb the repose of mankind. The obscure notions, the vague speculations of these multiplied creeds, would be matter of great indifference, if man was not taught to hold them as highly important to his welfare—if he did not draw from them conclusions pernicious to himself—if he did not learn from these theologians that he must sharpen his asperity against those who do not contemplate them in the same point of view with himself: as he perhaps, then, will never have a common standard, a fixed rule, a regular graduated scale, whereby to form his judgment on these points—as all efforts of the imagination must necessarily assume divers shapes, undergo a variety of modifications, which can never be assimilated to each other, it was little likely that mankind would at all times be able to understand each other on this subject; much less that they would be in accord in the opinions they should adopt. From hence that diversity of superstitions which in all ages have given rise to the most irrational disputes; which have engendered the most sanguinary wars; which have caused the most barbarous massacres; which have divided man from his fellow by the most rancorous animosities, that will perhaps never be healed; because he has been impelled to consider the peculiar tenets he adopted, not only as immediately essential to his individual welfare, but also as intimately connected with the happiness, closely interwoven with the tranquillity of the nation of which he was a citizen. That such contrariety of sentiment, such discrepancy of opinion should exist, is not in the least surprising; it is, in fact, the natural result of those physical causes to which, as long as he exists, he is at all times submitted. The man of a heated imagination cannot accommodate himself to the god of a phlegmatic, tranquil being: the infirm, bilious, discontented, angry mortal, cannot view him under the same aspect as he who enjoys a sounder constitution,—as the individual of a gay turn, who enjoys the blessing of content, who wishes to live in peace. An equitable, kind, compassionate, tender-hearted man, will not delineate to himself the same portrait of his god, as the man who is of an harsh, unjust, inflexible, wicked character. Each individual will modify his god after his own peculiar manner of existing, after his own mode of thinking, according to his particular mode of feeling. A wise, honest, rational man will always figure to himself his god as humane and just.

Nevertheless, as fear usually presided at the formation of those idols man set up for the object of his worship; as the ideas of these beings were generally associated with that of terror as the recollections of sufferings, which he attributed to them, often made him tremble; frequently awakened in his mind the most afflicting, reminiscence; as it sometimes filled him with inquietude, sometimes inflamed his imagination, sometimes overwhelmed him with dismay, the experience of all ages proves, that these vague idols became the most important of all considerations—was the affair which most seriously occupied the human race: that they every where spread consternation—produced the most frightful ravages, by the delirious inebriation resulting from the opinions with which they intoxicated the mind. Indeed, it is extremely difficult to prevent habitual fear, which of all human passions is the most incommodious, from becoming a dangerous leaven; which in the long run will sour, exasperate, and give malignancy to the most moderate temperament.

If a misanthrope, in hatred of his race, had formed the project of throwing man into the greatest perplexity,—if a tyrant, in the plenitude of his unruly desire to punish, had sought out the most efficacious means; could either the one or the other have imagined that which was so well calculated to gratify their revenge, as thus to occupy him unceasingly with objects not only unknown to him, but which no two of them should ever see with precisely the same eyes; which notwithstanding they should be obliged to contemplate as the centre of all their thoughts—as the only model of their conduct—as the end of all their actions—as the subject of all their research—as a thing of more importance to them than life itself; upon which all their present felicity, all their future happiness, must necessarily depend? Could the gods themselves, in their solicitude to punish the impious Prometheus, for having stolen fire from the sun, have imagined a more certain method of executing their wishes? Was not Pandora's box, though stuffed with evils, trifling when compared with this? That at least left hope, to the unfortunate Epimetheus; this effectually cut it off.

If man was subjected to an absolute monarch, to a sultan who should keep himself secluded from his subjects; who followed no rule but his own desires; who did not feel himself bound by any duty; who could for ever punish the offences committed against him; whose fury it was easy to provoke; who was irritated even by the ideas, the thoughts of his subjects; whose displeasure might be incurred without even their own knowledge; the name of such a sovereign would assuredly be sufficient to carry trouble, to spread terror, to diffuse consternation into the very souls of those who should hear it pronounced; his idea would haunt them every where—would unceasingly afflict them—would plunge them into despair. What tortures would not their mind endure to discover this formidable being, to ascertain the secret of pleasing him! What labour would not their imagination bestow, to discover what mode of conduct might be able to disarm his anger! What fears would assail them, lest they might not have justly hit upon the means of assuaging his wrath! What disputes would they not enter into upon the nature, the qualities of a ruler, equally unknown to them all! What a variety of means would not be adopted, to find favour in his eyes; to avert his chastisement!

Such is the history of the effects superstition has produced upon the earth. Man has always been panic-struck, because the systems adopted never enable him to form any correct opinion, any fixed ideas, upon a subject so material to his happiness; because every thing conspired either to give his ideas a fallacious turn, or else to keep his mind in the most profound ignorance; when he was willing to set himself right, when he was sedulous to examine the path which conducted to his felicity, when he was desirous of probing opinions so consequential to his peace, involving so much mystery, yet combining both his hopes and his fears, he was forbidden to employ the only proper method,—HIS REASON, guided by his experience; he was assured this would be an offence the most indelible. If he asked, Wherefore his reason had then been given him, since he was not to use it in matters of such high behest? he was answered, those were mysteries of which none but the initiated could be informed; that it sufficed for him to know, that the reason which he seemed so highly to prize, which he held in so much esteem, was his most dangerous enemy—his most inveterate, most determined foe. Where can be the propriety of such an argument? Can it really be that reason is dangerous? If so, the Turks are justified in their predilection for madmen: but to proceed, he is told that he must believe in the gods, not question the mission of their priests; in short, that he had nothing to do with the laws they imposed, but to obey them: when he then required that these laws might at least be made comprehensible to him; that he might be placed in a capacity to understand them; the old answer was returned, that they were *mysteries*; he must not inquire into them. But where is the necessity for mystery in points of such vast importance? He might, indeed, from time to time consult these oracles, when he was able to make the sacrifices demanded; he would then receive precepts for his conduct: these were always, however, given in such vague, indeterminate terms, that he had scarcely the chance of acting right. At different times the same oracles delivered different opinions: thus he had nothing, steady; nothing permanent, whereby to guide his steps; like a blind man left to himself in the streets, he was obliged to grope his way at the peril of his existence. This will serve to shew the urgent necessity there is for truth to throw its radiant lustre on systems big with so much importance; that are so calculated to corroborate the animosities, to confirm the bitterness of soul, between those whom nature intended should always act as brothers.

By the magical charms with which these idols were surrounded, the human species has remained either as if it was benumbed, in a state of stupid apathy, or else he has become furious with fanaticism: sometimes, desponding with fear, man cringed like a slave who bends under the scourge of an inexorable master, always ready to strike him; he trembled under a yoke made too ponderous for his strength: he lived in continual dread of a vengeance he was unceasingly striving to appease, without ever knowing when he had succeeded: as he was always bathed in tears, continually enveloped in misery—as he was never permitted to lose sight of his fears—as he was continually exhorted to nourish his alarm, he could neither labour for his own happiness nor contribute to that of others; nothing could exhilirate him; he became the enemy of himself, the persecutor of his fellow-creatures, because his felicity here below was interdicted; he passed his time in heaving the most bitter sighs; his reason being forbidden him, he fell into either a state of infancy or delirium, which submitted him to authority; he was destined to this servitude from the hour he quitted his mother's womb, until that in which he was returned to his kindred dust; tyrannical opinion bound him fast in her massive fetters; a prey to the terrors with which he was inspired, he appeared to have come upon the earth for no other purpose than to dream—with no other desire than to groan—with no other motives than to sigh; his only view seemed to be to injure himself; to deprive himself of every rational pleasure, to embitter his own existence; to disturb the felicity of others. Thus, abject, slothful, irrational, he frequently became wicked, under the idea of doing honour to his gods; because they instilled into his mind that it was his duty to avenge their cause, to sustain their honour, to propagate their worship.

Mortals were prostrate from race to race, before vain idols to which fear had given birth in the bosom of ignorance, during the calamities of the earth; they tremblingly adored phantoms which credulity had placed in the recesses of their own brain, where they found a sanctuary which time only served to strengthen; nothing could undeceive them; nothing was competent to make them feel, it was themselves they adored—that they bent the knee before their own work—that they terrified themselves with the extravagant pictures they had themselves delineated; they obstinately persisted in prostrating themselves, in perplexing themselves, in trembling; they even made a crime of endeavouring to dissipate their fears; they mistook the production of their own folly; their conduct resembled that of children, who having disfigured their own features, become afraid of themselves when a mirror reflects the extravagance they have committed. These notions so afflicting for themselves, so grievous to others, have their epoch from the calamities of man; they will continue, perhaps augment, until their mind, enlightened by discarded reason, illumined by truth, shall set in their true colours these various systems; until reflection guided by experience, shall attach no more importance to them, than is consistent with the happiness of society; until man, bursting the chains of superstition—recalling to mind the great end of his existence—taking a rational view of that which surrounds him, shall no longer refuse to contemplate nature under her true character; shall no longer persist in refusing to acknowledge she contains within herself the cause of that wonderful phenomena which strikes on the dazzled optics of man: until thoroughly persuaded of the weakness of their claim to the homage of mankind, he shall make one pious, simultaneous, mighty effort, and *overthrow the altars of Moloch and his priests.*

CHAP. IV.

Examination of the Proofs of the Existence of the Divinity, as given by CLARKE.

The unanimity of man in acknowledging the Divinity, is commonly looked upon as the strongest proof of his existence. There is not, it is said, any people on the earth who have not some ideas, whether true or false, of an all-powerful agent who governs the world. The rudest savages as well as the most polished nations, are equally obliged to recur by thought to the first cause of every thing that exists; thus it is affirmed, the cry of Nature herself ought to convince us of the existence of the Godhead, of which she has taken pains to engrave the notion in the minds of men: they therefore conclude, that the idea of God is innate.

Perhaps there is nothing of which man should be more sedulously careful than permitting a promiscuous assemblage of right with wrong—of suffering false conclusions to be drawn from true propositions; this will not improbably be found to be pretty much the case in this instance; the existence of the great *Cause of causes*, the *Parent of parents*, does not, I think, admit of any doubt in the mind of any one who has reasoned: but, if this existence did not rest upon better foundations than the unanimity of man on this subject, I am fearful it would not be placed upon so solid a rock as those who make this asseveration may imagine: the fact is, man is not generally agreed upon this point; if he was, superstition could have no existence; the idea of God cannot be *innate*, because, independent of the proofs offered on every side of the almost impossibility of innate ideas, one simple fact will set such an opinion for ever at rest, except with those who are obstinately determined not to be convinced by even their own arguments: if this idea was innate, it must be every where the same; seeing that that which is antecedent to man's being, cannot have experienced the modifications of his existence, which are posterior. Even if it were waived, that the same idea should be expected from all mankind, but that only every nation should have their ideas alike on this subject, experience will not warrant the assertion, since nothing can be better established than that the idea is not uniform even in the same town; now this would be an insuperable quality in an innate idea. It not unfrequently happens, that in the endeavour to prove too much, that which stood firm before the attempt, is weakened; thus a bad advocate frequently injures a good cause, although he may not be able to overturn the rights on which it is rested. It would, therefore, perhaps, come nearer to the point if it was said, "that the natural curiosity of mankind have in all ages, and in all nations, led him to seek after the primary cause of the phenomena he beholds; that owing to the variations of his climate, to the difference of his organization, the greater or less calamity he has experienced, the variety of his intellectual faculties, and the circumstances under which he has been placed, man has had the most opposite, contradictory, extravagant notions of the Divinity, but that he has uniformly been in accord in acknowledging both the existence, and the wisdom of his work—NATURE."

If disengaged from prejudice, we analyze this proof, we shall see that the universal consent of man, so diffused over the earth, actually proves little more than that he has been in all countries exposed to frightful revolutions, experienced disasters, been sensible to sorrows of which he has mistaken the physical causes; that those events to which he has been either the victim or the witness, have called forth his admiration or excited his fear; that for want of being acquainted with the powers of nature, for want of understanding her laws, for want of comprehending her infinite resources, for want of knowing the effects she must necessarily produce under given circumstances, he has believed these phenomena were due to some secret agent of which he has had vague ideas—to beings whom he has supposed conducted themselves after his own manner; who were operated upon by similar motives with himself.

The consent then of man in acknowledging a variety of gods, proves nothing, except that in the bosom of ignorance he has either admired the phenomena of nature, or trembled under their influence; that his imagination was disturbed by what he beheld or suffered; that he has sought in vain to relieve his perplexity, upon the unknown cause of the phenomena he witnessed, which frequently obliged him to quake with terror: the imagination of the human race has laboured variously upon these causes, which have almost always been incomprehensible to him; although every thing confessed his ignorance, his inability to define these causes, yet he maintained that he was assured of their existence; when pressed, he spoke of a spirit, (a word to which it was impossible to attach any determinate idea) which taught nothing but the sloth, which evidenced nothing but the stupidity of those who pronounced it.

It ought, however, not to excite any surprise that man is incapable of forming any substantive ideas, save of those things which act, or which have heretofore acted upon his senses; it is very evident that the only objects competent to move his organs are material,—that none but physical beings can furnish him with ideas,—a truth which has been rendered sufficiently clear in the commencement of this work, not to need any further proof. It will suffice therefore to say that the idea of God is not an innate, but an acquired notion; that it is the very nature of this notion to vary from age to age; to differ in one country from another; to be viewed variously by individuals. What do I say? It is, in fact, an idea hardly ever constant in the same mortal. This diversity, this fluctuation, this change, stamps it with the true character of an acquired opinion. On the other hand, the strongest proof that can be adduced that these ideas are founded in error, is, that man by degrees has arrived at perfectioning all the sciences which have any known objects for their basis, whilst the science of theology has not advanced; it is almost every where at the same point; men seem equally undecided on this subject; those who have most occupied themselves with it, have effected but little; they seem, indeed, rather to have rendered the primitive ideas man formed to himself on this head more obscure,—to have involved in greater mystery all his original opinions.

As soon as it is asked of man, what are the gods before whom he prostrates himself, forthwith his sentiments are divided. In order that his opinions should be in accord, it would be requisite that uniform ideas, analogous sensations, unvaried perceptions, should every where have given birth to his notions upon this subject: but this would suppose organs perfectly similar, modified by sensations which have a perfect affinity: this is what could not happen: because man, essentially different by his temperament, who is found under circumstances completely dissimilar, must necessarily have a great diversity of ideas upon objects which each individual contemplates so variously. Agreed in some general points, each made himself a god after his own manner; he feared him, he served him, after his own mode. Thus the god of one man, or of one nation, was hardly ever that of another man, or of another nation. The god of a savage, unpolished people, is commonly some material object, upon which the mind has exercised itself but little; this god appears very ridiculous in the eyes of a more polished community, whose minds have laboured more intensely upon the subject. A spiritual god, whose adorers despise the worship paid by the savage to a coarse, material object, is the subtle production of the brain of thinkers, who, lolling in the lap of polished society quite at their leisure, have deeply meditated, have long occupied themselves with the subject. The theological god, although for the most part incomprehensible, is the last effort of the human imagination; it is to the god of the savage, what an inhabitant of the city of Sybaris, where effiminacy and luxury reigned, where pomp and pageantry had reached their climax, clothed with a curiously embroidered purple habit of silk, was to a man either quite naked, or simply covered with the skin of a beast perhaps newly slain. It is only in civilized societies, that leisure affords the opportunity of dreaming—that ease procures the facility of reasoning; in these associations, idle speculators meditate, dispute, form metaphysics: the faculty of thought is almost void in the savage, who is occupied either with hunting, with fishing, or with the means of procuring a very precarious subsistence by dint of almost incessant labour. The generality of men, however, have not more elevated notions of the divinity, have not analyzed him more than the savage. A spiritual, immaterial God, is formed only to occupy the leisure of some subtle men, who have no occasion to labour for a subsistence. Theology, although a science so much vaunted, considered so important to the interests of man, is only useful to those who live at the expense of others; or of those who arrogate to themselves the privilege of thinking for all those who labour. This science becomes, in some polished societies, who are not on that account more enlightened, a branch of commerce extremely advantageous to its professors; equally unprofitable to the citizens; above all when these have the folly to take a very decided interest in their unintelligible system—in their discordant opinions.

What an infinite distance between an unformed stone, an animal, a star, a statue, and the abstracted Deity, which theology hath clothed with attributes under which it loses sight of him itself! The savage without doubt deceives himself in the object to which he addresses his vows; like a child he is smitten with the first object that strikes his sight—that operates upon him in a lively manner; like the infant, his fears are alarmed by that from which he conceives he has either received an injury or suffered disgrace; still his ideas are fixed by a substantive being, by an object which he can examine by his senses. The Laplander who adores a rock,—the negro who prostrates himself before a monstrous serpent, at least see the objects they adore. The idolater falls upon his knees before a statue, in which he believes there resides some concealed virtue, some powerful quality, which he judges may be either useful or prejudicial to himself; but that subtle reasoner, called a metaphysician, who in consequence of his unintelligible science, believes he has a right to laugh at the savage, to deride the Laplander, to scoff at the negro, to ridicule the idolater, doth not perceive that he is himself prostrate before a being of his own imagination, of which it is impossible he should form to himself any correct idea, unless, like the savage, he re-enters into visible nature, to clothe him with qualities capable of being brought within the range of his comprehension.

For the most part the notions on the Divinity, which obtain credit even at the present day, are nothing more than a general terror diversely acquired, variously modified in the mind of nations, which do not tend to prove any thing, save that they have received them from their trembling, ignorant ancestors. These gods have been successively altered, decorated, subtilized, by those thinkers, those legislators, those priests, who have meditated deeply upon them; who have prescribed systems of worship to the uninformed; who have availed themselves of their existing prejudices, to submit them to their yoke; who have obtained a dominion over their mind, by seizing on their credulity,—by making them participate in their errors,—by working on their fears; these dispositions will always be a necessary consequence of man's ignorance, when steeped in the sorrows of his heart.

If it be true, as asserted, that the earth has never witnessed any nation so unsociable, so savage, to be without some form of religious worship—who did not adore some god—but little will result from it respecting the Divinity. The word GOD, will rarely be found to designate more than the unknown cause of those effects which man has either admired or dreaded. Thus, this notion so generally diffused, upon which so much stress is laid; will prove little more than that man in all generations has been ignorant of natural causes,—that he has been incompetent, from some cause or other, to account for those phenomena which either excited his surprise or roused his fears. If at the present day a people cannot be found destitute of some kind of worship, entirely without superstition, who do not acknowledge a God, who have not adopted a theology more or less subtle, it is because the uninformed ancestors of these people have all endured misfortunes—have been alarmed by terrifying effects, which they have attributed to unknown causes—have beheld strange sights, which they have ascribed to powerful agents, whose existence they could not fathom; the details of which, together with their own bewildered notions, they have handed down to their posterity who have not given them any kind of examination.

It will readily be allowed, that the universality of an opinion by no means proves its truth. Do we not see a great number of ignorant prejudices, a multitude of barbarous errors, even at the present day, receive the almost universal sanction of the human race? Are not nearly all the inhabitants of the earth imbued with the idea of magic—in the habit of acknowledging occult powers—given to divination—believers in enchantment—the slaves to omens—supporters of witchcraft—thoroughly persuaded of the existence of ghosts? If some of the most enlightened persons are cured of these follies, they still find very zealous partizans in the greater number of mankind, who accredit them with the firmest confidence. It would not, however, be concluded by men of sound sense, in many instances not by the theologian himself, that therefore these chimeras actually have existence, although sanctioned with the credence of the multitude. Before Copernicus, there was no one who did not believe that the earth was stationary, that the sun described his annual revolution round it. Was, however, this universal consent of man upon a principle of astronomical science, which endured for so many thousand years, less an error on that account? Yet to have doubted the truth of such a generally-diffused opinion, one that had received the sanction of so many learned men—that was clothed with the sacred vestments of so many ages of credulity—that had been adopted by Moses, acknowledged by Solomon, accredited by the Persian magi—that Elijah himself had not refuted—that had obtained the fiat of the most respectable universities, the most enlightened legislators, the wisest kings, the most eloquent ministers; in short, a principle that embraced all the stability that could be derived from the universal consent of all ranks: to have doubted, I say, of this, would at one period have been held as the highest degree of profanation, as the most presumptuous scepticism, as an impious blasphemy, that would have threatened the very existence of that unhappy country from whose unfortunate bosom such a venomous, sacrilegious mortal could have arisen. It is well known what opinion was entertained of Gallileo for maintaining the existence of the antipodes. Pope Gregory excommunicated as atheists all those who gave it credit. Thus each man has his God: But do all these gods exist? In reply it will be said, somewhat triumphantly, each man hath his ideas of the sun, do all these suns exist? However narrow may be the pass by which superstition imagines it has thus guarded its favourite hypothesis, nothing will perhaps be more easy than the answer: the existence of the sun is a fact verified by the daily use of the senses; all the world see the sun; no one bath ever said there is no sun; nearly all mankind have acknowledged it to be both luminous and hot: however various may be the opinions of man, upon this luminary, no one has ever yet pretended there was more than one attached to our planetary system. But we may perhaps be told, there is a wide difference between that which can be contemplated by the visual organs, which can be understood by the sense of feeling, and that which does not come under the cognizance of any part of the organic structure of man. We must confess theology here has the advantage; that we are unable to follow it through its devious sinuosities; amidst its meandering labyrinths: but then it is the advantage of those who see sounds, over those who only hear them; of those who hear colours, over those who only see them; of the professors of a science, where every thing is built upon laws inverted from those common to the globe we inhabit; over those common understandings, who cannot be sensible to any thing that does not give an impulse to some of their organs.

If man, therefore, had the courage to throw aside his prejudices, which every thing conspires to render as durable as himself—if divested of fear he would examine coolly—if guided by reason he would dispassionately view the nature of things, the evidence adduced in support of any given doctrine; he would, at least, be under the necessity to acknowledge, that the idea of the Divinity is not innate—that it is not anterior to his existence—that it is the production of time, acquired by communication with his own species—that, consequently, there was a period when it did not actually exist in him: he would see clearly, that he holds it by tradition from those who reared him: that these themselves received it from their ancestors: that thus tracing it up, it will be found to have been derived in the last resort, from ignorant savages, who were our first fathers. The history of the world will shew that crafty legislators, ambitious tyrants, blood-stained conquerors, have availed themselves of the ignorance, the fears, the credulity of his progenitors, to turn to their own profit an idea to which they rarely attached any other substantive meaning than that of submitting them to the yoke of their own domination.

Without doubt there have been mortals who have dreamed they have seen the Divinity. Mahomet, I believe, boasted he had a long conversation with the Deity, who promulgated to him the system of the Mussulmans. But are there not thousands, even of the theologians, who will exhaust their breath, and fatigue their lungs with vociferating this man was a liar; whose object was to take advantage of the simplicity, to profit by the enthusiasm, to impose on the credulity of the Arabs; who promulgated for truths, the crazy reveries of his own distempered imagination? Nevertheless, is it not a truth, that this doctrine of the crafty Arab, is at this day the creed of millions, transmitted to them by their ancestors, rendered sacred by time, read to them in their mosques, adorned with all the ceremonies of superstitious worship; of which the inhabitants of a vast portion of the earth do not permit themselves for an instant to doubt the veracity; who, on the contrary, hold those who do not accredit it as dogs, as infidels, as beings of an inferior rank, of meaner capacities than themselves? Indeed that man, even if he were a theologian, would not experience the most gentle treatment from the infuriated Mahometan, who should to his face venture to dispute the divine mission of his prophet. Thus the ancestors of the Turk have transmitted to their posterity, those ideas of the Divinity which they manifestly received from those who deceived them; whose impositions, modified from age to age, subtilized by the priests, clothed with the reverential awe inspired by fear, have by degrees acquired that solidity, received that corroboration, attained that veteran stability, which is the natural result of public sanction, backed by theological parade.

The word God is, perhaps, among the first that vibrate on the ear of man; it is reiterated to him incessantly; he is taught to lisp it with respect; to listen to it with fear; to bend the knee when it is reverberated: by dint of repetition, by listening to the fables of antiquity, by hearing it pronounced by all ranks and persuasions, he seriously believes all men bring the idea with them into the world; he thus confounds a mechanical habit with instinct; whilst it is for want of being able to recal to himself the first circumstances under which his imagination was awakened by this name; for want of recollecting all the recitals made to him during the course of his infancy; for want of accurately defining what was instilled into him by his education; in short, because his memory does not furnish him with the succession of causes that have engraven it on his brain, that he believes this idea is really inherent to his being; innate in all his species. Iamblicus, indeed, who was a Pythagorean philosopher not in the highest repute with the learned world, although one of those visionary priests in some estimation with theologians, (at least if we may venture to judge by the unlimited draughts they have made on the bank of his doctrines) who was unquestionably a favourite with the emperor Julian, says, "that anteriorly to all use of reason, the notion of the gods is inspired by nature, and that we have even a sort of feeling of the Divinity, preferable to the knowledge of him." It is, however, uniformly by habit, that man admires, that he fears a being, whose name he has attended to from his earliest infancy. As soon as he hears it uttered, he without reflection mechanically associates it with those ideas with which his imagination has been filled by the recitals of others; with those sensations which he has been instructed to accompany it. Thus, if for a season man would be ingenuous with himself, he would concede that in the greater number of his race, the ideas of the gods, and of those attributes with which they are clothed, have their foundation, take their rise in, are the fruit of the opinions of his fathers, traditionally infused into him by education—confirmed by habit—corroborated by example—enforced by authority. That it very rarely happens he examines these ideas; that they are for the most part adopted by inexperience, propagated by tuition, rendered sacred by time, inviolable from respect to his progenitors, reverenced as forming part of those institutions he has most learned to value. He thinks he has always had them, because he has had them from his infancy; he considers them indubitable, because he is never permitted to question them—because he never has the intrepidity to examine their basis.

If it had been the destiny of a Brachman, or a Mussulman, to have drawn his first breath on the shores of Africa, he would adore, with as much simplicity, with as much fervour, the serpent reverenced by the Negroes, as he does the God his own metaphysicians have offered to his reverence. He would be equally indignant if any one should presumptuously dispute the divinity of this reptile, which he would have learned to venerate from the moment he quitted the womb of his mother, as the most zealous, enthusiastic fakir, when the marvellous wonders of his prophet should be brought into question; or as the most subtile theologian when the inquiry turned upon the incongruous qualities with which he has decorated his gods. Nevertheless, if this serpent god of the Negro should be contested, they could not at least dispute his existence. Simple as may be the mind of this dark son of nature, uncommon as may be the qualities with which he has clothed his reptile, he still may be evidenced by all who choose to exercise their organs of sight; not so with the theologian; he absolutely questions the existence of every other god but that which he himself has formed; which is questioned in its turn by his brother metaphysician. They are by no means disposed to admit the proofs offered by each other. Descartes, Paschal, and Doctor Samuel Clarke himself, have been accused of atheism by the theologians of their time. Subsequent reasoners have made use of their proofs, and even given them as extremely valid. Doctor Bowman published a work, in which he pretends all the proofs hitherto brought forward are crazy and fragile: he of course substitutes his own; which in their turn have been the subject of animadversion. Thus it would appear these theologians are not more in accord with themselves than they are with Turks or Pagans. They cannot even agree as to their proofs of existence: from age to age new champions arise, new evidence is adduced, the old discarded, or treated with contempt; profound philosophers, subtle metaphysicians, are continually attacking each other for their ignorance on a point of the very first importance. Amidst this variety of discussion, it is very difficult for simple winds, for those who steadily search after truth, who only wish to understand what they believe, to find a point upon which they can fix with reliance—a standard round which they may rally without fear of danger—a common measure that way serve them for a beacon to avoid the quicksands of delusion—the sophistry of polemics.

Men of very great genius have successively miscarried in their demonstrations; have been held to have betrayed their cause by the weakness of the arguments by which they have supported it; by the manner in which they have attempted to establish their positions. Thus many of them, when they believed they had surmounted a difficulty, had the mortification to find they had only given birth to an hundred others. They seem, indeed, not to be in a capacity to understand each other, or to agree among themselves, when they reason upon the nature and qualities of beings created by such a variety of imaginations, which each contemplates diversely, upon which the natural self-love of each disputant induces him to reject with vehement indignation every thing that does not fall in with his own peculiar mode of thinking—that does not quadrate either with his superstition or his ignorance, or sometimes with both.

The opponents of Clarke charge him with begging the question in his work on *The Being and Attributes of God*. They say he has pretended to prove this existence *a priori*, which they deem impossible, seeing there is nothing anterior to the first of causes; that therefore it can only be proved *a posteriori*, that is to say, by its effects. Law, in his *Inquiry into the Ideas of Space, Time, Immensity, &c.* has attacked him very triumphantly, for this manner of proof, which is stated to be so very repugnant to the school-men. His arguments have been treated with no more ceremony by Thomas D'Aquinas, John Scott, and others of the schools. At the present day I believe he is held in more respect—that his authority outweighs that of all his antagonists together. Be that as it may, those who have followed him have done nothing more than either repeat his ideas, or present his evidence under a new form. Tillotson argues at great length, but it would be rather difficult to understand which side of the question he adopts on this momentous subject; whether he is a Necessitarian, or among the opposers of Fatalism. Speaking of man, he says, "he is liable to many evils and miseries, which he can neither prevent or redress; he is full of wants, which he cannot supply, and compassed about with infirmities which he cannot remove, and obnoxious to dangers which he can never sufficiently provide against: he is apt to grieve for what he cannot help, and eagerly to desire what he is never able to obtain." If the proofs of Clarke, who has drawn them up in twelve propositions, are examined with attention, I think they may be fairly shielded from the reproach with which they have been loaded; it does not appear that he has proved his positions *a priori*, but *a posteriori*, according to rule. It seems clear, however, that he has mistaken the proof of the existence of the effects, for the proof of the existence of the cause: but here he seems to have more reason than his critics, who in their eagerness to prove that Clarke has not conformed to the rules of the schools, would entirely overlook the best, the surest foundation whereon to rest the existence of the *Great Cause of causes*, that *Parent of Parents*, whose wisdom shines so manifestly in nature, of which Clarke's work may be said to be such a masterly evidence. We shall follow, step by step, the different propositions in which this learned divine developes the received opinions upon the Divinity; which, when applied to nature, will be found to be so accurate, so correct, as to leave no further room to doubt either the existence or the wisdom of her great author, thus proved through her own existence. Dr. Clarke sets out with saying:

"*1st. Something has existed from all eternity.*"

This proposition is evident—hath no occasion for proofs. Matter has existed from all eternity, its forms alone are evanescent; matter is the great engine used by nature to produce all her phenomena, or rather it is nature herself. We have some idea of matter, sufficient to warrant the conclusion that this has always existed. First, that which exists, supposes existence essential to its being. That which cannot, annihilate itself, exists necessarily; it is impossible to conceive that that which cannot cease to exist, or that which cannot annihilate itself, could ever have had a beginning. If matter cannot be annihilated, it could not commence to be. Thus we say to Dr. Clarke, that it is matter, it is nature, acting by her own peculiar energy, of which no particle is ever in an absolute state of rest, which hath always existed. The various material bodies which this nature contains often change their form, their combination, their properties, their mode of action: but their principles or elements are indestructible—have never been able to commence. What this great scholar actually understands, when he makes the assertion "that an eternal duration is now actually past," is not quite so clear; yet he affirms, "that not to believe it would be a real and express contradiction." We may, however, safely admit his argument, "that when once any proposition is clearly demonstrated to, be true, it ought not to disturb us that there be perhaps some perplexing difficulties on the other side, which merely for want of adequate ideas of the manner of the existence of the things demonstrated, are not easily to be cleared."

2nd, *"There has existed from eternity some one unchangeable and independent Being."*

We may fairly inquire what is this Being? Is it independent of its own peculiar essence, or of those properties which constitute it such as it is? We shall further inquire, if this Being, whatever it may be, can make the other beings which it produces, or which it moves, act otherwise than they do, according to the properties which it has given them? And in this case we shall ask, if this Being, such as it way be supposed to be, does not act necessarily; if it is not obliged to employ indispensible means to fulfil its designs, to arrive at the end which it either has, or may be supposed to have in view? Then we shall say, that nature is obliged to act after her essence; that every thing which takes place in her is necessary; but that she is independent of her forms.

A man is said to be independent, when he is determined in his actions only by the general causes which are accustomed to move him; he is equally said to be dependent on another, when he cannot act but in consequence of the determination which this last gives him. A body is dependent on another body when it owes to it its existence, and its mode of action. A being existing from eternity cannot owe his existence to any other being; he cannot then be dependent upon him, except he owes his action to him; but it is evident that an eternal or self-existent Being contains in his own nature every thing that is necessary for him to act: then, matter being eternal, is necessarily independent in the sense we have explained; of course it hath no occasion for a mover upon which it ought to depend.

This eternal Being is also immutable, if by this attribute be understood that he cannot change his nature; but if it be intended to infer by it that he cannot change his mode of action or existence, it is without doubt deceiving themselves, since even in supposing an immaterial being, they would be obliged to acknowledge in him different modes of being, different volitions, different ways of acting; particularly if he was not supposed totally deprived of action, in which case he would be perfectly useless. Indeed it follows of course that to change his mode of action he must necessarily change his manner of being. From hence it will be obvious, that the theologians, in making their gods immutable, render them immoveable, consequently they cannot act. An immutable being, could evidently neither have successive volition, nor produce successive action; if this being hath created matter, or given birth to the universe, there must have been a time in which he was willing that this matter, this universe, should exist; and this time must have been preceded by another time, in which he was willing that it might not yet exist. If God be the author of all things, as well as of the motion and of the combinations of matter, he is unceasingly occupied in producing and destroying; in consequence, he cannot be called immutable, touching his mode of existing. The material world always maintains itself by motion, and the continual change of its parts; the sum of the beings who compose it, or of the elements which act in it, is invariably the same; in this sense the immutability of the universe is much more easy of comprehension, much more demonstrable than that of an other being to whom, they would attribute all the effects, all the mutations which take place. Nature is not more to be accused of mutability, on account of the succession of its forms, than the eternal Being is by the theologians, by the diversity of his decrees. Here we shall be able to perceive that, supposing the laws by which nature acts to be immutable, it does not require tiny of these logical distinctions to account for the changes that take place: the mutation which results, is, on the contrary, a striking proof of the immutability of the system which produces them; and completely brings mature under the range of this second proposition as stated by Dr. Clarke.

3dly, "That unchangeable and independent Being which has existed from eternity without any eternal cause of its existence, must be self-existent, that is, necessarily existing."

This proposition is merely a repetition of the first; we reply to it by inquiring, Why matter, which is indestructible, should not be self-existent? It is evident that a being who had no beginning, must be self-existent; if he had existed by another, he would have commenced to be; consequently he would not be eternal.

4thly, "What the substance or essence of that Being which is self-existent, or necessarily existing, is, we have no idea; neither is it at all possible for us to comprehend it."

Dr. Clarke would perhaps have spoken more correctly if he had said his essence is impossible to be known: nevertheless, we shall readily concede that the essence of matter is incomprehensible, or at least that we conceive it very feebly by the manner in which we are affected by it; but without this we should be less able to conceive the Divinity, who would then be impervious on any side. Thus it must necessarily be concluded, that it is folly to argue upon it, since it is by matter alone we can have any knowledge of him; that is to say, by which we can assure ourselves of his existence,— by which we can at all guess at his qualities. In short we must conclude, that every thing related of the Divinity, either proves him material, or else proves the impossibility in which the human mind will always find itself, of conceiving any being different from matter; without extent, yet omnipresent; immaterial, yet acting upon matter; spiritual, yet producing matter; immutable, yet putting every thing in activity, &c.

Indeed it must be allowed that the incomprehensibility of the Divinity does not distinguish him from matter; this will not be more easy of comprehension when we shall associate it with a being much less comprehensible than itself; we have some slender knowledge of it through some of its parts. We do not certainly know the essence of any being, if by that word we are to understand that which constitutes its peculiar nature. We only know matter by the sensations, the perceptions, the ideas which it furnishes; it is according to these that we judge it to be either favorable or unfavourable, following the particular disposition of our organs. But when a being does not act upon any part of our organic structure, it does not exist for us; we cannot, without exhibiting folly, without betraying our ignorance, without falling into obscurity, either speak of its nature, or assign its qualities; our senses are the only channel by which we could have formed the slightest idea of it; these not having received any impulse, we are, in point of fact, unacquainted with its existence. The incomprehensibility of the Divinity ought to convince man that it is a point at which he is bound to stop; indeed he is placed in a state of utter incapacity to proceed: this, however, would not suit with those speculators who are willing to reason upon him continually, to shew the depth of their learning,—to persuade the uninformed they understand that which is incomprehensible to all men; by which they expect to be able to submit him to their own views. Nevertheless, if the Divinity be incomprehensible, It would not be straining a point beyond its tension, to conclude that a priest, or metaphysician, did not comprehend him better than other men: it is not, perhaps, either the wisest or the surest way to become acquainted with him, to represent him to ourselves, by the imagination of a theologian.

5thly, "Though the substance, or essence of the self-existent Being, is in itself absolutely incomprehensible to us, yet many of the essential attributes of his nature are strictly demonstrable, as well as his existence. Thus, in the first place, the self-existent Being must of necessity be eternal."

This proposition differs in nothing from the first, except Dr. Clarke does not here understand that as the self-existent Being had no beginning, he can have no end. However this may be, we must ever inquire, Why this should not be matter? We shall further observe, that matter not being capable of annihilation, exists necessarily, consequently will never cease to exist; that the human mind has no means of conceiving how matter should originate from that which is not itself matter: is it not obvious, that matter is necessary; that there is nothing, except its powers, its arrangement, its combinations, which are contingent or evanescent? The general motion is necessary, but the given motion is not so; only during the season that the particular combinations subsist, of which this motion is the consequence, or the effect: we may be competent to change the direction, to either accelerate or retard, to suspend or arrest, a particular motion, but the general motion can never possibly be annihilated. Man, in dying, ceases to live; that is to say, he no longer either walks, thinks, or acts in the mode which is peculiar to human organization: but the matter which composed his body, the matter which formed his mind, does not cease to move on that account: it simply becomes susceptible of another species of motion.

6thly, "The self-existent Being must of necessity be infinite and omnipresent."

The word infinite presents only a negative idea—which excludes all bounds: it is evident that a being who exists necessarily, who is independent, cannot be limited by any thing which is out of himself; he must consequently be his own limits; in this sense we may say he is infinite.

Touching what is said of his omnipresence, it is equally evident that if there be nothing exterior to this being, either there is no place in which he must not be present, or that there will be only himself and the vacuum. This granted, I shall inquire if matter exists; if it does not at least occupy a portion of space? In this case, matter, or the universe, must exclude every other being who is not matter, from that place which the material beings occupy in space. In asking whether the gods of the theologians be by chance the abstract being which they call the vacuum or space, they will reply, no! They will further insist, that their gods, who are not matter, penetrate that which is matter. But it must be obvious, that to penetrate matter, it is necessary to have some correspondence with matter, consequently to have extent; now to have extent, is to have one of the properties of matter. If the Divinity penetrates matter, then he is material; by a necessary deduction he is inseparable from matter; then if he is omnipresent, he will be in every thing. This the theologian will not allow: he will say it is a mystery; by which I shall understand that he is himself ignorant how to account for his own positions; this will not be the case with making nature act after immutable laws; she will of necessity be every where, in my body, in my arm, in every other material being, because matter composes them all. The Divinity who has given this invariable system, will without any incongruous reasoning, without any subterfuge, be also present every where, inasmuch as the laws he has prescribed will unchangeably act through the whole; this does not seem inconsistent with reason to suppose.

7th, "The Self-existent Being must of necessity be but one."

If there he nothing exterior to a being who exists necessarily, it must follow that he is unique. It will be obvious that this proposition is the same with the preceding one; at least, if they are not willing to deny the existence of the material world.

8th, "The self-existent and original Cause of all things, must be an intelligent being."

Here Dr. Clarke most unquestionably assigneth a human quality: intelligence is a faculty appertaining to organized or animated beings, of which we have no knowledge out of these beings. To have intelligence, it is necessary to think; to think, it is requisite to have ideas; to have ideas, supposes senses; when senses exist they are material; when they are material, they cannot be a pure spirit, in the language of the theologian.

The necessary Being who comprehends, who contains, who produces animated beings, contains, includes, and produceth intelligence. But has the great whole a peculiar intelligence, which moveth it, which maketh it act, which determineth it in the mode that intelligence moves and determines animated bodies; or rather, is not this intelligence the consequence of immutable laws, a certain modification resulting from certain combinations of matter, which exists under one form of these combinations, but is wanting under another form? This is assuredly what nothing is competent absolutely, and demonstrably to prove. Man having placed himself in the first rank in the universe, has been desirous to judge of every thing after what he saw within himself, because he hath pretended that in order to be perfect it was necessary to be like himself. Here is the source of all his erroneous reasoning upon nature—the foundation of his ideas upon his gods. He has therefore concluded, perhaps not with the most polished wisdom, that it would be indecorous in himself, injurious to the Divinity, not to invest him with a quality which is found estimable in man—which he prizes highly—to which he attaches the idea of perfection—which he considers as a manifest proof of superiority. He sees his fellow-creature is offended when he is thought to lack intelligence; he therefore judges it to be the same with the Divinity. He denies this quality to nature, because he considers her a mass of ignoble matter, incapable of self-action; although she contains and produces intelligent beings. But this is rather a personification of an abstract quality, than an attribute of the Deity, with whose perfections, with whose mode of existence, he cannot by any possible means become acquainted according to the fifth proposition of Dr. Clarke himself. It is in the earth that is engendered those living animals called worms; yet we do not say the earth is a living creature. The bread which man eats, the wine that he drinks, are not themselves thinking substances; yet they nourish, sustain, and cause those beings to think, who are susceptible of this modification of their existence. It is likewise in nature, that is formed intelligent, feeling, thinking beings; yet it cannot be rationally said, that nature feels, thinks, and is intelligent after the manner of these beings, who nevertheless spring out of her bosom.

How! cries the metaphysician, the subtilizing philosopher, what! refuse to the Divinity, those qualities we discover in his creatures? Must, then, the work be more perfect than the workman? Shall God, who made the eye, not himself see? Shall God, who formed the ear, not himself hear! This at a superficial view appears insuperable: but are the questioners, however triumphantly they may make the inquiry, themselves aware of the length this would carry them, even if their queries were answered with the most unqualified affirmative? Have they sufficiently reflected on the tendency of this mode of reasoning? If this be admitted as a postulatum, are they prepared to follow it in all its extent? Suppose their argument granted, what is to be done with all those other qualities upon which man does not set so high a value? Are they also to be ascribed to the Divinity, because we do not refuse him qualities possessed by his creatures? By a parity of reasoning we should attach faculties that would be degrading to the Divinity. Thus it ever happens with those who travel out of the limits of their own knowledge; they involve themselves in perpetual contradictions which they can never reconcile; which only serve to prove that in arguing upon points, on which universal ignorance prevails, the result is constantly that all the deductions made from such unsteady principles, must of necessity be at war with each other, in hostility with themselves. Thus, although we cannot help feeling the profound wisdom, that must have dictated the system we see act with such uniformity, with such constancy, with such astonishing power, we cannot form the most slender idea of the particular nature of that wisdom; because if we were for an instant to assimilate it to our own, weak and feeble as it is, we should from that instant be in a state of contradiction; seeing we could not then avoid considering the evil we witness, the sorrow we experience, as a dereliction of this wisdom, which at least proves one great truth, *that we are utterly incapable of forming an idea of the Divinity*. But in contemplating things as our own experience warrants in whatever we do understand, in considering nature as acting by unchangeable laws, we find good and evil necessarily existing, without at all involving the wisdom of the great *Cause of causes*; who thus has no need to remedy that, which the further progress of the eternal system will regulate of itself, or which industry and patient research on our parts will enable us to discover the means of futurely avoiding.

9th, "*The self-existent and original Cause of all things, is not a necessary agent, but a being endued with liberty and choice.*"

Man is called free, when he finds within himself motives that determine him to action, or when his will meets no obstacle to the performance of that to which his motives have determined him. The necessary Being of which question is here made, doth he find no obstacles to the execution of the projects which are attributed to him? Is he willing, adopting their own hypothesis, that evil should be committed, or can he not prevent it? In this latter case he is not free; if his will does meet with obstacles, if he is willing to permit evil; then he suffers man to restrain his liberty, by deranging his projects; if he has not these projects, then they are themselves in error who ascribe them to him. How will the metaphysicians draw themselves out of this perplexing intricacy?

The further a theologian goes, whilst considering his gods as possessed of human qualities, as acting by mortal motives, the more he flounders—the greater the mass of contradiction he heaps together: thus if it be asked of him, can God reward crime, punish virtue, he will immediately answer, no! In this answer he will have truth: but then this truth, and the freedom which is ascribed to him, cannot, according to human ideas, exist together; because if this being cannot love vice, cannot hate virtue, and it is evident he cannot, he is in fact not more free than man himself. Again, God is said to have made a covenant with his creatures; now it is the very essence of a covenant to restrict choice; and that being must be considered a necessary agent who is under the necessity of fulfilling any given act. As it is impossible to suppose the Divinity can act irrationally, it must be conceded that as he made these laws, he is himself obliged to follow them: because if he was not, as we must again suppose he does nothing without a good reason, he would thereby imply, that the mode of action he adopted would be wiser; which would again involve a contradiction. The theologians fearing, without doubt, to restrain the liberty of the Divinity, have supposed it was necessary that he should not be bound by his own laws, in which they have shewn somewhat more ignorance of their subject than they imagined.

10th, "The self-existent Being, the supreme Cause of all things, must of necessity have infinite power."

As nature is adequate to produce every thing we see—as she contains the whole united power of the universe, her power has consequently no limits: the being who conferred this power cannot have less. But if the ideas of the theologians were adopted, this power would not appear quite so unlimited; since, according to them, man is a free agent, consequently has the means of acting contrary to this power, which at once sets a boundary to it. An equitable monarch is perhaps nothing less than he is a free agent; when he believes himself bound to act conformably to the laws, which he has sworn to observe, or which he cannot violate without wounding his justice. The theologian is a man who may be very fairly estimated neuter; because he destroys with one hand what he establishes with the other.

11th, "The Supreme Cause and Author of all things, must of necessity be infinitely wise."

As nature produces all things by certain immutable laws, it will require no great difficulty to allow that she may be infinitely wise: indeed, whatever side of the argument may be taken, this fact will result as a necessary consequence. It will hardly admit of a question that all things are produced by nature: if, therefore, we do not allow her wisdom to be first rate, it would be an insult to the Divinity, who gave her her system. If the theologian himself is to take the lead, he also admits that nature operates under the immediate auspices of his gods; whatever she does, must then, according to his own shewing, be executed with the most polished wisdom. But the theologian is not satisfied with going thus far: he will insist, not only that he knows what these things are, but also that he knows the end they have in view: this, unfortunately, is the rock he splits upon. According to his own admission, the ways of God are impenetrable to man. If we grant his position, what is the result? Why, that it is at random he speaks. If these ways are impenetrable, by what means did he acquire his knowledge of them? How did he discover the end proposed by the Deity? If they are not impenetrable, they then can be equally known to other men as to himself. The theologian would be puzzled to shew he has any more privileges in nature than his fellow mortals. Again, if he has asserted these things to be impenetrable, when they are not so, he is then in the situation that he has himself placed Mahomet: he is no longer worthy of being attended to, because he has swerved from veracity. It certainly is not very consistent with the sublime idea of the Divinity that he should be clothed with that weak, vain passion of man, called glory: the being who had the faculty of producing such a system as it operated in nature, could hardly be supposed to have such a frivolous passion as we know this to be in our fellows: and as we can never reason but after what we do know, it would appear nothing can be more inconsistent than thus continually heaping together our own feeble, inconsistent views, and then supposing the great *Cause of causes* acts by such futile rules.

12th, "The supreme Cause and Author of all things must of necessity be a being of infinite goodness, justice, and truth, and all other moral perfections, such as become the supreme governor and judge of the world."

We must again repeat that these are human qualities drawn from the model of man himself; they only suppose a being of the human species, who should be divested of what we call imperfections: this is certainly the highest point of view in which our finite minds are capable of contemplating the Divinity: but as this being has neither species nor cause, consequently no fellow creatures, he must necessarily be of an order so different to man, that human faculties can in no wise be appropriately assigned to him. The idea of perfection, as man understands it, is an abstract, metaphysical, negative idea, of which he has no archetype whereby to form a judgment: he would call that a perfect being, who, similar to himself, was wanting in those qualities which he finds prejudicial to him; but such a being would after all be no wore than a man. It is always relatively to himself, to his own mode of feeling and of thinking, that a thing is either perfect or imperfect; it is according to this, that in his eyes a thing is more or less useful or prejudicial; agreeable or disagreeable. Justice includes all moral perfections. One of the most prominent features of justice, in the ideas of man, is the equity of the relations subsisting between beings, founded upon their mutual wants. According to the theologian, his gods owe nothing to man. How then does he measure out his ideas of justice? For a monarch to say he owed nothing to his subjects, would be considered, even by this theologian himself, as rank injustice; because he would expect the fulfilment of duties on their part, without exercising those which devolved upon himself. Duties, according to the only idea man can form of them, must be reciprocal. It is rather stretching the human capabilities, to understand the relations between a pure spirit and material beings—between finity and infinity—between eternal beings and those which are transitory: thus it is, that metaphysics hold forth an inconceivable being by the very attributes with which they clothe him; for either he has these attributes, or he has them not: whether he has them or has them not, man can only understand them after his own powers of comprehension. If he does at all understand them, he cannot have the slightest idea of justice unaccompanied by duties, which are the very basis, the superstructure, the pillars upon which this virtue rests. Whether we are to view it as self-love or ignorance in the theologian, that he thus dresses up his gods after himself, it certainly was not the happiest effort of his imagination to work by an inverse rule: for, according to himself, the qualities he describes are all the negation of what he calls them. Doctor Clarke himself stumbles a little upon these points; he insists upon free agency, and uses this extraordinary method to support his argument; he says, "God is, by necessity, a free agent: and he can no more possibly cease to be so, than he can cease to exist. He must of necessity, every moment choose to act, or choose to forbear acting; because two contradictories cannot possibly be true at once. Man also is by necessity, not in the nature of things, but through God's appointment, a free agent. And it is no otherwise in his power to cease to be such, than by depriving himself of life." Will Doctor Clarke permit us to put one simple question: If to be obligated to do a certain given thing, is to be free, what is it to be coerced? Or if two contradictories cannot be true at once, by what rule of logic are we to measure the idea of that freedom which arises out of necessity. Supposing necessity to be what Dr. Johnson, (using Milton as his authority) says it is, "compulsion," "fatality," would it be considered a man was less restrained in his actions because he was only compelled to do what was right? The restraint would undoubtedly he beneficial to him, but it would not therefore render him more a free agent. If the Divinity cannot love wickedness, cannot hate goodness, (and surely the theologians themselves will not pretend he can,) then the power of choice has no existence as far as these two things are concerned; and this upon Clarke's own principle, because two contradictories cannot be true at once. Nothing could, I think, appear a greater contradiction, than the idea that the *Great Cause of causes* could by any possibility love vice: if such a monstrous principle could for a moment have existence, there would be an end of all the foundations of religion.

The Doctor is very little happier in reasoning upon *immateriality*. He says, by way of illustrating his argument, "that it is possible to infinite power to create an immaterial cogitative substance, endued with a power of beginning motion, and with a liberty of will or choice." Again, "that immaterial substances are not impossible; or, that a substance immaterial is not a contradictory notion. Now, whoever asserts that it is contradictory, must affirm that whatever is not matter is nothing; and that, to say any thing exists which is not matter, is saying that there exists something which is nothing, which in other words is plainly this,—that whatever we have not an idea of, is nothing, and impossible to be." It could, I am apt to believe, never have entered into any reasonable mind that a thing was impossible because he could have no idea of it:—many things, on the contrary, are possible, of which we have not the most slender notion: but it does not, I presume, flow consecutively out of this admission, that therefore every thing is, which is not impossible. Doctor Clarke then, rather begs the question on this occasion. In the schools it is never considered requisite to prove a negative; indeed, this is ranked by logicians amongst those things impossible to be, but it is considered of the highest importance to soundness of argument, to establish the affirmative by the most conclusive reasoning. Taking this for granted, we will apply the doctor's own reasoning. He says, "Nothing is that of which every thing, can truly be affirmed. So that the idea of nothing, if I may so speak, is absolutely the negative of all ideas; the idea, therefore, either of a finite or infinite nothing is a contradiction in terms." To affirm, of a thing with truth, it must be necessary to be acquainted with that thing. To have ideas, as we have already proved, it is necessary to have perceptions; to have perceptions, it is requisite to have sensations; to have sensations, requires organs. An idea cannot be, and not be, at the same moment: the idea of substance, it will scarcely be denied, is that of a thing solid, real, according to Dryden; capable of supporting accidents, according to Watts; something of which we can say that it is, according to Davies; body, corporeal nature, according to Newton; the idea of immaterial, according to Hooker, is incorporeal. How then am I to understand immaterial substance? Is it not, according to these definitions, that which cannot couple together? If a thing be immaterial, it cannot be a substance; if a substance, it cannot be immaterial: those I apprehend will not have many ideas, who do not see this is a complete negative of all ideas. If, therefore, on the outset, the doctor cannot find words, by which he can convey the idea of that of which he is so desirous to prove the existence, by what chain of reasoning does he flatter himself that he is to be understood? He will endeavour to draw out of this dilemma, by assuring as there are things which we can neither see nor touch, but which do not the less exist on that account. Granted: but from thence we can neither reason upon them, nor assign them qualities; we must at least either feel them or something like them, before we can have any idea of them: this, however, would not prove they were not substances, nor that substances can be immaterial. A thing may with great possibility exist of which we have no knowledge, and yet be material; but I maintain until we have a knowledge of it, it exists not for us, any more than colours exist for a man born blind; the man who has sight knows they do exist, can describe them to his dark neighbour; from this description the blind man may form some idea of them by analogy with what he himself already knows; or, perhaps, having a finer tact than his neighbour, he may be enabled to distinguish them by their surfaces; it would, therefore, be bad reasoning in the man born blind, to deny the existence of colours; because although these colours may have no relation with the senses in the absence of sight, they have with those who have it in their power to see and to know them: this blind man, however, would-appear a little ridiculous if he undertook to define them with all their gradations of shade; with all their variations under different masses of light. Again, if those who were competent to discriminate these modifications of matter called colours, were to define them to this blind man, as those modifications of matter called sound, would the blind man be able to have any conception of them? It certainly would not be wise in him to aver, that such a thing as colorific sound had no existence, was impossible; but at least he would be very justifiable in saying, they appeared contradictions, because he had some ideas of sound which did not at all aid him in forming those of colour; he would not, perhaps, be very inconclusive if he suspected the competency of his informer to the definition attempted, from his inability to convey to him in any distinct, understood terms, his own ideas of colours. The theologian is a blind man, who would explain to others who are also blind, the shades and colours of a portrait whose original he has not even stumbled upon in the dark. There is nothing incongruous in supposing that every thing which has existence is matter; but it requires the complete inversion of all our ideas, to conceive that which is immaterial; because, in point of fact, this would be a quality of which "nothing can with truth be affirmed."

It is, indeed true, that Plato, who was a great creator of chimeras, says, "those who admit nothing but what they can see and feel, are stupid ignorant beings, who refuse to admit the reality of the existence of invisible things." With all due deference to such an authority, we may still venture to ask, is there then no difference, no shade, no gradation, between an admission of possibilities and the proof of realities. Theology would then be the only science in which it is permitted to conclude that a thing is, as soon as it is possible to be. Will the assertion of either Clarke or Plato stand absolutely in place of all evidence? Would they themselves permit such to be convincing if used against them? The theologians evidently hold this Platonic, this dogmatical language; they have dreamed the dreams of their master; perhaps if they were examined a little, they would be found nothing more than the result of those obscure notions, those unintelligible metaphysics, adopted by the Egyptian, Chaldean, and Assyrian priests, among whom Plato drew up his philosophy. If, however, philosophy means that which we are led to suppose it does, by the great John Locke, it is "a system by which natural effects are explained." Taken in this sense we shall be under the necessity of agreeing, that the Platonic doctrines in no wise merit this distinction, seeing he has only drawn the human mind from the contemplation of visible nature, to plunge it into the unfathomable depths of invisibility—of intangibility—of suppositious speculation, where it can find little other food except chimeras or conjecture. Such a philosophy is rather fantastical, yet it would seem we are required to subscribe to its positions without being allowed to compare them with reason, to examine them through the medium of experience, to try the gold by the action of fire: thus we have in abundance the terms spirits, incorporeal substances, invisible powers, supernatural effects, innate ideas, mysterious virtues, possessed by demons, &c. &c. which render our senses entirely useless, which put to flight every thing like experience; while we are gravely told that "nothing is that, of which no thing can truly be affirmed." Whoever may be willing to take the trouble of reading the works of Plato and his disciples, such as Proclus, Iamblicus, Plotinus, and others, will not fail to find in them almost every doctrine, every metaphysical subject of the theologian; in fact, the theurgy of many of the modern superstitions, which for the most part seems to be little more than a slight variation of that adopted by the ethnic priests. Dreamers have not had that variety in their follies, that has generally been imagined. That some of these things should be extensively admitted, by no means affords proof of their existence. Nothing appears more facile than to make mankind admit the greatest absurdities, under the imposing name of mysteries; after having imbued him from his infancy with maxims calculated to hoodwink his reason—to lead him astray—to prevent him from examining that which he is told he must believe. Of this there cannot well exist a more decisive proof than the great extent of country, the millions of human beings who faithfully and without examination have adopted the idle dreams, the rank absurdities, of that arch impostor Mahomet. However this may be, we shall be obliged again to reply to Plato, and to those of his followers who impose upon us the necessity of believing that which we cannot comprehend, that, in order to know that a thing exists, it is at least necessary to have some idea of it; that this idea can only come to us by the medium of our senses; that consequently every thing of which our senses do not give us a knowledge, is in fact nothing for us; and can only rest upon our faith; upon that admission which is pretty generally, even by the theologian himself, considered as rather a sandy foundation whereon to erect the altar of truth: that if there be an absurdity in not accrediting the existence of that which we do not know, there is no less extravagance in assigning it qualities; in reasoning upon its properties; in clothing it with faculties, which may or may not be suitable to its mode of existence; in substituting idols of our own creation; in combining incompatible attributes, which will neither bear the test of experience nor the scrutiny of reason; and then endeavouring to make the whole pass current by dint of the word infinite, which we will now examine.

Infinite, according to Dennis, means "boundless, unlimited." Doctor Clarke thus describes it:—he says, "The self-existent being must be a most simple, unchangeable incorruptible being; without parts, figure, motion, divisibility, or any other such properties as we find in matter. For all these things do plainly and necessarily imply finiteness in their very notion, and are utterly inconsistent with complete infinity." Ingenuously, is it possible for man to form any true notion of such a quality? The theologians themselves acknowledge he cannot. Further, the Doctor allows, "That as to the particular manner of his being infinite, or every where present, in opposition to the manner of created things being present in such or such finite places, this is as impossible for our finite understandings to comprehend or explain, as it is for us to form an adequate idea of infinity." What is this, then, but that which no man can explain or comprehend? If it cannot be comprehended, it cannot be detailed; if it cannot be detailed, it is precisely "that of which nothing can with truth be affirmed;" and this is Dr. Clarke's own explanation of nothing. Indeed, is not the human mind obliged by its very nature to join limited quantities to other quantities, which it can only conceive as limited, in order to form to itself a sort of confused idea of something beyond its own grasp, without ever reaching the point of infinity, which eludes every attempt at definition? Then it would appear that it is an abstraction, a mere negation of limitation.

Our learned adversary seems to think it strange that the existence of incorporeal, immaterial substances, the essence of which we are not able to comprehend, should not be generally accredited. To enforce this belief, he says, "There is not so mean and contemptible a plant or animal, that does not confound the most enlarged understanding, upon earth: nay, even the simplest and plainest of all inanimate beings have their essence or substance hidden from us in the deepest and most impenetrable obscurity."

We shall reply to him,

First, That the idea of an immaterial substance; or being without extent, is only an absence of ideas, a negation of extent, as we have already shewn; that when we are told a being is not matter, they speak to us of that which is not, and do not teach us that which is; because by insisting that a being is such, that it cannot act upon any of our senses, they, in fact, inform us that we have no means of assuring ourselves whether such being exists or not.

Secondly, We shall avow without the least hesitation, that men of the greatest genius, of the most indefatigable research, are not acquainted with the essence of stones, plants, animals, nor with the secret springs which constitute some, which make others vegetate or act: but then at least we either feel them or see them; our senses have a knowledge of them in some respects; we can perceive some of their effects; we have something whereby to judge of them, either accurately or inaccurately; we can conceive that which is matter, however varied, however subtle, however minute, by analogy with other matter; but our senses cannot compass that which is immaterial on any side; we cannot by any possible means understand it; we have no means whatever of ascertaining its existence; consequently we cannot even form an idea of it; such a being is to us an occult principle, or rather a being which imagination has composed, by deducting from it every known quality. If we are ignorant of the intimate combination of the most material beings, we at least discover, with the aid of experience, some of their relations with ourselves: we have a knowledge of their surface, their extent, their form, their colour, their softness, their density; by the impressions they make on our senses, we are capable of discriminating them—of comparing them—of judging of them in some manner—of seeing them—of either avoiding or courting them, according to the different modes in which we are affected by them; we cannot apply any of these tests to immaterial beings; to spirits; neither can those men who are unceasingly talking to mankind of these inconceivable things.

Thirdly, We have a consciousness of certain modifications in ourselves, which we call sentiment, thought, will, passions: for want of being acquainted with our own peculiar essence; for want of precisely understanding the energy of our own particular organization, we attribute these effects to a concealed cause, distinguished from ourselves; which the theologians call a spiritual cause, inasmuch as it appears to act differently from our body. Nevertheless, reflection, experience, every thing by which we are enabled to form any kind of judgment, proves that material effects can only emanate from material causes. We see nothing in the universe but physical, material effects, these can only be produced by analogous causes; it is, then certainly more rational to attribute them to nature herself, of which we may know something, if we will but deign to meditate her with attention, rather than to spiritual causes, of which we must for ever remain ignorant, let us study them as long as we please.

If incomprehensibility be not a sufficient reason for absolutely denying the possibility of immateriality, it certainly is not of a cogency to establish its existence; we shall always be less in a capacity to comprehend a spiritual cause, than one that is material; because materiality is a known quality; spirituality is an occult, an unknown quality; or rather it is a mode of speech of which we avail ourselves to throw a veil over our own ignorance. We are repeatedly told that our senses only bring us acquainted with the external of things; that our limited ideas are not capable of conceiving immaterial beings: we agree frankly to this position; but then our senses do not even shew us the external of these immaterial substances, Which the theologians will nevertheless attempt to define to us; upon which they unceasingly dispute among themselves; upon which even until this day they are not in perfect unison with each other. The great John Locke in his familiar letters, says, "I greatly esteem all those who faithfully defend their opinions; but there are so few persons who, according to the manner they do defend them, appear fully convinced of the opinions they profess, that I am tempted to believe there are more sceptics in the world than are generally imagined."

Abady, one of the most strenuous supporters of immaterialism, says, "The question is not what incorporeity is, but whether it be." To settle this disputable point, it were necessary to have some data whereon to form our judgment; but how assure ourselves of the existence of that, of which we shall never be competent to have a knowledge? If we are not told what this is; if some tangible evidence be not offered to the human mind; how shall we feel ourselves capacitated to judge whether or not its existence be even possible? How form an estimate of that picture whose colours elude our sight, whose design we cannot perceive, whose features have no means of becoming familiar to our mind, whose very canvas refuses itself to our all research, of which the artist himself can afford no other idea, no other description, but that it is, although he himself can neither shew us how or where! We have seen the ruinous foundations upon which men have hitherto erected this fanciful idea of immateriality; we have examined the proofs which they have offered, if proofs they can be called, in support of their hypothesis; we have sifted the evidence they have been willing to have accredited, in order to establish their position; we have pointed out the numberless contradictions that result from their want of union on this subject, from the irreconcileable qualities with which they clothe their imaginary system. What conclusion, then, ought fairly, rationally, consistently, to be drawn from the whole? Can we, or can we not admit their argument to be conclusive, such as ought to be received by beings who think themselves sane? Will it allow any other inference than that it has no existence; that immateriality is a quality hitherto unproved; the idea of which the mind of man has no means of compassing? Still they will insist, "there are no contradictions between the qualities which they attribute to these immaterial substances; but there is a difference between the understanding of man and the nature of these substances." This granted, are they nearer the point at which they labour? What standard is it necessary man should possess, to enable him to judge of these substances? Can they shew the test that will lead to an acquaintance with them? Are not those who have thus given loose to their imagination, who have given birth to this system, themselves men? Does not the disproportion, of which they speak with such amazing confidence, attach to themselves as well as to others? If it needs an infinite mind to comprehend infinity—to form an idea of incorporeity—can the theologian himself boast he is in a capacity to understand it? To what purpose then is it they speak of these things to others? Why do they attempt descriptions of that which they allow to be indescribable? Man, who will never be an infinite being, will never be able to conceive infinity; if, then, he has hitherto been incompetent to this perfection of knowledge, can he reasonably flatter himself he will ever obtain it; can he hope under any circumstances to conquer that which according to the shewing of all is unconquerable?

Nevertheless it is pretended, that it is absolutely necessary to know these substances: but how prove the necessity of having a knowledge of that which is impossible to be known? We are then told that good sense and reason are sufficient to convince us of its existence: this is taking new ground, when the old has been found untenable: for we are also told that reason is a treacherous guide; one that frequently leads us astray; that in religious matters it ought not to prevail: at least then they ought to shew us the precise time when we must resume this reason. Shall we consult it again, when the question is, whether what they relate is probable; whether the discordant qualities which they unite are consistently combined; whether their own arguments have all that solidity which they would themselves wish them to possess? But we have strangely mistaken them if they are willing that we should recur to it upon these points; they will instead, insist we ought blindly to be directed by that which they vouchsafe to inform us; that the most certain road to happiness is to submit in all things to that which they have thought proper to decide on the nature of things, of which they avow their own ignorance, when they assert them to be beyond the reach of mortals. Thus it would appear that when we should consent to accredit these mysteries, it would never arise of our own knowledge; seeing this can no otherwise obtain but by the effect of demonstrable evidence; it would never arise from any intimate conviction of our minds; but it would be entirely on the word of the theologian himself, that we should ground our faith; that we should yield our belief. If these things are to the human species what colours are to the man born blind, they have at least no existence with relation to ourselves. It will avail the blind man nothing to tell him these colours have no less existence, because he cannot see them. But what shall we say of that portrait whose colours the blind man attempts to explain, whose features he is willing we should receive upon his authority, whose proportions are to be taken from his description, merely because we know he cannot behold them?

The Doctor, although unwilling to relinquish his subject, removes none of the difficulty when he asks, "Are our five senses, by an absolute necessity in the nature of the thing, all and the only possible ways of perception? And is it impossible and contradictory there should be any being in the universe, indued with ways of perception different from these that are the result of our present composition? Or are these things, on the contrary, purely arbitrary; and the same power that gave us these, may have given others to other beings, and might, if he had pleased have given to us others in this present state?" It seems perfectly unnecessary to the true point of the argument to reason upon what can or cannot be done: I therefore reply, that the fact is, we have but five senses: by the aid of these man is not competent to form any idea whatever of immateriality; but he is also in as absolute a state of ignorance, upon what might be his capabilities of conception, if he had more senses. It is rather acknowledging a weakness in his evidence, on the part of the Doctor, to be thus obliged to rest it upon the supposition of what might be the case, if man was a being different to what he is; in other words, that they would be convincing to mankind if the human race were not human beings. Therefore to demand what the Divinity could have done in such a case, is to suppose the thing in question, seeing we cannot form an idea how far the power of the Divinity extends: but we may be reasonably allowed to use the theological argument in elucidation; these men very gravely insist, upon what authority must be best known to themselves, "that God cannot communicate to his works that perfection which he himself possesses;" at the same moment they do not fail to announce his omnipotence. Will it require any capacity, more than is the common lot of a child, to comprehend the absurd contradiction of the two assertions? As beings possessing but five senses, we must then, of necessity, regulate our judgment by the information they are capable of affording us: we cannot, by any possibility, have a knowledge of those, which confer the capacity to comprehend beings, of an order entirely distinguished from that in which we occupy a place. We are ignorant of the mode in which even plants vegetate, how then be acquainted with that which has no affinity with ourselves? A man born blind, has only the use of four senses; he has not the right, however, of assuming it as a fact, there does not exist an extra sense for others; but he may very reasonably, and with great truth aver, that he has no idea of the effects which would be produced in him, by the sense which he lacks: notwithstanding, if this blind man was surrounded by other men, whose birth had also left them devoid or sight, might he not without any very unwarrantable presumption, be authorized to inquire of them by what right, upon what authority, they spoke to him of a sense they did not themselves possess; how they were enabled to reason, to detail the minutiae of that sensation upon which their own peculiar experience taught them nothing?

In short, we can again reply to Dr. Clarke, and to the theologians, that following up their own systems, the supposition is impossible, and ought not to be made, seeing that the Divinity, who according to their own shewing, made man, was not willing that he should have more than five senses; in other words, that he should be nothing but what he actually is; they all found the existence of these immaterial substances upon the necessity of a power that has the faculty to give a commencement to motion. But if matter has always existed, of which there does not seem to exist a doubt, it has always had motion, which is as essential to it as its extent, and flows from its primitive properties. Indeed the human mind, with its five senses, is not more competent to comprehend matter devoid of motion, than it is to understand the peculiar quality of immateriality: motion therefore exists only in and by matter; mobility is a consequence of its existence; not that the great whole can occupy other parts of space than it actually does; the impossibility of that needs no argument, but all its parts can change their respective situations—do continually change them; it is from thence results the preservation, the life of nature, which is always as a whole immutable: but in supposing, as is done every day, that matter is inert, that is to say, incapable of producing any thing by itself, without the assistance of a moving power, which sets it in motion, are we by any means enabled to conceive that material nature receives this activity from an agent, who partakes in nothing of material substance? Can man really figure to himself, even in idea, that that which has no one property of matter, can create matter, draw it from its own peculiar source, arrange it, penetrate it, give it play, guide its course? Is it not, on the contrary, more rational to the mind, more consistent with truth, more congenial to experience, to suppose that the being who made matter is himself material: is there the smallest necessity to suppose otherwise? Can it make man either better or worse, that he should consider the whole that exists as material? Will it in any manner make him a worse subject to his sovereign; a worse father to his children; a more unkind husband; a more faithless friend?

Motion, then, is co-eternal with matter: from all eternity the particles of the universe have acted and reacted upon each other, by virtue of their respective energies; of their peculiar essences; of their primitive elements; of their various combinations. These particles must have combined in consequence of their affinity; they must have been either attracted or repelled by their respective relations with each other; in virtue of these various essences, they must have gravitated one upon the other; united when they were analagous; separated when that analogy was dissolved, by the approach of heterogeneous matter; they must have received their forms, undergone a change of figure, by the continual collision of bodies. In a material world the acting powers must be material: in a whole every part of which is essentially in motion, there is no occasion for a power distinguished from itself; the whole must be in perpetual motion by its own peculiar energy. The general motion, as we have elsewhere proved, has its birth from the individual motion, which beings ever active must uninterruptedly communicate to each other. Thus every cause produces its effect; this effect in its turn becomes a cause, which in like manner produces an effect; this constitutes the eternal chain of things, which although perpetually changing in its detail, suffers no change in its whole.

Theology, after all, has seldom done more than personify this eternal series of motion; the principle of mobility inherent to matter: it has clothed this principle with human qualities, by which it has rendered it unintelligible: in applying these properties, they have taken no means of understanding how far they were suitable or not: in their eagerness to make them assimilate, they have extended them beyond their own conception; they have heaped them together without any judgment; and they have been surprised when these qualities, contradictory in themselves, did not enable them satisfactorily to account for all the phenomena they beheld; from thence they have wrangled; accused each other of imbecility; yet infuriated themselves against whoever had the temerity to question that which they did not themselves understand; in short, they have acted like a man who should insist that all other men should have precisely the same vision that he himself had dreamed.

Be this as it may, the greater portion of what either Dr. Clarke or the theologians tell us, becomes, in some respects, sufficiently intelligible as soon as applied to nature—to matter: it is eternal, that is to say, it cannot have had a commencement, it never will have an end; it is infinite, that is to say, we have no conception of its limits. Nevertheless, human qualities, which must be always borrowed from ourselves, and with others we have a very slender acquaintance, cannot be well suitable to the entire of nature; seeing that these qualities are in themselves modes of being, or modes which appertain only to particular beings: not to the great whole which contains them.

Thus, to resume the answers which have been given to Dr. Clarke, we shall say: *First*, we can conceive that matter has existed from all eternity, seeing that we cannot conceive it to have been capable of beginning. *Secondly*, that matter is independent, seeing there is nothing exterior to itself; that it is immutable, seeing it cannot change its nature, although it is unceasingly changing its form and its combinations. *Thirdly*, that matter is self-existent, since not being able to conceive it can be annihilated, we cannot possibly conceive it can have commenced to exist. *Fourthly*, that we do not know the essence, or the true nature of matter, although we have a knowledge of some of its properties; of some of its qualities: according to the mode in which they act upon us. *Fifthly*, that matter not having had a beginning, will never have an end, although its numerous combinations, its various forms, have necessarily a commencement and a period. *Sixthly*, that if all that exists, or every thing our mind can conceive is matter, this matter is infinite; that is to say, cannot be limited by any thing; that it is omnipresent, seeing there is no place exterior to itself, indeed, if there was a place exterior to it, that would be a vacuum. *Seventhly*, that nature is unique, although its elements or its parts may be varied to infinity, indued with properties extremely opposite; with qualities essentially different. *Eighthly*, that matter, arranged, modified, and combined in a certain mode, produces in some beings what we call intelligence, which is one of its modes of being, not one of its essential properties, *Ninthly*, that matter is not a free agent, since it cannot act otherwise than it does, in virtue of the laws of its nature, or of its existence; that consequently, heavy bodies must necessarily fall; light bodies by the same necessity rise; fire must burn; man must experience good and evil, according to the quality of the beings whose action he experiences. *Tenthly*, that the power or the energy of matter, has no other bounds than those which are prescribed by its own existence. *Eleventhly*, that wisdom, justice, goodness, &c. are qualities peculiar to matter combined and modified, as it is found in some beings of the human species; that the idea of perfection is an abstract, negative, metaphysical idea, or mode of considering objects, which supposes nothing real to be exterior to itself. *Twelfthly*, that matter is the principle of motion, which it contains within itself: since matter alone is capable of either giving or receiving motion: this is what cannot be conceived of immateriality or simple beings destitute of parts, devoid of extent, without mass, having no ponderosity, which consequently cannot either move itself or other bodies.

CHAP. V.

Examination of the Proofs offered by DESCARTES, MALEBRANCHE, NEWTON, &c.

If the evidence of Clarke did not prove satisfactory—if the theologians of his day disputed the manner in which he handled his subject—if they were disposed to think he had not established his argument upon proper foundations, it did not seem probable that either the system of Descartes, the sublime reveries of Malebranche, or the more methodical mode adopted by Newton, were at all likely to meet with a better reception; the same objections will lie against them all, that they have not demonstrated the existence of their immaterial substances; although they have incessantly spoken of them, as if they were things of which they had the most intimate knowledge. Unfortunately this is a rock which the most sublime geniuses have not been competent to avoid: the most enlightened men have done little more than stammer upon a subject which they have all concurred in considering of the highest importance; which they unceasingly hold forth as the most necessary for man to know; without at the same time considering he is not in a condition to occupy himself with objects inaccessible to his senses—which his mind, consequently, can never grasp—which his utmost research cannot bring into that tangible shape by which alone he can be enabled to form a judgment.

To the end that we may be convinced of that want of solidity which the greatest men have not known how to give to the proofs they have offered, but which they have successively imagined has established their positions, let us briefly examine what the most celebrated philosophers, what the most subtile metaphysicians have said. For this purpose we will begin with Descartes, the restorer of philosophy among the moderns, to whose sublime errors we are indebted for the effulgent truths of the Newtonian system. This great man himself tells us, "All the strength of argument which I have hitherto used to prove the existence of immaterial substances, consists in this, that I acknowledge it would not be possible, my nature was such as it is, that is to say, that I should have in me the idea of immateriality, if this incorporeity did not truly exist; this same immateriality, of which the idea is in me, possesses all those high perfections of which our mind can have some slight idea, without however being able to comprehend them." In another place he says, "We must necessarily conclude from this alone, that because I exist, and have the idea of immateriality, that is to say, of a most perfect being, the existence is therefore most evidently demonstrated." There are not, perhaps, many except Descartes himself, to whom this would appear quite so conclusive; who would be impressed with the conviction which he seems to imagine is so very substantive.

First, We shall reply to Descartes, it is not a warrantable deduction, that because we have an idea of a thing, we must therefore conclude it exists; to give validity to such a mode of reasoning would be productive of the greatest mischief; would, in fact, tend to subvert all human institutions. Our imagination presents us with the idea of a sphinx, or of an hippogriff, besides a thousand other fantastical beings; are we, on that authority, to insist that these things really exist? Is the mere circumstance of our having an idea of various parts of nature, discrepantly jumbled together, without any other evidence as to the assemblage, a sufficient warranty for calling upon mankind to accredit the existence of such heterogeneous masses? If a philosopher of the most consummate experience, of the greatest celebrity, one who enjoyed the confidence of mankind above every other, was to detail the faculties and perfections of these visionary beings, although he should hold them forth as the perfection of all natural combinations, would, I say, any reasonable being lend himself to the asseveration?

Secondly, It is obvious that the mere circumstance of existence, does not prove the absolute existence of any thing anterior to itself; although in man, as well as the other beings of nature, it is evidence that something has existed before him. If this argument was to be admitted, are they aware how far it, would carry them? To maintain that the existence of one being demonstrably proves the existence of an anterior being, would be, in fact, denying that any thing was self-existent. The fallacy of such a position is too glaring to need refutation.

Thirdly, It is not possible he should have a distinct, positive idea of immateriality, of which be, as well as the theologian, labours to prove the existence. It is impossible for man, for a material being, to form to himself a correct idea, or indeed any idea, of incorporeity; of a substance without extent, acting upon nature, which is corporeal; a truth which it may not be presuming too much to say we have already sufficiently proved.

Fourthly, It is equally impossible for man to have any clear, decided idea of perfection, of infinity, of immensity, and other theological attributes. To Descartes we must therefore reply as we have done to Dr. Clarke on his twelfth proposition.

Thus nothing can well be less conclusive than the proofs upon which Descartes rests the existence of immateriality. He gives it thought and intelligence, but how conceive these qualities without a subject to which they may adhere? He pretends that we cannot conceive it but "as a power which applies itself successively to the parts of the universe." Again, he says, "that an immaterial substance cannot be said to have extent, but as we say of fire contained in a piece of iron, which has not, properly speaking, any other extension than that of the iron itself." According to these notions we shall be justified in taxing him with having announced in a very clear, in a most unequivocal manner, that this is nature herself: this indeed is a pure Spinosism; it was decidedly on the principles of Descartes that Spinosa drew up his system; in fact it flows out of it consecutively.

We might, therefore, with great reason, accuse Descartes of atheism, seeing that he very effectually destroys the feeble proofs he adduces in support of his own hypothesis; we have solid foundation for insisting that his system overturns the idea of the creation, because if from the modification we subtract the subject, the modification itself disappears: and if, according to the Cartesians, this immateriality is nothing without nature, they are complete Spinosians, with another name. If incorporeity is the motive-power of this nature, it no longer exists independently; it, in fact, exists no longer than the subject to which it is inherent subsists. Thus no longer existing independently, it will exist only while the nature which it moves shall endure; without matter, without a subject to move, to preserve, what is to become of it, according to this doctrine, or rather according to this elucidation of a system which is in itself untenable?

It will be obvious from this, that Descartes, far from establishing on a rocky foundation the existence of this immateriality, totally destroys his own system. The same thing will necessarily happen to all those who reason upon his principles; they will always finish by confuting him, and by contradicting themselves. The same want of just inference, the same discrepancy, will obtrude themselves in the principles of the celebrated Father Malebranche; which, if considered with the slightest attention, appear to conduct directly to Spinosism; in fact, can any thing be more in unison with the language of Spinosa himself, than to say, as does Malebranche, "that the universe is only an emanation from God; that we see every thing in God, that every thing we see is only God; that God alone does every thing that is done; that all the action, with every operation that takes place in nature, is God himself; in a word, that God is every being and the only being." Is not this formally asserting that nature herself is God? Moreover, at the same time Malebranche assures us we see every thing in God, he pretends that it is not yet clearly demonstrated that matter and bodies have existence; that faith alone teaches us these mysteries, of which, without it, we should not have any knowledge whatever. In reply, it might be a very fair question, how the existence of the being who created matter can be demonstrated, if the existence of this matter itself be yet a problem? He himself acknowledges "that we can have no distinct demonstration of the existence of any other being than of that which is necessary;" he further adds, "that if it be closely examined, it will be seen, that it is not even possible to know with certitude, if God be or be not truly the creator of a material, of a sensible world." According to these notions, it is evident, that, following up the system of Malebranche, man has only his faith to guarantee the existence of the world; yet faith itself supposes its existence; if it be not, however, certain that it does exist, and the Bishop of Cloyne, Dr. Berkeley, has also held this in doubt, how shall we be persuaded that we must believe the oracles which have been delivered to a visionary world?

On the other hand, these notions of Malebranche completely overturns all the theological doctrines of free agency. How can the liberty of man's action be reconciled with the idea that it is the Divinity who is the immediate mover of nature; who actually gives impulse to matter and bodies, without whose immediate interference nothing takes place; who pre-determines his creatures to every thing they do? How can it be pretended, if this doctrine is to be accredited, that human souls have the faculty of forming thoughts—have the power of volition—are in a condition to move themselves—have the capacity to modify their existence? If it be supposed with the theologians, that the conservation of the creatures in the universe is a continued creation, must it not appear, that being thus perpetually recreated, they are enabled to commit evil? It will then be a self-evident fact, that, admitting the system of Malebranche, God does every thing, and that his creatures are no more than passive instruments in his hands. Under this idea they could not be answerable for their sins, because they would have no means of avoiding them. Under this notion they could neither have merit or demerit; they would be like a sharp instrument in their own hands, which whether it was applied to a good or to an evil purpose, it would attach to themselves, not to the instrument: this would annihilate all religion: it is thus that theology is continually occupied with committing suicide.

Let us now see, if the immortal Newton, the great luminary of science, the champion of astronomical truth, will afford us clearer notions, more distinct ideas, more certain evidence of the existence of immaterial substances. This great man, whose comprehensive genius unravelled nature, whose capacious mind developed her laws, seems to have bewildered himself, the instant he lost sight of them. A slave to the prejudices of his infancy, he had not the courage to hold the lamp of his own enlightened understanding to the agent theology has so gratuitously associated with nature; he has not been able to allow that her own peculiar powers were adequate to the production of that beautiful phenomena, he has with such masterly talents so luminously explained. In short, the sublime Newton himself becomes an infant when he quits physics, when he lays aside demonstration, to lose himself in the devious sinuosities, in the inextricable labyrinths, in the delusive regions of theology. This is the manner in which he speaks of the Divinity:

"This God," says he, "governs all, not as the soul of the world, but as the lord and sovereign of all things. It is in consequence of his sovereignty that he is called the Lord God, [Greek letters], *pantokrator*, the universal emperor. Indeed the word God is relative and relates itself with slaves; the Deity is the dominion or the sovereignty of God, not over his own body, as those think who look upon God as the soul of the world, but over slaves."

From this it will be seen that Newton, as well as the theologians, makes the Divinity a pure spirit, who presides over the universe as a monarch, as a lord paramount; that is to say, what man defines in earthly governors, despot, absolute princes, powerful monarchs, whose governments have no model but their own will, who exercise an unlimited power over their subjects, transformed into slaves; whom they usually compel to feel in a very grievous manner the weight of their authority. But according to the ideas of Newton, the world has not existed from eternity, the staves of God have been formed in the course of time; from this it would be a just inference, that before the creation of the world the god of Newton was a sovereign without subjects. Let us see if this truly great philosopher is more in unison with himself in the subsequent ideas which he delivers on this subject.

"The supreme God," he says, "is an eternal, infinite, and absolutely perfect being; but however perfect a being may be, if he has no sovereignty he is not the supreme God. The word God signifies Lord, but every lord is not god; it is the sovereignty of the spiritual Being which constitutes God; it is the true sovereignty which constitutes the true God; it is the supreme sovereignty which constitutes the supreme God; it is a false sovereignty which constitutes a false god. From true sovereignty, it follows, that the true God is living, intelligent, and powerful; and from his other perfections, it follows, that he is supremely or sovereignly perfect. He is eternal, infinite, omniscient; that is to say, he exists from eternity, and will never have an end; he governs all, and he knows every thing that is done, or that can be done. He is neither eternity nor infinity, but he is eternal and infinite; he is not space or duration, but he exists and is present." The term here used is *adest*, which appears to have been placed there to avoid saying that God is contained in space.

In all this unintelligible series, nothing is to be found but incredible efforts to reconcile the theological attributes, the abstract with the human qualities, which have been ascribed to the Divinity; we see in it negative qualities, which can no longer be suitable to man, given, however, to the Sovereign of nature, whom he has supposed a king. However it may be, this picture always supposes the Supreme God to have occasion for subjects to establish his sovereignty. It makes God stand in need of man for the exercise of his empire; without these, according to the text, he would not be a king; he could have had no empire when there was nothing: but if this description of Newton was just, if it really represented the Divinity, we might be very fairly permitted to ask, Does not this Spiritual King exercise his spiritual empire in vain, upon refractory beings, who do not at all times do that which he is willing they should; who are continually struggling against his power; who spread disorder in his states? This Spiritual Monarch, who is master of the minds, of the souls, of the wills, of the passions of his slaves, does he leave them the freedom of revolting against him? This infinite Monarch, who fills every thing with his immensity, who governs all, does he also govern the man who sins; does he direct his actions; is he in him when he offends his God? The devil, the false god, the evil principle, hath he not, according to this, a more extensive empire than the true God, whose projects, if we are to believe the theologians, he is unceasingly overturning? In earthly governments the true sovereign is generally considered to be him whose power in a state influences the greater number of his subjects. If, then, we could suppose him to be omnipresent, that is, present in all places, should we not say he was the sad witness to all the outrages committed against his authority, and we should not entertain a very exalted opinion of his power if he permitted them to continue. This, it is true, would be arguing upon a monarch of this world, still it would be the language held by observers.

Is the spirituality of the Divinity well supported by those who say he fills all space, who from that instant give him extent, ascribe to him volume, make him correspond with the various points of space? This is the very reverse of an immaterial substance.

"God is one," continues Newton, "and he is the same for ever, and every where, not only by his virtue alone, or by his energy, but also by his substance." But how are we to conceive that a being who is in continual activity, who produces all the changes which beings undergo, can always be himself the same? What is to be understood by either this virtue or this energy? These are relative terms, which do not present any clear, distinct idea to our mind, except as they apply to man: what are we, however, to understand by the divine substance? If this substance be spiritual, that is, devoid of extent, how can there exist in it any parts? How can it give impulse to matter, how set it in motion? How can it even be conceived by mortals?

Nevertheless Newton informs us, "that all things are contained in him, and are moved in him, but without reciprocity of action: God experiences nothing by the motion of bodies; these experience no resistance whatever by his omnipresence." It would here appear that he clothes the Divinity with that which bears the character of vacuum—of nothing; without that, it would be almost impossible not to have a reciprocal action or relation between these substances, which are either penetrated or encompassed on all sides. It must be obvious, that in this instance our scientific author does not distinctly understand himself.

He proceeds, "It is an incontestible truth, that God exists necessarily, and the same necessity obliges to exist always and every where: from whence it follows, that he is in every thing similar to itself; he is all eyes, all ears, all brains, all arms, all feeling, all intelligence, all action; but in a mode by no means human, by no means corporeal, and which is totally unknown to us. In the same manner as a blind man has no idea of colours, it is that we have no idea of the mode in which God feels and understands." The necessary existence of the Divinity is precisely the thing in question; it is this existence that it was needful to have verified by proofs as clear, by evidence as distinct, by demonstration as strong, as gravitation and attraction. One would have hardly thought it possible the expansive capabilities of Newton would not have compassed it. But oh, unrivalled genius! so mighty, so powerful, so colossal, while yet you was a geometrician; so insignificant, so weak, so inconsistent; when you became a theologian; that is to say, when you reasoned upon that which can neither be calculated, nor submitted to experience; how could you think of speaking to us on a subject which, by your own confession is to you just what a picture is to a man born blind? Wherefore quit nature, which had already explained to you so much? Why seek in imaginary spaces those causes, those powers, that energy, which she would have distinctly pointed out to you, had you been willing to have consulted her with your usual sagacity? The gigantic, the intelligent Newton, suffers himself to be hoodwinked—to be blinded by prejudice; he has not courage to look a question fairly in the face, when that question involves notions which habit has rendered sacred to him; he turns his eyes from truth, he casts behind him his experience, he lulls to sleep his reason, when it becomes necessary to probe opinions full of contradictions, yet fraught with the best interests of humanity.

Let us, however, continue to examine how far the most transcendent genius is capable of leading himself astray, when once he abandons experience, when once he chains up his reason, when once he suffers himself to be guided by his imagination.

"God," continues the father of modern philosophy, "is totally destitute of body and of corporeal figure; here is the reason why he cannot be either seen, touched, or understood; and ought not to be adored under any corporeal form." What idea, however, can be formed of a being who is resembled by nothing of which we have any knowledge? What are the relations that can be supposed to exist between such very dissimilar beings? When man renders this being his adoration, does he not, in fact, in despite of himself, make him a being similar to his own species; does he not suppose that, like himself, he is sensible to homage—to be won by presents—gained by flattery; in short, he is treated like a king of the earth, who exacts the respect, demands the fealty, requires the obedience of all who are submitted to him. Newton adds, "we have ideas of his attributes, but we do not know that it is any one substance; we only see the figures and the colours of bodies; we only hear sounds; we only touch the exterior surfaces; we only scent odours; we only taste flavours: no one of our senses, no one of our reflections, can shew us the intimate nature of substances: we have still less ideas of God."

If we have an idea of the attributes of God, it is only because we clothe him with those which belong to ourselves; which we never do more than aggrandize, which we only augment or exaggerate; we then mistake them for those qualities with which we were at first acquainted. If in all those substances which are pervious to our senses, we only know them by the effects they produce on us, after which we assign them qualities, at least these qualities are something tangible, they give birth to clear and distinct ideas. This superficial knowledge, however slender it may be, with which our senses furnish us, is the only one we can possibly have; constituted as we are, we find ourselves under the necessity of resting contented with it, and we discover that it is sufficient for our wants; but we have not even the most superficial idea of immateriality, or a substance distinguished from all those with which we have the slightest acquaintance. Nevertheless, we hear men hourly reasoning upon it, disputing about its properties, advancing its faculties, as if they had the most demonstrable evidence of the fact; tearing each other in pieces, because the one does not readily admit what the other asserts, upon a subject which no man is competent to understand.

Our author goes on "We only have a knowledge of God by his attributes, by his properties, by the excellent and wise arrangement which he has given to all things, and by their FINAL CAUSES: we admire him in consequence of his perfections." I repeat, that we have no real knowledge of the Divinity; that we borrow his attributes from ourselves; but it is evident these cannot be suitable to the Universal Being, who neither can have the same nature nor the same properties as particular beings; it is nevertheless after ourselves that we assign him intelligence, wisdom, perfection, in subtracting from them what we call defects. As to the order, or the arrangement of the universe, man finds it excellent, esteems it the perfection of wisdom, as long as it is favorable to his species; or when the causes which are co-existent with himself do not disturb his own peculiar existence; otherwise he is apt to complain of confusion, and final causes vanish: he then attributes to an immutable God, motives equally borrowed from his own peculiar mode of action, for deranging the beautiful order he so much admires in the universe. Thus it is always in himself, that is, in his own individual mode of feeling, that he draws up the ideas of the order, the wisdom, the excellence, the perfection which he ascribes to the Deity; whilst the good as well as the evil which take place in the world, are the necessary consequence of the essence of things; of the general, immutable laws of nature; in short, of the gravitation, of the repulsion of matter; of those unchangeable laws of motion, which Newton himself has so ably thrown into light; but which he has by a strange fatuity forborne to apply when the question was concerning the cause of these phenomena, which prejudice has refused to the capabilities of nature. He goes on, "We revere, and we adore God, on account of his sovereignty: we worship him like his slaves; a God destitute of sovereignty, of providence, and of final causes, would be no more than nature and destiny." It is true that superstition enjoins man to adore its gods like ignorant slaves, who tremble under a master whom they know not; he certainly prays to them on all occasions, sometimes requesting nothing less than an entire change in the essence of things, to gratify his capricious desires, and it is perhaps well for him they are not competent to grant his request: in the origin, as we have shewn, these gods were nothing more than nature acting by necessary laws, clothed under a variety of fables; or necessity personified under a multitude of names. However this may be, we do not believe that true religion, that sterling worship which renders man grateful, whilst it exalts the majesty of the Divinity, requires any such meanness from man that he should act like a slave; he is rather expected to sit down to the banquet prepared for him, with all the dignity of an invited guest; under the cheering consciousness of a welcome that is never accorded to slaves; nothing is required at his hands, but that he should conduct himself temperately in the banquetting-house; that he should be grateful for the good cheer he receives; that he should have virtue; (which we have already sufficiently explained is to render himself useful, by making others happy); that he should not by pertinaciously setting up whimsical opinions, and insisting on their adoption by his neighbour, disturb the harmony of the feast; that he should be sufficiently intelligent to know when he is really felicitous, and not seek to put down the gaiety of his fellow guests; but that he should rise from the board satisfied with himself, contented with others; in short, to comprise the whole in a trite axiom of one of the Greek philosophers, he should learn the invaluable secret, "to *bear* and *forbear*."

But to proceed. Newton tells us, "that from a physical and blind necessity, which should preside every where, and be always the same, there could not emanate any variety in the beings; the diversity which we behold, could only have its origin in the ideas and in the will of a being which exists necessarily;" but wherefore should not this diversity spring out of natural causes, from matter acting upon matter; the action of which either attracts and combines various yet analogous elements, or else separates beings by the intervention of those substances which have not a disposition to unite? Is not bread the result of the combination of flour, yeast and water? As for the blind necessity, as it is elsewhere said, we must acknowledge it is that of which we are ignorant, either of its properties or its energies; of which being blind ourselves we have no knowledge of its mode of action. Philosophers explain all the phenomena that occur by the properties of matter; and though they feel the want of a more intimate acquaintance with natural causes, they do not therefore the less believe them deducible from these properties or these causes. Are, therefore, the philosophers atheists, because they do not reply, it is God who is the author of these effects? Is the industrious workman, who makes gunpowder, to be challenged as an atheist, because he says the terrible effects of this destructive material, which inspired the native Americans with such awe, which raised in their winds such wonder, are to be ascribed to the junction of the apparently harmless substances of nitre, charcoal and sulpher, set in activity by the accession of trivial scintillations, produced from the collision of steel with flint, merely because some bigoted *Priest of the Sun*, who is ignorant of the composition, chooses to think it is not possible such a striking phenomenon could be the work of any thing short of the secret agents, whom he has himself appointed to govern the world?

"It is allegorically said that God sees, hears, speaks, smiles, loves, hates, desires, gives, receives, rejoices, grows angry, fights, makes, or fashions, &c. because all that is said of God, is borrowed from the conduct of man, by an imperfect analogy." Man has not been able to act otherwise, for want of being acquainted with nature and her eternal course: whenever he has imagined a peculiar energy which he has not been able to fathom, he has given it the name of God; and he has then made him act upon the self-same principles, as he himself would adopt, according to which he would act if he was the master. It is from this proneness to *Theanthropy*, that has flowed all those absurd, and frequently dangerous ideas, upon which are founded the superstitions of the world; who all adore in their gods either natural causes of which they are ignorant, or else powerful mortals of whose malice they stand in awe. The sequel will shew the fatal effects that have resulted to mankind from the absurd ideas they have very frequently formed to themselves of the Divinity; that nothing could be more degrading to him, more injurious to themselves, than the idea of comparing him to an absolute sovereign, to a despot, to a tyrant. For the present let us continue to examine the proofs offered in support of their various systems.

It is unceasingly repeated that the regular action, the invariable order, which reigns in the universe, the benefits heaped upon mortals, announce a wisdom, an intelligence, a goodness, which we cannot refuse to acknowledge, in the cause which produces these marvellous effects. To this we must reply, that it is unquestionably true that not only these things, but all the phenomena he beholds, indicate the existence of something gifted very superiorly to erring man; the great question, however, is one that perhaps will never be solved, what is this being? Is this question answered by heaping together the estimable qualities of man? Speaking with relation to ourselves, which is all that the theologian really does, although in such numerous regions he pretends to do a great deal more, we can apply the terms goodness, wisdom, intelligence, the best with which we are acquainted, to this being for the want of having those that may be appropriate; but I maintain, this does not, in point of fact, afford us one single idea of the *Great Cause of causes*; we admire his works; and knowing that what we approve highly in our own species, we attribute to their being wise, we say the Divinity displays wisdom. So far it is well; but this, after all, is a human quality. If we consult experience, we shall presently be convinced that our wisdom does not bear the least affinity to the actions attributed to the Divinity. To get at this a little closer, we must endeavour to find out what we do not call wisdom in man; this will help us to form an estimate, how very incompetent we are to describe the qualities of a being that differs so very materially from ourselves. We most certainly should not call him a wise man, who having built a beautiful residence, should himself set it on fire; and thus destroy what he had laboured so much to bring to perfection: yet this happens every day in nature, without its being in any manner a warrantry for us to charge her with folly. If therefore we were to form our judgments after our own puny ideas of wisdom, what should we say? Why, in point of fact, just what the man does, who, thinking he has had too much rain, implores fine weather? Which, properly translated, is neither more nor less than giving the Divinity to understand he best knows what is proper for himself. The just, the only fair inference to be drawn from this, is, that we positively know nothing about the matter; that those who pretend they do, would, if it was upon any other subject, he suspected of having an unsound mind. We do not mean to insist that we are in the right, but we mean to aver that the object of this work is not so much either to build up new systems, or to put down old ones, as by shewing man the inconclusiveness of his reasonings upon matters not accessible to his comprehension—to induce him to be more tolerant to his neighbour—to invite him to be less rancorous against those who do not see with his eyes—to hold forth to him motives for forbearance, against those whose system of faith may not exactly harmonize with his own—to render him less ferocious in support of opinions, which, if he will but discard his prejudices, he may find not so solidly bottomed as he imagines. All we know is scarcely more than that the motion we witness in the universe is the necessary consequence of the laws of matter; that the uniformity of this motion is evidence of their immutability; that it is not too much to say it cannot cease to act in the manner it does, as long as the same causes operate, governed by the same circumstances. We evidently see that motion, however regular in our mind, that order, however beautiful to our admiring optics, yields to what we term disorder, to that which we designate frightful confusion, as soon as new causes, not analogous to the preceding, either disturb or suspend their action. We further know that a better knowledge of nature, the consequence of time, the result of patient, laborious, physical researches, with the comparison of facts and the application of experience, has enabled man in many instances to divert from himself the evil effects of inevitable causes, which anterior to these discoveries overwhelmed his unhappy progenitors with ruin. How far these salutary developements are to be carried by industry, what may be achieved by honesty, what light is to be gathered from the recession of prejudice, the wisest among men is not competent to decide. Certain it is, that phenomena which for ages were supposed to denounce the anger of the Deity against mankind, are now well understood to be common effects of natural causes.

Order, as we have elsewhere shewn, is only the effects which result to ourselves from a series of motion; there cannot be any disorder relatively to the great whole; in which all that takes place is necessary; in which every thing is determined by laws which nothing can change. The order of nature may be damaged or destroyed relatively to ourselves, but it is never contradicted relatively to herself, since she cannot act otherwise than she does: if we attribute to her the evils we sustain, we are equally obliged to acknowledge we owe to her the good we experience.

It in said, that animals furnish a convincing proof of the powerful cause of their existence; that the admirable harmony of their parts, the mutual assistance they lend each other, the regularity with which they fulfill their functions, the preservation of these parts, the conservation of such complicated wholes, announce a workman who unites wisdom with power; in short, whole tracts of anatomy and botany have been copied to prove nothing more than that these things exist, for of the power that produced them there cannot remain a doubt. We shall never learn more from these erudite tracts, save that there exists in nature certain elements with an aptitude to attraction; a disposition to unite, suitable to form wholes, to induce combinations capable of producing very striking effects. To be surprised that the brain, the heart, the arteries, the veins, the eyes, the ears of an animal, act as we see them—that the roots of plants attract juices, or that trees produce fruit, is to be surprised that a tree, a plant, or an animal exists at all. These beings would not exist, or would no longer be that which we know they are, if they ceased to act as they do: this is what happens when they die. If the formation, the combination, the modes of action, variously possessed by these beings, if their conservation for a season, followed by their destruction or dissolution, prove any thing, it is the immutability of those laws which operate in nature: we cannot doubt the power of nature; she produces all the animals we behold, by the combination, of matter, continually in motion; the harmony that subsists between the component parts of these beings, is a consequence of the necessary laws of their nature, and of that which results from their combination. As soon as this accord ceases, the animal is necessarily destroyed: from this we must conclude that every mutation in nature is necessary; is only a consequence of its laws; that it could not be otherwise than it is, under the circumstances in which it is placed.

Man, who looks upon himself as the *chef d'oeuvre*, furnishes more than any other production a proof of the immutability of the laws of nature: in this sensible, intelligent, thinking being, whose vanity leads him to believe himself the sole object of the divine predilection, who forms his God after his own peculiar model, we see only a more inconstant, a more brittle machine; one more subject to be deranged by its extreme complication, than the grosser beings: beasts destitute of our knowledge, plants that vegetate, stones devoid of feeling, are in many respects beings more highly favored than man: they are at least exempted from the sorrows of the mind—from the torments of reflection—from that devouring, chagrin to which he is so frequently a prey. Who is he who would not be a plant or a stone, every time reminiscence forces upon his imagination the irreparable loss of a beloved object? Would it not be better to be an inanimate mass, than a restless, turbulent, superstitious being, who does nothing but tremble under the imaginary displeasure of beings of his own creation; who to support his own gloomy opinions, immolates his fellow creatures at the shrine of his idol; who ravages the country, and deluges the earth with the blood of those who happen to differ from him on a speculative point of an unintelligible creed? Beings destitute of life, bereft of feeling, without memory, not having the faculties of thought, at least are not afflicted by the idea of either the past, the present, or the future; they do not at any rate believe themselves in danger of becoming eternally unhappy, because they way have reasoned badly; or because they happened to be born in a land where truth has never yet shed its refulgent beams on the darkened mind of perplexed mortals.

Let it not then be said that we cannot have an idea of a work, without also having an idea of the workman, as distinguished from his work: the savage, when he first beheld the terrible operation of gunpowder, did not form the most distant idea that it was the work of a man like himself. Nature is not to be contemplated as a work of this kind; she is self-existent. In her bosom every thing is produced: she is an immense elaboratory, provided with materials, who makes the instruments of which she avails herself in her operations. All her works are the effects of her own energies; of those agents which she herself produces; of those immutable laws by which she sets every thing in activity. Eternal, indestructible elements, ever in motion, combine themselves variously, and thus give birth to all beings, to all the phenomena which fill the weak eyes of erring mortals with wonder and dismay; to all the effects, whether good or bad, of which man experiences the influence; to all the vicissitudes he undergoes, from the moment of his birth until that of his death; to order and to confusion, which he never discriminates but by the various modes in which he is affected: in short, to all those miraculous spectacles with which he occupies his meditation—upon which he exercises his reason—which frequently spread consternation over the surface of the earth. These elements need nothing when circumstances favour their junction, save their own peculiar properties, whether individual or united, with the motion that is essential to them, to produce all those phenomena which powerfully striking the senses of mankind, either fill him with admiration, or stagger him with alarm.

But supposing for a moment that it was impossible to conceive the work, without also conceiving the workman, who watches over his work, where must we place this workman? Shall it be interior or exterior to his production? Is he matter and motion, or is he only space or the vacuum? In all these cases either he would be nothing, or he would be contained in nature: as nature contains only matter and motion, it must be concluded that the agent who moves it is material; that he is corporeal; if this agent be exterior to nature, then we can no longer form any idea of the place which he occupieth: neither can we better conceive an immaterial being; nor the mode in which a spirit without extent can act upon matter from which it is separated. These unknown spaces, which imagination has placed beyond the visible world, can have no existence for a being, who with difficulty sees down to his feet; he cannot paint to his mind any image of the power which inhabit them; but if he is compelled to form some kind of a picture, he must combine at random the fantastical colours which he is ever obliged to draw from the world he inhabits: in this case he will really do no more than reproduce in idea, part or parcels of that which he has actually seen; he will form a whole which perhaps has no existence in nature, but which it will be in vain he strives to distinguish from her; to place out of her bosom. When he shall be ingenuous with himself, When he shall be no longer willing to delude others, he will be obliged to acknowledge, that the portrait he has painted, although in its combination it resembles nothing in the universe, is nevertheless in all its constituent members an exact delineation of that which nature presents to our view. Hobbes in his *Leviathan* says, "The universe, the whole mass of things, is corporeal, that is to say, body; and hath the dimensions of magnitude, namely, length, breadth, and depth: also every part of body is likewise body, and hath the like dimensions; and consequently every part of the universe is body; and that which is not body, is no part of the universe; and because the universe is all, that which is no part of it is nothing; and consequently no where: nor does it follow from hence, that spirits are nothing, for they have dimensions, and are therefore really bodies; though that name in common speech be given to such bodies only as are visible, or palpable, that is, that have some degree of opacity: but for spirits they call them incorporeal; which is a name of more honour, and may therefore with more piety be attributed to God himself, in whom we consider not what attribute expresseth best his nature, which is incomprehensible; but what best expresseth our desire to honour him."

It will be insisted that if a statue or a watch were shewn to a savage, who had never before seen either, he would not be able to prevent himself from acknowledging that these things were the works of some intelligent agent of greater ability, possessing more industry than himself: it will be concluded from thence, that we are in like manner obliged to acknowledge that the universe, that man, that the various phenomena, are the works of an agent, whose intelligence is more comprehensive, whose power far surpasses our own. Granted: who has ever doubted it? the proposition is self-evident; it cannot admit of even a cavil. Nevertheless we reply, in the *first place*, that it is not to be doubted that nature is extremely powerful; diligently industrious: we admire her activity every time we are surprised by the extent, every time we contemplate the variety, every time we behold those complicated effects which are displayed in her works; or whenever we take the pains to meditate upon them: nevertheless, she is not really more industrious in one of her works than she is in another; she is not fathomed with more ease in those we call her most contemptible productions, than she is in her most sublime efforts: we no more understand how she has been capable of producing a stone or a metal, than the means by which she organized a head like that of the illustrious Newton. We call that man industrious who can accomplish things which we cannot; nature is competent to every thing: as soon therefore as a thing exists, it is a proof she has been capable of producing it: but it is never more than relatively to ourselves that we judge beings to be industrious: we then compare them to ourselves; and as we enjoy a quality which we call intelligence, by the assistance of which we accomplish things, by which we display our diligence, we naturally conclude from it, that those works which most astonish us, do not belong to her, but are to be ascribed to an intelligent being like ourselves, but in whom we make the intelligence commensurate with the astonishment these phenomena excite in us; that is to say, in other words, to our own peculiar ignorance, and the weakness incident to our nature.

In the *second place*, we must observe, that the savage, to whom either the statue or the watch is brought, will or will not have ideas of human industry: if he has ideas of it, he will feel that this watch or this statue, way be the work of a being of his own species, enjoying faculties of which he is himself deficient: if he has no idea of it, if he has no comprehension of the resources of human art, when he beholds the spontaneous motion of the watch, he will be impressed with the belief that it is an animal, which cannot be the work of man. Multiplied experience confirms this mode of thinking which is ascribed to the savage. The Peruvians mistook the Spaniards for gods, because they made use of gunpowder, rode on horseback, and came in vessels which sailed quite alone. The inhabitants of the island of Tenian being ignorant of fire before the arrival of Europeans, the first time they saw it, conceived it to be an animal who devoured the wood. Thus it is, that the savage, in the same manner as many great and learned men, who believe themselves much more acute, will attribute the strange effects that strike his organs, to a genius or to a spirit; that is to say, to an unknown power; to whom he will ascribe capabilities of which he believes the beings of his own species are entirely destitute: by this he will prove nothing, except that he is himself ignorant of what man is capable of producing. It is thus that a raw unpolished people raise their eyes to heaven, every time they witness some unusual phenomenon. It is thus that the people denominate all those strange effects, with the natural causes of which they are ignorant, miraculous, supernatural, divine; but these are not by reasonable persons therefore considered proofs of what they assert: as the multitude are generally unacquainted with the cause of any thing, every object becomes a miracle in their eyes; at least they imagine God is the immediate cause of the good they enjoy—of the evil they suffer. In short, it is thus that the theologians themselves solve every difficulty that starts in their road; they ascribe to God all those phenomena, of the causes of which either they are themselves ignorant, or else unwilling that man should be acquainted with the source.

In the *third place*, the savage, in opening the watch, and examining its parts, will perhaps feel, that this machinery announces a work which can only be the result of human labour. He will perhaps perceive, that they very obviously differ from the immediate productions of nature, whom he has not observed to produce wheels made of polished metal. He will further notice, perhaps, that these parts when separated, no longer act as they did when they were combined; that the motion he so much admired, ceases when their union is broken. After these observations, he will attribute the watch to the ingenuity of man; that is to say, to a being like himself, of whom he has some ideas, but whom he judges capable to construct machines to which he is himself utterly incompetent. In short, he will ascribe the honour of his watch to a being known to him in some respects, provided with faculties very far superior to his own; but he will be at an immense distance from the belief, that this material work, whose ingenuity pleases him so much, can be the effect of an immaterial cause; or of an agent destitute of organs, without extent; whose action upon material beings cannot be within, the sphere of his comprehension. Nevertheless, man, when he cannot embrace the causes of things, does not scruple to insist that they are impossible to be the production of nature, although he is entirely ignorant how far the powers of this nature extend; to what her capabilities are equal. In viewing the world, we must acknowledge material causes for many of those phenomena which take place in it; those who study nature are continually adding fresh discoveries to this list of physical causes; science, as she enriches the intellectual stores of human enjoyment, every day throws a broader light on the energies of nature, which *prejudice*, aided by its almost inseparable companion, *ignorance*, would for ever bind down in the fetters of impotence.

Let us not, however, be told, that pursuing this hypothesis, we attribute every thing to a blind cause—to the fortuitous concurrence of atoms—to chance. Those only are called blind causes of which we know not either the combination, the laws, or the power. Those effects are called fortuitous, with whose causes man is unacquainted; to which his experience affords him no clue; which his ignorance prevents him from foreseeing. All those effects, of which he does not see the necessary connection with their causes, he attributes to chance. Nature is not a blind cause; she never acts by chance; nothing that she does would ever be considered fortuitous, by him who should understand her mode of action—who had a knowledge of her resources—who was intelligent in her ways. Every thing that she produces is strictly necessary—is never more than a consequence of her eternal, immutable laws; all is connected in her by invisible bonds; every effect we witness flows necessarily from its cause, whether we are in a condition to fathom it, or whether we are obliged to let it remain hidden from our view. It is very possible there should be ignorance on our part; but the words spirit, intelligence, will not remedy this ignorance; they will rather redouble it, by arresting our research; by preventing us from conquering those impediments which obstruct us in probing the natural causes of the effects, with which our visual faculties bring us acquainted.

This may serve for an answer to the clamour of those who raise perpetual objections to the partizans of nature, by unceasingly accusing them with attributing every thing to chance. Chance is a word devoid of sense, which furnishes no substantive idea; at least it indicates only the ignorance of its employers. Nevertheless, we are triumphantly told, it is reiterated continually, that a regular work cannot be ascribed to the concurrence of chance. Never, we are informed, will it be possible to arrive at the formation of a poem such as the Iliad, by means of letters thrown together promiscuously or combined at random. We agree to it without hesitation; but, ingenuously, are the letters which compose a poem thrown with the hand in the manner of dice? It would avail as much to say, we could not pronounce a discourse with the feet. It is nature, who combines according to necessary laws, under given circumstances, a head organized in a mode suitable to bring forth a poem: it is nature who assembles the elements, which furnish man with a brain competent to give birth to such a work: it is nature, who, through the medium of the imagination, by means of the passions, in consequence of the temperament which she bestows upon man, capacitates him to produce such a masterpiece of fancy; such a never-fading effort of the mind: it is his brain modified in a certain manner, crowded with ideas, decorated with images, made fruitful by circumstances, that alone can become the matrix in which a poem can be conceived—in which the matter of it can be digested: this is the only womb whose activity could usher to an admiring world, the sublime stanzas which develope the story of the unfortunate Priam, and immortalize their author. A head organized like that of Homer, furnished with the same vigour, glowing with the same vivid imagination, enriched with the same erudition, placed under the same circumstances, would necessarily, and not by chance, produce the poem of the Iliad; at least, unless it be denied that causes similar in every thing must produce effects perfectly identical. We should without doubt be surprised, if there were in a dice-box a hundred thousand dice, to see a hundred thousand sixes follow in succession; but if these dice were all cogged or loaded, our surprise would cease: the particles of matter may be compared to cogged dice, that is to say, always producing certain determinate effects under certain given circumstances; these particles being essentially varied in themselves, countless in their combinations, they are cogged in myriads of different modes. The head of Homer, or of Virgil, was no more than an assemblage of particles, possessing peculiar properties; or if they will, of dice cogged by nature; that is to say, of beings so combined, of matter so wrought, as to produce the beautiful poems of the Iliad or the Aeneid. As much may be said of all other productions: indeed, what are men themselves but cogged dice—machines into which nature has infused the bias requisite to produce effects of a certain description? A man of genius produces a good work, in the same manner as a tree of a good species, placed in a prolific soil, cultivated with care, grafted with judgment, produces excellent fruit.

Then is it not either knavery or puerility, to talk of composing a work by scattering letters with the hand; by promiscuously mingling characters; or gathering together by chance, that which can only result from a human brain, with a peculiar organization, modified after a certain manner? The principle of human generation does not develope itself by chance; it cannot be nourished with effect, expanded into life, but in the womb of a woman: a confused heap of characters, a jumble of symbols, is nothing more than an assemblage of signs, whose proper arrangement is adequate to paint human ideas; but in order that these ideas may be correctly delineated, it is previously requisite that they should have been conceived, combined, nourished, connected, and developed in the brain of a poet; where circumstances make them fructify, mature them, and bring them forth in perfection, by reason of the fecundity, generated by the genial warmth and the peculiar energy of the matrix, in which these intellectual seeds shall have been placed. Ideas in combining, expanding, connecting, and associating themselves, form a whole, like all the other bodies of nature: this whole affords us pleasure, becomes a source of enjoyment, when it gives birth to agreeable sensations in the mind; when it offers to our examination pictures calculated to move us in a lively manner. It is thus that the history of the Trojan war, as digested in the head of Homer, ushered into the world with all the fascinating harmony of numbers peculiar to himself, has the power of giving a pleasurable impulse to heads, who by their analogy with that of this incomparable Grecian, are in a capacity to feel its beauties.

From this it will be obvious, that nothing can be produced by chance; that no effect can exist without an adequate cause for its existence; that the one must ever be commensurate with the other. All the works of nature grow out of the uniform action of invariable laws, whether our mind can with facility follow the concatenation of the successive causes which operate; or whether, as in her more complicated productions, we find ourselves in the impossibility of distinguishing the various springs which she sets in motion to give birth to her phenomena. To nature, the difficulty is not more to produce a great poet, capable of writing an admirable poem, than to form a glittering stone or a shining metal which gravitates towards a centre. The mode she adopts to give birth to these various beings, is equally unknown to us, when we have not meditated upon it; frequently the most sedulous attention, the most patient investigation affords us no information; sometimes, however, the unwearied industry of the philosopher is rewarded, by throwing into light the most mysterious operations. Thus the keen penetration of a Newton, aided by uncommon diligence, developed the starry system, which, for so many thousand years, had eluded the research of all the astronomers by whom he was preceded. Thus the sagacity of a Harvey giving vigour to his application, brought out of the obscurity in which for almost countless centuries it had been buried, the true course pursued by the sanguinary fluid, when circulating through the veins and arteries of man, giving activity to his machine, diffusing life through his system, and enabling him to perform those actions which so frequently strike an astonished world with wonder and regret. Thus Gallileo, by a quickness of perception, a depth of reasoning peculiar to himself, held up to an admiring world, the actual form and situation of the planet we inhabit; which until then had escaped the observation of the most profound geniuses—the most subtle metaphysicians—the whole host of priests; which when first promulgated was considered so extraordinary, so contradictory to all the then received opinions, either sacred or profane, that he was ranked as an atheist, as an impious blasphemer, to hold communion with whom, would secure to the communers a place in the regions of everlasting torment; in short, it was held an heresy of such an indelible dye, that notwithstanding the infallibility of his sacred function, Pope Gregory, who then filled the papal chair, excommunicated all those who had the temerity to accredit so abominable a doctrine.

Man is born by the necessary concurrence of those elements suitable to his construction; he increases in bulk, corroborates his system, expands his powers, in the same manner as a plant or a stone; which as well as himself, are augmented in their volume, invigorated in their capabilities, by the addition of homogeneous matter, that exists within the sphere of their attraction. Man feels, thinks, receives ideas, acts after a certain manner, that is to say, according to his organic structure, which is peculiar to himself; that renders him susceptible of modifications, of which the stone and the plant are utterly incapable. On the other hand, the organization of these beings is of a nature to enable them to receive other modifications, which man is not more capacitated to experience, than the stone or the plant are those which constitute him what he is. In consequence of this peculiar arrangement, the man of genius produces works of merit; the plant when it is healthy yields delicious fruits the stone when it is placed in a suitable matrix possesses a glittering brilliance which dazzles the eyes of mortals; each in their sphere of action both surprise and delight us; because we feel that they excite in us sensations, that harmonize with what we call order; in consequence of the pleasure they infuse, by the rarity, by the magnitude, and by the variety of the effects which they occasion us to experience. Nevertheless, that which is found most admirable in the productions of nature, that which is most esteemed in the actions of man, most highly valued in animals, most sought after in vegetation, most in request among fossils, is never more than the natural effects of the different particles of matter, diversely arranged, variously combined, submitted to numerous modifications; from matter thus united result organs, brains, temperament, taste, talents, all the multifarious properties, all the multitudinous qualities, which discriminate the beings whose multiplied activity make up the sum of what is designated animated nature.

Nature then produces nothing but what is necessary; it is not by fortuitous combinations, by chance throws, that she exhibits to our view the beings we behold; all her throws are sure, all the causes she employs have infallibly their effects. Whenever she gives birth to extraordinary, marvellous, rare beings, it is, that the requisite order of things the concurrence of the necessary productive causes, happens but seldom. As soon as those beings exist, they are to be ascribed to nature, equally with the most familiar of her productions; to nature every thing is equally possible, equally facile, when she assembles together the instruments or the causes necessary to act. Thus it seems presumption in man to set limits to the powers of nature, which he so very imperfectly understands. The combinations, or if they will, the throws that she makes in an eternity of existence, can easily produce all the beings that have existed: her eternal march must necessarily bring forth, again and again, the most astonishing circumstances; the most rare occurrences; those most calculated to rouse the wonder, to elicit the admiration of beings, who are only in a condition to give them a momentary consideration; who can get nothing more than a glimpse, without ever having either the leisure or the means to search into causes, which lie hid from their weak eyes, in the depths of Cimmerian obscurity. Countless throws during eternity, with elements and combinations varied almost to infinity, quite with relation to man, suffice to produce every thing of which he has a knowledge, with multitudes of other effects, of which he will never have the least conception.

Thus, we cannot too often repeat to the metaphysicians, to the supporters of immateriality, to the inconsistent theologians, who commonly ascribe to their adversaries the most ridiculous opinions, in order to obtain an easy, short-lived triumph in the prejudiced eyes of the multitude; or in the stagnant minds of those who never examine deeply; that chance is nothing but a word, as well as many other words, imagined solely to cover the ignorance of those to whom the course of nature is inexplicable—to shield the idleness of others who are too slothful to seek into the properties of acting causes. It is not chance that has produced the universe, it is self-existent; nature exists necessarily from all eternity: she is omnipotent because every thing is produced by her energies; she is omnipresent, because she fills all space; she is omniscient, because every thing can only be what it actually is; she is immovable, because as a whole she cannot be displaced; she is immutable, because her essence cannot change, although her forms may vary; she is infinite, because she cannot have any bounds; she is all perfect, because she contains every thing: in short, she has all the abstract qualities of the metaphysician, all the moral faculties of the theologian, without involving any contradiction, since that which is the assemblage of all, must of necessity contain the properties of all.

However concealed may be her ways, the existence of nature is indubitable; her mode of action is in some respects known to us. Experience amply demonstrates we might, if we were more industrious, become better acquainted with her secrets; but with an immaterial substance, with a pure spirit, the mind of man can never become familiar: he has no means by which he can picture to himself this incomprehensible, this inconceivable quality: in despite therefore of the roundness of assertion adopted by the theologian, notwithstanding all the subtilties of the metaphysician, it will always be for man, while he remains such as he now is, in the language of Doctor Samuel Clarke, that, *of which nothing can with truth be affirmed.*

CHAP. VI.

Of Pantheism; or of the Natural Ideas of the Divinity.

The false principle that matter is not self-existent; that by its nature it is in an impossibility to move itself; consequently incompetent to the production of those striking phenomena which arrest our wondering eyes in the wide expanse of the universe; it will be obvious, to all who seriously attend to what has preceded, is the origin of the proofs upon which theology rests the existence of immateriality. After these suppositions, as gratuitous as they are erroneous, the fallacy of which we have exposed elsewhere, it has been believed that matter did not always exist, but that its existence, as well as its motion, is a production of time; due to a cause distinguished from itself; to an unknown agent to whom it is subordinate. As man finds in his own species a quality which he calls intelligence, which presides over all his actions, by the aid of which he arrives at the end he proposes to himself; he has clothed this invisible agent with this quality, which he has extended beyond the limits of his own conception: he magnified it thus, because, having made him the author of effects of which he found himself incapable, he did not conceive it possible that the intelligence he himself possessed, unless it was prodigiously amplified, would be sufficient to account for those productions, to which his erring judgment led him to conclude the natural energy of physical causes were not adequate.

As this agent was invisible, as his mode of action was inconceivable, he made him a spirit, a word that really means nothing more than that he is ignorant of his essence, or that he acts like the breath of which he cannot trace the motion. Thus, in speaking of spirituality, he designated an occult quality, which he deemed suitable to a concealed being, whose mode of action was always imperceptible to the senses. It would appear, however, that originally the word spirit was not meant to designate immateriality; but a matter of a more subtile nature than that which acted coarsely on the organs: still of a nature capable of penetrating the grosser matter—of communicating to it motion—of instilling into it active life—of giving birth to those combinations—of imparting to them those modifications, which his organic structure rendered him competent to discover. Such was, as has been shewn, that all-powerful Jupiter, who in the theology of the ancients, was originally destined to represent the etherial, subtile matter that penetrates, vivifies, and gives activity to all the bodies of which nature is the common assemblage.

It would be grossly deceiving ourselves to believe that the idea of spirituality, such as the subtilty of dreaming metaphysicians present it in these days, was that which offered itself to our forefathers in the early stages of the human mind. This immateriality, which excludes all analogy with any thing but itself—which bears no resemblance to any thing of which man is capacitated to have a knowledge, was, as we have already observed, the slow, the tardy fruit of his imagination, after he had quitted experience, and renounced his reason. Men reared in luxurious leisure, unceasingly meditating, without the assistance of those natural helps with which attentive observation would have furnished them, by degrees arrived at the formation of this incomprehensible quality, which is so fugitive, that although man has been compelled to reverence it, to accredit it against all the evidence of his senses, they have never yet been enabled to give any other explanation of its nature, than by using a term to which it is impossible to attach any intelligible idea. Seraphis said, with tears in his eyes, "that in making him adopt the opinion of spirituality, they had deprived him of his God." Many fathers of the church have given a human form to the Divinity, and treated all those as heretics who made him spiritual. Thus by dint of reasoning, by force of subtilizing, the word spirit no longer presents any one image upon which the mind can fix itself; when they are desirous to speak of it, it becomes impossible to understand them, seeing that each visionary paints it after his own manner; and in the portrait he forms, consults only his own temperament, follows nothing but his own imagination, adopts nothing but his own peculiar reveries; the only point in which they are at all in unison, is in assigning to it inconceivable qualities, which they naturally enough believe are best suited to the incomprehensible beings they have delineated: from the incompatible heap of these qualities, generally resulted a whole, whose existence they thus rendered impossible. In short, this word, which has occupied the research of so many learned and intelligent men; which is considered of such importance to mankind, has been, in consequence of theological reveries, always fluctuating: these never bearing the least resemblance to each other, it has become destitute of any fixed sense, a mere sound, to which each who echoes it affixes his own peculiar ideas, which are never in harmony with those of his neighbour; which indeed are not even steady in himself, but like the camelion, assume the colour of every differing circumstance. This unintelligible word has been substituted for the more intelligible one of matter; man, when clothed with power, has entertained the most rancorous antipathies, pursued the most barbarous persecutions, against those who have not been enabled to contemplate this changeable idea under the same point of view with himself.

There have, however, been men who had sufficient courage to resist this torrent of opinion—to oppose themselves to this delirium; who have believed, that the object which was announced as the most important for mortals, as the sole object worthy of their thoughts, demanded an attentive examination; who apprehended that if experience could be of any utility, if judgment could afford any advantage, if reason was of any use whatever, it must, most unquestionably be, to consider this quality so opposed to every thing in nature, which was said to regulate all the beings which she contains. These quickly saw they could not subscribe to the general opinion of the uninformed, who never examine any thing, who take every thing upon the credit of others; much less was it consistent with sound sense to agree with their guides, who, either deceivers or deceived, forbade others to submit it to the scrutiny of reason; who were themselves frequently in an utter incapacity to pass it under such an ordeal. Thus some thinkers, disgusted with the obscure and contradictory notions which others had through habit mechanically attached to this incomprehensible property, had the temerity to shake off the yoke which had been imposed upon them from their infancy: calling reason to their aid against those terrors with which they alarmed the ignorant, revolting at the hideous descriptions under which they attempted to defend their hypothesis, they had the intrepidity to tear the veil of delusion; to rend asunder the barriers of imposture; they considered with calm resolution, this formidable prejudice, contemplated with a serene eye this unsupported opinion, examined with cool deliberation this fluctuating notion, which had become the object of all the hopes, the source of all the fears, the spring of all the quarrels which distracted the mind, and disturbed the harmony of blind, confiding mortals.

The result of these inquiries has uniformly been, a conviction that no rational proof has ever been adduced in support of this hypothesis; that from the nature of the thing itself, none can be offered; that an incorporeity is inconceivable to corporeal beings; that these only behold nature acting after invariable laws, in which every thing is material; that all the phenomena of which the world is the theatre, spring out of natural causes; that man as well as all the other beings is the work or this nature, is only an instrument in her hand, obliged to accomplish the eternal decrees of an imperious necessity.

Whatever efforts the philosopher makes to penetrate the secrets of nature, he never finds more, as we have many times repeated, than matter; various in itself, diversely modified in consequence of the motion it undergoes. Its whole, as well as its parts, displays only necessary causes producing necessary effects, which flow necessarily one out of the other: of which the mind, aided by experience, is more or less competent to discover the concatenation. In virtue of their specific properties, all the beings that come under our review, gravitate towards a centre—attract analogous matter—repel that which is unsuitable to combination—mutually receive and give impulse—acquire qualities—undergo modifications which maintain them in existence for a season—are born and dissolved by the operation of an inexorable decree, that obliges every thing, we behold to pass into a new mode of existence. It is to these continued vicissitudes that are to be ascribed all the phenomena, whether trivial or of magnitude; ordinary or extraordinary; known or unknown; simple or complicated; which are operated in the universe. It is by these mutations alone that we have any knowledge of nature: she is only mysterious to those who contemplate her through the veil of prejudice: her course is always simple to those who look at her without prepossession.

To attribute the effects to which we are witnesses, to nature, to matter, variously combined with the motion that is inherent to it, is to give them an intelligible and known cause; to attempt to penetrate deeper, is to plunge ourselves into imaginary regions, where we find only a chaos of obscurities—where we are lost in an unfathomable abyss of incertitude. Let us then be content with contemplating nature, who, being self-existent, must in her essence possess motion; which cannot be conceived without properties, from which result perpetual action and re-action; or those continual efforts which give birth to such a numerous train of circumstances; in which a single molecule cannot be found, that does not necessarily occupy the place assigned to it, by immutable and necessary laws—that is for an instant in an absolute state of repose. What necessity can there exist to seek out of matter for a power to give it play, since its motion flows as necessarily out of its existence as its bulk, its form, its gravity, &c. since nature in inaction would no longer be nature?

If it be demanded, How can we figure to ourselves, that matter by its own peculiar energy can produce all the effects we witness? I shall reply, that if by matter it is obstinately determined to understand nothing but a dead, inert mass, destitute of every property, incapable of moving itself, we shall no longer have a single idea of matter; we shall no longer be able to account for any thing. As soon, however, as it exists, it must have properties; as soon as it has properties, without which it could not exist, it must act by virtue of those properties; since it is only by its action we can have a knowledge of its existence, be conscious of its properties. It is evident that if by matter be understood that which it is not, or if its existence be denied, those phenomena which strike our visual organs cannot be attributed to it. But if by nature be understood (that which she really is), an heap of existing matter, possessing various properties, we shall be obliged to acknowledge that nature must be competent to move herself; by the diversity of her motion, must have the capability, independent of foreign aid, to produce the effects we behold; we shall find that nothing can be made from nothing; that nothing is made by chance; that the mode of action of every particle of matter, however minute, is necessarily determined by its own peculiar, or by its individual properties.

We have elsewhere said, that that which cannot be annihilated—that which in its nature is indestructible—cannot have been inchoate, cannot have had a beginning to its existence, but exists necessarily from all eternity; contains within itself a sufficient cause for its own peculiar existence. It becomes then perfectly useless to seek out of nature a cause for her action which is in some respects known to us; with which indefatigable research may, judging of the future by the past, render us more familiar. As we know some of the general properties of matter; as we can discover some of its qualities, wherefore should we seek its motion in an unintelligible cause, of which we are not in a condition to become acquainted with any one of its properties? Can we conceive that immateriality could ever draw matter from its own source? Impossible; it is not within the grasp of human intellect. If creation is an eduction from nothing, there must have been a time when matter had not existence; there must consequently be a time when it will cease to be: this latter is acknowledged by many theologians themselves to be impossible. Do those who are continually talking of this mysterious act of omnipotence, by which a mass of matter has been, all at once, substituted to nothing, perfectly understand what they tell us? Is there a man on earth who conceives that a being devoid of extent can exist, become the cause of the existence of beings who have extent—act upon matter—draw it from his own peculiar essence—set it in motion? In truth, the more we consider theology, the more we must be convinced that it has invented words destitute of sense; substituted sounds to intelligible realities.

For want of consulting experience, for want or studying nature, for want of examining the material world, we have plunged ourselves into an intellectual vacuum, which we have peopled with chimeras, We have not stooped to consider matter, to study its different periods, to follow it through its numerous, changes. We have either ridiculously or knavishly confounded dissolution, decomposition, the separation of the elementary particles of bodies, with their radical destruction; we have been unwilling to see that the elements are indestructible; although the forms are fleeting, and depend upon transitory combination. We have not distinguished the change of figure, the alteration of position, the mutation of texture, to which matter is liable, from its annihilation, which is impossible; we have falsely concluded, that matter Was not a necessary being—that it commenced to exist—that this existence was derived from that which possessed nothing in common with itself—that that which was not substance, could give birth to that which is. Thus an unintelligible name has been substituted for matter, which furnishes us with true ideas of nature; of which at each instant we experience the influence, of which we undergo the action, of which we feel the power, and of which we should have a much better knowledge, if our abstract opinions did not continually fasten a bandage over our eyes.

Indeed the most simple notions of philosophy shew us, that, although bodies change and disappear, nothing is however lost in nature; the various produce of the decomposition of a body serves for elements, supplies materials, forms the basis, lays the foundation for accretions, contributes to the maintenance of other bodies. The whole of nature subsists, and is conserved only by the circulation, the transmigration, the exchange, the perpetual displacement of insensible atoms—the continual mutation of the sensible combinations of matter. It is by this palingenesia, this regeneration, that the great whole, the mighty macrocosm subsists; who, like the Saturn of the ancients, is perpetually occupied with devouring her own children.

It will not then be inconsistent with observation, repugnant to reason, contrary to good sense, to acknowledge that matter is self-existent; that it acts by an energy peculiar to itself; that it will never be annihilated. Let us then say, that matter is eternal; that nature has been, is, and ever will be occupied with producing and destroying; with doing and undoing; with combining and separating; in short, with following a system of laws resulting from its necessary existence. For every thing that she doth, she needs only to combine the elements of matter; these, essentially diverse, necessarily either attract or repel each other; come into collision, from whence results either their union or dissolution; by the same laws that one approximates, the other recedes from their respective spheres of action. It is thus that she brings forth plants, fossils, animals, men; thus she gives existence to organized, sensible, thinking beings, as well as to those who are destitute of either feeling or thought. All these act for the season of their respective duration, according to immutable laws, determined by their various properties; arising out of their configuration; depending on their masses; resulting from their ponderosity, &c. Here is the true origin of every thing which is presented to our view; this indicates the mode by which nature, according to her own peculiar powers, is in a state to produce all those astonishing effects which assail our wondering eyes; all that phenomena to which mankind is the witness; as well as all the bodies who act diversely upon the organs with which he is furnished, of which he can only judge according to the manner in which these organs are affected. He says they are good, when they are analogous to his own mode of existence—when they contribute to the maintenance of the harmony of his machine: he says they are bad, when they disturb this harmony. It is thus he ascribes views, ideas, designs, to the being he supposes to be the power by which nature is moved; although all the experience we are able to collect, unequivocally proves, that she acts after an invariable, eternal code of laws.

Nature is destitute of those views which actuate man; she acts necessarily, because she exists: her system is immutable, and founded upon the essence of things. It is the essence of the seed of the male, composed of primitive elements, which serve for the basis of an organized being, to unite itself with that of the female; to fructify it; to produce, by this combination, a new organized being; who, feeble in his origin, not having yet acquired a sufficient quantity of material particles to give him consistence, corroborates himself by degrees; strengthens himself by the daily accretion of analogous matter; is nourished by the modifications appropriate to his existence: matured by the continuation of circumstances calculated to give vigour to his frame; thus he lives, thinks, acts, engenders in his turn other organized beings similar to himself. By a consequence of his temperament and of physical laws, this generation does not take place, except when the circumstances necessary to its production find themselves united. Thus this procreation is not operated by chance; the animal does not fructify, but with an animal of his own species, because this is the only one analogous to himself, who unites the qualities, who combines the circumstances, suitable to produce a being resembling himself; without this he would not produce any thing, or he would only give birth to a being who would be denominated a monster, because it would be dissimilar to himself. It is of the essence of the grain of plants, to be impregnated by the pollen or seed of the stygma of the flower; in this state of copulation they in consequence develope themselves in the bowels of the earth; expand by the aid of water; shoot forth by the accession of heat; attract analogous particles to corroborate their system: thus by degrees they form a plant, a shrub, a tree, susceptible of that life, filled with that motion, capable of that action which is suitable to vegetable existence. It is of the essence of particular particles of earth, homogeneous in their nature, when separated by circumstances, attenuated by water, elaborated by heat, to unite themselves in the bosom of mountains, with other atoms which are analogous; to form by their aggregation, according to their various affinities, those bodies possessing more or less solidity; having more or less purity, which are called diamonds, chrystals, stones, metals, minerals. It is of the essence of exhalations raised by the heat of the atmosphere, to combine, to collect themselves, to dash against each other, and either by their union or their collision to produce meteors, to generate thunder. It is of the essence of some inflammable matter to gather itself together, to ferment in the caverns of the earth, to increase its active force by augmenting its heat, and then explode, by the accession of other matter suitable to the operation, with that tremendous force which we call earthquakes; by which mountains are destroyed; cities overturned; the inhabitants of the plains thrown into a state of consternation; these full of alarm, unused to meditate on natural effects, unconscious of the extent of physical powers, stretch forth their hands in dismay, heave the most desponding sighs, utter aloud their complaints, and earnestly implore a cessation of those evils, which nature, acting by necessary laws, obliges them to experience as necessarily as she does those benefits by which she fills them with the most extravagant joy. In short, it is of the essence of certain climates to produce men so organized, whose temperament is so modified, that they become either extremely useful or very prejudicial to their species, in the same manner as it is the property of certain portions of the land, to bring forth either delicious fruits or dangerous poisons.

In all this nature acts necessarily; she pursues an undeviating course, which we are bound to consider the perfection of wisdom; because she exists necessarily, has her modes of action determined by certain, invariable laws, which themselves flow out of the constituent properties of the various beings she contains, and those circumstances, which the eternal motion she is in must necessarily bring about. It is ourselves who have a necessary aim, which is our own conservation; it is by this that we regulate all the ideas we form to ourselves of the causes acting in nature; it is according to this standard we judge of every thing we see or feel. Animated ourselves, existing after a certain manner, possessing a soul endowed with rare and peculiar qualities, we, like the savage, ascribe a soul and animated life to every thing that acts upon us. Thinking and intelligent ourselves, we give these, faculties to those beings whom we suppose to be more powerful than mortals; but as we see the generality of matter incapable of modifying itself, we suppose it must receive its impulse from some concealed agent, some external cause, which our imagination pictures as similar to ourselves. Necessarily attracted by that which is advantageous to us, repelling by an equal necessity that which is prejudicial to our manner of existence; we cease to reflect that our modes of feeling are due to our peculiar organization, modified by physical causes: in this state, either of inattention or ignorance, we mistake the natural results of our own peculiar structure, for instruments employed by a being whom we clothe with our own passions—whom we suppose actuated by our own views—who, possessing our ideas, embraces a mode of thinking and acting similar to ourselves.

If after this it be asked, What is the end of nature? We shall reply that on this head we are ignorant; that it is more than probable no man will ever fathom the secret; but we shall also say, it is evidently to exist, to act, to conserve her whole. If then it be demanded, Wherefore she exists? We shall again reply, of this we know nothing at present, possibly never shall; but we shall also say, she exists necessarily, that her operations, her motion, her phenomena, are the necessary consequences of her necessary existence. There necessarily exists something; this is nature or the universe, this nature necessarily acts as she does. If it be wished to substitute any other word for nature, the question will still remain as it did, as to the cause of her existence; the end she has in view. It is not by changing of terms that a geometrician can solve problems; one word will throw no more light on a subject than another, unless that word carries a certain degree of conviction in the ideas which it generates. As long as we speak of matter, if we cannot develope all its properties, we shall at least have fixed, determinate ideas; something tangible, of which we have a slight knowledge, that we can submit to the examination of our senses: but from the moment we begin to talk of immateriality, of incorporeity, from thence our ideas become confused; we are lost in a labyrinth of conjecture—we have no one means of seizing the subject on any side—we are, after the most elaborate arguments, after the most subtle reasoning, obliged to acknowledge we cannot form the most slender opinion respecting it, that has any thing substantive for its support. In short, that it is precisely that thing "of which every thing may be denied, but of which nothing can with truth be affirmed." Let us clothe this incomprehensible being with whatever qualities we may, it will be always in ourselves we seek the model; they will be our own faculties that we delineate, our own passions that we describe. In like manner man, as long as he is ignorant, will always conjecture that it is for himself alone the universe was formed; not withstanding, he has nothing more to do, than to open his eyes in order to be undeceived. He will then see, that he undergoes a common destiny, equally partakes with all other beings of the benefits, shares with them without exception the evils of life; like them he is submitted to an imperious necessity, inexorable in its decrees; which is itself nothing more than the sum total of those laws which nature herself is obliged to follow.

Thus every thing proves that nature, or matter, exists necessarily; that it cannot in any moment swerve from those laws imposed upon it by its existence. If it cannot be annihilated, it cannot have been inchoate. The theologian himself agrees that it requires a miracle to annihilate an atom. But is it possible to derogate from the necessary laws of existence? Can that which exists necessarily, act but according to the laws peculiar to itself? Miracle is another word invented to shield our own sloth, to cover our own ignorance; it is that by which we wish to designate those rare occurrences, those solitary effects of natural causes, whose infrequency do not afford us means of diving into their springs. It is only saying by another expression, that an unknown cause hath by modes which we cannot trace, produced an uncommon effect which we did not expect, which therefore appears strange to us. This granted, the intervention of words, far from removing the ignorance in which we found ourselves with respect to the power and capabilities of nature, only serves to augment it, to give it more durability. The creation of matter becomes to our mind as incomprehensible, and appears as impossible as its annihilation.

Let us then conclude that all those words which do not present to the mind any determinate idea, ought to be banished the language of those who are desirous of speaking so as to be understood; that abstract terms, invented by ignorance, are only calculated to satisfy men destitute of experience; who are too slothful to study nature, too timid to search into her ways; that they are suitable only to content those enthusiasts, whose curious imagination pleases itself with making fruitless endeavours to spring beyond the visible world; who occupy themselves with chimeras of their own creation: in short, that these words are useful only to those whose sole profession it is to feed the ears of the uninformed with pompous sounds, that are not comprehended by themselves—upon the sense of which they are in a state of perpetual hostility with each other—upon the true meaning of which they have never yet been able to come to a common agreement; which each sees after his own peculiar manner of contemplating objects, in which there never was, nor probably never will be, the least harmony of feeling.

Man is a material being; he cannot consequently have any ideas, but of that which like himself is material; that is to say, of that which is in a capacity to act upon his organs, which has some qualities analogous with his own. In despite of himself, he always assigns material properties to his gods; the impossibility he finds in compassing them, has made him suppose them to be spiritual; distinguished from the material world. Indeed he, must be content, either not to understand himself, or he must have material ideas of the Divinity; the human mind may torture itself as long as it pleases, it will never, after all its efforts, be enabled to comprehend, that material effects can emanate from immaterial causes; or that such causes can have any relation with material beings. Here is the reason why man, as we have seen, believes himself obliged to give to his gods, these morals which he so much so highly esteems, in those beings of his race, who are fortunate enough to possess them: he forgets that a being who is spiritual, adopting the theological hypothesis, cannot from thence either have his organization, or his ideas; that it cannot think in his mode, nor act after his manner; that consequently it cannot possess what he calls intelligence, wisdom, goodness, anger, justice, &c. as he himself understands those terms. Thus, in truth, the moral qualities with which he has clothed the Divinity, supposes him material, and the most abstract theological notions, are, after all, founded upon a direct, undeniable *Anthropomorphism.*

In despite of all their subtilties, the theologians cannot do otherwise; like all the beings of the human species, they have a knowledge of matter alone: they have no real idea of a pure spirit. When they speak of the intelligence, of the wisdom, of the designs of their gods, they are always those of men which they describe, that they obstinately persist in giving to beings, of which, according to their own shewing, to the evidence they themselves adduce, their essence does not render them susceptible; who if they had those qualities with which they clothe them, would from that very moment cease to be incorporeal; would be in the truest sense of the word, substantive matter. How shall we reconcile the assertion, that beings who have not occasion for any thing—who are sufficient to them selves—whose projects must be executed as soon as they are formed; can have volition, passions, desires? How shall we attribute anger to beings without either blood or bile? How can we conceive an omnipotent being (whose wisdom we admire in the striking order he has himself established in the universe,) can permit that this beautiful arrangement should be continually disturbed, either by the elements in discord, or by the crimes of human beings? In short, this being cannot have any one of the human qualities, which always depend upon the peculiar organization of man—upon his wants—upon his institutions, which are themselves always relative to the society in which he lives. The theologian vainly strives to aggrandize, to exaggerate in idea, to carry to perfection by dint of abstraction, the moral qualities of man; they are unsuitable to the Divinity; in vain it is asserted they are in him of a different nature from what they are in his creatures; that they are perfect; infinite; supreme; eminent; in holding this language, they no longer understand themselves; they can have no one idea of the qualities they are describing, seeing that man can never have a conception of them, but inasmuch as they bear an analogy to the same qualities in himself.

It is thus that by force of metaphysical subtilty, mortals have no longer any fixed, any determinate idea of the beings to which they have given birth. But little contented with understanding physical causes, with contemplating active nature; weary of examining matter, which experience proves is competent to the production of every thing, man has been desirous to despoil it of the energy which it is its essence to possess, in order to invest it in a pure spirit; in an immaterial substance; which he is under the necessity of re-making a material being, whenever he has an inclination either to form an idea of it to himself, or make it understood by others. In assembling the parts of man, which he does no more than enlarge, which he swells out to infinity, he believes he forms an immaterial being, who, for that reason, acquires the capability of performing all those phenomena, with the true causes of which he is ignorant; nevertheless those operations of which he does comprehend the spring, he as sedulously denies to be due to the powers of this being; time, therefore, according to these ideas, as he advances the progress of science, as he further developes the secrets of nature, is continually diminishing the number of actions ascribed to this being—is constantly circumscribing his sphere of action. It is upon the model of the human soul that he forms the soul of nature, or that secret agent from which she receives impulse. After having made himself double, he makes nature in like manner twofold, and then he supposes she is vivified by an intelligence, which he borrows from himself, Placed in an impossibility of becoming acquainted with this agent, as well as with that which he has gratuitously distinguished from his own body; he has invented the word spiritual to cover up his ignorance; which is only in other words avowing it is a substance entirely unknown to him. From that moment, however, he has no ideas whatever of what he himself has done; because he first clothes it with all the qualities he esteems in his fellows, and then destroys them by an assurance, that they in no wise resemble the qualities he has been so anxious to bestow. To remedy this inconvenience, he concludes this spiritual substance much more noble than matter; that its prodigious subtilty, which he calls simplicity, but which is only the effect of metaphysical abstraction, secures it from decomposition, from dissolution, from all those revolutions, to which material bodies, as produced by nature, are evidently exposed.

It is thus, that man always prefers the marvellous to the simple; the unintelligible to the intelligible; that which he cannot comprehend, to that which is within the range of his understanding; he despises those objects which are familiar to him; he estimates those alone with which he is incapable of having any intercourse: that of which he has only confused vague ideas, he concludes must contain something important for him to know—must have something supernatural in its construction. In short, he needs mystery to move his imagination—to exercise his mind—to feed his curiosity; which never labours harder, than when it is occupied with enigmas impossible to be guessed at; which from that very circumstance, he judges to be extremely worthy of his research. This, without doubt, is the reason he looks upon matter, which he has continually under his eyes, which he sees perpetually in action, eternally changing its form, as a contemptible thing—as a contingent being, that does not exist necessarily; consequently, that cannot exist independently: this is the reason why he has imagined a spirit, which he will never be able to conceive; which on that account he declares to be superior to matter; which he roundly asserts to be anterior to nature, and the only self-existent being. The human wind found food in these mystical ideas, they unceasingly occupied it; the imagination had play, it embellished them after its own manner: ignorance fed itself with the fables to which these mysteries gave rise; habit identified them with the existence of man himself: when each could ask the other concerning these ideas, without any one being in a capacity to return a direct answer, he felt himself gratified, he immediately concluded that the general impossibility of reply stamped them with the wondrous faculty of immediately interesting his welfare; of involving his most prominent interests, more than all the things put together, with which he had any possible means of becoming intimately acquainted. Thus they became necessary to his happiness; he believed he fell into a vacuum without them; he became the decided enemy to all those who endeavoured to lead him back to nature, which he had learned to despise; to consider only as an impotent mass, an heap of inert matter, not possessing any energy but what it received from causes exterior to itself; as a contemptible assemblage of fragile combinations, whose forms were continually subject to perish.

In distinguishing nature from her mover, man has fallen into the same absurdity as when he separated his soul from his body; life from the living being; the faculty of thought from the thinking being: deceived on his own peculiar nature, having taken up an erroneous opinion upon the energy of his own organs, he has in like manner been deceived upon the organization of the universe; he has distinguished nature from herself; the life of nature from living nature; the action of nature from active nature. It was this soul of the world—this energy of nature—this principle of activity, which man first personified, then separated by abstraction; sometimes decorated with imaginary attributes; sometimes with qualities borrowed from his own peculiar essence. Such were the aerial materials of which man availed himself to construct the incomprehensible, immaterial substances, which have filled the world with disputes—which have divided man from his fellow—which to this day he has never been able to define, even to his own satisfaction. His own soul was the model. Deceived upon the nature of this, he never had any just ideas of the Divinity, who was, in his mind, nothing more than a copy exaggerated or disfigured to that degree, as to make him mistake the prototype upon which it had been originally formed.

If, because man has distinguished himself from his own existence, it has been impossible for him ever to form to himself any true idea of his own nature; it is also because he has distinguished nature from herself, that both herself and her ways have been mistaken. Man has ceased to study nature, that he might, recur by thought to a substance which possesses nothing in common with her; this substance he has made the mover of nature, without which she would not be capable of any thing; to whom every thing that takes place in her system, must be attributed; the conduct of this being has appeared mysterious, has been held up as marvellous, because he seemed to be a continual contradiction: when if man had but recurred to the immutability of the laws of nature, to the invariable system she pursues, all would have appeared intelligible; every thing would have been reconciled; the apparent contrariety would have vanished. By thus taking a wrong view of things, wisdom and intelligence appeared to be opposed by confusion and disorder; goodness to be rendered nugatory by evil; while all is only just what it must inevitably be, under the given circumstances. In consequence of these erroneous opinions, in the place of applying himself to the study of nature, to discover the method of obtaining her favors, or to seek the means of throwing aside his misfortunes; in the room of consulting his experience; in lieu of labouring usefully to his own happiness; he has been only occupied with expecting these things by channels through which they do not flow; he has been disputing upon objects be never can understand, while he has totally neglected that which was within the compass of his own powers; which he might have rendered propitious to his views, by a more industrious application of his own talent; by a patient investigation, for the purpose of drawing at the fountain of truth, the limpid balsam that alone can heal the sorrows or his heart.

Nothing could be well more prejudicial to his race, than this extravagant theory; which, as we shall prove, has become the source of innumerable evils. Man has been for thousands of years trembling before idols of his own creation—bowing down before them with the most servile homage—occupied with disarming their wrath—sedulously employed in propitiating their kindness, without ever advancing a single step on the road he so much desires to travel. He will perhaps continue the same course for centuries to come, unless by some unlooked for exertion on his part, he shall happen to discard the prejudices which blind him; to lay aside his enthusiasm for the marvellous; to quit his fondness for the enigmatical; rally round the standard of his reason: unless, taking experience for his guide, he march undauntedly forward under the banner of truth, and put to the rout that host of unintelligible jargon, under the cumbrous load of which he has lost sight of his own happiness; which has but too frequently prevented him from seeking the only means adequate either to satisfy his wants, or to ameliorate the evils which he is necessarily obliged to experience.

Let us then re-conduct bewildered mortals to the altar of nature; let us endeavour to destroy that delusion which the ignorance of man, aided by a disordered imagination, has induced him to elevate to her throne; let us strive to dissipate that heavy mist which obscures to him the paths of truth; let us seek to banish from his mind those visionary ideas which prevent him from giving activity to his experience; let us teach him if possible not to seek out of nature herself, the causes of the phenomena he admires—to rest satisfied that she contains remedies for all his evils—that she has manifold benefits in store for those, who, rallying their industry, are willingly patiently to investigate her laws—that she rarely withholds her secrets from the researches of those who diligently labour to unravel them. Let us assure him that reason alone can render him happy; that reason is nothing more than the science of nature, applied to the conduct of man in society; that this reason teaches that every thing is necessary; that his pleasures as well as his sorrows are the effects of nature, who in all her works follows only laws which nothing can make her revoke; that his interest demands he should learn to support with equanimity of mind, all those evils which natural means do not enable him to put aside. In short, let us unceasingly repeat to him, it is in rendering his fellow creature happy, that he will himself arrive at a felicity he will in vain expect from others, when his own conduct refuses it to him.

Nature is self-existent; she will always exist; she produces every thing; contains within herself the cause of every thing; her motion is a necessary consequence of her existence; without motion we could form no conception of nature; under this collective name we designate the assemblage of matter acting by virtue of its peculiar energies. Every thing proves to us, that it is not out of nature man ought to seek the Divinity. If we have only an incomplete knowledge of nature and her ways—if we have only superficial, imperfect ideas of matter, how shall we be able to flatter ourselves with understanding or having any certain notions of immateriality, of beings so much more fugitive, so much more difficult to compass, even by thought, than the material elements; so much more shy of access than either the constituent principles of bodies, their primitive properties, their various modes of acting, or their different manner of existing? If we cannot recur to first causes, let its content ourselves with second causes, with those effects which we can submit to experience, let us collect the facts with which we have an acquaintance; they will enable us to judge of what we do not know: let us at least confine ourselves to the feeble glimmerings of truth with which our senses furnish us, since we do not possess means whereby to acquire broader masses of light.

Do not let us mistake for real sciences, those which have no other basis than our imagination; we shall find that such can at most be but visionary: let us cling close to nature which we see, which we feel, of which we experience the action; of which at least we understand the general laws. If we are ignorant of her detail, if we cannot fathom the secret principles she employs in her most complicated productions, we are at least certain she acts in a permanent, uniform, analogous, necessary manner. Let us then observe this nature; let us watch her movements; but never let us endeavour to quit the routine she prescribes for the beings of our species: if we do, we shall not only be obliged to return, but we shall also infallibly be punished with numberless errors, which will darken our mind, estrange us from reason; the necessary consequence will be countless sorrows, which we may otherwise avoid. Let us consider we are sensible parts of a whole, in which the forms are only produced to be destroyed; in which combinations are ushered into life, that they may again quit it, after having subsisted for a longer or a shorter season. Let us look upon nature as an immense elaboratory which contains every thing necessary for her action; who lacks nothing requisite for the production of all the phenomena she displays to our sight. Let us acknowledge her power to be inherent in her essence; amply commensurate to her eternal march; fully adequate to the happiness of all the beings she contains. Let us consider her as a whole, who can only maintain herself by what we call the discord of the elements; that she exists by the continual dissolution and re-union of her parts; that from this springs the universal harmony; that from this the general stability has its birth. Let us then re-establish omnipotent nature, so long mistaken by man, in her legitimate rights. Let us place her on that adamantine throne, which it is for the felicity of the human race she should occupy. Let us surround her with those ministers who can never deceive, who can never forfeit our confidence—*Justice and Practical Knowledge*. Let us listen to her eternal voice; she neither speaks ambiguously, nor in an unintelligible language; she may be easily comprehended by the people of all nations; because *Reason* is her faithful interpreter. She offers nothing to our contemplation but immutable truths. Let us then for ever impose silence on that enthusiasm which leads us astray; let us put to the blush that imposture which would riot on our credulity; let us discard that gloomy superstition, which has drawn us aside from the only worship suitable to intelligent beings. Above all, never let us forget that the temple of happiness can only be reached through the groves of virtue, which surround it on every side; that the paths which lead to these beautiful walks can only be entered by the road of experience, the portals of which are alone opened to those who apply to them the key of truth: this key is of very simple structure, has no complicated intricacy of wards, and is easily formed on the anvil of social intercourse, merely by *not doing unto others that which you would not wish they should do unto you.*

CHAP. VII.

Of Theism.—Of the System of Optimism.—Of final Causes.

Very few men have either the courage or the industry to examine opinions, which every one is in agreement to acknowledge; there is scarcely any one who ventures to doubt their truth, even when no solid arguments have been adduced in their support. The natural supineness of man readily receives them without examination upon the authority of others—communicates them to his successors in the season of their infancy; thus is transmitted from race to race, notions which once having obtained the sanction of time, are contemplated as clothed with a sacred character, although perhaps to an unprejudiced mind, who should be bent on searching into their foundation, no proofs will appear, that they ever were verified. It is thus with immateriality: it has passed current from father to son for many ages, without these having done any thing more than habitually consign to their brain those obscure ideas which were at first attached to it, which it is evident, from the admission even of its advocates, can never be removed, to admit others of a more enlightened nature. Indeed how can it possibly be, that light can be thrown upon an incomprehensible subject: each therefore modifies it after his own manner; each gives it that colouring that most harmonizes with his own peculiar existence; each contemplates it under that perspective which is the issue of his own particular vision: this from the nature of things cannot be the same in every individual: there must then of necessity be a great contrariety in the opinions resulting. It is thus also that each man forms to himself a God in particular, after his own peculiar temperament—according to his own natural dispositions: the individual circumstances under which he is found, the warmth of his imagination, the prejudices he has received, the mode in which he is at different times affected, have all their influence in the picture he forms. The contented, healthy man, does not see him with the same eyes as the man who is chagrined and sick; the man with a heated blood, who has an ardent imagination, or is subject to bile, does not pourtray him under the same traits as he who enjoys a more peaceable soul, who has a cooler fancy, who is of a more phlegmatic habit. This is not all; even the same individual does not view him in the same manner at different periods of his life: he undergoes all the variations of his machine—all the revolutions of his temperament—all those continual vicissitudes which his existence experiences. The idea of the Divinity is said to be innate; on the contrary, it is perpetually fluctuating in the mind of each individual; varies every moment in all the beings of the human species; so much so, that there are not two who admit precisely the same Deity; there is not a single one, who, under different circumstances, does not see him variously.

Do not then let us be surprised at the variety of systems adopted by mankind on this subject; it ought not to astonish us that there is so little harmony existing among men upon a point of such consequence; it ought not to appear strange that so much contradiction should prevail in the various doctrines held forth; that they should have such little consistency, such slender connection with each other; that the professors should dispute continually upon the rectitude of the opinions adopted by each: they must necessarily wrangle upon that which each contemplates so variously—upon which there is hardly a single mortal who is constantly in accord with himself.

All men are pretty well agreed upon those objects which they are enabled to submit to the test of experience; we do not hear any disputes upon the principles of geometry; those truths that are evident, that are easily demonstrable, never vary in our mind; we never doubt that the part is less than the whole; that two and two make four; that benevolence is an amiable quality; that equity is necessary to man in society. But we find nothing but perpetual controversy upon all those systems which have the Divinity for their object; they are full of incertitude; subject to continual variations: we do not see any harmony either in the principles of theology, or in the principles of its graduates. Even the proofs offered of his existence have been the subject of cavil; they have either been thought too feeble, have been brought forward against rule, or else have not been taken up with sufficient zeal to please the various reasoners who advocate the cause; the corollaries drawn from the premises laid down, are not the same in any two nations, scarcely in two individuals; the thinkers of all ages, in all countries, are perpetually in rivalry with each other; unceasingly quarrel upon all the points of religion; can never agree either upon their theological hypotheses, or upon the fundamental truths which should serve for their basis; even the attributes, the very qualities ascribed, are as warmly contested by some, as they are zealously defended by others.

These never-ending disputes, these perpetual variations, ought, at least, to convince the unprejudiced, that the ideas of the Divinity have neither the generally-admitted evidence, nor the certitude which are attributed to them; on the contrary, these contrarieties in the opinions of the theologians, if submitted to the logic of the schools, might be fatal to the whole of them: according to that mode of reasoning, which at least has the sanction of our universities, all the probabilities in the world cannot acquire the force of a demonstration; a truth is not made evident but when constant experience, reiterated reflection, exhibits it always under the same point of view; the evidence of a proposition cannot be admitted unless it carries with it a substantive demonstration; from the constant relation which is made by well constituted senses, results that evidence, that certitude, which alone can produce full conviction: if the major proposition of a syllogism should be overturned by the minor, the whole falls to the ground. Cicero, who is no mean authority on such a subject, says expressly, "No reasoning can render that false, which experience has demonstrated as evident." Wolff, in his Ontology, says; "That which is repugnant in itself, cannot possibly be understood; that those things which are in themselves contradictions, must always be deficient of evidence." St. Thomas says, "Being, is all that which is not repugnant to existence."

However it may be with these qualities, which the theologians assign to their immaterial beings, whether they may be irreconcileable, or whether they are totally incomprehensible, what can result to the human species in supposing them to have intelligence and views? Can an universal intelligence, whose care must be equally extended to every thing that exists, have more direct, more intimate relations with man, who only forms an insensible portion of the great whole? Can we seriously believe that it is to make joyful the insects, to gratify the ants of his garden, that the Monarch of the universe has constructed and embellished his habitation? Would our feeble eyes, therefore, become stronger—would our narrow views of things be enlarged—should we be better capacitated to understand his projects—could we with more certitude divine his plans, enter into his designs—would our exility of judgment be competent to measure his wisdom, to follow the eternal order he has established? Will those effects, which flow from his omnipotence, emanate from his providence—whether we estimate them as good, or whether we tax them as evil—whether we consider them beneficial, or view them as prejudicial—be less the necessary results of his wisdom, of his justice, of his eternal decrees? In this case can we reasonably suppose that a Being, so wise, so just, so intelligent, will derange his system, change his plan, for such weak beings as ourselves? Can we rationally believe we have the capacity to address worthy prayers, to make suitable requests, to point out proper modes of conduct to such a Being? Can we at all flatter ourselves that to please us, to gratify our discordant wishes, he will alter his immutable laws? Can we imagine that at our entreaty he will take from the beings who surround us their essences, their properties, their various modes of action? Have we any right to expect he will abrogate in our behalf the eternal laws of nature, that he will disturb her eternal march, arrest her ever-lasting course, which his wisdom has planned; which his goodness has conferred; which are, in fact, the admiration of mankind? Can we hope that in our favour fire will cease to burn, when we approximate it too closely; that fever shall not consume our habit, when contagion has penetrated our system; that gout shall not torment us, when an intemperate mode of life shall have amassed the humours that necessarily result from such conduct; that an edifice tumbling in ruins shall not crush us by its fall, when we are within the vortex of its action? Will our vain cries, our most fervent supplications, prevent a country from being unhappy, when it shall be devastated by an ambitious conqueror; when it shall be submitted to the capricious will of unfeeling tyrants, who bend it beneath the iron rod of their oppression?

If this infinite intelligence gives a free course to those events which his wisdom has prepared; if nothing happens in this world but after his impenetrable designs; we ought silently to submit; we have in fact nothing to ask; we should be madmen to oppose our own weak intellect to such capacious wisdom; we should offer an insult to his prudence if we were desirous to regulate them. Man must not flatter himself that he is wiser than his God; that he is in a capacity to make him change his will; with having power to determine him to take other means than those which he has chosen to accomplish his decrees. An intelligent Divinity can only have taken those measures which embrace complete justice; can only have availed himself of those means which are best calculated to arrive at his end; if he was capable of changing them, he could neither be called wise, immutable, nor provident. If it was to be granted, that the Divinity did for a single instant suspend those laws which he himself has given, if he was to change any thing in his plan, it would be supposing he had not foreseen the motives of this suspension; that he had not calculated the causes of this change; if he did not make these motives enter into his plan, it would be saying he had not foreseen the causes that render them necessary: if he has foreseen them without making them part of his system, it would be arraigning the perfection of the whole. Thus in whatever manner these things are contemplated, under whatever point of view they are examined, it is evident that the prayers which man addresses to the Divinity, which are sanctioned by the different modes of worship, always suppose he is supplicating a being whose wisdom and providence are defective; in fact, that his own is more appropriate to his situation. To suppose he is capable of change in his conduct, is to bring his omniscience into question; to vitally attack his omnipotence; to arraign his goodness; at once to say, that he either is not willing or not competent to judge what would be most expedient for man; for whose sole advantage and pleasure they will, notwithstanding, insist he created the universe: such are the inconsistent doctrines of theology; such the imbecile efforts of metaphysics.

It is, however, upon these notions, extravagant as they may appear, ill directed as they assuredly are, inconclusive as they must be acknowledged by unprejudiced minds, that are founded all the superstitions and many of the religions of the earth. It is by no means an uncommon sight, to see man upon his knees before an all-wise God, whose conduct he is endeavouring to regulate; whose decrees he wishes to avert; whose plan he is desirous to reform. These inconsistent objects he is occupied with gaining, by means equally repugnant to sound sense; equally injurious to the dignity of the Divinity: adopting his own sensations as the criterion of the feelings of the Deity; in some places he tries to win him to his interests by presents; sometimes we behold even the princes of the earth attempting to direct his views, by offering him splendid garments, upon which their own fatuity sets an inordinate value, merely because they have laboured at them themselves; some strive to disarm his justice by the most splendid pageantry; others by practices the most revolting to humanity; some think his immutability will yield to idle ceremonies; others to the most discordant prayers; it not unfrequently happens that to induce him to change in their favour his eternal decrees, those who have opposite interests to promote, each returns him thanks for that which the others consider as the greatest curse that can befal them. In short, man is almost every where prostrate before an omnipotent God, who, if we were to judge by the discrepancy of their requests, never has rendered his creatures such as they ought to be; who to accomplish his divine views has never taken the proper measures, who to fulfil his wisdom has continual need of the admonitions of man, conveyed either in the form of thanks or prayers.

We see, then, that superstition is founded upon manifest contradictions, which man must always fall into when he mistakes the natural causes of things—when he shall attribute the good or evil which he experiences to an intelligent cause, distinguished from nature, of which he will never be competent to form to himself any certain ideas. Indeed, man will always be reduced, as we have so frequently repeated, to the necessity of clothing his gods with his own imbecile qualities: as he is himself a changeable being, whose intelligence is limited; who, placed in divers circumstances, appears to be frequently in contradiction with himself; although he thinks he honours his gods in giving them his own peculiar qualities, he in fact does nothing more than lend them his own inconstancy, cover them with his own weakness, invest them with his own vices. It is thus that in reasoning, he is unable to account for the necessity of things—that he imagines there is a confusion which his prayers will have a tendency to remove—that he thinks the evils of life more than commensurate with the good: he does not perceive that an undeviating system, by operating upon beings diversely organized, whose circumstances are different, whose modes of action are at variance, must of necessity sometimes appear to be inimical to the interests of the individual, while it embraces the general good of the whole. The theologian may subtilize, exaggerate, render as unintelligible as he pleases, the attributes with which he clothes his divinities, he will never be able to remove the contradictions which arise from the discordant qualities which he thus heaps together; neither will he be able to give man any other mode of judging than what arises from the exercise of his senses, such as they are actually found. He will never be able to furnish the idea of an immutable being, while he shall represent this being as capable of being irritated and appeased by the prayers of mortals. He will never delineate the features of omnipotence under the portrait of a being who cannot restrain the actions of his inferiors. He will never hold up a standard of justice, while he shall mingle it with mercy, however amiable the quality; or while he shall represent it as punishing those actions, which the perpetrators were under the necessity of committing. Neither will he be able, under any circumstances, to make a finite mind comprehend infinity; much less when he shall represent this infinity as bounded by finity itself.

From this it will be obvious, that immaterial substances, such as are depicted by the theologians, can only be looked upon as the offspring of a metaphysical brain, unsupported by any of those proofs which are usually required to establish the propositions laid down among men; all the qualities which they ascribe to them, are only those which are suitable to material substances; all the abstract properties with which they invest them, are incomprehensible by material beings; the whole taken together, is one confused mass of contradictions: they have held forth to man, that it highly imported to his interests to know, to understand these substances; he has consequently set his intellect in action to discover some means of compassing an end, said to be so consequential to his welfare; he has, however, been unable to make any progress, because no clue could be offered to him of the road he must pursue; all was mere assertion unsupported by evidence; the whole was enveloped in complete darkness, into which the least scintillation of light could never penetrate. Notwithstanding, as soon as man believes himself greatly interested in knowing a thing, he labors to form to himself an idea of that, the knowledge of which he thinks so important; if insuperable obstacles impede his inquiries—if difficulties of a magnitude to alarm his industry intervene—if with immense labour he makes but little progress, then the slender success that attends his research, aided by a slothful disposition, while it wearies his diligence disposes him to credulity. It was thus, that a crafty ambitious Arab, subtle and knavish in his manners, insinuating in his address, profiting by this credulous inclination, made his countrymen adopt his own fanciful reveries as permanent truths, of which it was not permitted them for an instant to doubt; following up these opinions with enthusiasm, he stimulated them on to become conquerors; obliging the conquered to lend themselves to his system, he gave currency to a creed, invented solely for the purpose of enslaving mankind, which now spreads over immense regions inhabited by a numerous population, although like other systems it does not escape sectarianism, having above seventy branches. Thus ignorance, despair, sloth, the want of reflecting habits, place the human race in a state of dependance upon those who build up systems, while upon the objects which are the foundations, they have no one settled idea: once adopted, however, whenever these systems are brought into question, man either reasons in a very strange manner, or else is the dupe of very deceitful arguments: when they are agitated, and he finds it impossible to understand what is said concerning them when his mind cannot embrace the ambiguity of these doctrines, he imagines those who speak to him are better acquainted with the objects of their discourse than himself; these seizing the favourable opportunity, do not let it slip, they reiterate to him with Stentorian lungs, "That the most certain way is to agree with what they tell him; to allow himself to be guided by them;" in short, they persuade him to shut his eyes, that he may with greater perspicuity distinguish the road he is to travel: once arrived at this influence, they indelibly fix their lessons; irrevocably chain him to the oar; by holding up to his view the punishments intended for him by these imaginary beings, in case he refuses to accredit, in the most liberal manner, their marvellous inventions; this argument, although it only supposes the thing in question, serves to close his mouth—to put an end to his research; alarmed, confused, bewildered, he seems convinced by this victorious reasoning—attaches to it a sacredness that fills him with awe—blindly conceives that they have much clearer ideas of the subject than himself—fears to perceive the palpable contradictions of the doctrines announced to him, until, perhaps, some being, more subtle than those who have enslaved him, by labouring the point incessantly, attacking him on the weak side of his interest, arrives at throwing the absurdity of his system into light, and finally succeeds by inducing him to adopt that of another set of speculators. The uninformed man generally believes his priests have more senses than himself; he takes them for superior beings; for divine men. He only sees that which these priests inform him he must contemplate; to every thing else his eyes are completely hoodwinked; thus the authority of the priests frequently decides, without appeal, that which is useful perhaps only to the priesthood.

When we shall be disposed to recur to the origin of things, we shall ever find that it has been man's imagination, guided by his ignorance, under the influence of fear, which gave birth to his gods; that enthusiasm or imposture have generally either embellished or disfigured them; that credulity readily adopted the fabulous accounts which interested duplicity promulgated respecting them; that these dispositions, sanctioned by time, became habitual. Tyrants finding their advantage in sustaining them, have usually established their power upon the blindness of mankind, and the superstitious fears with which it is always accompanied. Thus, under whatever point of view it is considered, it will always be found that *error cannot be useful to the human species.*

Nevertheless, the happy enthusiast, when his soul is sensible of its enjoyments, when his softened imagination has occasion to paint to itself a seducing object, to which he can render thanks for the kindness he experiences, will ask, "Wherefore deprive me of a being that I see under the character of a sovereign, filled with wisdom, abounding in goodness? What comfort do I not find in figuring to myself a powerful, intelligent, indulgent monarch, of whom I am the favorite; who continually occupies himself with my welfare—unceasingly watches over my safety—who perpetually administers to my wants—who always consents that under him I shall command the whole of nature? I believe I behold him constantly showering his benefits on man; I see his Providence labouring for his advantage without relaxation; he covers the earth with verdure to delight him; he loads the trees with delicious fruits to gratify his palate; he fills the forests with animals suitable to his nourishment; he suspends over his head planets with innumerable stars, to enlighten him by day, to guide his erring steps by night; he extends around him the azure firmament to gladden his sight; he decorates the meadows with flowers to please his fancy; he causes crystal fountains to flow with limpid streams to slake his thirst; he makes rivulets meander through his lands to fructify the earth; he washes his residence with noble rivers, that yield him fish in abundance. Ah! suffer me to thank thee, Author of so many benefits: do not deprive me of my charming sensations. I shall not find my illusions so sweet, so consolatory in a severe destiny—in a rigid necessity—in a blind inanimate matter—in a nature destitute of intelligence, devoid of feeling."

"Wherefore," will say the unfortunate, from whom his destiny has rigorously withheld those benefits which have been lavished on so many others; "wherefore ravish from me an error that is dear to me? Wherefore annihilate to me a being, whose consoling idea dries up the source of my tears—who serves to calm my sorrows? Wherefore deprive me of an object which I represent to myself as a compassionate, tender father; who reproves me in this world, but into whose arms I throw myself with confidence, when the whole of nature appears to have abandoned me? Supposing it no more than a chimera, the unhappy have occasion for it, to guarantee them against frightful despair: is it not cruel, is it not inhuman, to be desirous of plunging them into a vacuum, by seeking to undeceive them? Is it not an useful error, preferable to those truths which deprive the mind of every consolation, which do not hold forth any relief from its sorrows?"

Thus will equally reason the Negro, the Mussulman, the Brachman, and others. We shall reply to these enthusiasts, no! truth can never render you unhappy; it is this which really consoles us; it is a concealed treasure, much superior to all the superstitions ever invented by fear; it can cheer the heart; give it courage to support the burthens of life; make us smile under adversity; elevate the soul; render it active; furnishes it with means to resist the attacks of fate; to combat misfortunes with success. This will shew clearly that the good and evil of life are distributed with an equal hand, without respect to man's peculiar comforts; that all beings are equally regarded in the universe; that every thing is submitted to necessary laws; that man has no right whatever to think himself a being peculiarly favoured—who is exempted from the common operations of the eternal routine; that it is folly to think he is the only being considered—one for whose enjoyment alone every thing is produced; an attention to facts will suffice to put an end to this delusion, however pleasant may be the indulgence of such a notion; the most superficial glance of the eye will be sufficient to undeceive us in the idea, that he is the *final cause* of the creation—the constant object of the labours of nature, or of its Author. Let us seriously ask him, if he does not witness good constantly blended with evil? If he does not equally partake of them with the other beings in nature? To be obstinately bent to see only the evil, is as irrational as to be willing only to notice the good. Providence seems to be just as much occupied for one class of beings as for another. We see the calm succeed the storm; sickness give place to health; the blessings of peace follow the calamities of war; the earth in every country bring forth roots necessary for the nourishment of man, produce others suitable to his destruction. Each individual of the human species is a compound of good and bad qualities; all nations present a varied spectacle of virtues, growing up beside vices; that which gladdens one being, plunges another into sadness—no event takes place that does not give birth to advantages for some, to disadvantages for others. Insects find a safe retreat in the ruin of the palace, which crushes man in its fall; man by his death furnishes food for myriads of contemptible insects; animals are destroyed by thousands that he may increase his bulk; linger out for a season a feverish existence. We see beings engaged in perpetual hostility, each living at his neighbour's expence; the one banquetting upon that which causes the desolation of the other; some luxuriously growing into flesh upon the misery which wears others into skeletons—profiting by misfortunes, rioting upon disasters, which ultimately, reciprocally destroy them. The most deadly poisons spring up beside the most wholesome fruits the earth equally nourishes the fatal steel which terminates man's career, and the fruitful corn that prolongs his existence; the bane and its antidote are near neighbours, repose on the same bosom, ripen under the same sun, equally court the hand of the incautious stranger. The rivers which man believes flow for no other purpose than to irrigate his residence, sometimes swell their waters, overtop their banks, inundate his fields, overturn his dwelling, and sweep away the flock and shepherd. The ocean, which he vainly imagines was only collected together to facilitate his commerce supply him with fish, and wash his shores; often wrecks his ships, frequently bursts its boundaries, lays waste his lands, destroys the produce of his industry, and commits the most frightful ravages. The halcyon, delighted with the tempest, voluntarily mingles with the storm; rides contentedly upon the surge; rejoiced by the fearful howlings of the northern blast, plays with happy buoyancy upon the foaming billows, that have ruthlessly dashed in pieces the vessel of the unfortunate mariner; who, plunged into an abyss of misery, with tremulous emotion clings to the wreck; views with horrific despair, the premature destruction of his indulged hopes; sighs deeply at the thoughts of home; with aching heart, thinks of the cherished friends his streaming eyes will never more behold in an agony of soul dwells upon the faithful affection of an adored wife, who will never again repose her drooping head upon his manly bosom; grows wild with the appalling remembrance of beloved children, his wearied arms will never more encircle with parental fondness; then sinks for ever, the unhappy victim of circumstances that fill with glee the fluttering bird, who sees him yield to the overwhelming force of the infuriate waves. The conqueror displays his military skill, fights a sanguinary battle, puts his enemy to the rout, lays waste his country, slaughters thousands of his fellows, plunges whole districts into tears, fills the land with the moans of the fatherless, the wailings of the widow, in order that the crows may have a banquet—that ferocious beasts may gluttonously gorge themselves with human gore—that worms may riot in luxury.

Thus when there is a question concerning an agent we see act so variously; whose motives seem sometimes to be advantageous, sometimes disadvantageous for the human race; at least each individual will judge after the peculiar mode in which he is himself affected; there will consequently be no fixed point, no general standard in the opinions men will form to themselves. Indeed our mode of judging will always be governed by our manner of seeing, by our way of feeling. This will depend upon our temperament, which itself springs out of our organization, and the peculiarity of the circumstances in which we are placed; these can never be the same for all the beings of our species. These individual modes of being affected, then, will always furnish the colours of the portrait which man may paint to himself of the Divinity; it must therefore be obvious they can never be determinate—can have no fixity—can never be reduced to any graduated scale; the inductions which they may draw from them, can never be either constant or uniform; each will always judge after himself, will never see any thing but himself or his own peculiar situation in the picture he delineates.

This granted, the man who has a contented, sensible soul, with a lively imagination, will paint the Divinity under the most charming traits; he will believe that he sees in the whole of nature nothing but proofs of benevolence, evidence of goodness, because it will unceasingly cause him agreeable sensations. In his poetical extacy he will imagine he every where perceives the impression of a perfect intelligence—of an infinite wisdom—of a providence tenderly occupied with the welfare of man; self-love joining itself to these exalted qualities, will put the finishing hand to his persuasion, that the universe is made solely for the human race; he will strive in imagination to kiss with transport the hand from which he believes he receives so many benefits; touched with his kindness, gratified with the perfume of roses whose thorns he does not perceive, or which his extatic delirium prevents him from feeling, he will think he can never sufficiently acknowledge the necessary effects, which he will look upon as indubitable testimony of the divine predilection for man. Completely inebriated with these feelings, this enthusiast will not behold those sorrows, will not notice that confusion of which the universe is the theatre: or if it so happens, he cannot prevent himself from being a witness, he will be persuaded that in the views of an indulgent providence, these calamities are necessary to conduct man to a higher state of felicity; the reliance which he has in the Divinity, upon whom he imagines they depend, induces him to believe, that man only suffers for his good; that this being, who is fruitful in resources, will know how to make him reap advantage from the evils which he experiences in this world: his mind thus pre-occupied, from thence sees nothing that does not elicit his admiration call forth his gratitude; excite his confidence; even those effects which are the most natural, the most necessary, appear in his eyes miracles of benevolence; prodigies of goodness: he shuts his eyes to the disorders which could bring these amiable qualities into question: the most cruel calamities, the most afflicting events, the most heart-rending circumstances, cease to be disorders in his eyes, and do nothing, more than furnish him with new proofs of the divine perfections; he persuades himself that what appears defective or imperfect, is only so in appearance; he admires the wisdom, acknowledges the bounty of the Divinity, even in those effects which are the most terrible for his race—most suitable to discourage his species—most fraught with misery for his fellow.

It is, without doubt, to this happy disposition of the human mind, in some beings of his order, that is to be ascribed the system of *Optimism*, by which enthusiasts, furnished with a romantic imagination, seem to have renounced the evidence of their senses: to find that even for man every thing is good in nature, where the good has constantly its concomitant evil, and where minds less prejudiced, less poetical, would judge that every thing is only that which it can be—that the good and the evil are equally necessary—that they have their source in the nature of things; moreover, in order to attribute any particular character to the events that take place, it would be needful to know the aim of the whole; now the whole cannot have an aim, because if it had a tendency, an aim, or end, it would no longer be the whole, seeing that that to which it tended would be a part not included.

It will be asserted by some, that the evils which we behold in this world are only relative, merely apparent; that they prove nothing against the good: but does not man almost uniformly judge after his own mode of feeling; after his manner of co-existing with those causes by which he is encompassed; which constitute the order of nature with relation to himself; consequently, he ascribes wisdom and goodness to all that which affects him pleasantly, disorder to that state of things by which he is injured. Nevertheless every thing which we witness in the world conspires to prove to us, that whatever is, is necessary; that nothing is done by chance; that all the events, good or bad, whether for us or for beings of a different order, are brought about by causes acting after certain and determinate laws; that nothing can he a sufficient warrantry in us to clothe with any one of our human qualities, either nature or the motive-power which has been given to her.

With respect to those who pretend that supreme wisdom will know how to draw the greatest benefits for us, even out of the bosom of those calamities which it is permitted we shall experience in this world; we shall ask them, if they are themselves the confidents of the Divinity; or upon what they found these assertions so flattering to their hopes? They will, without doubt, tell us they judge by analogy; that from the actual proofs of goodness and wisdom, they have a just right to conclude in favour of future bounty. Would it not be a fair reply to ask, If they reason by analogy, and man has not been rendered completely happy in this world, what analogy informs them he will be so in another? If, according to their own shewing, man is sometimes made the victim of evil in his present existence, in order that he may attain a greater good, does not analogical reasoning, which they say they adopt, clearly warrant a deduction, that the same afflictions, for the same purposes, will be equally proper, equally requisite in the world to come?

Thus this language founds itself upon ruinous hypotheses, which have for their bases only a prejuced imagination. It, in fact, signifies nothing more than that man once persuaded, without any evidence, of his future happiness, will not believe it possible he can be permitted to be unhappy: but might it not be inquired what testimony does he find, what substantive knowledge has he obtained of the peculiar good that results to the human species from those sterilities, from those famines, from those contagions, from those sanguinary conflicts, which cause so many millions of men to perish; which unceasingly depopulate the earth, and desolate the world we inhabit? Is there any one who has sufficient compass of comprehension to ascertain the advantages that result from the evils that besiege us on all sides? Do we not daily witness beings consecrated to misfortune, from the moment they quitted the womb of the parent who brought them into existence, until that which re-committed them to the earth, to sleep in peace with their fathers; who with great difficulty found time to respire; lived the constant sport of fortune; overwhelmed with affliction, immersed in grief, enduring the most cruel reverses? Who is to measure the precise quantity of misery required to derive a certain portion of good? Who is to say when the measure of evil will be full which it is necessary to suffer?

The most enthusiastic Optimists, the *Theists* themselves, the partizans of *Natural Religion*, as well as the most credulous and superstitious, are obliged to recur to the system of another life, to remedy the evils man is decreed to suffer in the present; but have they really any just foundation to suppose the next world will afford him a happiness denied him in this? If it is necessary to recur to a doctrine so little probable as that of a future existence, by what chain of reasoning do they establish their opinion, that when he shall no longer have organs, by the aid of which he is at present alone enabled either to enjoy or to suffer, he shall be able to compensate the evils he has endured; to enjoy a felicity, to partake of a pleasure this organic structure has refused him while on his pilgrimage through the land of his fathers.

From this it will be seen, that the proofs of a sovereign intelligence, or of a magnified human quality drawn from the order, from the harmony, from the beauty of the universe, are never more than those which are derived from men who are organized and modified after a certain mode; or whose cheerful imagination is so constructed as to give birth to agreeable chimeras which they embellish according to their fancy: these illusions, however, must be frequently dissipated even in themselves, whenever their machine becomes deranged; when sorrows assail them, when misfortune corrodes their mind; the spectacle of nature, which under certain circumstances has appeared to them so delightful, so seducing, must then give place to disorder, must yield to confusion. A man of melancholy temperament, soured by misfortunes, made irritable by infirmities, cannot view nature and her author under the same perspective, as the healthy man of a sprightly humour, who is contented with every thing. Deprived of happiness, the fretful man can only find disorder, can see nothing but deformity, can find nothing but subjects to afflict himself with; he only contemplates the universe as the theatre of malice, as the stage for tyrants to execute their vengeance; he grows superstitious, he gives way to credulity, and not unfrequently becomes cruel, in order to serve a master whom he believes he has offended.

In consequence of these ideas, which have their growth in an unhappy temperament, which originate in a peevish humour, which are the offspring of a disturbed imagination, the superstitious are constantly infected with terror, are the slaves to mistrust, the creatures of discontent, continually in a state of fearful alarm. Nature cannot have charms for them; her countless beauties pass by unheeded; they do not participate in her cheerful scenes; they look upon this world, so marvellous to the happy man, so good to the contented enthusiast, as a *valley of tears*, in which a vindictive fate has placed them only to expiate crimes committed either by themselves or by their fathers; they consider themselves as sent here for no other purpose than to be the sharers of calamity; the sport of a capricious fortune; that they are the children of sorrow, destined to undergo the severest trials, to the end that they may everlastingly arrive at a new existence, in which they shall be either happy or miserable, according to their conduct towards the ministers of a being who holds their destiny in his hands. These dismal notions have been the source of all the irrational systems that have ever prevailed; they have given birth to the most revolting practices, currency to the most absurd customs. History abounds with details of the most atrocious cruelties, under the imposing name of public worship; nothing has been considered either too fantastical or too flagitious by the votaries of superstition. Parents have immolated their children; lovers have sacrificed the objects of their affection; friends have destroyed each other: the most bloody disputes have been fomented; the most interminable animosities have been engendered, to gratify the whim of implacable priests, who by crafty inventions have obtained an influence over the people; to please blind zealots, who have never been able either to give fixity to their ideas, or to define their own feelings. Idle dreamers nourished with bile, intoxicated with theologic fury—atrabilarians, whose melancholic humour frequently disposes them to wickedness—visionaries, whose devious imaginations, heated with intemperate zeal, generally leads them to the extremes of fanaticism, working upon ignorance, whose usual bias is credulity, have incessantly disturbed the harmony of mankind, kindled the inextinguishable flame of discord, and in an almost uninterrupted succession, strewed the earth with the mangled carcasses of the multitudinous victims to mad-brained error, whose only crime has been their incapacity to dream according to the rules prescribed by these infuriate maniacs; although these have never been uniform—never assimilated in any two countries—never borne the same features in any two ages, nor even had the united concurrence of the persecuting contemporaries.

It is then in the diversity of temperament, arising from variety of organization—in the contrariety of passions, springing out of this miscellany, modified by the most opposite circumstances, that must be sought the difference we find in the opinions of the theist, the optimist, the happy enthusiast, the zealot, the devotee, the superstitious of all denominations; they are all equally irrational—the dupes of their imagination—the blind children of error. What one contemplates under a favorable point of view, the other never looks upon but on the dark side; that which is the object of the most sedulous research to one set, is that which the others most seek to avoid: each insists he is right; no one offers the least shadow of substantive proof of what he asserts; each points out the great importance of his mission, yet cannot even agree with his colleagues in the embassy, either upon the nature of their instructions, or the means to be adopted. It is thus whenever man sets forth a false supposition, all the reasonings he makes on it are only a long tissue of errors, which entail on him an endless series of misfortunes; every time he renounces the evidence of his senses, it is impossible to calculate the bounds at which his imagination will stop; when he once quits the road of experience, when he travels out of nature, when he loses sight of his reason, to strike into the labyrinths of conjecture, it is difficult to ascertain where his folly will lead him—into what mischievous swamps this *ignis fatuus* of the mind may beguile his wandering steps. It is certainly true, the ideas of the happy enthusiast will be less dangerous to himself, less baneful to others, than those of the atrabilarious fanatic, whose temperament may render him both cowardly and cruel; nevertheless the opinions of the one and of the other will not be less chimerical; the only difference will be, that of the first will produce agreeable, cheerful dreams; while that of the second will present the most appalling visions, terrific spectres, the fruit of a peevish transport of the brain: there will, however, never be more than a step between them all; the smallest revolution in the machine, a slight infirmity, an unforeseen affliction, suffices to change the course of the humours—to vitiate the temperament—to endanger the organization—to overturn the whole system of opinions of the happiest. As soon as the portrait is found disfigured, the beautiful order of things is overthrown relatively to himself; melancholy grapples him—pusillanimity benumbs his faculties—by degrees plunges, him into the rankest depths of gloomy superstition; he then degenerates into all those irregularities which are the dismal harvest of fanatic ignorance ploughed with credulity.

Those ideas, which have no archetype but in the imagination of man, must necessarily take their complexion from his own character; must be clothed with his own passions; must constantly follow the revolutions of his machine; be lively or gloomy; favourable or prejudicial; friendly or inimical; sociable or savage; humane or cruel; according as he whose brain they inhabit shall himself be disposed; in fact, they can never be more than the shadow of the substance he himself interposes between the light and the ground on which they are thrown. A mortal plunged from a state of happiness into misery, whose health merges into sickness, whose joy is changed into affliction, cannot in these vicissitudes preserve the same ideas; these naturally depend every instant upon the variations, which physical sensations oblige his organs to undergo. It will not therefore appear strange that these opinions should be fluctuating, when they depend upon the state of the nervous fluid, upon the greater or less portion of igneous matter floating in the sanguinary vessels.

Theism, or what is called *Natural Religion*, cannot have certain principles; those who profess it must necessarily be subject to vary in their opinions—to fluctuate in their conduct, which flows out of them. A system founded upon wisdom and intelligence, which can never contradict itself, when circumstances change will presently be converted into fanaticism; rapidly degenerate into superstition; such a system, successively meditated by enthusiasts of very distinct characters, must of necessity experience vicissitudes, and quickly depart from its primitive simplicity. The greater part of those philosophers who have been disposed to substitute theism for superstition, have not felt that it was formed to corrupt itself—to degenerate. Striking examples, however, prove this fatal truth. Theism is almost every where corrupted; it has by degrees given way to those superstitions, to those extravagant sects, to those prejudicial opinions with which the human species is degraded. As soon as man consents to acknowledge invisible powers out of nature, upon which his restless mind will never be able invariably to fix his ideas—which his imagination alone will be capable of painting to him; whenever he shall not dare to consult his reason relatively to those powers, it must necessarily be, that the first false step leads him astray, that his conduct as well as his opinions becomes in the long run perfectly absurd.

Those are usually called Theists, who, undeceived upon the greater number of grosser errors to which the uninformed, the superstitiously ignorant, tend the most determined support, simply hold the notion of unknown agents endowed with intelligence, wisdom, power and goodness, in short, full of infinite perfections, whom they distinguish from nature, but whom they clothe after their own fashion; to whom they ascribe their own limited views; whom they make act according to their own absurd passions. The religion of Abraham appears to have originally been a kind of theism, imagined to reform the superstition of the Chaldeans; Moses modified it, and gave it the Judaical form. Socrates was a theist, who lost his life in his attack on polytheism; his disciple Aristocles, or Plato, as he was afterwards called from his large shoulders, embellished the theism of his master, with the mystical colours which he borrowed from the Egyptian and Chaldean priests, which he modified in his own poetical brain, and preserved a remnant of polytheism. The disciples of Plato, such as Proclus, Ammonius, Jamblicus. Plotinus, Longinus, Porphyrus, and others, dressed it up still more fantastically, added a great deal of superstitious mummery, blended it with magic, and other unintelligible doctrines. The first doctors of Christianity were Platonists, who combined the reformed Judaism with the philosophy taught in Academia. Mahomet, in combating the polytheism of his country, seems to have been desirous of restoring the primitive theism of Abraham, and his son Ishmael; yet this has now seventy-two sects. Thus it will be obvious, that theism has no fixed point, no standard, no common measure more than other systems: that it runs from one supposition to another, to find in what manner evil has crept into the world. Indeed it has been for this purpose, which perhaps after all will never be satisfactorily explained, that the doctrine of free-agency was introduced; that the fable of Prometheus and the box of Pandora was imagined; that the history of the Titans was invented; notwithstanding, it must be evident that these things as well as all the other trappings of superstition, are not more difficult of comprehension than the immaterial substances of the theists; the mind who can admit that beings devoid of parts, destitute of organs, without bulk, can move matter, think like man, have the moral qualities of human nature, need not hesitate to allow that ceremonies, certain motions of the body, words, rites, temples, statues, can equally contain secret virtues; has no occasion to withhold its faith from the concealed powers of magic, theurgy, enchantments, charms, talismans, &c.; can shew no good reason why it should not accredit inspirations, dreams, visions, omens, soothsayers, metamorphoses, and all the host of occult sciences: when things so contradictory to the dictates of reason, so completely opposed to good sense are freely admitted, there can no longer be an thing which ought to possess the right to make credulity revolt; those who give sanction to the one, may without much hesitation believe whatever else is offered to their credence. It would be impossible to mark the precise point at which imagination ought to arrest itself—the exact boundary that should circumscribe belief—the true dose of folly that may be permitted them; or the degree of indulgence that can with safety be extended to those priests who are in the habit of teaching so variously, so contradictorily, what man ought to think on the subjects they handle so advantageously to themselves; who when it becomes a question what remuneration is due from mankind for their unwearied exertions in his favour, are, in spite of all their other differences, in the most perfect union; except perhaps when they come to the division of the spoil: in this, indeed, the apple of discord sometimes takes a tremendous roll. Thus it will be clear that there can be no substantive grounds for separating the theists from the most superstitious; that it becomes impossible to fix the line of demarcation, which divides them from the most credulous of men; to shew the land-marks by which they can be discriminated from those who reason with the least conclusive persuasion. If the theist refuses to follow up the fanatic in every step of his cullibility, he is at least more inconsequent than the last, who having admitted upon hearsay an inconsistent, whimsical doctrine, also adopts upon report the ridiculous, strange means which it furnishes him. The first sets forth with an absurd supposition, of which he rejects the necessary consequences; the other admits both the principle and the conclusion. There are no degrees in fiction any more than in truth. If we admit the superstition, we are bound to receive every thing which its ministers promulgate, as emanating from its principle. None of the reveries of superstition embrace any thing more incredible than immateriality; these reveries are only corollaries drawn with more or less subtilty from unintelligible subjects, by those who have an interest in supporting the system. The inductions which dreamers have made, by dint of meditating on impenetrable materials, are nothing more than ingenious conclusions, which have been drawn with wonderful accuracy, from unknown premises, that are modestly offered to the sanction of mankind by enthusiasts, who claim an unconditional assent, because they assure us no one of the human race is in a capacity either to see, feel, or comprehend the object of their contemplation. Does not this somewhat remind us of what Rabelais describes as the employment of Queen Whim's officers, in his fifth book and twenty-second chapter?

Let us then acknowledge, that the man who is this most credulously superstitious, reasons in a more conclusive manner, or is at least more consistent in his credulity, than those, who, after having admitted a certain position of which they have no one idea, stop short all at once, and refuse to accredit that system of conduct which is the immediate, the necessary result of a radical and primitive error. As soon as they subscribe to a principle fatally opposed to reason, by what right do they dispute its consequences, however absurd they may be found? We cannot too often repeat, for the happiness of mankind, that the human mind, let it torture itself as much as it will, when it quits visible nature leads itself astray; for want of an intelligent guide it wanders in tracks that bewilder its powers, and is quickly obliged, to return into that with which it has at least some, acquaintance. If man mistakes nature and her energies, it is because he does not sufficiently study her—because he does not submit to the test of experience the phenomena he beholds; if he will obstinately deprive her of motion, he can no longer have any ideas of her. Does, he, however, elucidate his embarrassments, by submitting her action to the agency of a being of which he makes himself the model? Does he think he forms a god, when he assembles into one heterogeneous mass, his own discrepant qualities, magnified until his optics are no longer competent to recognize them, and then unites to them certain abstract properties of which he cannot form to himself any one conception? Does he, in fact, do more than collect together that which becomes, in consequence of its association, perfectly unintelligible? Yet, strange as it may appear, when he no longer understands himself—when his mind, lost in its own fictions, becomes inadequate to decipher the characters he has thus promiscuously assembled—when he has huddled together a heap of incomprehensible, abstract qualities, which he is obliged to acknowledge are the mere creatures of imagination, not within the reach of human intellect, he firmly persuades himself he has made a most accurate and beautiful portrait of the Divinity; he ostentatiously displays his picture, demands the eulogy of the spectator, and quarrels with all those who do not agree to adulate his creative powers, by adopting the inconceivable being he holds forth to their worship; in short, to question the existence of his extravaganza, rouses his most bitter reproaches; elicits his everlasting scorn; entails on the incredulous his eternal hatred.

On the other hand, what could we expect from such a being, as they have supposed him to be? What could we consistently ask of him? How make an immaterial being, who has neither organs, space, point, or contact, understand that modification of matter called voice? Admit that this is the being who moves nature—who establishes her laws—who gives to beings their various essences—who endows them with their respective properties; if every thing that takes place is the fruit of his infinite providence—the proof of his profound wisdom, to what end shall we address our prayers to him? Shall we solicit him to acknowledge that the wisdom and providence with which we have clothed him, are in fact erroneous, by entreating him to alter in our favour his eternal laws? Shall we give him to understand our wisdom exceeds his own, by asking, him for our pleasure to change the properties of bodies—to annihilate his immutable decrees—to trace back the invariable course of things—to make beings act in opposition to the essences with which he has thought it right to invest them? Will he at our intercession prevent a body ponderous and hard by its nature, such as a stone, for example, from wounding, in its fall a sensitive being such as the human frame? Again, should we not, in fact, challenge impossibilities, if the discordant attributes brought into union by the theologians were correct; would not immutability oppose itself to omnipotence; mercy to the exercise of rigid justice; omniscience, to the changes that might be required in foreseen plans? In physics, in consequence of the general research after a perpetual motion, science has drawn forth the discovery, that by amalgamating metals of contrary properties, the contractile powers of one kind, under given circumstances which cause the dilation of the other, by their opposite tendencies neutralize the actual effects of each, taken separately, and thus produce an equality in the oscillations, that, neither possessed individually.

It will perhaps, be insisted, that the infinite science of the Creator of all things, is acquainted with resources in the beings he has formed, which are concealed from imbecile mortals; that consequently without changing any thing, either in the laws of nature, or in the essence of things, he is competent to produce effects which surpass the comprehension of our feeble understanding; that these, effects will in no wise be contrary to that order which he himself has established in nature. Granted: but then I reply, *first*, that every thing which is conformable to the nature of things, can neither be called supernatural nor miraculous: many things are, unquestionably, above our comprehension; but then all that is operated in the world is natural—grows out of those immutable laws by which nature is regulated. In the *second* place, it will be requisite to observe, that by the word miracle an effect is designed, of which, for want of understanding nature, she is believed incapable. In the *third* place, it is worthy of remark, that the theologians, almost universally, insist that by miracle is meant not an extraordinary effort of nature, but an effect directly opposite to her laws, which nevertheless they equally challenge to have been prescribed by the Divinity. Buddaeus says, "a miracle is an operation by which the laws of nature, upon which depend the order and the preservation of the universe, are suspended." If, however, the Deity, in those phenomena that most excite our surprise, does nothing more than give play to springs unknown to mortals, there is, then, nothing in nature, which, in this sense, may not be looked upon as a miracle; because the cause by which a stone falls is as unknown to us, as that which makes our globe turn on its own axis. Thus, to explain the phenomena of nature by a miracle, is, in other words, to say we are ignorant of the actuating causes; to attribute them to the Divinity, is to agree we do not comprehend the resources of nature: it is little better than accrediting magic. To attribute to a sovereignly intelligent, immutable, provident, wise being, those miracles by which he derogates from his own laws, is at one blow to annihilate all these qualities: it is an inconsistency that would shame a child. It cannot be supposed that omnipotence has need of miracles to govern the universe, nor to convince his creatures, whose minds and hearts must be in his own hands. The last refuge of the theologian, when driven off all other ground, is the possibility of every thing he asserts, couched in the dogma, "that nothing is impossible to the Divinity." He makes this asseveration with a degree of self-complacency, with an air of triumph, that would almost persuade one he could not be mistaken; most assuredly, with those who dip no further than the surface, he carries complete conviction. But we must take leave to examine a little the nature of this proposition, and we do apprehend that a very slight degree of consideration will shew that it is untenable. In the *first* place, as we have before observed, the possibility of a thing by no means proves its absolute existence: a thing may be extremely possible, and yet not be.

Secondly, if this was once to become an admitted argument, there would be, in fact, an end of all morality and religion. The Bishop of Chester, Doctor John Wilkins, says, "would not such men be generally accounted out of their wits, who could please themselves by entertaining actual hopes of any thing, merely upon account of the possibility of it, or torment themselves with actual fears of all such evils as are possible? Is there any thing imaginable wore wild and extravagant amongst those in bedlam than this would be?" *Thirdly*, the impossibility would reasonably appear to be on the other side, so far from nothing being impossible, every thing that is erroneous would seem to be actually so; the Divinity could not possibly either love vice, cherish crime, be pleased with depravity, or commit wrong; this decidedly turns the argument against them; they must either admit the most monstrous of all suppositions, or retire from behind the shield with which they have imagined they rendered themselves invulnerable.

To those who may be inclined to inquire, whether it would not be better that all things were operated by a good, wise, intelligent Being, than by a blind nature, in which not one consoling quality is found; by a fatal necessity always inexorable to human intreaty? It may be replied, *first*, that our interest does not decide the reality of things, and that when this should be even wore advantageous than it is pointed out, it would prove nothing. *Secondly*, that as we are obliged to admit some things are operated by nature, it is certainly on the side of probability that she performs the others; especially as her capabilities are more substantively proved by every age as it advances. *Thirdly*, that nature duly studied furnishes every thing necessary to render us as, happy as our essence admits. When, guided by experience, we shall consult her, with cultivated reason; she will discover to us our duties, that is to say, the indispensable means to which her eternal and necessary laws have attached our preservation, our own happiness, and that of society. It is decidedly in her bosom that we shall find wherewith to satisfy our physical wants; whatever is out of nature, can have no existence relatively to ourselves.

Nature, then, is not a step-mother to us; we do not depend upon an inexorable destiny. Let us therefore endeavour to become more familiar with her resources; she will procure us a multitude of benefits when we shall pay her the attention she deserves: when we shall feel disposed to consult her, she will supply us with the requisites to alleviate both our physical and moral evils: she only punishes us with rigour, when, regardless of her admonitions, we plunge into excesses that disgrace us. Has the voluptuary any reason to complain of the sharp pains inflicted by the gout, when experience, if he had but attended to its counsels, has so often warned him, that the grossness of sensual indulgence must inevitably amass in his machine those humours which give birth to the agony he so acutely feels? Has the superstitious bigot any cause for repining at the misery of his uncertain ideas, when an attentive examination of that nature, he holds of such small account, would have convinced him that the idols under whom he trembles, are nothing but personifications of herself, disguised under some other name? It is evidently by incertitude, discord, blindness, delirium, she chastises those who refuse to, acknowledge the justice of her claims.

In the mean time, it cannot be denied, that a pure Theism, or what is called Natural Religion, may not be preferable to superstition, in the same manner as reform has banished many of the abuses of those countries who have embraced it; but there is nothing short of an unlimited and inviolable liberty of thought, that can permanently assure the repose of the mind. The opinions of men are only dangerous when they are restrained, or when it is imagined necessary to make others think as we ourselves think. No opinions, not even those of superstition itself, would be dangerous, if the superstitious did not think themselves obliged to enforce their adoption, or had not the power to persecute those who refused. It is this prejudice, which, for the benefit of mankind, it is essential to annihilate; and if the thing be not achievable, then the next object which philosophy may reasonably propose to itself, will be to make the depositaries of power feel that they never ought to permit their subjects to commit evil for either superstitious or religious opinions. In this case, wars would be almost unheard of amongst men: instead of beholding the melancholy spectacle of man cutting the throat of his fellow man, because this cannot see with his eyes, we shall witness him essentially labouring to his own happiness by promoting that of his neighbour; cultivating the earth in peace; quietly bringing forth the productions of nature, instead of puzzling his brain with theological disputes, which can never be of the smallest advantage, except to the priests. It must be a self-evident truth, that an argument by men, upon that which is not accessible to man, *could only have been invented by knaves, who, like the professors of legerdemain, were determined to riot luxuriously on the ignorance and credulity of mankind.*

CHAP. VIII.

Examination of the Advantages which result from Man's Notions on the Divinity.—Of their Influence upon Mortals;—upon Politics;—upon Science;—upon the Happiness of Nations, and that of Individuals.

The slender foundation of those ideas which men form to themselves of their gods, must have appeared obvious in what has preceded; the proofs which have been offered in support of the existence of immaterial substances, have been examined; the want of harmony that exists in the opinions upon this subject, which all concur in agreeing to be equally impossible to be known to the inhabitants of the earth, has been shewn; the incompatibility of the attributes with which, theology has clothed incorporeity, has been explained. It has been proved, that the idols which man sets up for adoration, have usually had their birth, either in the bosom of misfortune, when ignorance was at a loss to account for the calamities of the earth upon natural principles, or else have been the shapeless fruit of melancholy, working upon an alarmed mind, coupled with enthusiasm and an unbridled imagination. It has been pointed out how these prejudices, transmitted by tradition from father to son, grafting themselves upon infant minds, cultivated by education, nourished by fear, corroborated by habit, have been maintained by authority; perpetuated by example. In short, every thing must have distinctly evidenced to us, that the ideas of the gods, so generally diffused over the earth, has been little more than an universal delusion of the human race. It remains now to examine if this error has been useful.

It needs little to prove error can never be advantageous for mankind; it is ever founded upon his ignorance, which is itself an acknowledged evil; it springs out of the blindness of his mind to acknowledged truths, and his want of experience, which it must be admitted are prejudicial to his interests: the more importance, therefore, he shall attach to these errors, the more fatal will be the consequences resulting from their adoption. Bacon, the illustrious sophist, who first brought philosophy out of the schools, had great reason when he said, "The worst of all things is deified error." Indeed, the mischiefs springing from superstition or religious errors, have been, and always will be, the most terrible in their consequences—the most extensive in their devastation. The more these errors are respected, the more play they give to the passions; the more value is attached to them, the more the mind is disturbed; the more they are insisted upon, the more irrational they render those, who are seized with the rage for proselytism; the more they are cherished, the greater influence they have on the whole conduct of our lives. Indeed, there can he but little likelihood that he who renounces his reason, in the thing which he considers as most essential to his happiness, will listen to it on any other occasion.

The slightest reflection will afford ample proof to this sad truth: in those fatal notions which man has cherished on this subject, are to be traced the true sources of all those prejudices, the fountain of all those sorrows, to which he is the victim. Nevertheless, as we have elsewhere said, utility ought to be the only standard, the uniform scale, by which to form a judgment on either the opinions, the institutions, the systems, or the actions of intelligent beings; it is according to the measure of happiness which these things procure for us, that we ought either to cover them with our esteem, or expose them to our contempt. Whenever they are useless it is our duty to despise them; as soon as they become pernicious, it is imperative to reject them; reason imperiously prescribes that our detestation should be commensurate with the evils which they cause.

Taking these principles for a land-mark, which are founded on our nature, which must appear incontestible to every reasonable being, with experience for a beacon, let us coolly examine the effects which these notions have produced on the earth. We have already, in more than one part of the work, given a glimpse of the doctrine of that morals, which having only for object the preservation of man, and his conduct in society, can have nothing, in common with imaginary systems: it has been shewn, that the essence of a sensitive, intelligent, rational being, properly meditated, would discover motives competent to moderate the fury of his passions—to induce him to resist his vicious propensities—to make him fly criminal habits—to invite him to render himself useful to those beings for whom his own necessities have a continual occasion; thus, to endear himself to his, fellow mortals, to become respectable in his own esteem. These motives will unquestionably be admitted to possess more solidity, to embrace greater, potency, to involve more truth, than those which are borrowed from systems that want stability; that assume more shapes than there are languages; that are not tangible to the tact of humanity; that must of necessity present a different perspective to all who shall view them through the medium of prejudice. From what has been advanced, it will be felt that education, which should make man in early life contract good habits, adopt favorable dispositions, fortified by a respect for public opinion, invigorated by ideas of decency, strengthened by wholesome laws, corroborated by the desire of meriting the friendship of others, stimulated by the fear of losing his own esteem, would be fully adequate to accustom him to a laudable conduct, amply sufficient to divert him from even those secret crimes, from which he is obliged to punish himself by remorse; which costs him the most incessant labour to keep concealed, by the dread of that shame, which must always follow their publicity. Experience demonstrates in the clearest manner, that the success of a first crime disposes him to commit a second; impunity leads on to the third, this to a lamentable sequel that frequently closes a wretched career with the most ignominious exhibition; thus the first delinquency is the commencement of a habit: there is much less distance from this to the hundredth, than from innocence to criminality: the man, however, who lends himself to a series of bad actions, under even the assurance of impunity, is most woefully deceived, because he cannot avoid castigating himself: moreover, he cannot know at what point of iniquity he shall stop. It has been shewn, that those punishments which society, for its own preservation, has the right to inflict on those who disturb its harmony, are more substantive, more efficacious, more salutary in their effects, than all the distant torments held forth by the priests; they intervene a more immediate obstacle to the stubborn propensities of those obdurate wretches, who, insensible to the charms of virtue, are deaf to the advantages that spring from its practice, than can be opposed by the denunciations, held forth in an hereafter existence, which he is at the same moment taught may be avoided by repentance, that shall only take place when the ability to commit further wrong has ceased. In short, one would be led to think it obvious to the slightest reflection, that politics, founded upon the nature of man, upon the principles of society, armed with equitable laws, vigilant over morals, faithful in rewarding virtue, constant in visiting crime, would be more suitable to clothe ethics with respectability, to throw a sacred mantle over moral goodness, to lend stability to public virtue, than any authority that can be derived from contested systems, the conduct of whose professors frequently disgrace the doctrines they lay down, which after all seldom do more than restrain those whose mildness of temperament effectually prevents them from running into excess; those who, already given to justice, require no coercion. On the other hand, we have endeavoured to prove that nothing can be more absurd, nothing actually more dangerous, than attributing human qualities to the Divinity which cannot but choose to find themselves in a perpetual contradiction.

Plato has said "that virtue consists in resembling God." But how is man to resemble a being, who, it is acknowledged, is incomprehensible to mankind—who cannot be conceived by any of those means, by which he is alone capable of having perceptions? If this being, who is shewn to man under such various aspects, who is said to owe nothing to his creatures, is the author of all the good, as well as all the evil that takes place, how can he be the model for the conduct of the human race living together in society? At most he can only follow one side of the character, because among his fellows, he alone is reputed virtuous who does not deviate in his conduct from justice; who abstains from evil; who performs with punctuality those duties he owes to his fellows. If it be taken up, and insisted he is not the author of the evil, only of the good, I say very well: that is precisely what I wanted to know; you thereby acknowledge he is not the author of every thing; we are no longer at issue; you are inconclusive to your own premises, consequently ought not to demand an implicit reliance on what you choose to assert.

But, replies the subtle theologian, that is not the affair; you must seek it in the creed I have set forth—in the religion of which I am a pillar. Very good: Is it then actually in the system of fanatics, that man should draw up his ideas of virtue? Is it in the doctrines which these codes hold forth, that he is to seek for a model? Alas! do they not pourtray their idols: under the most unwholesome colours; do they not represent them as following their caprice in every thing, who love or hate, who choose or reject, who approve or condemn according to their whim, who delight in carnage, who send discord amongst men, who act irrationally, who commit wantonness, who sport with their feeble subjects, who lay continual snares for them, who rigorously interdict the use of their reason? What, let us seriously ask, would become of morality, if men proposed to themselves such portraits for models!

It was, however, for the most part, systems of this temper that nations adopted. At was in consequence of these principles that what has been called religion in most countries, was far removed from being favourable to morality; on the contrary, it often shook it to its foundation—frequently left no vestige of its existence. It divided man, instead of drawing closer the bonds of union; in the place of that mutual love, that reciprocity of succour, which ought ever to distinguish human society, it introduced hatred and persecution; it made them seize every opportunity to cut each other's throat for speculative opinions, equally irrational; it engendered the most violent heart-burnings—the most rancorous animosities—the most sovereign contempt. The slightest difference in their received opinions rendered them the most mortal enemies; separated their interests for ever; made them despise each other; and seek every means to render their existence miserable. For these theological conjectures, nations become opposed to nations; the sovereign frequently armed himself against his subjects; subjects waged war with their sovereign; citizens gave activity to the most sanguinary hostility against each other; parents detested their offspring; children plunged the pointed steel, the barbed arrow, into the bosoms of those who gave them existence; husbands and wives disunited, became the scourges of each other; relations forgetting the ties of consanguinity, tore each other to pieces, or else reciprocally consigned them to oblivion; all the bonds of society were rent asunder; the social compact was broken up; society committed suicide: whilst in the midst of this fearful wreck—regardless of the horrid shrieks called forth by this dreadful confusion—unmindful of the havock going forward on all sides—each pretended that he conformed to the views of his idol, detailed to him by his priest—fulminated by the oracles. Far from making himself any reproach, for the misery he spread abroad, each lauded his own individual conduct; gloried in the crimes he committed in support of his sacred cause.

The same spirit of maniacal fury pervaded the rites, the ceremonies, the customs, which the worship, adopted by superstition, placed so much above all the social virtues. In one country, tender mothers delivered up their children to moisten with their innocent blood the altars of their idols; in another, the people assembled, performed the ceremony of consolation to their deities, for the outrages they committed against them, and finished by immolating to their anger human victims; in another, a frantic enthusiast lacerated his body, condemned himself for life to the most rigorous tortures, to appease the wrath of his gods. The Jupiter of the Pagans was a lascivious monster; the Moloch of the Phenicians was a cannibal; the savage idol of the Mexican requires thousands of mortals to bleed on his shrine, in order to satisfy his sanguinary appetite.

Such are the models superstition holds out to the imitation of man; is it then surprising that the name of these despots became the signal for madbrained enthusiasm to exercise its outrageous fury; the standard under which cowardice wreaked its cruelty; the watchword for the inhumanity of nations to muster their barbarous strength; a sound which spreads terror wherever its echo could reach; a continual pretext for the most barefaced breaches of public decorum; for the most shameless violation of the moral duties? It was the frightful character men gave of their gods, that banished kindness from their hearts—virtue from their conduct—felicity from their habitations—reason from their mind: almost every where it was some idol, who was disturbed by the mode in which unhappy mortals thought; this armed them with poignards against each other; made them stifle the cries of nature; rendered them barbarous to themselves; atrocious to their fellow creatures: in short, they became irrational, breathed forth vengeance, outraged humanity, every time that, instigated by the priest, they were inclined to imitate the gods of their idolatry, to display their zeal, to render themselves acceptable in their temples.

It is not, then, in such systems, man ought to seek either for models of virtue, or rules of conduct suitable to live in society. He needs human morality, founded upon his own nature; built upon invariable experience; submitted to reason. The ethics of superstition will always he prejudicial to the earth; cruel masters cannot be well served, but by those who resemble them: what then becomes of the great advantages which have been imagined resulted to man, from the notions which have been unceasingly infused into him of his gods? We see that almost all nations acknowledge them; yet, to conform themselves to their views, they trampled under foot the clearest rights of nature—the most evident duties of humanity; they appeared to act as if it was only by madness the most incurable—by folly the most preposterous—by the most flagitious crimes, committed with an unsparing hand, that they hoped to draw down upon themselves the favor of heaven—the blessings of the sovereign intelligence they so much boast of serving with unabated zeal; with the most devotional fervor; with the most unlimited obedience. As soon, therefore, as the priests give them to understand their deities command the commission of crime, or whenever there is a question of their respective creeds, although they are wrapt in the most impenetrable obscurity, they make it a duty with themselves to unbridle their rancour—to give loose to the most furious passions; they mistake the clearest precepts of morality; they credulously believe the remission of their own sins will be the reward of their transgressions against their neighbour. Would it not be better to be an inhabitant of Soldania in Africa, where never yet form of worship entered, or the name of God resounded, than thus to pollute the land with superstitious castigation—with the enmity of priests against each other?

Indeed, it is not generally in those revered mortals, spread over the earth to announce the oracles of the gods, that will be found the most sterling virtues. These men, who think themselves so enlightened, who call themselves the ministers of heaven, frequently preach nothing but hatred, discord, and fury in its name: the fear of the gods, far from having a salutary influence over their own morals, far from submitting them to a wholesome discipline, frequently do nothing more than increase their avarice, augment their ambition, inflate their pride, extend their covetousness, render them obstinately stubborn, and harden their hearts. We may see them unceasingly occupied in giving birth to the most lasting animosities, by their unintelligible disputes. We see them hostilely wrestling with the sovereign power, which they contend is subordinate to their own. We see them arm the chiefs of nations against the legitimate magistrates; distribute to the credulous multitude the most mortal weapons, to massacre each other in the prosecution of those futile controversies, which sacerdotal vanity clothes with the most interesting importance. Do these men, who advance the beauty of their theories, who menace the people with eternal vengeance, avail themselves of their own marvellous notions to moderate their pride—to abate their vanity—to lessen their cupidity—to restrain their turbulence—to bring their vindictive humours under control? Are they, even in those countries where their empire is established upon pillars of brass, fixed on adamantine rocks, decorated with the most curious efforts of human ingenuity—where the sacred mantle of public opinion shields them with impunity—where credulity, planted in the hot-bed of ignorance, strikes the roots of their authority into the very centre of the earth; are they, I would ask, the enemies to debauchery, the foes to intemperance, the haters of those excesses which they insist a severe God interdicts to his adorers? On the contrary, are they not seen to be emboldened in crime; intrepid in iniquity; committing the most shameful atrocities; giving free scope to their irregularities; indulging their hatred; glutting their vengeance; exercising the most savage cruelties on the miserable victims to their cowardly suspicion? In short, it may be safely advanced, without fear of contradiction, that scarcely any thing is more frequent, than that those men who announce these terrible creeds—who make men tremble under their yoke—who are unceasingly haranguing upon the eternity and dreadful nature of their punishments—who declare themselves the chosen ministers of their oracular laws—who make all the duties of morality centre in themselves; are those whom superstition least contributes to render virtuous; are men who possess the least milk of human kindness; the fewest feelings of tenderness; who are the most intolerant to their neighbours; the most indulgent to themselves; the most unsociable in their habits; the most licentious in their manners; the most unforgiving in their disposition. In contemplating their conduct, we should be tempted to accredit, that they were perfectly undeceived with respect to the idols whom they serve; that no one was less the dupe to those menaces which they so solemnly pronounce in their name, than themselves. In the hands of the priests of almost all countries, their divinities resembled the head of Medusa, which, without injuring him who shewed it, petrified all others. The priests are generally the most crafty of men, and many among them are substantively wicked.

Does the idea of these avenging, these remunerating systems, impose upon some princes of the earth, who found their titles, who rest their power upon them; who avail themselves of their terrific power to intimidate their subjects; to make the people, often rendered unhappy by their caprice, hold them in reverence? Alas! the theological, the supernatural ideas, adopted by the pride of some sovereigns, have done nothing more than corrupt politics—than metamorphose, them into an abject tyranny. The ministers of these idols, always tyrants themselves, or the cherishers of despots, are unceasingly crying out to monarchs that they are the images of the Divinity. Do they not inform the credulous multitude that heaven is willing they should groan under the most cruel bondage; writhe under the most multifarious injustice; that to suffer is their inheritance; that their princes have the indubitable right to appropriate the goods, dispose of the persons, coerce the liberty; command the lives of their subjects? Do not some of these chiefs of nations, thus poisoned in the name of deified idols, imagine that every indulgence of their wayward humour is freely permitted to them? At once competitors, representatives, and rivals of the celestial powers, do they not, in some instances, exercise after their example the most arbitrary despotism? Do they not, in the intoxication into which sacerdotal flattery has plunged them, think that like their idols, they are not accountable to man for their actions, that they owe nothing to the rest of mortals, that they are bound by no bonds but their own unruly will, to their miserable subjects?

Then it is evident that it is to theological notions, to the loose flattery of its ministers, that are to be ascribed the despotism, the tyrannical injustice, the corruption, the licentiousness of some princes, and the blindness of those people, to whom in heaven's name they interdict the love of liberty; who are forbid to labour effectually to their own happiness; to oppose themselves to violence, however flagrant; to exercise their natural rights, however conducive to their welfare. These intoxicated rulers, even while adoring their avenging gods, in the act of bending others to their worship, do not scruple to outrage them by their irregularities—by their want of moral virtue. What morality is this, but that of men who offer themselves as living images, as animated representatives of the Divinity? Are those monarchs, then, who are habitually unjust, who wrest without remorse the bread from the hands of a famished people, to administer to the profligacy of their insatiable courtiers—to pamper the luxury of the vile instruments of their enormities, atheists? Are, then, those ambitious conquerors, who not contented with oppressing their own slaves, carry desolation, spread misery, deal out death among the subjects of others, atheists? Do we not witness in some of those potentates who rule over nations by *divine right*, (a patent of power, which every usurper claims as his own) ambitious mortals, whose exterminating fury nothing can arrest; with hearts perfectly insensible to the sorrows of mankind; with minds without energy; with souls without virtue; who neglect their most evident duties, with which they do not even deign to become acquainted; powerful men, who insolently set themselves above the rules of equity; knaves who make a sport of honesty? Generally speaking, is there the least sincerity in the alliances which these rulers form among themselves? Do they ever last longer than for the season of their convenience? Do we find substantive virtues adorn those who most abjectly submit themselves to all the follies of superstition? Do they not tax each other as violators of property—as faithlessly aggrandizing themselves at the expence of their neighbour; in fact, do we not see them endeavouring to surprise, anxious to over-reach, ready to injure each other, without being arrested by the menaces of their creeds, or at all yielding to the calls of humanity? In general, they are too haughty to be humane; too inflated with ambition to be virtuous; they make a code for themselves, which they cannot help violating. Charles the Fifth used to say, "that being a warrior, it was impossible for him to have either conscience or religion." His general, the Marquis de Piscaire, observed, that "nothing was more difficult, than to serve at one and the same time, the god *Mars* and *Jesus Christ.*" Indeed, nothing can be more opposed to the true spirit of Christianity than the profession of arms; notwithstanding the Christian princes have the most numerous armies, and are in perpetual hostility with each other: perhaps the clergy themselves do not hold forth the most peaceable examples of the doctrine they teach; they sometimes wrangle for tithes, dispute for trifling enjoyments, quarrel for worldly opinion, with as much determined obstinacy, with as, much settled rancour, with as little charity, as could possibly inhabit the bosom of the most unenlightened Pagan, whose ignorance they despise—whose superstition they rank as the grossest effort of idolatrous debasement. It might almost admit of doubt whether they would be quite pleased to see the mild maxims of the Evangelists, the true Christian meekness, rigidly followed—whether they might not think the complete working of their own system would clash with their own immediate interests? Is it a demonstrable axiom that the ministers of the Christian faith do not think soldiers are beings extremely well calculated to give efficacy to their doctrine—solidity to their advantages—durability to their claims? Be this as it may, priests as well as monarchs have occasionally waged war for the most futile interests; impoverished a people from the anti-christian motives; wrested from each other with all the venom of furies, the bloody remnant of the nations they have laid waste; in fact, to judge by their conduct on certain occasions, it might have been a question if they were not disputing who should have the credit of making the greater number of miserable beings upon earth. At length, either wearied with their own fury, exhausted by their own devouring passions, or compelled by the stern hand of necessity, they have permitted suffering humanity to take breath; they have allowed the miseries concomitant on war, to cease for an instant their devastating havoc; they have made peace in the name of that God, whose decrees, as attested by themselves, they have been so wantonly outraging,—still ready, however, to violate their most solemn pledges, when the smallest interest could offer them a pretext.

Thus it will be obvious, in what manner the idea of the Divinity operates on the priest, as well as upon those who are called his images; who insist they have no account to render but to him alone. Among these representatives of the Divine Majesty, it is with difficulty during thousands of years we find some few who have equity, sensibility, virtue, or even the most ordinary talent. History points out some of these vicegerents of the Deity, who in the exacerbation of their delirious rage, have insisted upon displacing him, by exalting themselves into gods; and exacting the most obsequious worship; who have inflicted the most cruel torments on those who have opposed themselves to their madness, and refused to acknowledge the Divinity of their persons. These men, whose licentiousness knew no limits, from the impunity which attended their actions, notwithstanding they had learned to despise public opinion, to set decency at defiance, to indulge in the most shameless vice: in spite of the power they possessed; of the homage they received; of the terror they inspired: although they had learned to counterfeit, with great effect, the whole catalogue of human virtues; found it impossible, even with the addition of their enormous wealth, wrenched from the necessities of laborious honesty, to counterfeit the animating blush, which modest merit brings forth, when eulogized by some happy being whose felicity he has occasioned, by following the great law of nature—which says, "*love thy neighbour as thyself.*" On the contrary, we see them grow listless with satiety; disgusted with their own inordinate indulgences; obliged to recur to strange pleasures, to awaken their benumbed faculties; to run headlong into the most costly follies, in the fruitless attempt to keep up the activity of their souls, the spring of which they had for ever relaxed, by the profligacy of their enjoyment.

History, although it describes a multitude of vicious rulers, whose irregular propensities were of the most mischievous consequence to the human race, nevertheless, shews us but few who have been atheists. The annals of nations, on the contrary, offer to our view great numbers of superstitious princes, governed by their mistresses, led by unworthy favorites, leagued with priests, who passed their lives plunged in luxury; indulging the most effeminate pursuits; following the most childish pleasures; pleased with ostentatious show; slaves even to the fashion of the vestments that covered them; but strangers to every manly virtue; insensible to the sorrows of their subjects; although uniformly good to their hungry courtiers, invariably kind to those cringing sycophants who surrounded their persons, and poisoned their ears with the most fulsome flattery: in short, superstitious persecutors, who, to render themselves acceptable to their priests, to expiate their own shameful irregularities, added to all their other vices that of tyrannizing over the mind, of fettering the conscience, of destroying their subjects for their opinions, when they were in hostility with their own received doctrines. Indeed, superstition in princes frequently allied itself with the most horrid crimes; they have almost all professed religion, although very few of them have had a just knowledge of morality—have practiced any useful substantive virtue. Superstitious notions, on the contrary, often serve to render them more blind, to augment their evil inclinations; to set them at a greater distance from moral goodness. They for the most part believe themselves assured of the favor of heaven; they think they faithfully serve their gods, that the anger of their divinities is appeased, if for a short season they shew themselves attached to futile customs—lend themselves to absurd rites—perform some ridiculous duties, which superstition imposes on them, with a view to obtain their assistance in the prosecution of its own plans, very rarely in strict unison with their immediate interest. Nero, the cruel, sanguinary, matricidal Nero, his hands yet reeking with the blood of that unfortunate being who had borne him in her womb, who had, with agonizing pains, given the monster to the world that plunged the dagger in her heart, was desirous to be initiated into the *Eleusinian Mysteries*. The odious Constantine himself, found in the priests, accomplices disposed to expiate his crimes. The infamous Philip, whose ungovernable ambition caused him to be called the daemon of the south, whilst he assassinated his wife and son, caused the throats of the wretched Batavians to be cut for their religious opinions. It is thus, that the priests of superstition sometimes persuade sovereigns they can atone for crimes, by committing others of a more atrocious kind—of an increased magnitude.

It would be fair to conclude, from the conduct of so many princes, who had so much superstition, but so slender a portion of virtue, that the notion of their gods, far from being useful to them, only served to render them wore corrupt—to make them more abominable than they already were; that the idea of an avenging power, placed in the perspective of futurity, imposed but little restraint on the turbulence of deified tyrants, who were sufficiently powerful not to fear the reproaches of their subjects—who had the insensibility to be deaf to the censure of their fellows—who were gifted with an obduracy of soul, that prevented their having compassion for the miseries of mankind, from whom they fancied themselves so pre-eminently distinguished; which, in fact, they were, if crime can be allowed for the standard of distinction. Neither heaven nor earth furnishes a balsam of sufficient efficacy to heal the inveterate wounds of beings cankered to this degree: for such chronic diseases, there is "no balm in Gilead:" there is no curb sufficiently coercive to rein in the passions, to which superstition itself gives activity; which only makes them more unruly; renders them more inveterately rash. Whenever men flatter themselves with easily expiating their sins—when they soothe themselves with the consolitary idea of appeasing the anger of the gods by a show of earnestness, they then deliver themselves up, with the most unrestrained freedom, to the bent of their criminal pursuits. The most dissolute men are frequently in appearance extremely attached to superstition: it furnishes them with a means of compensating by ceremonies, that of which they are deficient in morals: it is much easier for them to adopt a faith, to believe in a doctrine, to conform themselves to certain rituals, than to renounce their habits, resist their passions, or relinquish the pursuit of that pleasure, which results to unprincipled minds from the prosecution of the most diabolical schemes.

Under chiefs, depraved even by superstition, nations continued necessarily to be corrupted. The great conformed themselves to the vices of their masters; the example of these distinguished men, whom the uninformed erroneously believe to be happy, was followed by the people; courts thus became the sinks from whence issued the epidemic contagion of licentious indulgence. The law only held forth pictures of honesty; the dispensers of jurisprudence were partial, partook of the mania of the times, were labouring under the general disease; Justice suffered her balance to rust, occasionally removed her bandage, although she always wore it in the presence of the poor; genuine ideas of equity had grown into disuse; distinct notions of right and wrong became troublesome and unfashionable; education was neglected; it served only to produce prejudiced beings, grounded in ignorance—devotees, always ready to injure themselves—fanatics, eager to shew their zeal ever willing to annoy their unfortunate neighbours. Superstition, sustained by tyranny, ousted every other feeling, hoodwinked its destined victims, rendered those tractable whom it had the intention to despoil. Whoever doubts of these truisms, has only to turn over the pages of history, he will find myriads of evidence to much more than is here stated. Machiavel, in his *Political Discourses upon Titus Livius*, labours the point hard, to shew the utility of superstition to the Roman Republic: unfortunately, however, the examples he brings forward in its support, incontestibly prove that none but the senate profited by the infatuation of the people, who availed itself of their blindness more effectually to bend them to its yoke.

Thus it was that nations, destitute of equitable laws, deficient in the administration of justice, submitted to irrational government, continued in slavery by the monarch, chained up in ignorance by the priest, for want of enlightened institutions, deprived of reasonable education, became corrupt, superstitious, and flagitious. The nature of man, the just interests of society, the real advantage of the sovereign, the true happiness of the people, once mistaken, were completely lost sight of; the morality of nature, founded upon the essence of man living in society, was equally unknown; lay buried under an enormous load of prejudice, that no common efforts were competent to remove. It was entirely forgotten that man has wants; that society was formed that he might, with greater security, facilitate the means of satisfying them; that government, to be legitimate, ought to have for object, the happiness—for end, the means of maintaining the indivisibility of the community; that consequently it ought to give activity to springs, full play to motives suitable to have a favorable influence over sensible beings. It was quite overlooked, that virtue faithfully rewarded, vice as regularly visited, had an elastic force, of which the public authorities could efficaciously avail themselves, to determine their citizens to blend their interests; to work out their own felicity, by labouring to the happiness of the body of which they were members. The social virtues were unknown, the *amor patriae* became a chimera. Men thus associated, thus blinded by their superstitious bias, credulously believed their own immediate interest consisted in injuring each other; they were solely occupied with meriting the favor of those men, who fatally accreditted the doctrine of clerical flatterers, of silver-toned courtiers, which taught that they wore distinctly interested in injuring the whole.

This is the mode in which the human heart has become perverted; here is the genuine source of moral evil; the hot-bed of that epidemical depravity, the cause of that hereditary corruption, the fountain of that inveterate delinquency, which pervaded the earth; rendering the abundance of nature nothing better than a curse; blasting the fairest prospects of humanity; degrading man below the beast of the forest; sinking his intellectual faculties in the most savage barbarity; rendering him the vile instrument of lawless ambition; the wretched tool by which the fetters of his species were firmly rivetted; obliging him to moisten his harvest with the bitter tears of the most abject slavery. For the purpose of remedying so many crying evils, grown insupportable, recourse was had to new superstitions. Notwithstanding this alone had produced them, it was still imagined, that the menaces of heaven would restrain passions which every thing conspired to rouse in all hearts; fatuity persuaded monarchs that ideal, metaphysical barriers, terrible fables, distant phantoms, would be competent to curb those inordinate desires, to rein in that impetuous propensity to crime, that rendered society incommodious to itself; credulity fancied that invisible powers would be more efficacious, than those visible motives that evidently invited mortals to the commission of mischief. Every thing was understood to be achieved, by occupying man's mind with gloomy chimeras, with vague, undefinable terrors, with avenging angels; and politics madly believed that its own interests grew out of the blind submission of its subjects, to the ministers of these delusive doctrines.

What was the result? Nations had only sacerdotal laws; theological morality; accommodated to the interests of the hierarchy—suitable to the views of subtle priests: who substituted reveries for realities, opinions for reason, rank fallacies for sterling truths; who made ceremonies supply the place of virtue; a pious blindness supersede the necessity of an enlightened understanding; undermined the sacredness of oaths, and placed fanaticism on the altars of sociability. By a necessary consequence of that confidence which the people were compelled to give to the ministers of superstition, two distinct authorities were established in each state, who were substantially at variance, in continual hostility with each other. The priest fought the sovereign with the formidable weapon of opinion; it generally proved sufficiently powerful to shake the most established thrones. Thus, although the hierarchy was unceasingly admonishing the people to submit themselves to the divine authority of their sovereigns, because it was derived immediately from heaven, yet, whenever it so happened that the monarch did not repay their advocacy, by blindly yielding his own authority to the supervisance of the priests, these made no scruple of threatening him with loss of his temporalities; fulminated their anathemas, interdicted his dominions, and sometimes went the length of absolving his subjects from allegiance. Superstition, in general, only upholds despotism, that it may with greater certainty direct its blows against its enemies; it overthrows it whenever it is found to clash with its interests. The ministers of invisible powers preach up obedience to visible powers, only when they find these humbly devoted to themselves. Thus the sovereign was never at rest, but when abjectly cringing to his priest, he tractably received his lessons—lent himself to his frantic zeal—and piously enabled him to carry on the furious occupation of proselytism. These priests, always restless, full of ambition, burning with intolerance, frequently excited the sovereign to ravage his own states—encouraged him to tyranny: when, pursuing this sacerdotal mania, he feared to have outraged humanity, to have incurred the displeasure of heaven, he was quickly reconciled to himself, upon promise of undertaking some distant expedition, for the purpose of bringing some unfortunate nation within the pale of their own particular creed. When the two rival powers united themselves, morality gained nothing by the junction; the people were neither more happy, nor more virtuous; their morals, their welfare, their liberty, were equally overwhelmed by the combined powers. Thus, superstitious princes always felt interested in the maintenance of theological opinions, which were rendered flattering to their vanity, favorable to their power. Like the grateful perfumes of Arabia, that are used to cover the ill scent of a deadly poison, the priest lulled them into security by administering to their sensualities; these, in return, made common cause with him: fully persuaded that the superstition which they themselves adopted, must be the most wholesome for their subjects, most conducive to their interests, those who refused to receive the boon, thus gratuitously forced upon them, were treated as enemies, held up to public scorn, and rendered the victims of punishment. The most superstitious sovereign became, either politically or through piety, the executioner of one part of his slaves; he was taught to believe it a sacred duty to tyrannize over the mind—to overwhelm the refractory—to crush the enemy of his priest, under an idea that he was therefore hostile to his own authority. In cutting the throats of these unfortunate sceptics, he imagined he at once discharged his obligations to heaven, and gave security to his own power. He did, not perceive, that by immolating victims to his priest, he in fact strengthened the arm of his most formidable foe—the real enemy to his authority—the rival of his greatness—the least subjected of his subjects.

But the prevalence of these false notions, with which both the minds of the sovereign and the people were prepossessed, it was found that every thing in society concurred to gratify the avidity, to bolster the pride, to glut the vengeance of the sacerdotal order: every where, it was to be observed, that the most turbulent, the most dangerous, the most useless men, were those who were the most amply rewarded. The strange spectacle presented itself, of beholding those who were born the bitterest enemies to sovereign power, cherished by its fostering care—honoured at its hands: the most rebellious subjects were looked upon as the pillars of the throne; the corrupters of the people were rendered the exclusive masters of education; the least laborious of the citizens were richly rewarded for their idleness—munificently remunerated for the most futile speculations—held in respect for their fatal discord—gorged with benefits for their inefficacious prayers: they swept off the fat of the land for their expiations, so destructive to morals, so calculated to give permanency to crime. Thus, by a strange fatuity, the viper that could, and frequently did, inflict the most deadly sting on the bosom of confiding credulity, was pampered and nourished by the unsuspecting hand of its destined victim.

For thousands of years, nations as well as sovereigns were emulously despoiling themselves to enrich the expounders of superstition; to enable them to wallow in abundance: they loaded them with honors, decorated them with titles, invested them with privileges, granted them immunities, for no other purpose than to make them bad citizens, unruly subjects, mischievous beings, who revenged upon society the advantages they had received. What was the fruit that kings and people gathered from their imprudent kindness? What was the harvest these men yielded to their labour? Did princes really become more powerful; were nations rendered more happy; did they grow more flourishing; did men become more rational? No! Unquestionably, the sovereign lost the greater portion of his authority; he was the slave of his priest; and when he wished to preserve the remnant that was left, or to recover some part of what had been wrested from him, he was obliged to be continually wrestling against the men his own indulgence, his own weakness, had furnished with means, to set his authority at defiance: the riches of society were lavished to support the idleness, maintain the splendour, satiate the luxury of the most useless, the most arrogant, the most dangerous of its members.

Did the morals of the people improve under the pastoral care of these guides, who were so liberally rewarded? Alas! the superstitious never knew them, their fanatic creed had usurped the place of every virtue; its ministers, satisfied with upholding the doctrines, with preserving the ceremonies so useful to their own interests, only invented fictitious crimes—multiplied painful penances—instituted absurd customs; to the end, that they might turn even the transgressions of their slaves to their own immediate profit. Every where they exercised a monopoly of expiatory indulgences; they made a lucrative traffic of pretended pardons from above; they established a tariff, according to which crime was no longer contraband, but freely admitted upon paying the customs. Those subjected to the heaviest impost, were always such as the hierarchy judged most inimical to its own stability; you might at a very easy rate obtain permission to attack the dignity of the sovereign, to undermine the temporal power, but it was enormously dear to be allowed to touch even the hem of the sacerdotal garments. Thus heresy, sacrilege, &c. were considered crimes of a much deeper dye, that fixed an indelible stain on the perpetrator, alarmed the mind of the priestly order, much more seriously than the most inveterate villainy, the most determined delinquency, which more immediately involved the true interests of society. Thence the ideas of the people were completely overturned, imaginary crimes terrified them, while real crimes had no effect upon their obdurate hearts. A man, whose opinions were at variance with the received doctrines, whose abstract systems did not harmonize with those of his priest, was more loathed than a corrupter of youth; more abhorred than an assassin; more hated than an oppressor; was held in greater contempt than a robber; was punished with greater rigor than the seducer of innocence. The acme of all wickedness, was to despise that which the priest was desirous should be looked upon as sacred. The celebrated Gordon says, "the most abominable of heresies, is to believe there is any other god than the clergy." The civil laws concurred to aid this confusion of ideas; they inflicted the most serious penalties, punished in the most atrocious manner those unknown crimes which imagination had magnified into the most flagitious actions; heretics, infidels, were brought to the stake, and publicly burnt with the utmost refinement of cruelty; the brain was tortured to find means of augmenting the sufferings of the unhappy victims to sacerdotal fury; whilst calumniators of innocence, adulterers, depredators of every description, knaves of all kinds, were at a trifling cost absolved from their past iniquity, and opened a new account of future delinquency.

Under such instructors what could become of youth? The period of juvenility was shamefully sacrificed to superstition. Man, from his earliest infancy, was poisoned with unintelligible notions; fed with mysteries; crammed with fables; drenched with doctrines, in which he was compelled to acquiesce without being able to comprehend. His brain was disturbed with phantoms, alarmed with chimeras, rendered frantic by visions. His genius was cramped with puerile pursuits, mechanical devotions, sacred trifles. Superstition at length so fascinated the human mind, made such mere automata of mankind, that the people consented to address their gods in a dialect they did not themselves understand: women occupied their whole lives in singing Latin, without comprehending a word of the language; the people assisted very punctually, without being competent to explain any part of the worship, under an idea that it was taken kindly they should thus weary themselves; that it was sufficient to shew their persons in the sacred temples, which were beautifully decorated to fascinate their senses. Thus man wasted his most precious moments in absurd customs; spent his life in idle ceremonies; his bead was crowded with sophisms, his mind was loaded with errors; intoxicated with fanaticism, he was the declared enemy to reason; for ever prepossessed against truth, the energy of his soul was resisted by shackles too ponderous for its elasticity; the spring gave way, and he sunk into sloth and wretchedness: from this humiliating state he could never again soar; he could no longer become useful either to himself or to his associates: the importance he attached to his imaginary science, or rather the systematic ignorance which served for its basis, rendered it impossible for the most fertile soil to produce any thing but thorns; for the best proportioned tree to yield any thing but crabs.

Does a superstitious, sacerdotal education, form intrepid citizens, intelligent fathers of families, kind husbands, just masters, faithful servants, loyal subjects, pacific associates? No! it either makes peevish enthusiasts or morose devotees, who are incommodious to themselves, vexatious to others: men without principle, who quickly pour the waters of Lethe over the terrors with which they have been disturbed; who know no moral obligation, who respect no virtue. Thus superstition, elevated above every thing else, held forth the fanatical dogma, "Better to obey the gods than men;" in consequence, man believed he must revolt against his prince, detach himself from his wife, detest his children, estrange himself from his friends, cut the throats of his fellow-citizens, every time they questioned the veracity of his faith: in short, a superstitious education, when it had its effect, only served to corrupt the juvenile heart—to fascinate youthful winds with its pageantry—to degrade the human soul—to make man mistake the duties he owed to himself, his obligations to society, his relations with the beings by whom he was surrounded.

What advantages might not nations have reaped, if they would have employed on useful objects, those riches, which ignorance has so shamefully lavished on the expounders of superstition; which fatuity has bestowed on the most useless ceremonies? What might not have been the progress of genius, if it had enjoyed those ample remunerations, granted during so many ages to those priests who at all times opposed its elevation? What perfection might not science have attained, what height might not the arts have reached, if they had had the same succours that were held forth with a prodigal hand to enthusiasm and futility? Upon what rocks might not morality have been rested, what solid foundations might not politics have found, with what majestic grandeur might not truth have illumined the human horizon, if they had experienced the same fostering cares, the same animating countenance, the same public sanction, which accompanied imposture—which was showered upon fanaticism—which shielded falsehood from the rude attack of investigation—which gave impunity to its ministers?

It is then obvious, that superstitious, theological notions, have not produced any of those solid advantages that have been held forth; if may be doubted whether they were not always, and ever will remain, contrary to healthy politics, opposed to sound morality; they frequently change sovereigns into restless, jealous, mischievous, divinities; they transform their subjects into envious, wicked slaves, who by idle pageantry, by futile ceremonies, by an exterior acquiescence in unintelligible opinions, imagine themselves amply compensated for the evil they commit against each other. Those who have never had the confidence to examine these sublimated opinions; those who feel persuaded that their duties spring out of these abstruse doctrines; those who are actually commanded to live in peace, to cherish each other, to lend mutual assistance, to abstain from evil, and to do good, presently lose sight of these sterile speculations, as soon as present interests, ungovernable passions, inveterate habits, or irresistible whims, hurry them away. Where are we to look for that equity, that union of interest, that peace, that concord, which these unsettled notions, supported by superstition, backed with the full force of authority, promise to the societies placed under their surveillance? Under the influence of corrupt courts, of time-serving priests, who, either impostors or fanatics, are never in harmony with each other, are only to be discerned vicious men, degraded by ignorance—enslaved by criminal habits—swayed by transient interests—guided by shameful pleasures—sunk in a vortex of dissipation; who do not even think of the Divinity. In despite of his theological ideas, the subtle courtier continues to weave his dark plots, labours to gratify his ambition, seeks to satisfy his avidity, to indulge his hatred, to wreak his vengeance, to give full swing to all the passions inherent to the perversity of his being: maugre that frightful hell, of which the idea alone makes her tremble, the woman of intrigue persists in her amours; continues her harlotry, revels in her adulteries. Notwithstanding their dissipated conduct, their dissolute manners, their entire want of moral principle, the greater part of those who swarm in courts, who crowd in cities, would recoil with horror, if the smallest doubt was exhibited of the truth of that creed which they outrage every moment, of their lives. What advantage, then, has resulted to the human race from those opinions, so universal, at the same time so barren? They seem rarely to have had any other kind of influence than to serve as a pretext for the most dangerous passions—as a mantle of security for the most criminal indulgences. Does not the superstitious despot, who would scruple to omit the least part of the ceremonies of his persuasion, on quitting the altars at which he has been sacrificing, on leaving the temple where they have been delivering the oracles and terrifying crime in the name of heaven, return to his vices, reiterate his injustice, increase his political crimes, augment his transgressions against society? Issuing from the sacred fane, their ears still ringing with the doctrines they have heard, the minister returns to his vexations, the courtier to his intrigues, the courtezan to her prostitution, the publican to his extortions, the merchant to his frauds, the trader to his tricks.

Will it be pretended that those cowardly assassins, those dastardly robbers, those miserable criminals, whom evil institutions, the negligence of government, the laxity of morals, continually multiply; from whom the laws, in many instances too sanguinary, frequently wrest their existence; will it, I say, be pretended that the malefactors who regularly furnish the gibbets, who daily crowd the scaffolds, are either incredulous or atheists? No! Unquestionably, these unfortunate beings, these wretched outcasts, these children of turpitude, firmly believe in God; his name has been repeated to them from their infancy; they have been informed of the punishment destined for sinners: they have been habituated in early life to tremble at his judgments; nevertheless they have outraged society; their unruly passions, stronger than their fears, not having been coerced by visible motives, have not, for much more cogent reasons, been restrained by those which are invisible: distant, concealed punishments will never be competent to arrest those excesses which present and assured torments are incapable of preventing.

In short, does not every day's experience furnish us the lesson, that men, persuaded that an all-seeing Deity views them, hears them, encompasses them, do not on that account arrest their progress when the furor exists, either for gratifying their licentious passions, or committing the most dishonest actions? The same individual who would fear the inspection of the meanest of his fellows, whom the presence of another man would prevent from committing a bad action, from delivering himself up to some scandalous vice, freely sins, cheerfully lends himself to crime, when he believes no eyes beholds him but those of his God. What purpose, then, does the conviction of the omniscience, the ubiquity, the omnipotence of the Divinity answer, if it imposes much less on the conduct of the human being, than the idea of being overlooked by the least of his fellow men? He who would not have the temerity to commit a crime, even in the presence of a child, will make no scruple of boldly committing it, when he shall have only his God for a witness. These facts, which are indubitable, ill serve for a reply to those who insist that the fear of God is more suitable to restrain the actions of men, than wholesome laws, with strict discipline. When man believes he has only his God to dread, he commonly permits nothing to interrupt his course.

Those persons who do not in the least suspect the power of superstitious notions, who have the most perfect reliance on their efficacy, very rarely, however, employ them, when they are desirous to influence the conduct of those who are subordinate to them; when they are disposed to re-conduct them to the paths of reason. In the advice which a father gives to his vicious, criminal son, he rather represents to him the present temporal inconveniencies to which his conduct exposes him, than the danger he encounters in offending an avenging God; he points out to him the natural consequences of his irregularities, his health damaged by debaucheries; the loss of his reputation by criminal pursuits; the ruin of his fortune by gambling; the punishments of society, &c. Thus the DEICOLIST himself, on the most important occasions of life, reckons more stedfastly upon the force of natural motives, than upon those supernatural inducements furnished by superstition: the same man, who vilifies the motives that an atheist can have to do good and abstain from evil, makes use of them himself on this occasion, because he feels they are the most substantive he can employ.

Almost all men believe in an avenging and remunerating God; yet nearly in all countries the number of the wicked bears a larger proportion than that of the good. If the true cause of this general corruption be traced, it will be more frequently found in the superstitious notions inculcated by theology, than in those imaginary sources which the various superstitions have invented to account for human depravity. Man is always corrupt wherever he is badly governed; wherever superstition deifies the sovereign, his government becomes unworthy: this perverted and assured of impunity, necessarily render his people miserable; misery, when it exceeds the point of endurance, as necessarily renders them wicked. When the people are submitted to irrational masters, they are never guided by reason. If they are blinded by priests, who are either deceived or impostors, their reason become useless. Tyrants, when combined with priests, have generally been successful in their efforts to prevent nations from becoming enlightened—from seeking after truth—from ameliorating their condition—from perfectioning their morals; and never has the union smiled upon liberty: the people, unable to resist the mighty torrent produced by the confluence of two such rivers, have usually sunk into the most abject slavery. It is only by enlightening the mass of mankind, by demonstrating truth, that we can promise to render him better; that we can indulge the hope of making him happy. It is by causing both sovereigns and subjects to feel their true relations with each other, that their actual interests will be improved; that their politics will be perfectioned: it will then be felt and accredited, that the true art of governing mortals, the sure method of gaining their affections, is not the art of blinding them, of deceiving them, or of tyrannizing over them. Let us, then, good humouredly consult reason, avail ourselves of experience, interrogate nature; we shall, perhaps, find what is requisite to be done, in order to labour efficaciously to the happiness of the human race.

We shall most assuredly perceive, that error is the true source of the evils which embitter our existence; that it is in cheering the hearts, in dissipating those vain phantoms which alarm the ignorant, in laying the axe to the root of superstition, that we can peaceably seek after truth; that it is only in the conflagration of this baneful tree, we can ever expect to light the torch which shall illumine the road to felicity. Then let man study nature; observe her immutable laws; let him dive into his own essence; let him cure himself of his prejudices: these means will conduct him by a gentle declivity to that virtue, without which he must feel he can never be permanently happy in the world he inhabits.

If man could once cease to fear, from that moment he would be truly happy. Superstition is a domestic enemy which he always carries within himself: those who will seriously occupy themselves with this formidable phantom, must be content to endure continual agonies, to live in perpetual inquietude: if they will neglect the objects most worthy of interesting them, to run after chimeras, they will commonly pass a melancholy existence, in groaning, in praying, in sacrificing, in expiating faults, either real or imaginary, which they believe calculated to offend their priests; frequently in their irrational fury they will torment themselves, they will make it a duty to inflict on their own persons the most barbarous punishments: but society will reap no benefit from these mournful opinions—from the tortures of these pious irrationals; because their mind, completely absorbed by their gloomy reveries, their time dissipated in the most absurd ceremonies, will leave them no opportunity of being really advantageous to the community of which they are members. The most superstitions men are commonly misanthropists, quite useless to the world, and very injurious to themselves: if ever they display energy, it is only to devise means by which they can increase their own affliction; to discover new methods to torture their mind; to find out the most efficacious means to deprive themselves of those objects which their nature renders desirable. It is common in the world to behold penitents, who are intimately persuaded that by dint of barbarous inflictions on their own persons, by means of a lingering suicide, they shall merit the favor of heaven. Madmen of this species are to be seen every where; superstition has in all ages, in all places, given birth to the most cruel extravagances, to the most injurious follies.

If, indeed, these irrational devotees only injure themselves, and deprive society of that assistance which they owe to it, they without doubt do less mischief than those turbulent, zealous fanatics, who, infuriated with their superstitious ideas, believe themselves bound to disturb the world, to commit actual crimes, to sustain the cause of what they denominate the true faith. It not unfrequently happens that in outraging morality, the zealous enthusiast supposes he renders himself agreeable to his God. He makes perfection consist either in tormenting himself, or in rending asunder, in favour of his fanatical ideas, the most sacred ties that connect mortals with each other.

Let us, then, acknowledge, that the notions of superstition, are not more suitable to procure the welfare, to establish the content, to confirm the peace of individuals, than they are of the society of which they are members. If some peaceable, honest, inconclusive enthusiasts, find either comfort or consolation in them, there are millions who, more conclusive to their principles, are unhappy during their whole life; who are perpetually assailed by the most melancholy ideas; to whom their disordered imagination shews these notions, as every instant involving them in the most cruel punishments. Under such formidable systems, a tranquil, sociable devotee, is a man who has not reasoned upon them.

In short, every thing serves to prove, that superstitious opinions have the strongest influence over men; that they torment them unceasingly, divide them from their dearest connections, inflame their minds, envenom their passions, render them miserable without ever restraining their actions, except when their own temperament proves too feeble to propel them forward: all this holds forth one great lesson, that *superstition is incompatible with liberty, and can never furnish good citizens.*

CHAP. IX.

Theological Notions cannot be the Basis of Morality.—Comparison between Theological Ethics and Natural Morality.—Theology prejudicial to the human Mind.

Felicity is the great end of human existence; a supposition therefore, to be actually useful to man, should render him happy. By what parity of reasoning can he flatter himself that an hypothesis, which does not facilitate his happiness in his present duration, may one day conduct him to permanent bliss? If mortals only sigh, tremble, and groan in this world, of which they have a knowledge, upon what foundation is it they expect a more felicitous existence hereafter, in a world of which they know nothing? If man is every where the child of calamity, the victim to necessary evil, the unhappy sufferer under an immutable system, ought he reasonably to indulge a greater confidence in future happiness?

On the other hand, a supposition which should throw light on every thing, which should supply an easy solution to all the questions to which it could be applied, when even it should not be competent to demonstrate the certitude, would probably be true: but that system which should only obscure the clearest notions, render more insoluble the problems desired to be resolved by its means, would most assuredly be looked upon as fallacious; as either useless or dangerous. To be convinced of this principle, let us examine, without prejudice, if the theological ideas of the Divinity have ever given the solution to any one difficulty. Has the human understanding progressed a single step by the assistance of this metaphysical science? Has it not, on the contrary, had a tendency to obscure the wore certain science of morals? Has it not, in many instances, rendered the most essential duties of our nature problematical? Has it not in a great measure confounded the notions of virtue and vice, of justice and injustice? Indeed, what is virtue, in the eyes of the generality of theologians? They will instantly reply, "that which is conformable to the will of the incomprehensible beings who govern nature." But way it not be asked, without offence to the individual opinions of any one, what are these beings, of whom they are unceasingly talking, without having the capacity to comprehend them? How can we acquire a knowledge of their will? They will forthwith reply, with a confidence that is meant to strike conviction on uninformed minds, by recounting what they are not, without even attempting to inform us what they are. If they do undertake to furnish an idea of them, they will heap upon their hypothetical beings a multitude, of contradictory, incompatible attributes, with which they will form a whole, at once impossible for the human mind to conceive or else they will refer to oracles, by which they insist their intentions have been promulgated to mankind. If, however, they are requested to prove the authenticity of these oracles, which are at such variance with each other, they will refer to miracles in support of what they assert: these miracles, independent of the difficulty there must exist to repose in them our faith, when, as we have seen, they are admitted even by the theologians themselves, to be contrary to the intelligence, the immutability, to the omnipotency of their immaterial substances, are, moreover, warmly disputed by each particular sect, as being impositions, practised by the others for their own individual advantage. As a last resource, then, it will be necessary to accredit the integrity, to rely on the veracity, to rest on the good faith of the priests, who announce these oracles. On this again, there arises two almost insuperable difficulties, in the *first* place, who shall assure us of their actual mission? are we quite certain none of them may be mistaken? how shall we be justified in giving credence to their powers? are they not these priests themselves, who announce to us that they are the infallible interpreters of a being whom they acknowledge they do not at all know? In the *second* place, which set of these oracular developements are we to adopt? For to give currency to the whole, would, in point of fact, annihilate them entirely; seeing, that no two of them run in unison with each other. This granted, the priests, that is to say, men extremely suspicious, but little in harmony with each other, will be the arbiters of morality; they will decide (according to their own uncertain knowledge, after their various passions, in conformity to the different perspectives under which they view these things,) on the whole system of ethics; upon which absolutely rests the repose of the world—the sterling happiness of each individual. Would this be a desirable state? would it be that from which humanity has the best founded prospect of that felicity, which is the desired object of his research? Again; do we not see that either enthusiasm or interest is the only standard of their decisions? that their morals are as variable as their caprice? those who listen to them, very rarely discover to what line they will adhere. In their various writings, we have evidence of the most bitter animosities; we find continual contradictions; endless disputes upon what they themselves acknowledge to be the most essential points; upon those premises, in the substantive proof of which their whole system depends; the very beings they depict as their source of their various creeds, are pourtrayed as variable as themselves; as frequently changing their plans as these are their arguments. What results from all this to a rational man? It will be natural for him to conclude, that neither inconstant gods, nor vacillating priests, whose opinions are more fluctuating than the seasons, can be the proper models of a moral system, which should be as regular, as determinate, as invariable as the laws of nature herself; as that eternal march, from which we never see her derogate.

No! Arbitrary, inconclusive, contradictory notions, abstract, unintelligible speculations, can never be the sterling bases of the ethical science! They must be evident, demonstrable principles, deduced from the nature of man, founded upon his wants, inspired by rational education, rendered familiar by habit, made sacred by wholesome laws, that will flash conviction on our mind, render systems useful to mankind, make virtue dear to us—that will people nations with honest men—fill up the ranks with faithful subjects—crowd them with intrepid citizens. Incomprehensible beings can present nothing to our imagination, save vague ideas, which will never embrace any common point of union amongst those who shall contemplate them. If these beings are painted as terrible, the mind is led astray; if changeable, it always precludes us from ascertaining the road we ought to pursue. The menaces held forth by those, who, in despite of their own assertions, say they are acquainted with the views, with the determination of these beings, will seldom do more than render virtue unpleasant; fear alone will then make us practise with reluctance, that which reason, which our own immediate interest, ought to make us execute with pleasure. The inculcation of terrible ideas will only serve to disturb honest persons, without in the least arresting the progress of the profligate, or diverting the course of the flagitious: the greater number of men, when they shall be disposed to sin, to deliver themselves up to vicious propensities, will cease to contemplate these terrific ideas, will only behold a merciful God, who is filled with goodness, who will pardon the transgressions of their weakness. Man never views things but on that side which is most conformable to his desires.

The goodness of God cheers the wicked; his rigour disturbs the honest man. Thus, the qualities with which theology clothes its immaterial substances, themselves turn out disadvantageous to sound morality. It is upon this infinite goodness that the most corrupt men will have the audacity to reckon, when they are either hurried along by crime, or given up to habitual vice. If, then, they are reminded of their criminal courses, they reply, "God is good, his mercy is infinite, his clemency boundless:" thus it may be said that religion itself is pressed into the service of vice, by the children of turpitude. Superstition, above all, rather abets crime than represses it, by holding forth to mortals that by the assistance of certain ceremonies, the performance of certain rites, the repetition of certain prayers, aided by the payment of certain sums of money, they can appease the anger of their gods, assuage the wrath of heaven, wash out the stains of their sins, and be received with open arms into the happy number of the elect—be placed in the blissful abodes of eternity. In short, do not the priests of superstition universally affirm, that they possess infallible secrets, for reconciling the most perverse to the pale of their respective systems?

It must be concluded from this, that however these systems are viewed, in whatever manner they are considered, they cannot serve for the basis of morality, which in its very nature is formed to be invariably the same. Irascible systems are only useful to those who find an interest in terrifying the ignorance of mankind, that they may advantage themselves of his fears—profit by his expiations. The nobles of the earth, who are frequently men not gifted with the most exemplary morals—who do not on all occasions exhibit the most perfect specimens of self-denial—who would not, perhaps, be at all times held up as mirrors of virtue, will not see these formidable systems, when they shall be inclined to listen to their passions; to lend themselves to the indulgence of their unruly desires: they will, however, feel no repugnance to make use of them to frighten others, to the end that they may preserve unimpaired their superiority; that they may keep entire their prerogatives; that they may more effectually bind them to servitude. Like the rest of mankind, they will see their God under the traits of his benevolence; they will always believe him indulgent to those outrages they may commit against their fellows, provided they shew due respect for him themselves: superstition will furnish them with easy means to turn aside his Wrath; its ministers seldom omit a profitable opportunity, to expiate the crimes of human nature.

Morality is not made to follow the caprices of the imagination, the fury of the passions, the fluctuating interests of men: it ought to possess stability; to be at all times the same, for all the individuals of the human race; it ought neither to vary in one country, nor in one race from another: neither superstition nor religion, has a privilege to make its immutability subservient to the changeable laws of their systems. There is but one method to give ethics this solidity; it has been more than once pointed out in the course of this work: it is only to be founded upon the nature of man, bottomed upon his duties, rested upon the relations subsisting between intelligent beings, who are in love, with their happiness, who are occupied with their own preservation, who live together in society that they may With greater facility ascertain these ends. In short we must take for the basis of morality the necessity of things.

In weighing these principles, which are self evident, confirmed by constant experience, approved by reason, drawn from nature herself, we shall have an undeviating tone of conduct; a sure system of morality, that will never be in contradiction with itself. Man will have no occasion to recur to theological speculations to regulate his conduct in the visible world. We shall then be capacitated to reply to those who pretend that without them there can be no morality. If we reflect upon the long tissue of errors, upon the immense chain of wanderings, that flow from the obscure notions these various systems hold forth—of the sinister ideas which superstition in all countries inculcates; it would be much more conformable to truth to say, that all sound ethics, all morality, either useful to individuals or beneficial to society, is totally incompatible with systems which never represent their gods but under the form of absolute monarchs, whose good qualities are continually eclipsed by dangerous caprices. Consequently, we shall be obliged to acknowledge, that to establish morality upon a steady foundation, we must necessarily commence by at least quitting those chimerical systems upon which the ruinous edifice of supernatural morality has hitherto been constructed, which during such a number of ages, has been so uselessly preached up to a great portion of the inhabitants of the earth.

Whatever may have been the cause that placed man in his present abode, that gave him the faculties he possesses; whether the human species be considered as the work of nature, or whether it be supposed that he owes his existence to an intelligent being, distinguished from nature; the existence of man, such as he is, is a fact; we behold in him a being who thinks, who feels, who has intelligence, who loves himself, who tends to his own conservation, who in every moment of his duration strives to render his existence agreeable; who, the more easily to satisfy his wants and to procure himself pleasure, congregates in society with beings similar to himself; of whom his conduct can either conciliate the favour, or draw upon him the disaffection. It is, then, upon these general sentiments, inherent in his nature, which will subsist as long as his race shall endure, that we ought to found morality; which is only a science embracing, the duties of men living together in society.

These duties have their spring in our nature, they are founded upon our necessities, because we cannot reach the goal of happiness, if we do not employ the requisite means: these means constitute the moral science. To be permanently felicitous, we must so comport ourselves as to merit the affection, so act as to secure the assistance of those, beings with whom we are associated; these will only accord us their love, lend us their esteem, aid us in our projects, labour to our peculiar happiness, but in proportion as our own exertions shall be employed for their advantage. It is this necessity, flowing naturally out of the relations of mankind, that is called MORAL OBLIGATION. It is founded upon reflection, rested upon those motives competent to determine sensible, intelligent beings, to pursue that line of conduct, which in best calculated to achieve that happiness towards which they are continually verging. These motives in the human species, never can be other than the desire, always regenerating, of procuring good and avoiding evil. Pleasure and pain, the hope of happiness, or the fear of misery, are the only motives suitable to have an efficacious influence on the volition of sensible beings. To impel them towards this end, it is sufficient these motives exist and be understood to have a knowledge of them, it is only requisite to consider our own constitution: according to this, we shall find we can only love those actions, approve that conduct, from whence result actual and reciprocal utility; this constitutes VIRTUE. In consequence, to conserve ourselves, to make our own happiness, to enjoy security, we are compelled to follow the routine which conducts to this end; to interest others in our own preservation, we are obliged to display an interest in theirs; we must do nothing that can have a tendency to interrupt that mutual co-operation which alone can lead to the felicity desired. Such is the true establishment of moral obligation.

Whenever it is attempted to give any other basis to morality than the nature of man, we shall always deceive ourselves; none other can have the least stability; none can be more solid. Some authors, even of great integrity, have thought, that to give ethics more respectability in the eyes of man, to render more inviolable those duties which his nature imposes on him, it was needful to clothe them with the authority of a being whom they have made superior to nature—whom they have rendered more powerful than necessity. Theology, seizing on these ideas, with its own general want of just inference, has in consequence invaded morality; has endeavoured to connect it with its various systems. By some it has been imagined, this union would render virtue more sacred; that the fear attached to invisible powers, who govern nature, would lend more weight, would give more efficacy to its laws; in short, it has been believed that man, persuaded, of the necessity of the moral system, seeing it united with superstition, would contemplate superstition itself as necessary to his happiness. Indeed it is the supposition that these systems are essential to morality, that sustains the theological ideas—that gives permanency to the greater part of all the creeds on earth; it is erroneously imagined that without them man would neither understand nor practise the duties he owes to others. This prejudice once established, gives currency to the opinion that the vague ideas growing out of these systems are in such a manner connected with morality, are so linked with the actual welfare of society, that they cannot be attacked without overturning the social duties that bind man to his fellow. It is thought that the reciprocity of wants, the desire of happiness, the evident interests of the community, would be mere skeleton motives, devoid of all active energy, if they did not borrow their substance from these various systems; if they were not invested with the force derived from these numerous creeds; if they were not clothed with the sanction of those ideas which have been made the arbiters of all things.

Nothing, however, is more borne out by the evidence of experience, nothing has more thoroughly impressed itself on the minds of reflecting men, than the danger always arising from connecting truth with fiction; the known with the unknown; the delirium of enthusiasm, with the tranquillity of reason. Indeed what has resulted from the confused alliance, from the marvellous speculations, which theology has made with the most substantive realities? of mixing up its evanescent conjectures with the confirmed aphorisms of time? The imagination bewildered, has mistaken truth: superstition, by aid of its gratuitous suppositions, has commanded nature—made reason bow, under its bulky yoke,—submitted man to its own peculiar caprices; very frequently in the name of its gods obliged him to stifle his nature, to piously violate the most sacred duties of morality. When these superstitions have been desirous of restraining mortals whom they had previously hood-winked, whom they had rendered irrational, it gave them only ideal curbs, imaginary motives; it substituted unsubstantial causes, for those which were substantive; marvellous supernatural powers, for those which were natural, and well understood; it supplied actual realities, by ideal romances and visionary fables. By this inversion of principle, morality had no longer any fixed basis: nature, reason, virtue, demonstration, were laid prostrate before the most undefinable systems; were made to depend upon oracular promulgations, which never spake distinctly; indeed, they generally silenced reason, were often delivered by fanatics, which time proved to be impostors; by those who, always adopting the appellation of inspired beings, gave forth nothing but the wanderings of their own delirium, or else were desirous of profiting by the errors which they themselves instilled into mankind. Thus these men became deeply interested in preaching abject submission, non-resistance, passive-obedience, factitious virtues, frivolous ceremonies; in short, an arbitrary morality, conformable to their own reigning passions; frequently prejudicial to the rest of the human race.

It was thus, in making ethics flow from these various systems, they in point of fact submitted it to the dominant passions of men, who had a direct interest in moulding it to their own advantage. In being disposed to found it upon undemonstrated theories, they founded it upon nothing; in deriving it from imaginary sources, of which each individual forms to himself his own notion, generally adverse to that of his neighbour; in resting it upon obscure oracles, always delivered ambiguously, frequently interpreted by men in the height of delirium, sometimes by knaves, who had immediate interests to promote, they rendered it unsteady—devoid of fixed principle,—too frequently left it to the mercy of the most crafty of mankind. In proposing to man the changeable creeds of the theologians for a model, they weakened the moral system of human actions; frequently annihilated that which was furnished by nature; often substituted in its place nothing but the most perplexing incertitude; the most ruinous inconsistency. These systems, by the qualities which are ascribed, to them, become inexplicable enigmas, which each expounds as best suits himself;

which each explains after his own peculiar mode of thinking; in which the theologian ever finds that which most harmonizes with his designs; which he can bend to his own sinister purposes; which he offers as irrefragible evidence of the rectitude of those actions, which at bottom have nothing but his own advantage in view. If they exhort the gentle, indulgent, equitable man, to be good, compassionate, benevolent; they equally excite the furious, who is destitute of these qualities, to be intolerant, inhuman, pitiless. The morality of these systems varies in each individual; differs in one country from another; in fact, those actions which some men look upon as sacred, which they have learned to consider meritorious, make others shudder with horror—fill them with the most painful recollections. Some see the Divinity filled with gentleness and mercy; others behold him as full of wrath and fury, whose anger is to be assuaged by the commission of the most shocking cruelties.

The morality of nature is clear, it is evident even to those who outrage it. It is not thus with superstitious morality; this is as obscure as the systems which prescribe it; or rather as fluctuating as the passions, as changeable as the temperaments, of those who expound them; if it was left to the theologians, ethics ought to be considered as the science of all others the most problematical, the most unsteady, the most difficult to bring to a point; it would require the most profound, penetrating genius, the most active, vigorous mind, to discover the principles of those duties man owes to himself, that he ought to exercise towards others; this would render the sources of the moral system attainable by a very small number of individuals; would effectually lock them up in the cabinets of the metaphysicians; place them under the treacherous guardianship of priests: to derive it from those systems, which are in themselves undefinable, with the foundations of which no one is actually acquainted, which each contemplates after his own mode, modifies after his own peculiar ideas, is at once to submit it to the caprice of every individual; it is completely to acknowledge, we know not from whence it is derived, nor whence it has its principles. Whatever may be the agent upon whom they make nature, or the beings she contains, to depend; with whatever power they way suppose him invested, it is very certain that man either does, or does not exist; but as soon as his existence is acknowledged, as soon as it is admitted to be what it actually is, when he shall be allowed to be a sensible being living in society, in love with his own felicity, they cannot without either annihilating him, or new modelling him, cause him to exist otherwise than he does. Therefore, according to his actual essence, agreeable to his absolute qualities, conformable to those modifications which constitute him a being, of the human species, morality becomes necessary to him, and the desire of conserving himself will make him prefer virtue to vice, by the same necessity that he prefers pleasure to pain. If, following up the doctrine of the theologians, "that man hath occasion for supernatural grace to enable him to do good," it must be very injurious to sound principles of morality; because he will always wait for "the call from above," to exercise that virtue, which is indispensable to his welfare. Tertullian, nevertheless says expressly, "wherefore will ye trouble yourselves, seeking after the law of God, whilst ye have that which is common to all the world, and which is written on the tablets of nature?"

To say, that man cannot possess any moral sentiments without embracing the discordant systems offered to his acceptance, is, in point of fact, saying, that he cannot distinguish virtue from vice; it is to pretend that without these systems, man would not feel the necessity of eating to live, would not make the least distinction, would be absolutely without choice in his food: it is to pretend, that unless he is fully acquainted with the name, character, and qualities of the individual who prepares a mess for him, he is not competent to discriminate whether this mess be agreeable or disagreeable, good or bad. He who does not feel himself satisfied what opinions to adopt, upon the foundation and moral attributes of these systems, or who even formally denies them, cannot at least doubt his own existence-his own functions—his own qualities—his own mode of feeling—his own method of judging; neither can he doubt the existence of other organized beings similar to himself; in whom every thing discovers to him qualities analogous with his own; of whom he can, by certain actions, either gain the love or incur the hatred—secure the assistance or attract the ill-will—merit the esteem or elicit the contempt; this knowledge is sufficient to enable him to distinguish moral good and evil. In short, every man enjoying a well-ordered organization, possessing the faculty of making true experience, will only need to contemplate himself in order to discover what he owes to others: his own nature will enlighten him much more effectually upon his duties, than those systems in which he will consult either his own unruly passions, those of some enthusiast, or those of an impostor. He will allow, that to conserve himself, to secure his own permanent welfare, he is frequently obliged to resist the blind impulse of his own desires; that to conciliate the benevolence of others, he must act in a mode conformable to their advantage; in reasoning thus, he will find out what virtue actually is; if he puts his theory into practice, he will be virtuous; he will be rewarded for his conduct by the harmony of his own machine; by the legitimate esteem of himself, confirmed by the good opinion of others, whose kindness he will have secured: if he acts in a contrary mode, the trouble that will ensue, the disorder of his frame, will quickly warn him that nature, thwarted by his actions, disapproves his conduct, which is injurious to himself; to which he will be obliged to add the condemnation of others, who will hate him. If the wanderings of his mind prevent him from seeing the more immediate consequences of his irregularities, neither will he perceive the distant rewards, the remote punishments, which these systems hold forth; because they will never speak to him so distinctly as his conscience, which will either reward or punish him on the spot. Theology has never yet known how to give a true definition of virtue: according to it, it is an effort of grace, that disposes man to do that which is agreeable to the Divinity. But what is this grace? How doth it act upon man? How shall we know what is agreeable to a Divinity who is incomprehensible to all men?

Every thing that has been advanced evidently proves, that superstitious morality is an infinite loser when compared with the morality of nature, with which, indeed, it is found in perpetual contradiction. Nature invites man to love himself, to preserve his existence, to incessantly augment the sum of his happiness: superstition teaches him to be in love only with formidable doctrines, calculated to generate his dislike; to detest himself; to sacrifice to his idols his most pleasing sensations—the most legitimate pleasures of his heart. Nature counsels man to consult reason, to adopt it for his guide; superstition pourtrays this reason as corrupted, as a treacherous director, that will infallibly lead him astray. Nature warns him to enlighten his understanding, to search after truth, to inform himself of his duties; superstition enjoins him not to examine any thing, to remain in ignorance, to fear truth; it persuades him there are no relations so important to his interest, as those which subsist between himself and systems which he can never understand. Nature tells the being who is in love with his welfare, to moderate his passions, to resist them when they are found destructive to himself, to counteract them by substantive motives collected from experience; superstition desires a sensible being to have no passions, to be an insensible mass, or else to combat his propensities by motives borrowed from the imagination, which are as variable as itself. Nature exhorts man to be sociable, to love his fellow creatures, to be just, peaceable, indulgent, benevolent, to permit his associates to freely enjoy their opinions; superstition admonishes him to fly society, to detach himself from his fellow mortals, to hate them when their imagination does not procure them dreams conformable to his own; to break through the most sacred bonds, to maintain his own opinions, or to frustrate those of his neighbour; to torment, to persecute, to massacre, those who will not be mad after his own peculiar manner. Nature exacts that man in society should cherish glory, labour to render himself estimable, endeavour to establish an imperishable name, to be active, courageous, industrious; superstition tells him to be abject, pusillanimous, to live in obscurity, to occupy himself with ceremonies; it says to him, be useless to thyself, and do nothing for others. Nature proposes to the citizen, for his model, men endued with honest, noble, energetic souls, who have usefully served their fellow citizens; superstition recommends to his imitation mean, cringing sycophants; extols pious enthusiasts, frantic penitents, zealous fanatics, who for the most ridiculous opinions have disturbed the tranquility of empires. Nature urges the husband to be tender, to attach himself to the company of his mate, to cherish her in his bosom; superstition makes a crime of his susceptibility, frequently obliges him to look upon the conjugal bonds as a state of pollution, as the offspring of imperfection. Nature calls to the father to nurture his children, to cherish their affection, to make them useful members of society; superstition advises him to rear them in fear of its systems, to hoodwink them, to make them superstitious, which renders them incapable of actually serving society, but extremely well calculated to disturb its repose. Nature cries out to children to honor their parents, to listen to their admonitions, to be the support of their old age; superstition says, prefer the oracles; in support of the systems of which you are an admitted member, trample father and mother under your feet. Nature holds out to the philosopher that he should occupy himself with useful objects, consecrate his cares to his country, make advantageous discoveries, suitable to perfect the condition of mankind; superstition saith, occupy thyself with useless reveries; employ thy time in endless dispute; scatter about with a lavish hand the seeds of discord, calculated to induce the carnage of thy fellows; obstinately maintain opinions which thou thyself canst never understand. Nature points out to the perverse man, that he should blush for his vices, that he should feel sorrow for his disgraceful propensities, that he should be ashamed of crime; it shews him, that his most secret irregularities will necessarily have an influence over his own felicity; superstition crieth to the most corrupt men, to the most flagitious mortals, "do not irritate the gods, whom thou knowest not; but if, peradventure, against their express command, thou dost deliver thyself up to crime, remember that their mercy is infinite, that their compassion endureth for ever, that therefore they may be easily appeased; thou hast nothing more to do than to go into their temples, prostrate thyself before their altars, humiliate thyself at the feet of their ministers; expiate thy transgressions by largesses, by sacrifices, by offerings, by ceremonies, and by prayer; these things done with a willing spirit, and a contrite heart, will pacify thine own conscience, and cleanse thee in the eyes of heaven."

The rights of the citizen, or the man in society, are not less injured by superstition, which is always in contradiction with sound politics. Nature says distinctly to man, "thou art free; no power on earth can justly deprive thee of thy rights, without thine own consent; and even then, thou canst not legitimately make thyself a slave to thy like." Superstition tells him he is a slave, condemned to groan all his life under the iron rod of the representatives of its system. Nature commands man to love the country which gave him birth, to serve it faithfully, to blend his interests with it, to unite against all those who shall attempt to injure it; superstition generally orders him to obey without murmur the tyrants who oppress it, to serve them against its best interests, to merit their favors by contributing to enslave their fellow citizens to their ungovernable caprices: notwithstanding these general orders, if the sovereign be not sufficiently devoted to the priest, superstition quickly changes its language, it then calls upon subjects to become rebels; it makes it a duty in them to resist their masters; it cries out to them, "it is better to obey the gods than men." Nature acquaints princes that they are men: that it is not by their capricious whims that they can decide what is just; that it is not their wayward humours that can mark what is unjust; that the public will maketh the law. Superstition often insinuates to them that they are gods, to whom nothing in this world ought to offer resistance; sometimes, indeed, it transforms them into tyrants, whom enraged heaven is desirous should be immolated to its wrath.

Superstition corrupts princes; these corrupt the law, which, like themselves, becomes unjust; from thence institutions are perverted; education only forms men who are worthless, blinded with prejudice, smitten with vain objects, enamoured of wealth, devoted to pleasures, which they must obtain by iniquitous means: thus nature, mistaken, is disdained; virtue is only a shadow quickly sacrificed to the slightest interest, while superstition, far from remedying these evils to which it has given birth, does nothing more than render them still more inveterate; or else engenders sterile regrets which it presently effaces: thus, by its operation, man is obliged to yield to the force of habit, to the general example, to the stream of those propensities, to those causes of confusion, which conspire to hurry all his species, who are not willing to renounce their own welfare, on to the commission of crime.

Here is the mode by which superstition, united with politics, exert their efforts to pervert, abuse, and poison the heart of man; the generality of human institutions appear to have only for their object to abase the human character, to render it more flagitiously wicked. Do not then let us be at all astonished if morality is almost every where a barren speculation, from which every one is obliged to deviate in practice, if he will not risk the rendering himself unhappy. Men can only have sound morals, when, renouncing his prejudices, he consults his nature; but the continued impulse which his soul is every moment receiving, on the part of more powerful motives, quickly compels him to forget those ethical rules which nature points out to him. He is continually floating between vice and virtue; we behold him unceasingly in contradiction with himself; if, sometimes, he justly appreciates the value of an honest, upright conduct, experience very soon shews him, that this cannot lead him to any thing, which he has been taught to desire, on the contrary, that it may be an invincible obstacle to the happiness which his heart never ceases for an instant to search after. In corrupt societies it is necessary to become corrupt, in order to become happy.

Citizens, led astray at the same time both by their spiritual and temporal guides, neither knew reason nor virtue. The slaves both of their superstitious systems, and of men like themselves, they had all the vices attached to slavery; kept in a perpetual state of infancy, they had neither knowledge nor principles; those who preached virtue to them, knew nothing of it themselves, and could not undeceive them with respect to those baubles in which they had learned to make their happiness consist. In vain they cried out to them to stifle those passions which every thing conspired to unloose: in vain they made the thunder of the gods roll to intimidate men whose tumultuous passions rendered them deaf. It was soon discovered that the gods of the heavens were much less feared than those of the earth; that the favour of the latter procured a much more substantive welfare than the promises of the former; that the riches of this world were more tangible than the treasures reserved for favorites in the next; that it was much more advantageous for men to conform themselves to the views of visible powers than to those of powers who were not within the compass of their visual faculties.

Thus society, corrupted by its priests, guided by their caprice, could only bring forth a corrupt offspring. It gave birth to avaricious, ambitious, jealous, dissolute citizens, who never saw any thing happy but crime; who beheld meanness rewarded; incapacity honoured; wealth adored; debauchery held in esteem; who almost every where found talents discouraged; virtue neglected; truth proscribed; elevation of soul crushed; justice trodden under foot; moderation languishing in misery; liberality of mind obligated to groan under the ponderous bulk of haughty injustice.

In the midst of this disorder, in this confusion of ideas, the precepts of morality could only be vague declamations, incapable of convincing any one. What barrier could superstition, with its imaginary motives, oppose to the general corruption? When it spake reason, it could not be heard; its gods themselves were not sufficiently powerful to resist the torrent; its menaces failed of effect, on those hearts which every thing hurried along to crime; its distant promises could not counterbalance present advantages; its expiations, always ready to cleanse mortals from their sins, emboldened them to persevere in their criminal pursuits; its frivolous ceremonies calmed their consciences; its zeal, its disputes, its caprices, only multiplied the evils, with which society found itself afflicted; only gave them an inveteracy that rendered them more widely mischievous; in short, in the most vitiated nations there was a multitude of devotees, and but very few honest men. Great and small listened to the doctrines of superstition, when they appeared favorable to their dominant passions; when they were desirous to counteract them, they listened no longer. Whenever superstition was conformable to morality, it appeared incommodious, it was only followed when it either combatted ethics or destroyed them. The despot himself found it marvellous, when it assured him he was a god upon earth; that his subjects were born to adore him alone, to administer to his phantasms. He neglected it when it told him to be just; from thence he saw it was in contradiction with itself, that it was useless to preach equity to a deified mortal; besides, he was assured the gods would pardon every thing, as soon as he should consent to recur to his priests, always ready to reconcile them; the most wicked of their subjects reckoned in the same manner upon their divine assistance: thus superstition, far from restraining vice, assured its impunity; its menaces could not destroy the effects which its unworthy flattery had produced in princes; these same menaces could not annihilate the hope which its expiations had furnished to all. Sovereigns, either inflated with pride, or always confident of washing out their crimes by timely sacrifices, no longer actually feared their gods; become gods themselves, they believed they were permitted any thing against poor pitiful mortals, whom they no longer considered under any other light than as playthings destined for their earthly amusement.

If the nature of man was consulted in his politics which supernatural ideas have so woefully depraved, it would completely rectify those false notions that are entertained equally by sovereigns and by subjects; it would contribute more amply than all the superstitions existing, to render society happy, powerful, and flourishing under rational authority. Nature would teach man, it is for the purpose of enjoying a greater portion of happiness, that mortals live together in society; that it is its own preservation, its own immediate felicity, that society should have for its determinate, unchangeable object: that without equity, a nation only resembles a congregation of enemies; that his most cruel foe, is the man who deceives him in order that he may enslave him; that the scourges most to be feared, are those priests who corrupt his chiefs, who, in the name of the gods assure them of impunity for their crimes: she would prove to him that association is a misfortune under unjust, negligent, destructive governments.

This nature, interrogated by princes, would teach them they are men and not gods; that their power is only derived from the consent of other men; that they themselves are citizens, charged by other citizens, with the care of watching over the safety of the whole; that the law ought to be only the expression of the public will; that it is never permitted them to counteract nature, or to thwart the invariable end of society. This nature would make monarchs feel, that to be truly great, to be decidedly powerful, they ought to command elevated, virtuous souls; not minds degraded by despotism, vitiated by superstition. This nature would teach sovereigns, that in order to be cherished by their subjects, they ought to afford them succour; to cause them to enjoy those benefits which their wants render imperative, that they should at all times maintain them, inviolably, in the possession of their rights, of which they are the appointed defenders—of which they are the constituted guardians. This nature would prove to all those princes who should deign to consult her, that it is only by good actions, by kindness, they can either merit the love, or secure the attachment of the people; that oppression does nothing more than raise up enemies against them; that violence only makes their power unsteady; that force, however brutally used, cannot confer on them any legitimate right; that beings essentially in love with happiness, must sooner or later finish by revolting against an authority that establishes itself by injustice; that only makes itself felt by the outrage it commits: this is the manner in which nature, the sovereign of all beings, in whose system all are equal, would speak to one of these superb monarchs, whom flattery has deified:—"Untoward, headstrong child! Pigmy, so proud of commanding pigmies! Have they then assured thee that thou art a god? Have they flattered thee that thou art something supernatural? Know there is nothing superior to myself. Contemplate thine own insignificance, acknowledge thine impotence against the slightest of my blows. I can break thy sceptre; I can take away thine existence; I can level thy throne with the dust; I can scatter thy people; I can destroy even the earth which thou inhabitest; and yet thou hast the folly to believe thou art a god. Be then, again, thyself; honestly avow that thou art a man, formed to submit to my laws equally with the meanest of thy subjects. Learn then, and never let it escape thy memory, that thou art the man of thy people; the minister of thy nation; the interpreter of its laws; the executer of its will; the fellow-citizen of those whom thou hast the right of commanding, only because they consent to obey thee, in view of that well being which thou promisest to procure for them. Reign, then, on these conditions; fulfil thy sacred engagements. Be benevolent: above all, equitable. If thou art willing to have thy power assured to thee, never abuse it; let it be circumscribed by the immovable limits of eternal justice. Be the father of thy people, and they will cherish thee as thy children. But, if unmindful of thy duties, thou neglectest them; if negligent of thine own interest, thou separatest them from those of thy great family, if thou refusest to thy subjects that happiness which thou owest them; if, heedless of thy own security, thou armest thyself against them; thou shall be like all tyrants, the slave to gloomy care, the bondman of alarm, the vassal of cruel suspicion: thou wilt become the victim to thine own folly. Thy people, reduced to despair, shorn of their felicity, will no longer acknowledge thy divine rights. In vain, then, thou wouldst sue for aid to that superstition which hath deified thee; it can avail nothing with thy people, whom sharp misery had rendered deaf;

heaven will abandon thee to the fury of those enemies to which thy frenzy shall have given birth. Superstitious systems can effect nothing against my irrevocable decrees, which will that man shall ever irritate himself against the cause of his sorrows."

In short, every thing would make known to rational princes, that they have no occasion for superstition to be faithfully obeyed on earth; that all the powers contained in these systems will not sustain them when they shall act the tyrant; that their true friends are those who undeceive the people in their delusions; that their real enemies are those who intoxicate them with flattery—who harden them in crime—who make the road to heaven too easy for them—who feed them with fanciful, chimerical doctrines, calculated to make them swerve from those cares, to divert them from those sentiments, which they justly owe to their nations.

It is then, I repeat it, only by re-conducting man to nature, that we can procure him distinct notions, evident opinions, certain knowledge; it is only by shewing him his true relations with his fellows, that we can place him on the road to happiness. The human mind, blinded by theology, has scarcely advanced a single step. Man's superstitious systems have rendered him sceptical on the most demonstrable truths. Superstition, while it pervaded every thing, while it had an universal influence, served to corrupt the whole: philosophy, dragged in its train, although it swelled its triumphant procession, was no longer any thing but an imaginary science: it quitted the real world to plunge into the sinuosities of the ideal, inconceivable labyrinths of metaphysics; it neglected nature, who spontaneously opened her book to its examination, to occupy itself with systems filled with spirits, with invisible powers, which only served to render all questions more obscure; which, the more they were probed, the more inexplicable they became; which took delight in promulgating that which no one was competent to understand. In all difficulties it introduced the Divinity; from thence things only became more and more perplexed, until nothing could be explained. Theological notions appear only to have been invented to put man's reason to flight; to confound his judgment; to deceive his mind; to overturn his clearest ideas in every science. In the hands of the theologian, logic, or the art of reasoning, was nothing more than an unintelligible jargon, calculated to support sophism, to countenance falsehood, to attempt to prove the most palpable contradictions. Morality, as we have seen, became wavering and uncertain, because it was founded on ideal systems, never in harmony with themselves, which, on the contrary, were continually contradicting their own most positive assertions. Politics, as we have elsewhere said, were cruelly perverted by the fallacious ideas given to sovereigns of their actual rights. Jurisprudence was determinately submitted to the caprices of superstition, which shackled labour, chained down human industry, controuled activity, and fettered the commerce of nations. Every thing, in short, was sacrificed to the immediate interests of these theologians: in the place of every rational science, they taught nothing but an obscure, quarrelsome metaphysics, which but too often caused the blood of those unhappy people to flow copiously who were incapable of understanding its hallucinations.

Born an enemy to experience, theology, that supernatural science, was an invincible obstacle to the progress of the natural sciences, as it almost always threw itself in their way. It was not permitted to experimental philosophy, to natural history, to anatomy, to see any thing but through the jaundiced eye of superstition. The most evident facts were rejected with disdain, proscribed with horror, when ever they could not be made to quadrate with the idle hypotheses of superstition. Virgil, the Bishop of Saltzburg, was condemned by the church, for having dared to maintain the existence of the antipodes; Gallileo suffered the most cruel persecutions, for asserting that the sun did not make its revolution round the earth. Descartes was obliged to die in a foreign land. Priests, indeed, have a right to be the enemies to the sciences; the progress of reason must, sooner or later, annihilate superstitious ideas. Nothing that is founded upon nature, that is bottomed upon truth, can ever be lost; while the systems of imaginations, the creeds of imposture, must be overturned. Theology unceasingly opposed itself to the happiness of nations—to the progress of the human mind—to useful researches—to the freedom of thought; it kept man in ignorance; all his steps being guided by it, he was no more than a tissue of errors. Indeed, is it resolving a question in natural philosophy, to say that an effect which excites our surprise, that an unusual phenomenon, that a volcano, a deluge, a hurricane, a comet, &c. are either signs of divine wrath, or works contrary to the laws of nature? In persuading nations, as it has done, that the calamities, whether physical or moral, which they experience, are the effects of the divine anger, or chastisements which his power inflicts on them, has it not, in fact, prevented them from seeking after remedies for these evils? Would it not have been more useful to have studied the nature of things, to have sought in nature herself, or in human industry, for succours against those sorrows with which mortals are afflicted, than to attribute the evil which man experiences to an unknown power, against whose will it cannot be supposed there exists any relief? The study of nature, the search after truth, elevates the soul, expands the genius, is calculated to render man active, to make him courageous. Theological notions appear to have been made to debase him, to contract his mind, to plunge him into despondence. In the place of attributing to the divine vengeance those wars, those famines, those sterilities, those contagions, that multitude of calamities, which desolate the earth; would it not have been more useful, more consistent with truth, to have shewn man that these evils were to be ascribed to his own folly, or rather to the unruly passions, to the want of energy, to the tyranny of some princes, who sacrifice nations to their frightful delirium? The irrational people, instead of amusing themselves with expiations for their pretended crimes, seeking to render themselves acceptable to imaginary powers; should they not rather have sought in a more healthy administration, the true means of avoiding those scourges, to which they were the victims? Natural evils demand natural remedies: ought not experience then long since to have convinced mortals of the inefficacy of supernatural remedies, of expiatory sacrifices, of fastings, of processions, &c. which almost all the people of the earth have vainly opposed to the disasters which they experienced?

Let us then conclude, that theology with its notions, far from being useful to the human species, is the true source of all those sorrows which afflict the earth of all those errors by which man is blinded; of those prejudices which benumb mankind; of that ignorance which renders him credulous; of those vices which torment him; of those governments which oppress him. Let us be fully persuaded that those theological, supernatural ideas, with which man is inspired from his infancy, are the actual causes of his habitual folly; are the springs of his superstitious quarrels; of his sacred dissensions; of his inhuman persecutions. Let us, at length, acknowledge, that they are these fatal ideas which have obscured morality; corrupted politics; retarded the progress of the sciences; annihilated happiness; banished peace from the bosom of mankind, Then let it be no longer dissimulated, that all those calamities, for which man turns his eyes towards heaven, bathed in tears, have their spring in the imaginary systems he has adopted: let him, therefore, cease to expect relief from them; let him seek in nature, let him search in his own energies, those resources, which superstition, deaf to his cries, will never procure for him. Let him consult the legitimate desires of his heart, and he will find that which he oweth to himself, also that which he oweth to others; let him examine his own essence, let him dive into the aim of society, from thence he will no longer be a slave; let him consult experience, he will find truth, and he will discover, that *error can never possible render him happy.*

CHAP. X.

Man can form no Conclusion from the Ideas which are offered him of the Divinity.—Of their want of just Inference.—Of the Inutility of his Conduct.

It has been already stated, that ideas to be useful, must be founded upon truth; that experience must at all times demonstrate their justice: if, therefore, as we have proved, the erroneous ideas which man has in almost all ages formed to himself of the Divinity, far from being of utility, are prejudicial to morality, to politics, to the happiness of society, to the welfare of the individuals who compose it, in short, to the progress of the human understanding; reason, and our interest, ought to make us feel the necessity of banishing from our mind these illusive, futile opinions, which can never do more than confound it—which can only disturb the tranquillity of our hearts. In vain should we flatter ourselves with arriving at the correction of theological notions; erroneous in their principles, they are not susceptible of reform. Under whatever shape an error presents itself, as soon as man shall attach an undue importance to it, it will, sooner or later, finish by producing consequences dangerous in proportion to their extent. Besides, the inutility of those researches, which in all ages have been made after the true nature of the Divinity, the notions that have hitherto been entertained, have done little more than throw it into greater obscurity, even to those who have most profoundly meditated on the subject; then, ought not this very inutility to convince us that this subject is not within the reach of our capacity that this being will not be better known to us, or by our descendants, than it hath been to our ancestors, either the most savage or the most ignorant? The object, which of all others man has at all times reasoned upon the most, written upon the most, nevertheless remains the least known; far from progressing in his research, time, with the aid of theological ideas, has only rendered it more impossible to be conceived. If the Divinity be such as dreaming theology depicts, he must himself be a Divinity who is competent to form an idea of him. We know little of man, we hardly know ourselves, or our own faculties, yet we are disposed to reason upon a being inaccessible to our senses. Let us, then, travel in peace over the line described for us by nature, without having a wish to diverge from it, to hunt after vague systems; let us occupy ourselves with our true happiness; let us profit of the benefits spread before us; let us labour to multiply them, by diminishing the number of our errors; let us quietly submit to those evils we cannot avoid, and not augment them by filling our mind with prejudices calculated to lead us astray. When we shall give it serious reflection, every thing will clearly prove that the pretended science of theology is, in truth, nothing but presumptuous ignorance, masked under pompous, unintelligible words. In short, let us terminate unfruitful researches; be content at least to acknowledge our invincible ignorance; it will clearly be more substantively advantageous, than an arrogant science, which has hitherto done little more than sow discord on the earth—affliction in the heart of man.

In supposing a sovereign intelligence who governs the world; in supposing a Divinity who exacts from his creatures that they should have a knowledge of him, that they should understand his attributes, his wisdom, his power; who is desirous they should render him homage; it must be allowed, that no man on earth in this respect completely fulfils the views of providence. Indeed, nothing is more demonstrable than the impossibility in which the theologians find themselves, to form to their mind any idea whatever of the Divinity. Procopius, the first bishop of the Goths, says in the most solemn manner: "I esteem it a very foolish temerity to be disposed to penetrate into the knowledge of the nature of God;" and further on he acknowledges, "that he has nothing more to say of him, except that he is perfectly good. He who knoweth more, whether he be ecclesiastic or layman, has only to tell it." The weakness, the obscurity of the proofs offered, of the systems attributed to him, the manifest contradictions into which they fall, the sophisms, the begging of the question, which are employed, evidently prove they are themselves in the greatest incertitude upon the nature of that being with whom it is their profession to occupy their thoughts: even the author of *A New View of Society* acknowledges, "that up to this moment it is, not possible yet to say which is right or which is wrong: that had any one of the various opposing systems which until this day have governed the world, and disunited man from man, been true, without any mixture of error; that system, very speedily after its public promulgation, would have pervaded society, and compelled all men to have acknowledged its truth." But granting that they have a knowledge of this being, that his essence, his attributes, his systems, were so fully demonstrated to them, as no longer to leave any doubt in their mind, do the rest of the human race enjoy the same advantages? Are they, in fact, in a condition to be charged with this knowledge? Ingenuously, how many persons are to be found in the world, who have the leisure, the capacity, the penetration, necessary to understand what is meant to be designated under the name of an immaterial being—of a pure spirit, who moveth matter without being himself matter; who is the motive of all the powers of nature, without being contained in nature—without being able to touch it? Are there, in the most religious societies, many persons who are competent to follow their spiritual guides, in the subtle proofs which they adduce in evidence of their creeds, upon which they bottom their systems of theology?

Without question very few men are capable of profound, connected meditation; the exercise of intense thought is, for the greater number, a species of labour as painful as it is unusual. The people, obliged to toil hard, in order to obtain subsistence, are commonly incapable of reflection; nobles, men of the world, women, young people, occupied with their own immediate affairs, taken up with gratifying their passions, employed in procuring themselves pleasure, as rarely think deeply as the uninformed. There are not, perhaps, two men in an hundred thousand, who have seriously asked themselves the question, *What it is they understand by the word God?* Whilst it is extremely rare to find persons to whom the nature of God is a problem. Nevertheless, as we have said, conviction supposes that evidence alone has banished doubt from the mind. Where, then, are the web who are convinced of the rectitude of these systems? Who are those in whom we shall find the complete certitude of these truths, so important to all? Who are the persons, who have given themselves an accurate account of the ideas they have formed upon the Divinity, upon his attributes, upon his essence? Alas! throughout the whole world, are only to be seen some speculators, who, by dint of occupying themselves with the idea, have, with great fatuity, believed they have discovered something decisive in the confused, unconnected wanderings of their own imagination; they have, in consequence, endeavoured to form a whole, which, chimerical as it is, they have accustomed themselves to consider as actually existing: by force of musing upon it, they have sometimes persuaded themselves they, saw it distinctly; these have not unfrequently succeeded in making others believe, their reveries, although they may not have mused upon it quite so much as themselves.

It is seldom more than hearsay, that the mass of the people adopt either the systems of their fathers, or of their priests: authority, confidence, submission, habit, take place of conviction—supersede proof; they prostrate themselves before idols, lend themselves to different creeds, because their ancestors have taught them to fall down, and worship; but never do they inquire wherefore they bend the knee: it is only because, in times far distant, their legislators, their guides, have imposed it upon them as a duty; these have said, "adore and believe those gods, whom ye cannot comprehend; yield yourselves in this instance to our profound wisdom; we know more than ye do respecting the Divinity." But wherefore, it might be inquired, should I take this system upon your authority? It is, they will reply, because the gods will have it thus; because they will punish you, if you dare to resist. But are not these gods the thing in question? Nevertheless, man has always been satisfied with this circle of errors; the idleness of his mind made him find it most easy to yield to the judgment of others. All superstitions are uniformly founded upon error, established by authority; equally forbid examination; are equally indisposed to permit that man should reason upon them; it is power that wills he should unconditionally accredit them: they are rested solely upon the influence of some few men, who pretend to a knowledge of things, which they admit are incomprehensible for all their species; who, at the same time, affirm they are sent as missionaries to announce them to the inhabitants of the earth: these inconceivable systems, formed in the brain of some enthusiastic persons, have most unquestionably occasion for men to expound them to their fellows. Man is generally credulous as a child upon those objects which relate to superstition; he is told he must believe them; as he generally understands nothing of the matter, he imagines he runs no risk in joining sentiments with his priest, whom he supposes has been competent to discover what he himself is not able to comprehend. The most rational people argue thus: "What shall I do? What interest can so many persons have to deceive?" But, seriously, does this prove that they do not deceive? They may do it from two motives: either because they are themselves deceived, or because they have a great interest in deceiving. By the confession of the theologians themselves, man is, for the greater part, without *religion*: he has only *superstition*. Superstition, according to them, "is a worship of the Divinity, either badly understood or irrational," or else, "worship rendered to a false Divinity." But where are the people or the clergy who will allow, either that their Divinity is false, or their worship irrational? How shall it be decided who is right, or who is wrong? It is evident that in this affair great numbers must be wrong. Indeed, Buddaeus, in his *Treatise on Atheism*, tells us, "in order that a religion may be true, not only the object of the worship must be true, but we must also have a just idea of it. He, then, who adoreth God without knowing him, adoreth him in a perverse and corrupt manner, and is generally guilty of superstition." This granted, would it not be fair to demand of the theologians, if they themselves can boast of having a *just idea* or real knowledge of the Divinity?

Admit for a moment they have, would it not then be evident, that it is for the priest, for the inspired, for the metaphysician, that this idea, which is said to be so necessary for the whole human race, is exclusively reserved? If we examine, however, we shall not find any harmony among the theological notions of these various inspired men, or of that hierarchy which is scattered over the earth: even those who make a profession of the same system, are not in unison upon the leading points. Are they ever contented with the proofs offered by their colleagues? Do they unanimously subscribe to each other's ideas? Are they agreed upon the conduct to be adopted; upon the manner of explaining their texts; upon the interpretation of the various oracles? Does there exist one country upon the whole earth, where the science of theology is actually perfectioned?—where the ideas of the Divinity are rendered so clear, as not to admit of cavil? Has this science obtained any of that steadiness, any of that consistency, any of that uniformity, which is found attached to other branches of human knowledge; even to the most futile arts, or to those trades which are most despised? Has the multitude of subtle distinctions, with which theology in some countries is filled throughout; have the words spirit, immateriality, incorporeity, predestination, grace, with other ingenious inventions, imagined by sublime thinkers, who during so many ages have succeeded each other, actually had any other effect than to perplex things; to render the whole obscure; decidedly unintelligible? Alas! do, they not offer practical demonstration, that the science held forth as the most necessary to man, has not, hitherto, been able to acquire the least degree of stability; has remained in the most determined state of indecision; has entirely failed in obtaining solidity? For thousands of years the most idle dreamers have been relieving each other, meditating on systems, diving into concealed ways, inventing hypothesis suitable to develope this important enigma. Their slender success has not at all discouraged theological vanity; the priests have always spoken of it as of a thing with which they were most intimately acquainted; they have disputed with all the pertinancy of demonstrated argument; they have destroyed each other with the most savage barbarity; yet, notwithstanding, to this moment, this sublime science remains entirely unauthenticated; almost unexamined. Indeed, if things were coolly contemplated, it would be obvious that these theories are not formed for the generality of mankind, who for the most part are utterly incompetent to comprehend the aerial subtilities upon which they rest. Who is the man, that understandeth any thing of the fundamental principles of these systems? Whose capacity embraces spirituality, immateriality, incorporeity, or the mysteries of which he is every day informed? Are there many persons who can boast of perfectly understanding the state of the question, in those theological disputations, which have frequently had the potency to disturb the repose of mankind? Nevertheless, even women believe themselves obliged to take part in the quarrels excited by these idle speculators, who are of less actual utility, to society, than the meanest artizan.

Man would, perhaps, have been too happy, if confining himself to those visible objects which interest him, he had employed half that energy which he has wasted in researches after incomprehensible systems, upon perfectioning the real sciences; in giving consistency to his laws; in establishing his morals upon solid foundations; in spreading a wholesome education among his fellows. He would, unquestionably, have been much wiser, more fortunate, if he had agreed to let his idle, unemployed guides quarrel among themselves unheeded; if he had permitted them to fathom those depths calculated to astound the mind, to amaze the intellect, without intermeddling with their irrational disputes. But it is the essence of ignorance, to attach great importance to every thing which it doth not understand. Human vanity makes the mind bear up against difficulties. The more an object eludes our inquiry, the more efforts we make to compass it; because from thence our pride is spurred on, our curiosity is set afloat, our passions are irritated, and it assumes the character of being highly interesting to us. On the other hand, the more continued, the more laborious our researches have been, the more importance we attach to either our real or our pretended discoveries; the more we are desirous not to have wasted our time; besides, we are always ready warmly to defend the soundness of our own judgment. Do not let us then be surprised at the interest that ignorant persons have at all times taken in the discoveries of their priests; nor at the obstinate pertinacity which they have ever manifested in their disputes. Indeed, in combating for his own peculiar system, each only fought for the interests of his own vanity, which of all human passions is the most quickly alarmed, the most calculated to lead man on to the commission of great follies.

Theology is truly the vessel of the Danaides. By dint of contradictory qualities, by means of bold assertions, it has so shackled its own systems as to render it impossible they should act. Indeed, when even we should suppose the existence of these theological systems, the reality of codes so discordant with each other and with themselves, we can conclude nothing from them to authorize the conduct, or sanction the mode of worship which they prescribe. If their gods are infinitely good, wherefore should we dread them? If they are infinitely wise, what reason have we to disturb ourselves with our condition? If they are omniscient, wherefore inform them of our wants, why fatigue them with our requests? If they are omnipresent, of what use can it be to erect temples to them? If they are lords of all, why make sacrifices to them; why bring them offerings of what already belongs to them? If they are just, upon what foundation believe that they will punish those creatures whom they have filled with imbecility? If their grace works every thing in man, what reason can there be why he should be rewarded? If they are omnipotent, how can they be offended; how can we resist them? If they are rational, how can the enrage themselves against blind mortals, to whom they have left the liberty of acting irrationally? If they are immutable, by what right shall we pretend to make them change their decrees? If they are inconceivable, wherefore should we occupy ourselves with them? If the knowledge of these systems be the most necessary thing, wherefore are they not more evident, more consistent, more manifest?

This granted, he who can undeceive himself on the afflicting notions of these theories, hath this advantage over the credulous, trembling, superstitious mortal—that he establishes in his heart a momentary tranquility, which, at least, rendereth him happy in this life. If the study of nature hath banished from his mind, those chimeras with which the superstitions man is infested, he, at least, enjoys a security of which this sees himself deprived. In consulting this nature, his fears are dissipated, his opinions, whether true or false, acquire a steadiness of character; a calm succeeds the storm, which panic terror, the result of wavering notions, excite in the hearts of all men who occupy themselves with these systems. If the human soul, cheered by philosophy, had the boldness to consider things coolly; it would no longer behold the universe submitted to implacable systems, under which man is continually trembling. If he was rational, he would perceive that in committing evil he did not disturb nature; that he either injureth himself alone, or injures other beings capable of feeling the effects of his conduct, from thence he would know the line of his duties; he would prefer virtue to vice, for his own permanent repose: he would, for his own satisfaction, for his own felicity in this world, find himself deeply interested in the practice of moral goodness; in rendering virtue habitual; in making it dear to the feeling of his heart: his own immediate welfare would be concerned in avoiding vice, in detesting crime, during the short season of his abode among intelligent, sensible beings, from whom he expects his happiness. By attaching himself to these rules, he would live contented with his own conduct; he would be cherished by those who are capable of feeling the influence of his actions; he would expect without inquietude the term when his existence should have a period; he would have no reason to dread the existence which *might* follow the one he at present enjoys: he would not fear to be deceived in his reasonings. Guided by demonstration, led gently along by honesty, he would perceive, that he could have nothing to dread from a beneficent Divinity, who would not punish him for those involuntary errors which depend upon the organization, which without his own consent he has received.

Such a man so conducting himself, would have nothing to apprehend, whether at the moment of his death, he falls asleep for ever; or whether that sleep is only a prelude to another existence, in which he shall find himself in the presence of his God. Addressing himself to the Divinity, he might with confidence say,

"O God! Father, who hath rendered thyself invisible to thy child! Inconceivable, hidden Author of all, whom I could not discover! Pardon me, if my limited understanding hath not been able to know thee, in a nature, where every thing hath appeared to me to be necessary! Excuse me, if my sensible heart hath not discerned thine august traits among those numerous systems which superstitious mortals tremblingly adore: if, in that assemblage of irreconcileable qualities, with which the imagination hath clothed thee, I could only see a phantom. How could my coarse eyes perceive thee in nature, in which all my senses have never been able to bring me acquainted but with material beings, with, perishable forms? Could I, by the aid of these senses, discover thy spiritual essence, of which no one could furnish me any idea? Could my feeble brain, obliged to form its judgments after its own capacity, discern thy plans, measure thy wisdom, conceive thine intelligence, whilst the universe presented to my view a continued mixture of order and confusion—of good and evil—of formation and destruction? Have I been able to render homage to the justice of thy priests, whilst I so frequently beheld crime triumphant, virtue in tears? Could I possibly acknowledge the voice of a being filled with wisdom, in those ambiguous, puerile, contradictory oracles, published in thy name in the different countries of the earth I have quitted? If I have not known thy peculiar existence, it is because I have not known either what thou couldst be, where thou couldst be placed, or the qualities which could be assigned thee. My ignorance is excusable, because it was invincible: my mind could not bend itself under the authority of men, who acknowledged they were as little enlightened upon thine essence as myself; who were for ever disputing among themselves; who were in harmony only in imperiously crying out to me, to sacrifice to them that reason which thou hadst given to me; But, oh God! If thou cherishest thy creatures, I also, like thee, have cherished them; I have endeavoured to render them happy, in the sphere in which I have lived. If thou art the author of reason, I have always listened to it—have ever endeavoured to follow it; if virtue pleaseth thee, my heart hath always honoured it; I have never willingly outraged it: when my powers have permitted me, I have myself practised it; I was an affectionate husband, a tender father, a sincere friend, a faithful subject, a zealous citizen; I have held out consolation to the afflicted; and if the foibles of my nature have been either injurious to myself or incommodious to others, I have not at least made the unfortunate groan under the weight of my injustice. I have not devoured the substance of the poor—I have not seen without pity the widow's tears; I have not heard without commiseration the cries of the orphan. If thou didst render man sociable, if thou was disposed that society should subsist, if thou wast desirous the community might be happy, I have been the enemy to all who oppressed him, the decided foe to all those who deceived him, in order that they might advantage themselves of his misfortunes.

"If I have not thought properly of thee, it is because my understanding could not conceive thee; if I have spoken ill of thy systems, it is because my heart, partaking too much of human nature, revolted against the odious portrait under which they depicted thee. My wanderings have been the effect of the temperament which thou hast given me; of the circumstances in which, without my consent, thou hast placed me; of those ideas, which in despite of me, have entered into my mind. As thou art good, as thou art just, (as we are assured thou art) thou wilt not punish me for the wanderings of mine imagination; for faults caused by my passions, which are the necessary consequence of the organization which I have received from thee. Thus I cannot doubt thy justice, I cannot dread the condition which thou preparest for me. Thy goodness cannot have permitted that I should incur punishment for inevitable errors. Thou wouldst rather prevent my being born, than have called me into the rank of intelligent beings, there to enjoy the fatal liberty of rendering myself eternally unhappy."

It is thus that a disciple of nature, who, transported all at once into the regions of space, should find himself in the presence of his God, would be able to speak, although he should not have been in a condition to lend himself to all the abstract systems of theology which appear to have been invented for no other purpose than to overturn in his mind all natural ideas. This illusory science seems bent an forming its systems in a manner the most contradictory to human reason; notwithstanding we are obliged to judge in this world according to its dictates; if, however, in the succeeding world, there is nothing conformable to this, what can be of more inutility, than to think of it or reason upon it? Besides, wherefore should we leave it to the judgment of men, who are, themselves, only enabled to act after our manner?

Without a very marked derangement of our organs, our sentiments hardly ever vary upon those objects which either our senses experience, or which reason has clearly demonstrated, In whatever circumstances we are found, we have no doubt either upon the whiteness of snow, the light of day, or the utility of virtue. It is not so with those objects which depend solely upon our imagination—which are not proved to us by the constant evidence of our senses; we judge of them variously, according to the dispositions in which we find ourselves. These dispositions fluctuate by reason of the involuntary impulse which our organs every instant receive, on the part of an infinity of causes, either exterior to ourselves, or else contained within our own frame. These organs are, without our knowledge, perpetually modified, either relaxed or braced by the density, more or less, of the atmosphere; by heat and by cold; by dryness and by humidity; by health and by sickness; by the heat of the blood; by the abundance of bile; by the state of the nervous system, &c. These various causes have necessarily an influence upon the momentary ideas, upon the instantaneous thoughts, upon the fleeting opinions of man, He is, consequently, obliged to see under a great variety of hues, those objects which his imagination presents to him; without it all times having the capacity to correct them by experience: to compare them by memory. This, without doubt, is the reason why man is continually obliged to view his gods, to contemplate his superstitious systems, under such a diversity of aspects, in different periods of his existence. In the moment, when his fibres find themselves disposed to he tremulous, he will be cowardly, pusillanimous; he will think of these systems only with fear and trembling. In the moment, when these same fibres shall have more tension, he will possess more firmness, he will then view these systems with greater coolness. The theologian will call his pusillanimity, "inward feeling;" "warning from heaven;" "secret inspiration;" but he who knoweth man, will say that this is nothing more than a mechanical motion, produced by a physical or natural cause. Indeed, it is by a pure physical mechanism, that we can explain all the revolutions that take place in the system, frequently from one minute to another; all the fluctuations in the opinions of mankind; all the variations of his judgment: in consequence of which we sometimes see him reasoning justly, sometimes in the most irrational manner.

This is the mode by which, without recurring to grace, to inspirations, to visions, to supernatural notions, we can render ourselves an account of that uncertain, that wavering state into which we sometimes behold persons fall, when there is a question respecting their superstition, who are otherwise extremely enlightened. Frequently, in despite of all reasoning, momentary dispositions re-conduct them to the prejudices of their infancy, upon which on other occasions they appear to be entirely undeceived. These changes are very apparent, especially under infirmities, in sickness, or at approach of death. The barometer of the understanding is then frequently obliged to fall. Those chimeras which he despised, or which in a state of health, he set down at their true value, are then realized. He trembles, because his machine is enfeebled; he is irrational because his brain is incapable of fulfilling its functions with exactitude. It is evident these are the actual causes of those changes which the priests well know how to make use of against what they call incredulity; from which they draw proofs of the reality of their sublimated opinions. Those conversions, or those alterations, which take place, in the ideas of man, have always their origin in some derangement of his machine; brought on either by chagrin or by some other natural or known cause.

Submitted to the continual influence of physical causes, our systems invariably follow the variations of the body; we reason well when the body is healthy—when it is soundly constituted; we reason badly when the corporeal faculties are deranged; from thence our ideas become disconnected, we are no longer equal to the task of associating them with precision; we are incapable of finding principles, or to draw from them just inferences; the brain, in fact, is shaken; we no longer contemplate any thing under its actual point of view. It is a man of this kind, who does not see things in frosty weather, under the same traits as when the season is cloudy, or when it is rainy; he does not view them in the same manner in sorrow as in gaiety; when in company as when alone. Good sense suggests to us, that it is when the body is sound, when the mind is undisturbed by any mist, that we can reason with accuracy; this state can furnish us with a general standard, calculated to regulate our judgment; even to rectify our ideas, when unexpected causes shall make them waver.

If the opinions even of the same individual, are fluctuating, subject to vaccillate, how many changes must they experience in the various beings who compose the human race? If there do not, perhaps, exist two persons who see a physical object under the same exact form or colour, what much greater variety must they not have in their mode of contemplating those things which have existence only in their imagination? What an infinity of combinations, what a multitude of ideas, must not minds essentially different, form to themselves when they endeavour to compose an ideal being, which each moment of their existence must present to them under a different aspect? It would, then, be a most irrational enterprise, to attempt to prescribe to man what he ought to think of superstition, which is entirely under the cognizance of his imagination; for the admeasurement of which, as we have very frequently repeated, mortals will never have any common standard. To oppugn the superstitious opinions of man, is to commence hostilities with his imagination—to attack his fancy—to be at war with his organization—to enter the lists with his habits, which are of themselves sufficient to identify with his existence, the most absurd, the most unfounded ideas. The more imagination man has, the greater enthusiast he will be in matters of superstition; reason will have the less ability to undeceive him in his chimeras. In proportion as his fancy is powerful, these chimeras themselves will become food necessary to its ardency. In fine, to battle with the superstitious notions of man, is to combat the passions he usually indulges for the marvellous; it is to assail him on that side where he is least vulnerable; to force him in that position where he unites all his strength—where he keeps the most vigilant guard. In despite of reason, those persons who have a lively imagination, are perpetually re-conducted to those chimeras which habit renders dear to them, even when they are found troublesome; although they should prove fatal. Thus a tender soul hath occasion for a God that loveth him; the happy enthusiast needeth a God who rewardeth him; the unfortunate visionary wants a God who taketh part in his sorrows; the melancholy devotee requireth a God who chastiseth him, who maintaineth him in that trouble which has become necessary to his diseased organization; the frantic penitent exacteth a God, who imposes upon him an obligation to be inhuman towards himself; whilst the furious fanatic would believe himself unhappy, if he was deprived of a God who commanded him to make others experience the effect of his inflamed humours, of his unruly passions.

He is, without question, a less dangerous enthusiast who feeds himself with agreeable illusions, than he whose soul is tormented with odious spectres. If a placid, tender soul, does not commit ravages in society, a mind agitated by incommodious passions, cannot fail to become, sooner or later, troublesome to his fellow creatures. The God of a Socrates, or a Fenelon, may be suitable to souls as gentle as theirs; but he cannot be that of a whole nation, in which it is extremely rare men of their temper are found: if honest men only view their gods as fitted with benefits; vicious, restless, inflexible individuals, will give them their own peculiar character, from thence will authorize themselves to indulge, a free course to their passions. Each will view his deities with eyes only open to his own reigning prejudice; the number of those who will paint them as afflicting will always be greater, much more to be feared, than those who shall delineate them under seducing colors: for one mortal that those ideas will render happy, there will be thousands who will be made miserable; they will, sooner or later, become an inexhaustible source of contention; a never failing spring of extravagant folly; they will disturb the mind of the ignorant, over whom impostors will always gain ascendancy—over whom fanatics will ever have an influence: they will frighten the cowardly, terrify the pussillanimous, whose imbecility will incline them to perfidy, whose weakness will render them cruel; they will cause the most upright to tremble, who, even while practising virtue, will fear incurring the divine displeasure; but they will not arrest the progress of the wicked, who will easily cast them aside, that they may the more commodiously deliver themselves up to crime; or who will even take advantage of these principles, to justify their transgression. In short, in the hands of tyrants, these systems will only serve to crush the liberty of the people; will be the pretext for violating, with impunity, all equitable rights. In the hands of priests they will become talismans, suitable to intoxicate the mind; calculated to hoodwink the people; competent to subjugate equally the sovereign as the subject; in the hands of the multitude, they will be a two-edged sword, with which they will inflict, at the same moment, the most dreadful wounds on themselves—the most serious injuries on their associates.

On the other hand, these theological systems, as we have seen, being only an heap of contradictions, which represent the Divinity under the most incompatible characters, seem to doubt his wisdom, when they invite mortals to address their prayers to him, for the gratification of their desires; to pray to him to grant that which he has not thought it proper to accord to them. Is it not, in other words, to accuse him with neglecting his creatures? Is it not to ask him to alter the eternal decrees of his justice; to change the invariable laws which he hath himself determined? Is it not to say to him, "O, my God! I acknowledge thy wisdom, thine omniscience, thine infinite goodness; nevertheless, thou forgettest thy servant; thou losest sight of thy creature; thou art ignorant, or thou feignest ignorance, of that which he wanteth: dost thou not see that I suffer from the marvellous arrangement, which thy wise laws have made in the universe? Nature, against thy commands, actually renders my existence painful: change then, I beseech thee, the essence which thy will has given to all beings. Grant that the elements, at this moment, lose in my favor their distinguishing properties; so order it, that heavy bodies shall not fall, that fire shall not burn, that the brittle frame which I have received at thine hands, shall not suffer those shocks which it every instant experiences. Rectify, I pray thee, for my happiness, the plan which thine infinite prudence hath marked out from all eternity." Such is very nearly the euchology which man adopts; such are the discordant, absurd requests which he continually puts up to the Divinity, whose wisdom he extols; whose intelligence he holds forth to admiration; whose providence he eulogizes; whose equity he applauds; whilst he is hardly ever contented with the effects of the divine perfections.

Man is not more consequent in those thanksgivings which he believes himself obliged to offer to the throne of grace. Is it not just, he exclaims, to thank the Divinity for his kindness? Would it not be the height of ingratitude to refuse our homage to the Author of our existence; to withhold our acknowledgements from the Giver of every thing that contributes to render it agreeable? But does he not frequently offer up his thanksgivings for actions that overwhelm his neighbour with misery? Does not the husbandman on the hill, return thanks for the rain that irrigates his lands parched with drought, whilst the cultivator of the valley is imploring a cessation of those showers which deluge his fields—that render useless the labour of his hands? Thus each becomes thankful for that which his own limited views points out to him as his immediate interest, regardless of the general effect produced by those circumstances on the welfare of his fellows. Each believes that it is either a peculiar dispensation of providence in his own favor, or a signal of the heavenly wrath directed against himself; whilst the slightest reflection would clearly evince it to be nothing more than the inevitable order of things, which take place without the least regard to his individual comforts. From this it will be obvious, that these systems do not teach their votaries, practically, to love their neighbour as themselves. But in matters of superstition, mortals never reason; they only follow the impulse of their fears; the direction of their imagination; the force of their temperament; the bent of their own peculiar passions; or those of the guides, who have acquired the right of controling their understanding. Fear has generally created these systems; terror unceasingly accompanies them; it is impossible to reason while we tremble.

We do not, however, flatter ourselves that reason will be capable, all at once, to deliver the human race from those errors with which so many causes united have contributed to poison him. The vainest of all projects would be the expectation of curing, in an instant, those epidemical follies, those hereditary fallacies, rooted during so many ages; continually fed by ignorance; corroborated by custom; borne along by the passions made inveterate by interest; grounded upon the fears, established upon the ever regenerating calamities of nations. The ancient disasters of the earth gave birth to the first systems of theology, new revolutions would equally produce others; even if the old ones should chance to be forgotton. Ignorant, miserable, trembling beings, will always either form to themselves systems, or else adopt those which imposture shall announce—which fanaticism shall be disposed to give them.

It would therefore be useless to propose more than to hold out reason to those who are competent to understand it; to present truth to those who can sustain its lustre; who can with serenity contemplate its refulgent beauty; to undeceive those who shall not be inclined to oppose obstacles to demonstration; to enlighten those who shall not desire pertinaciously to persist in error. Let us, then, infuse courage into those who want power to break with their illusions; let us cheer up the honest man, who is much more alarmed by his fears than the wicked, who, in despite of his opinions, always follows the rule of his passions: let us console the unfortunate, who groans under a load of prejudices which he has not examined: let us dissipate the incertitude of those whose doubts render them unhappy; who ingenuously seek after truth, but who find in philosophy itself only wavering opinions little calculated to determine their fluctuating minds. Let us banish from the man of genius those chimerical speculations which cause him to waste his time; let us wrest his gloomy superstition from the intimidated mortal, who, duped by his vain fears, becomes useless to society; let us remove from the atrabilarious being those systems that afflict him, that exasperate his mind, that do nothing more than kindle his anger against his incredulous neighbour; let us tear from the fanatic those terrible ideas which arm him with poniards against the happiness of his fellows; let us pluck from tyrants, let us snatch from impostors, those opinions which enable them to terrify, to enslave, and to despoil the human species. In removing from honest men their formidable notions let us not encourage those of the wicked, who are the enemies of society; let us deprive the latter of those illegitimate sources, upon which they reckon to expiate their transgressions; let us substitute actual, present terrors, to those which are distant and uncertain to those which do not arrest the most licentious excesses; let us make the profligate blush at beholding themselves what they really are; let the ministers of superstition tremble at finding their conspiracies discovered; let them dread the arrival of the day, when mortals, cured of those errors with which they have abused them, will no longer be enslaved by their artifice.

If we cannot induce nations to lay aside their inveterate prejudices, let us, at least, endeavour to prevent them from relapsing into those excesses, to the commission of which superstition has so frequently hurried them; let mankind form to himself chimeras, if he cannot do without them; let him think as he may feel inclined, provided his reveries do not make him forget that he is a man; that he does not cease to remember that a sociable being is not formed to resemble the most ferocious animals. Let us try to balance the fictitious interests of superstition, by the more immediate advantages of the earth. Let sovereigns, as well as their subjects, at length acknowledge that the benefits resulting from truth, the happiness arising from justice, the tranquillity springing out of wholesome laws, the blessings to be derived from a rational education, the superiority to be obtained from a physical, peaceable morality, are much more substantive than those they vainly expect from their respective superstitious systems, Let them feel, that advantages so tangible, benefits so precious, ought not to be sacrificed to uncertain hopes, so frequently contradicted by experience. In order to convince themselves of these truths, let every rational man consider the numberless crimes which superstition has caused upon our globe; let them study the frightful history of theology: let them read over the biography of its more odious ministers, who have too often fanned the spirit of discord—kindled the flame of fury—stirred up the raging fire of madness: let the prince and the people, at least, sometimes learn to resist the demoniacal passions of these interpreters of unintelligible systems, which they acknowledge they do not themselves at all understand, especially when they shall invoke them to be inhuman; when they shall preach up intolerance; when they invite them to barbarity; above all, when they shall command them, in the name of their gods, to stifle the cries of nature; to put down the voice of equity; to be deaf to the remonstrances of reason; to be blind to the interest of society.

Feeble mortals! led astray by error, how long will ye permit your imagination, so active, so prompt to seize on the marvellous, to continue to seek out of the universe pretexts to render you baneful to yourselves, injurious to the beings with whom ye live in society? Wherefore do ye not follow in peace, the simple, easy route marked out for ye by nature? To what purpose do ye scatter thorns on the road of life? What avails it, that ye multiply those sorrows to which your destiny exposes ye? What advantages can ye derive from systems with which the united efforts of the whole human species have not been competent to bring ye acquainted? Be content, then, to remain ignorant of that, which the human mind is not formed to comprehend; which human intellect is not adequate to embrace: occupy yourselves with truth; learn the invaluable art of living happy; perfection your morals; give rationality to your governments; simplify your laws, and rest them on the pillars of justice; watch over education, and see that it is of an invigorating quality; give attention to agriculture, and encourage beneficial improvements; foster those sciences which are actually useful, and place their professors in the most honorable stations; labor with ardour, and munificently reward those whose assiduity promotes the general welfare; oblige nature by your industry to open her immense stores, to become propitious to your exertions; do these things, and the gods will oppose nothing to your felicity. Leave to idle thinkers, to soporific dreamers, to waking visionaries, to useless enthusiasts, the unproductive task, the unfruitful occupation, of fathoming depths, from which ye ought sedulously to divert your attention; enjoy with moderation, the benefits attached to your present existence; augment their number when reason sanctions the multiplication; but never attempt to spring yourselves forward, beyond the sphere destined for your action. If you must have chimeras, permit your fellow creatures to have theirs also; but never cut the throats of your brethren, when, they cannot rave in your own manner. If ye will have unintelligible systems, if ye cannot be contented without marvellous doctrines, if the infirmities of your nature require an invisible crutch, adopt such as may best suit with your humour; select those which you may think most calculated to support your tottering frame; if ye can, let your own imagination give birth to them; but do not insist on your neighbours making the same choice with yourself: do not suffer these imaginary theories to infuriate your mind: let them not so far intoxicate your understandings, as to make ye mistake the duties ye owe to the real beings with whom ye are associated. Always remember, that amongst these duties, the foremost, the most consequential, the most immediate in its bearing upon the felicity of the human race, stands, *a reasonable indulgence for the foibles of others.*

CHAP. XI.

Defence of the Sentiments contained in this Work.—Of Impiety.—Do there exist Atheists?

What has been said in the course of this work, ought sufficiently to undeceive those who are capable of reasoning on the prejudices to which they attached so much importance. But the most evident truths frequently crouch under fear; are kept at bay by habit; prove abortive against the force of enthusiasm. Nothing is more difficult to remove from its resting place than error, especially when long prescription has given it full possession of the human mind. It is almost unassailable when supported by general consent; when it is propagated by education; when it has acquired inveteracy by custom: it commonly resists every effort to disturb it, when it is either fortified by example, maintained by authority, nourished by the hopes, or cherished by the fears of a people, who have learned to look upon these delusions as the most potent remedies for their sorrows. Such are the united forces which sustain the empire of unintelligible systems over the inhabitants of this world; they appear to give stability to their throne; to render their power immoveable; to make their reign as lasting as the human race.

We need not, then, be surprised at seeing the multitude cherish their own blindness; encourage their superstitious notions; exhibit the most sensitive fear of truth. Every where we behold mortals obstinately attached to phantoms from which they expect their happiness; notwithstanding these fallacies are evidently the source of all their sorrows. Deeply smitten with the marvellous, disdaining the simple, despising that which is easy of comprehension, but little instructed in the ways of nature, accustomed to neglect the use of their reason, the uninformed, from age to age, prostrate themselves before those invisible powers which they have been taught to adore. To these they address their most fervent prayers; implore them in their misfortunes, offer them the fruits of their labour; they are unceasingly occupied either with thanking their vain idols for benefits they have not received at their bands, or else in requesting from them favors which they can never obtain. Neither experience nor reflection can undeceive them; they do not perceive these idols, the work of their own hands, have always been deaf to their intreaties; they ascribe it to their own conduct; believe them to be violently irritated: they tremble, groan out the most dismal lamentations; sigh bitterly in their temples; strew their altars with presents; load their priests with their largesses; it never strikes their attention that these beings, whom they imagine so powerful, are themselves submitted to nature; are never propitious to their wishes, but when nature herself is favourable. It is thus that nations are the accomplices of those who deceive them; are themselves as much opposed to truth as those who lead them astray.

In matters of superstition, there are very few persons who do not partake, more or less, of the opinions of the illiterate. Every man who throws aside the received ideas, is generally considered a madman; is looked upon as a presumptuous being, who insolently believes himself much wiser than his associates. At the magical sound of superstition, a sudden panic, a tremulous terror takes possession of the human species: whenever it is attacked, society is alarmed; each individual imagines he already sees the celestial monarch lift his avenging arm against the country in which rebellious nature has produced a monster with sufficient temerity to brave these sacred opinions. Even the most moderate persons tax with folly, brand with sedition, whoever dares combat with these imaginary systems, the rights of which good sense has never yet examined. In consequence, the man who undertakes to tear the bandeau of prejudice, appears an irrational being—a dangerous citizen; his sentence is pronounced with a voice almost unanimous; the public indignation, roused by fanaticism, stirred up by imposture, renders it impossible for him to be heard in his defence; every one believes himself culpable, if he does not exhibit his fury against him; if he does not display his zeal in hunting him down; it is by such means man seeks to gain the favor of the angry gods, whose wrath is supposed to be provoked. Thus the individual who consults his reason, the disciple of nature, is looked upon as a public pest; the enemy to superstition is regarded as the enemy to the human race; he who would establish a lasting peace amongst men, is treated as the disturber of society; the man who would be disposed to cheer affrighted mortals by breaking those idols, before whom prejudice has obliged them to tremble, is unanimously proscribed as an atheist. At the bare name of atheist the superstitious man quakes; the deist himself is alarmed; the priest enters the judgement chair with fury glaring in his eyes; tyranny prepares his funeral pile, the vulgar applaud the punishments which irrational, partial laws, decree against the true friend of the human species.

Such are the sentiments which every man must expect to excite, who shall dare to present his fellow creatures with that truth which all appear to be in search of, but which all either fear to find, or else mistake what we are disposed to shew it to them. But what is this man, who is so foully calumniated as an atheist? He is one who destroyeth chimeras prejudicial to the human race; who endeavours to re-conduct wandering mortals back to nature; who is desirous to place them upon the road of experience; who is anxious that they should actively employ their reason. He is a thinker, who, having meditated upon matter, its energies, its properties, its modes of acting, hath no occasion to invent ideal powers, to recur to imaginary systems, in order to explain the phenomena of the universe—to develope the operations of nature; who needs not creatures of the imagination, which far from making him better understand nature, do no more than render it wholly inexplicable, an unintelligible mass, useless to the happiness of mankind.

Thus, the only men who can have pure, simple, actual ideas of nature, are considered either as absurd or knavish speculators. Those who form to themselves distinct, intelligible notions of the powers of the universe, are accused of denying the existence of this power: those who found every thing that is operated in this world, upon determinate, immutable laws, are accused with attributing every thing to chance; are taxed with blindness, branded with delirium, by those very enthusiasts themselves, whose imagination, always wandering in a vacuum, regularly attribute the effects of nature to fictitious causes, which have no existence but in their own heated brain; to fanciful beings of their own creation; to chimerical powers, which they obstinately persist in preferring to actual, demonstrable causes. No man in his proper senses can deny the energy of nature, or the existence of a power by virtue of which matter acts; by which it puts itself in motion; but no man can, without renouncing his reason, attribute this power to an immaterial substance; to a power placed out of nature; distinguished from matter; having nothing in common with it. Is it not saying, this power does not exist, to pretend that it resides in an unknown being, formed by an heap of unintelligible qualities, of incompatible attributes, from whence necessarily results a whole, impossible to have existence? Indestructible elements, the atoms of Epicurus, of which it is said the motion, the collision, the combination, have produced all beings, are, unquestionably, much more tangible than the numerous theological systems, broached in various parts of the earth. Thus, to speak precisely, they are the partizans of imaginary theories, the advocates of contradictory beings, the defenders of creeds, impossible to be conceived, the contrivers of substances which the human mind cannot embrace on any side, who are either absurd or knavish; those enthusiasts, who offer us nothing but vague names, of which every thing is denied, of which nothing is affirmed, are the real *Atheists*; those, I say, who make such beings the authors of motion, the preservers of the universe, are either blind or irrational. Are not those dreamers, who are incapable of attaching any one positive idea to the causes of which they unceasingly speak, true deniers? Are not those visionaries, who make a pure nothing the source of all beings, men really groping in the dark? Is it not the height of folly to personify abstractions, to organize negative ideas, and then to prostrate ourselves before the figments of our own brain?

Nevertheless, they are men of this temper who regulate the opinions of the world; who hold up to public scorn, those who are consistent to principle; who expose to the most infuriate vengeance, those who are more rational than themselves. If you will but accredit those profound dreamers, there is nothing short of madness, nothing on this side the most complete derangement of intellect, that can reject a totally incomprehensible motive-power in nature. Is it, then, delirium to prefer the known to the unknown? Is it a crime to consult experience, to call in the evidence of our senses, in the examination of that which we are informed is the most important to be understood? Is it a horrid outrage to address ourselves to reason; to prefer its oracles to the sublime decisions of some sophists, who themselves acknowledge they do not comprehend any thing of the systems they announce? Nevertheless, according to these men, there is no crime more worthy of punishment—there is no enterprize more dangerous to morals—no treason more substantive against society, than to despoil these immaterial substances, which they know nothing about, of those inconceivable qualities which these learned doctors ascribe to them—of that equipage with which a fanatical imagination has furnished them—of those miraculous properties with which ignorance, fear, and imposture have emulated each other in surrounding them: there is nothing more impious than to call forth man's reason upon superstitious creeds; nothing more heretical than to cheer up mortals against systems, of which the idea alone is the source of all their sorrows; there is nothing more pious, nothing more orthodox, than to exterminate those audacious beings who have had sufficient temerity to attempt to break an invisible charm that keeps the human species benumbed in error: if we are to put faith in the asseverations of the hierarchy, to be disposed to break man's chains is to rend asunder his most sacred bonds.

In consequence of these clamours, perpetually renovated by the disciples of imposture, kept constantly afloat by the theologians, reiterated by ignorance, those nations, which reason, in all ages, has sought to undeceive, have never dared to hearken to its benevolent lessons: they have stood aghast at the very name of physical truth. The friends of mankind were never listened to, because they were the enemies to his superstition—the examiners of the doctrines of his priest. Thus the people continued to tremble; very few philosophers had the courage to cheer them; scarcely any one dared brave public opinion; completely inoculated by superstition, they dreaded the power of imposture, the menaces of tyranny, which always sought to uphold themselves by delusion. The yell of triumphant ignorance, the rant of haughty fanaticism, at all time stifled the feeble voice of the disciple of nature; his lessons were quickly forgotten; he was obliged to keep silence; when he even dared to speak, it was frequently only in an enigmatical language, perfectly unintelligible to the great mass of mankind.

How should the uninformed, who with difficulty compass the most evident truths, those that are the most distinctly announced, be able to comprehend the mysteries of nature, presented under half words, couched under intricate emblems.

In contemplating the outrageous language which is excited among theologians, by the opinions of those whom they choose to call atheists; in looking at the punishments which at their instigation were frequently decreed against them, should we not be authorized to conclude, that these doctors either are not so certain as they say they are, of the infallibility of their respective systems; or else that they do not consider the opinions of their adversaries so absurd as they pretend? It is always either distrust, weakness, or fear, frequently the whole united, that render men cruel; they have no anger against those whom they despise; they do not look upon folly as a punishable crime. We should be content with laughing at an irrational mortal, who should deny the existence of the sun; we should not think of punishing him, unless we had, ourselves, taken leave of our senses. Theological fury never proves more than the imbecility of its cause. Lucian describes Jupiter, who disputing with Menippus, is disposed to strike him to the earth with his thunder; upon which the philosopher says to him, "Ah! thou vexest thyself, thou usest thy thunder! then thou art in the wrong." The inhumanity of these men-monsters, whose profession it was to announce chimerical systems to nations, incontestibly proves, that they alone have an interest in the invisible powers they describe; of which they successfully avail themselves to terrify, mortals: they are these tyrants of the mind, however, who, but little consequent to their own principles, undo with one hand that which they rear up with the other: they are these profound logicians who, after having formed a deity filled with goodness, wisdom and equity, traduce, disgrace, and completely annihilate him, by saving he is cruel, capricious, unjust, and despotic: this granted, these men are truly impious; decidedly heretical.

He who knoweth not this system, cannot do it any injury, consequently cannot be called impious. "To be impious," says Epicurus, "is not to take away from the illiterate the gods which they have; it is to attribute to these gods the opinions of the vulgar." To be impious is to insult systems which we believe; it is knowingly to outrage them. To be impious, is to admit a benevolent, just God, at the same time we preach up persecution and carnage. To be impious, is to deceive men in the name of a Deity, whom we make use of as a pretext for our own unworthy passions. To be impious, is to speak falsely on the part of a God, whom we suppose to be the enemy of falsehood. In fine, to be impious, is to make use of the name of the Divinity in order to disturb society—to enslave it to tyrants—to persuade man that the cause of imposture is the cause of God; it is to impute to God those crimes which would annihilate his divine perfections. To be impious, and irrational, at the same time, is to make, by the aggregation of discrepant qualities, a mere chimera of the God we adore.

On the other hand, to be pious, is to serve our country with fidelity; it is to be useful to our fellow creatures; to labour to the welfare of society. Every one can put in his claim to this piety, according to his faculties; he who meditates can render himself useful, when he has the courage to announce truth—to attack error—to battle those prejudices which everywhere oppose themselves to the happiness of mankind; it is to be truly useful, it is even a duty, to wrest from the hands of mortals those homicidal weapons which wretched fanatics so profusely distribute among them; it is highly praiseworthy to deprive imposture of its influence; it is loving our neighbour as ourself to despoil tyranny of its fatal empire over opinion, which at all times it so successfully employs to elevate knaves at the expence of public happiness; to erect its power upon the ruins of liberty; to establish unruly passions upon the wreck of public security. To be truly pious, is religiously to observe the wholesome laws of nature; to follow up faithfully those duties which she prescribes to us; in short, to be pious is to be humane, equitable, benevolent: it is to respect the rights of mankind. To be pious and rational at the same time, is to reject those reveries which would be competent to make us mistake the sober counsels of reason.

Thus, whatever fanaticism, whatever imposture may say, he who denieth the solidity of systems which have no other foundation than an alarmed imagination; he who rejecteth creeds continually in contradiction with themselves; he who banisheth from his heart, doctrines perpetually wrestling with nature, always in hostility with reason, ever at war with the happiness of man; he, I repeat, who undeceiveth himself on such dangerous chimeras, when his conduct shall not deviate from those invariable rules which sound morality dictates, which nature approves, which reason prescribes, may be fairly reputed pious, honest, and virtuous. Because a man refuseth to admit contradictory systems, as well as the obscure oracles, which are issued in the name of the gods, does it then follow, that such a man refuses to acknowledge the evident, the demonstrable laws of nature, upon which he depends, of which he in obliged to fulfil the necessary duties, under pain of being punished in this world; whatever he may be in the in the next? It is true, that if virtue could by any chance consist in an ignominious renunciation of reason, in a destructive fanaticism, in useless customs, the atheist, as he is called, could not pass for a virtuous being: but if virtue actually consists in doing to society all the good of which we are capable, this miscalled atheist may fairly lay claim to its practice: his courageous, tender soul, will not be found guilty, for hurling his legitimate indignation against prejudices, fatal to the happiness of the human species.

Let us listen, however, to the imputations which the theologians lay upon those men they falsely denominate atheists; let us coolly, without any peevish humour, examine the calumnies which they vomit forth against them: it appears to them that atheism, (as they call differing in opinion from themselves,) is the highest degree of delirium that can assail the human mind; the greatest stretch of perversity that can infect the human heart; interested in blackening their adversaries, they make incredulity the undeniable offspring of folly; the absolute effect of crime. "We do not," say they to us, "see those men fall into the horrors of atheism, who have reason to hope the future state will be for them a state of happiness." In short, according to these metaphysical doctors, it is the interest of their passions which makes them seek to doubt systems, at whose tribunals they are accountable for the abuses of this life; it is the fear of punishment which is alone known to atheists; they are unceasingly repeating the words of a Hebrew prophet, who pretends that nothing but folly makes men deny these systems; perhaps, however, if he had suppressed his negation, he would have more closely aproximated the truth. Doctor Bentley, in his *Folly of Atheism*, has let loose the whole Billingsgate of theological spleen, which he has scattered about with all the venom of the most filthy reptiles: if he and other expounders are to be believed, "nothing is blacker than the heart of an atheist; nothing is more false than his mind. Atheism," according to them, "can only be the offspring of a tortured conscience, that seeks to disengage itself from the cause of its trouble. We have a right", says Derham, "to look upon an atheist as a monster among rational beings; as one of those extraordinary productions which we hardly ever meet with in the whole human species; and who, opposing himself to all other men, revolts not only against reason and human nature, but against the Divinity himself."

We shall simply reply to all these calumnies by saying, it is for the reader to judge if the system which these men call atheism, be as absurd as these profound speculators (who are perpetually in dispute on the uninformed, ill organized, contradictory, whimsical productions of their own brain) would have it believed to be! It is true, perhaps, that the system of naturalism hitherto has not been developed in all its extent: unprejudiced persons however, will, at least, be enabled to know whether the author has reasoned well or ill; whether or not he has attempted to disguise the most important difficulties; distinctly to see if he has been disingenuous; they will be competent to observe if, like unto the enemies of human reason, he has recourse to subterfuges, to sophisms, to subtle discriminations, which ought always to make it suspected of those who use them, either that they do not understand or else that they fear the truth. It belongs then to candour, it is the province of disinterestedness, it is the duty of reason to judge, if the natural principles which have been here ushered to the world be destitute of foundation; it is to these upright jurisconsults that a disciple of nature submits his opinions: he has a right to except against the judgment of enthusiasm; he has the prescription to enter his caveat against the decision of presumptuous ignorance; above all, he is entitled to challenge the verdict of interested knavery. Those persons who are accustomed to think, will, at least find reasons to doubt many of those marvellous notions, which appear as incontestable truths only to those, who have never assayed them by the standard of good sense.

We agree with Derham, that atheists are rare; but then we also say, that superstition has so disfigured nature, so entangled her rights—enthusiasm has so dazzled the human mind-terror has so disturbed the heart of man—imposture has so bewildered his imagination—tyranny has so enslaved his thoughts: in fine, error, ignorance, and delirium have so perplexed and confused the clearest ideas, that nothing is more uncommon than to find men who have sufficient courage to undeceive themselves on notions which every thing conspires to identify with their very existence. Indeed, many theologians in despite of those bitter invectives with which they attempt to overwhelm the men they choose to call atheists, appear frequently to have doubted whether any ever existed in the world. Tertullian, who, according to modern systems, would be ranked as an atheist, because he admitted a corporeal God, says, "Christianity has dissipated the ignorance in which the Pagans were immersed respecting the divine essence, and there is not an artizan among the Christians who does not see God, and who does not know him." This uncertainty of the theologic professors was, unquestionably, founded upon those absurd ideas, which they ascribe to their adversaries, whom they have unceasingly accused with attributing every thing to chance—to blind causes—to dead, inert matter, incapable of self-action. We have, I think, sufficiently justified the partizans of nature against these ridiculous accusations; we have throughout the whole proved, and we repeat it, that chance is a word devoid of sense, which as well as all other unintelligible words, announces nothing but ignorance of actual causes. We have demonstrated that matter is not dead; that nature, essentially active and self-existent, has sufficient energy to produce all the beings which she contains—all the phenomena we behold. We have, throughout, made it evident that this cause is much more tangible, more easy of comprehension, than the inconceivable theory to which theology assigns these stupendous effects. We have represented, that the incomprehensibility of natural effects was not a sufficient reason for assigning to them a system still more incomprehensible than any of those of which, at least, we have a slight knowledge. In fine, if the incomprehensibility of a system does not authorize the denial of its existence, it is at least certain that the incompatibility of the attributes with which it is clothed, authorizes the assertion, that those which unite them cannot be any thing more than chimeras, of which the existence is impossible.

This granted, we shall be competent to fix the sense that ought to be attached to the name of atheist; which, notwithstanding, the theologians lavish on all those who deviate in any thing from their opinions. If, by atheist, be designated a man who denieth the existence of a power inherent in matter, without which we cannot conceive nature, and if it be to this power that the name of God is given, then there do not exist any atheists, and the word under which they are denominated would only announce fools. But if by atheists be understood men without enthusiasm; who are guided by experience; who follow the evidence of their senses; who see nothing in nature but what they actually find to have existence, or that which they are capacitated to know; who neither do, nor can perceive any thing but matter essentially active, moveable, diversely combined, in the full enjoyment of various properties, capable of producing all the beings who display themselves to our visual faculties, if by atheists be understood natural philosophers, who are convinced that without recurring to chimerical causes, they can explain every thing, simply by the laws of motion; by the relation subsisting between beings; by their affinities; by their analogies; by their aptitude to attraction; by their repulsive powers; by their proportions; by their combinations; by their decomposition: if by atheists be meant these persons who do not understand what *Pneumatology* is, who do not perceive the necessity of spiritualizing, or of rendering incomprehensible, those corporeal, sensible, natural causes, which they see act uniformly; who do not find it requisite to separate the motive-power from the universe; who do not see, that to ascribe this power to an immaterial substance, to that whose essence is from thenceforth totally inconceivable, is a means of becoming more familiar with it: if by atheists are to be pourtrayed those men who ingenuously admit that their mind can neither receive nor reconcile the union of the negative attributes and the theological abstractions, with the human and moral qualities which are given to the Divinity; or those men who pretend that from such an incompatible alliance, there could only result an imaginary being; seeing that a pure spirit is destitute of the organs necessary to exercise the qualities, to give play to the faculties of human nature: if by atheists are described those men who reject systems, whose odious and discrepant qualities are solely calculated to disturb the human species—to plunge it into very prejudicial follies: if, I repeat it, thinkers of this description are those who are called atheists, it is not possible to doubt their existence; and their number would be considerable, if the light of sound natural philosophy was more generally diffused; if the torch of reason burnt more distinctly; or if it was not obscured by the theological bushel: from thence, however, they would be considered neither as irrational; nor as furious beings, but as men devoid of prejudice, of whose opinions, or if they prefer it, whose ignorance, would be much more useful to the human race, than those ideal sciences, those vain hypotheses, which for so many ages have been the actual causes of all man's tribulation.

Doctor Cudworth, in his *Intellectual System*, reckons four species of atheists among the ancients.

First.—The disciples of Anaximander, called *Hylopathians*, who attributed every thing to matter destitute of feeling. His doctrine was, that men were born of earth united with water, and vivified by the beams of the sun; his crime seems to have been, that he made the first geographical maps and sun-dials; declared the earth moveable and of a cylindrical form.

Secondly.—The *Atomists*, or the disciples of Democritus, who attribute every thing, to the concurrence of atoms. His crime was, having first taught that the milky way was occasioned by the confused light from a multitude of stars.

Thirdly.—The *Stoics*, or the disciples of Zeno, who admitted a blind nature acting after certain laws. His crime appears to be, that he practised virtue with unwearied perseverance, and taught that this quality alone would render mankind happy.

Fourthly.—The *Hylozoists*, or the disciples of Strato, who attributed life to matter. His crime consisted in being one of the most acute natural philosophers of his day, enjoying high favour with Ptolemy Philadelphus, an intelligent prince, whose preceptor be was.

If, however, by atheists, are meant those men, who are obliged to avow, that they have not one idea of the system they adore, or which they announce to others; who cannot give any satisfactory account, either of the nature or of the essence of their immaterial substances; who can never agree amongst themselves on the proofs which they adduce in support of their System; on the qualities or on the modes of action of their incorporeities, which by dint of negations they render a mere nothing; who either prostrate themselves, or cause others to bow down, before the absurd fictions of their own delirium: if, I say, by atheists, be denominated men of this stamp, we shall be under the necessity of allowing, that the world is filled with them: we shall even be obliged to place in this number some of the most active theologians, who are unceasingly reasoning upon that Which they do not understand; who are eternally disputing upon points which they cannot demonstrate; who by their contradictions very efficaciously undermine their own systems; who annihilate all their own assertions of perfection, by the numberless imperfections with which they clothe them; who rebel against their gods by the atrocious character under which they depict them. In short, we shall be able to consider as true atheists, those credulous, weak persons, who upon hearsay and from tradition, bend the knee before idols, of whom they have no other ideas, than those which are furnished them by their spiritual guides, who themselves acknowledge that they comprehend nothing about the matter.

What has been said amply proves that the theologians themselves have not always known the sense they could affix to the word atheist; they have vaguely attacked, in an indistinct manner, calumniated with it, those persons whose sentiments and principles were opposed to their own. Indeed, we find that these sublime professors, always infatuated with their own particular opinions, have frequently been extremely lavish in their accusations of atheism, against all those whom they felt a desire to injure; whose characters it was their pleasure to paint in unfavourable colours; whose doctrines they wished to blacken; whose systems they sought to render odious: they were certain of alarming the illiterate, of rousing the antipathies of the silly, by a loose imputation, or by a word, to which ignorance attaches the idea of horror, merely because it is unacquainted with its true sense. In consequence of this policy, it has been no uncommon spectacle to see the partizans of the same sect, the adorers of the same gods, reciprocally treat each other as atheists, in the fervour of their theological quarrels; to be an atheist, in this sense, is not to have, in every point, exactly the same opinions as those with whom we dispute, either on superstitious or religious subjects. In all times the uninformed have considered those as atheists, who did not think upon the Divinity precisely in the same manner as the guides whom they were accustomed to follow. Socrates, the adorer of a unique God, was no more than an atheist in the eyes of the Athenian people.

Still more, as we have already observed, those persons have frequently been accused of atheism, who have taken the greatest pains to establish the existence of the gods, but who have not produced satisfactory proofs: when their enemies wished to take advantage of them, it was easy to make them pass for atheists, who had wickedly betrayed their cause, by defending it too feebly. The theologians have frequently been very highly incensed against those who believed they had discovered the most forcible proof of the existence of their gods, because they were obliged to discover that their adversaries could make very contrary inductions from their propositions; they did not perceive that it was next to impossible not to lay themselves open to attack, in establishing principles visibly founded upon that which each man sees variously. Thus Paschal says, "I have examined if this God, of whom all the world speaks, might not have left some marks of himself. I look every where, and every where I see nothing but obscurity. Nature offers one nothing, that may not be a matter of doubt and inquietude. If I saw nothing in nature which indicated a Divinity, I should determine with myself, to believe nothing about it. If every where I saw the sign of a creator, I should repose myself in peace, in the belief of one. But seeing too much to deny, and too little to assure me of his existence, I am in a situation that I lament, and in which I have an hundred times wished, that if a God doth sustain nature, he would give unequivocal marks of it, and that if the signs which he hath given be deceitful, that he would suppress them entirely; that he said all or nothing, to the end that I might see which side I ought to follow."

In a word, those who have most vigorously taken up the cause of the theological systems, have been taxed with atheism and irreligion; the most zealous partizans have been looked upon as deserters, have been contemplated as traitors; the most orthodox theologians have not been able to guarantee themselves from this reproach; they have mutually bespatered each other; prodigally lavished, with malignant reciprocity, the most abusive terms: nearly all have, without doubt, merited these invectives, if in the term atheist be included those men who have not any idea of their various systems, that does not destroy itself, whenever they are willing to submit it to the touchstone of reason. From whence we may conclude, without subjecting ourselves to the reproach of being hasty, that error will not stand the test of investigation; that it will not pass the ordeal of comparison; that it is in its hues a perfect chamelion; that consequently it can never do more than lead to the most absurd deductions: that the most ingenious systems, when they have their foundations in hallucination, crumble like dust under the rude band of the assayer; that the most sublimated doctrines, when they lack the substantive quality of rectitude, evaporate under the scrutiny of the sturdy examiner, who tries them in the crucible; that it is not by levelling abusive language against those who investigate sophisticated theories, they will either be purged of their absurdities, acquire solidity, or find an establishment to give them perpetuity; that moral obliquities, can never be made rectilinear by the mere application of unintelligible terms, or by the inconsiderate jumble of discrepant properties, however gaudy the assemblage: in short, that the only criterion of truth is, *that it is ever consistent with itself.*

CHAP. XII.

Is what is termed Atheism compatible with Morality?

After having proved the existence of those whom the superstitious bigot, the heated theologian, the inconsequent theist, calls *atheists*, let us return to the calumnies which are so profusely showered upon them by the deicolists. According to Abady, in his *Treatise on the Truth of the Christian Religion*, "an atheist cannot be virtuous: to him virtue is only a chimera; probity no more than a vain scruple; honesty nothing but foolishness;—he knoweth no other law than his interest: where this sentiment prevails, conscience is only a prejudice; the law of nature only an illusion; right no more than an error; benevolence hath no longer any foundation; the bonds of society are loosened; the ties of fidelity are removed; friend is ready to betray friend; the citizen to deliver up his country; the son to assassinate his father, in order to enjoy his inheritance, whenever they shall find occasion, and that authority or silence shall shield them from the arm of the secular power, which alone is to be feared. The most inviolable rights, and most sacred laws, must no longer be considered, except as dreams and visions." Such, perhaps, would be the conduct, not of a feeling, thinking, reflecting being, susceptible of reason; but of a ferocious brute, of an irrational wretch, who should not have any idea of the natural relations which subsist between beings, reciprocally necessary to each other's happiness. Can it actually be supposed, that a man capable of experience, furnished with the faintest glimmerings of sound sense, would lend himself to the conduct which is here ascribed to the atheist; that is to say, to a man who is conversant with the evidence of facts; who ardently seeks after truth; who is sufficiently susceptible of reflection, to undeceive himself by reasoning upon those prejudices which every one strives to shew him as important; which all voices endeavour to announce to him as sacred? Can it, I repeat, be supposed, that any enlightened, any polished society, contains a citizen so completely blind, not to acknowledge his most natural duties; so very absurd, not to admit his dearest interests; so completely besotted not to perceive the danger he incurs in incessantly disturbing his fellow creatures; or in following no other rule, than his momentary appetites? Is not every human being who reasons in the least possible manner, obliged to feel that society is advantageous to him; that he hath need of assistance; that the esteem of his fellows is necessary to his own individual happiness; provoked, that he has every thing to fear from the wrath of his associates; that the laws menace whoever shall dare to infringe them? Every man who has received a virtuous education, who has in his infancy experienced the tender cares of a parent; who has in consequence tasted the sweets of friendship; who has received kindness; who knows the worth of benevolence; who sets a just value upon equity; who feels the pleasure which the affection of our fellow creatures procures for us; who endures the inconveniences which result from their aversion who smarts under the sting which is inflicted by their scorn, is obliged to tremble at losing, by his measures, such manifest advantages—at incurring such, imminent danger. Will not the hatred of others, the fear of punishment, his own contempt of himself, disturb his repose every time that, turning, inwardly upon his own conduct, he shall contemplate it under the same perspective as does his neighbour? Is there then no remorse but for those who believe in incomprehensible systems? Is the idea that we are tinder the eye of beings of whom we have but vague notions, more forcible than the thought that we are viewed by our fellow men; than the fear of being detected by ourselves; than the dread of exposure; than the cruel necessity of becoming despicable in our own eyes; than the wretched alternative, to be constrained to blush guiltily, when we reflect on our wild career, and the sentiments which it must infallibly inspire?

This granted, we shall reply deliberately to this Abady, that an atheist is a man who understands nature, who studies her laws; who knows his own nature; who feels what it imposes upon him. An atheist hath experience; this experience proves to him every moment that vice can injure him; that his most concealed faults, his most secret dispositions, may be detected—may display his character in open day; this experience proves to him that society is useful to his happiness; that his interest authoritatively demands he should attach himself to the country that protects him, which enables him to enjoy in security the benefits of nature; every thing shews him that in order to be happy he must make himself beloved; that his parent is for him the most certain of friends; that ingratitude would remove him from his benefactor; that justice is necessary to the maintenance of every association; that no man, whatever way he his power, can be content with himself, when he knows he is an object of public hatred. He who has maturely reflected upon himself, upon his own nature, upon that of his associates, upon his own wants, upon the means of procuring them, cannot prevent himself from becoming acquainted with his duties—from discovering the obligations he owes to himself, as well as those which he owes to others; from thence he has morality, he has actual motives to confirm himself to its dictates; he is obliged to feel, that these duties are imperious: if his reason be not disturbed by blind passions, if his mind be not contaminated by vicious habits, he will find that virtue is the surest road to felicity. The atheists, as they are styled, or the fatalists, build their system upon necessity: thus, their moral speculations, founded upon the nature of things, are at least much more permanent, much more invariable, than those which only rest upon systems that alter their aspect according to the various dispositions of their adherents—in conformity with the wayward passions of those who contemplate, them. The essence of things, and the immutable laws of nature, are not subject to fluctuate; it is imperative with the atheist, as he is facetiously called by the theologian, to call whatever injures himself either vice or folly; to designate that which injures others, crime; to describe all that is advantageous to society, every thing which contributes to its permanent happiness, virtue.

It will be obvious, then, that the principles of the miscalled atheist are much less liable to be shaken, than those of the enthusiast, who shall have studied a baby from his earliest Infancy; who should have devoted not only his days, but his nights, to gleaning the scanty portion of actual information that he scatters through his volumes; they will have a much more substantive foundation than those of the theologian, who shall construct his morality upon the harlequin scenery of systems that so frequently change, even in his own distempered brain. If the atheist, as they please to call those who differ in opinion with themselves, objects to the correctness, of—their systems, he cannot deny his own existence, nor that of beings similar to himself, by whom he is surrounded; he cannot doubt the reciprocity of the relations that subsist between them; he cannot question the duties which spring out of these relations; Pyrrhonism, then, cannot enter his mind upon the actual principles of morality; which is nothing more than the science of the relations of beings living together in society.

If, however, satisfied with a barren, speculative knowledge of his duties, the atheist of the theologian should not apply them in his conduct—if, hurried along by the current of his ungovernable passions—if, borne forward by criminal habits—if, abandoned to shameful vices-if, possessing a vicious temperament, which he has not been sedulous to correct—if, lending himself to the stream of outrageous desires, he appears to forget his moral obligations, it by no means follows, either that he hath no principles, or that his principles are false: it can only be concluded from such conduct, that in the intoxication of his passions, in the delirium of his habits, in the confusion of his reason, he does not give activity to doctrines grounded upon truth; that he forgets to give currency to ascertained principles; that he may follow those propensities which lead him astray. In this, indeed, he will have dreadfully descended to the miserable level of the theologian, but he will nevertheless find him the partner of his folly—the partaker of his insanity—the companion of his crime.

Nothing is, perhaps, more common among men, than a very marked discrepancy between the mind and the heart; that is to say, between the temperament, the passions, the habits the caprices, the imagination, and the judgment, assisted by reflection. Nothing is, in fact, more rare, than to find these harmoniously running upon all fours with each other; it is, however, only when they do, that we see speculation influence practice. The most certain virtues are those which are founded upon the temperament of man. Indeed, do we not every day behold mortals in contradiction with themselves? Does not their more sober judgment unceasingly condemn the extravagancies to which their undisciplined passions deliver them up? In short, doth not every thing prove to us hourly, that men, with the very best theory, have sometimes the very worst practice; that others with the most vicious theory, frequently adopt the most amiable line of conduct? In the blindest systems, in the most atrocious superstitions, in those which are most contrary to reason, we meet with virtuous men, the mildness of whose character, the sensibility of whose hearts, the excellence of whose temperament, re conducts them to humanity, makes them fall back upon the laws of nature, in despite of their furious theories. Among the adorers of the most cruel, vindictive, jealous gods, are found peaceable, souls, who are enemies to persecution; who set their faces against violence; who are decidedly opposed to cruelty: among the disciples of a God filled with mercy, abounding in clemency, are seen barbarous monsters; inhuman cannibals: nevertheless, both the one and the other acknowledge, that their gods ought to serve them for a model. Wherefore, then, do they not in all things conform themselves? It is because the most wicked systems cannot always corrupt a virtuous soul; that those which are most bland, most gentle in their precepts, cannot always restrain hearts driven along by the impetuosity of vice. The organization will, perhaps, be always more potent than either superstition or religion. Present objects, momentary interests, rooted habits, public opinion, have much more efficacy than unintelligible theories, than imaginary systems, which themselves depend upon the organic structure of the human frame.

The point in question then is, to examine if the principles of the atheist, as he is erroneously called, be true, and not whether his conduct be commendable? An atheist, having an excellent theory, founded upon nature, grafted upon experience, constructed upon reason, who delivers himself up to excesses, dangerous to himself, injurious to society, is, without doubt, an inconsistent man. But he is not more to be feared than a superstitious bigot; than a zealous enthusiast; or than even a religious man who, believing in a good, confiding in an equitable, relying on a perfect God, does not scruple to commit the most frightful devastations in his name. An atheistical tyrant would assuredly not be more to be dreaded than a fanatical despot. An incredulous philosopher, however, is not so mischievous a being as an enthusiastic priest, who either fans the flame of discord among his fellow subjects, or rises in rebellion against his legitimate monarch. Would, then, an atheist clothed with power, be equally dangerous as a persecuting priest-ridden king; as a savage inquisitor; as a whimsical devotee; or, as a morose bigot? These are assuredly more numerous in the world than atheists, as they are ludicrously termed, whose opinions, or whose vices are far from being in a condition to have an influence upon society; which is ever too much hoodwinked by the priest, too much blinded by prejudice, too much the slave of superstition, to be disposed to give them a patient hearing.

An intemperate, voluptuous atheist, is not more dangerous to society than a superstitions bigot, who knows how to connect licentiousness, punic faith, ingratitude, libertinism, corruption of morals, with his theological notions. Can it, however, be ingeniously imagined, that a man, because he is falsely termed an atheist, or because he does not subscribe to the vengeance of the most contradictory systems, will therefore be a profligate debaucheé, malicious, and persecuting; that he will corrupt the wife of his friend; will turn his own wife adrift; will consume both his time and his money in the most frivolous gratifications; will be the slave to the most childish amusements; the companion of the most dissolute men; that he will discard all his old friends; that he will select his bosom confidents from the brazen betrayers of their native land—from among the hoary despoilers of connubial happiness—from out of the ranks of veteran gamblers; that he will either break into his neighbour's dwelling, or cut his throat; in short, that he will lend himself to all those excesses, the most injurious to society, the most prejudicial to himself, the most deserving public castigation? The blemishes of an atheist, then, as the theologian styles him, have not any thing more extraordinary in them than those of the superstitious man; they possess nothing with which his doctrine can be fairly reproached. A tyrant, who should be incredulous, would not be a more incommodious scourge to his subjects, than a theological autocrat, who should wield his sceptre to the misery of his people. Would the nation of the latter feel more happy, from the mere circumstance that the tyger who governed it believed in the most abstract systems, heaped the most sumptuous presents on the priests, and humiliated himself at their shrine? At least it must be acknowledged, according to the shewing of the theologian himself, that under the dominion of the atheist, a nation would not have to apprehend superstitious vexations; to dread persecutions for opinion; to fear proscriptions for ill-digested systems; neither would it witness those strange outrages that have sometimes been Committed for the interests of heaven, even under the mildest monarchs. If it was the victim to the turbulent passions of an unbelieving prince, the sacrifice to the folly of a sovereign who should be an infidel, it would not, at least, suffer from his blind infatuation, for theological systems which he does not understand; nor from his fanatical zeal, which of all the passions that infest monarchs, is ever the most destructive, always the most dangerous. An atheistical tyrant, who should persecute for opinions, would be a man not consistent with his own principles; he could not exist; he would not, indeed, according to the theologian, be an atheist at most, he would only furnish one more example, that mortals much more frequently follow the blind impulse of their passions, the more immediate stimulus of their interest, the irresistible torrent of their temperament, than their speculations, however grave, however wise. It is, at least, evident, that an atheist has one pretext less than a credulous prince, for exercising his natural wickedness.

Indeed, if men condescended to examine things coolly, they would find that on this earth the name of God is but too frequently made use of as a motive to indulge the worst of human passions. Ambition, imposture, and tyranny, have often formed a league to avail themselves of its influence, to the end that they might blind the people, and bend them beneath a galling yoke: the monarch sometimes employs it to give a divine lustre to his person—the sanction of heaven to his rights—the confidence of its votaries to his most unjust, most extravagant whims. The priest frequently uses it to give currency to his pretensions, to the end that he may with impunity gratify his avarice, minister to his pride, secure his independence. The vindictive, enraged, superstitious being, introduces the cause of his gods, that he may give free scope to his fury, which he qualifies with zeal. In short, superstition becomes dangerous, because it justifies those passions, lends legitimacy to those crimes, holds forth as commendable those excesses, of which it does not fail to gather the fruit: according to its ministers, every thing is permitted to revenge the most high: thus the name of the Divinity is made use of to authorize the most baneful actions, to palliate the most injurious transgressions. The atheist, as he is called, when he commits crimes, cannot, at least, pretend that it is his gods who command them, or who clothe them with the mantle of their approval, this is the excuse the superstitious being offers for his perversity; the tyrant for his persecutions; the priest for his cruelty, and for his sedition; the fanatic for the ebullition of his boiling passions; the penitent for his inutility.

"They are not," says Bayle, "the general opinions of the mind, but the passions, which determine us to act." Atheism, as it is called, is a system which will not make a good man wicked but it may, perhaps, make a wicked man good. "Those," says the same author, "who embraced the sect of Epicurus, did not become debaucheés because they had adopted the doctrine of Epicurus; they only lent themselves to the system, then badly understood, because they were debaucheés." In the same manner, a perverse man may embrace atheism, because he will flatter himself, that this system will give full scope to his passions: he will nevertheless be deceived. Atheism, as it is called, if well understood, is founded upon nature and upon reason, which never can, like superstition, either justify or expiate the crimes of the profligate.

From the diffusion of doctrines which make morality depend upon unintelligible, incomprehensible systems, that are proposed to man for a model, there has unquestionably resulted very great inconvenience. Corrupt souls, in discovering, how much each of these suppositions are erroneous or doubtful, give loose to the rein of their vices, and conclude there are not more substantive motives for acting well; they imagine that virtue, like these fragile systems, is merely chimerical; that there is not any cogent solid reason for practising it in this world. Nevertheless, it must be evident, that it is not as the disciples of any particular tenet, that we are bound to fulfil the duties of morality; it is as men, living together in society, as sensible beings seeking to secure to ourselves a happy existence, that we should feel the moral obligation. Whether these systems maintain their ground, or whether the do not, our duties will remain the same; our nature, if consulted, will incontestibly prove, that *vice is a decided evil, that virtue is an actual, a substantial good.*

If, then, there be found atheists who have denied the distinction of good and evil, or who have dared to strike at the foundations of morality; we ought to conclude, that upon this point they have reasoned badly; that they have neither been acquainted with the nature of man, nor known the true source of his duties; that they have falsely imagined that ethics, as well as theology, was only an ideal science; that the fleeting systems once destroyed, there no longer remained any bonds to connect mortals. Nevertheless, the slightest reflection would have incontestibly proved, that morality is founded upon immutable relations subsisting between sensible, intelligent, sociable beings; that without virtue, no society can maintain itself; that without putting the curb on his desires, no mortal can conserve himself: man is constrained from his nature to love virtue, to dread crime, by the same necessity that obliges him to seek happiness, and fly from sorrow: thus nature compels him to place a distinction between those objects which please, and those objects Which injure him. Ask a man, who is sufficiently irrational to deny the difference between virtue and vice, if it would be indifferent to him to be beaten, robbed, calumniated, treated with ingratitude, dishonoured by his wife, insulted by his children, betrayed by his friend? His answer will prove to you, that whatever he may say, he discriminates the actions of mankind; that the distinction between good and evil, does not depend either upon the conventions of men, or upon the ideas which they may have of particular systems; upon the punishments or upon the recompenses which attend mortals in a future existence.

On the contrary, an atheist, as he is denominated, who should reason with justness, would feel himself more interested than another in practising those virtues to which he finds his happiness attached in this world. If his views do not extend themselves beyond the limits of his present existence, he must, at least, desire to see his days roll on in happiness and in peace. Every man, who during the calm of his passions, falls back upon himself, will feel that his interest invites him to his own preservation; that his felicity rigorously demands he should take the necessary means to enjoy life peaceably that it becomes an imperative duty to himself to keep his actual abode free from alarm; his mind untainted by remorse. Man oweth something to man, not merely because he would offend any particular system, if he was to injure his fellow creature; but because in doing him an injury he would offend a man; would violate the laws of equity; in the maintenance of which every human being finds himself interested.

We every day see persons who are possessed of great talents, who have very extensive knowledge, who enjoy very keen penetration, join to these advantages a very corrupt heart; who lend, themselves to the most hideous vices: their opinions may be true in some respects, false in a great many others; their principles may be just, but their inductions are frequently defective; very often precipitate. A man may embrace sufficient knowledge to detect some of his errors, yet command too little energy to divest himself of his vicious propensities. Man is a being whose character depends upon his organization, modified by habit—upon his temperament, regulated by education—upon his propensities, marshalled by example—upon his; passions, guided by his government; in short, he is only what transitory or permanent circumstances make him: his superstitious ideas are obliged to yield to this temperament; his imaginary systems feel a necessity to accommodate themselves to his propensities; his theories give way to his interests. If the system which constitutes man an atheist in the eyes of this theologic friend, does not remove him from the vices with which he was anteriorly tainted, neither does it tincture him with any new ones; whereas, superstition furnishes its disciples with a thousand pretexts for committing evil without repugnance; induces them even to applaud themselves for the commission of crime. Atheism, at least, leaves men such as they are; it will neither increase a man's intemperance, nor add to his debaucheries, it will not render him more cruel than his temperament before invited him to be: whereas superstition either lacks the rein to the most terrible passions, gives loose to the most abominable suggestions, or else procures easy expiations for the most dishonourable vices. "Atheism," says Chancellor Bacon, "leaves to man reason, philosophy, natural piety, laws, reputation, and every thing that can serve to conduct him to virtue; but superstition destroys all these things, and erects itself into a tyranny over the understandings of men: this is the reason why atheism never disturbs the government, but renders man more clear-sighted, as seeing nothing beyond the bounds of this life." The same author adds, "that the times in which men have turned towards atheism, have been the most tranquil; whereas superstition has always inflamed their minds, and carried them on to the greatest disorders;

because it infatuates the people with novelties, which wrest from and carry with them all the authority of government."

Men, habituated to meditate, accustomed to make study a pleasure, are not commonly dangerous citizens: whatever may be their speculations, they never produce sudden revolutions upon the earth. The winds of the people, at all times susceptible to be inflamed by the marvellous, their dormant passions liable to be aroused by enthusiasm, obstinately resist the light of simple truths; never heat themselves for systems that demand a long train of reflection—that require the depth of the most acute reasoning. The system of atheism, as the priests choose to denominate it, can only be the result of long meditation; the fruit of connected study; the produce of an imagination cooled by experience: it is the child of reason. The peaceable Epicurus never disturbed Greece; his philosophy was publicly taught in Athens during many centuries; he was in incredible favour with his countrymen, who caused statues to be erected to him; he had a prodigious number of friends, and his school subsisted for a very long period. Cicero, although a decided enemy to the Epicureans, gives a brilliant testimony to the probity both of Epicurus and his disciples, who were remarkable for the inviolable friendship they bore each other. In the time of Marcus Aurelius, there was at Athens a public professor of the philosophy of Epicurus, paid by that emperor, who was himself a stoic. Hobbes did not cause blood to flow in England, although in his time, religious fanaticism made a king perish on the scaffold. The poem of Lucretius caused no civil wars in Rome; the writings of Spinosa did not excite the same troubles in Holland as the disputes of Gomar and D'Arminius. In short, we can defy the enemies to human reason to cite a single example, which proves in a decisive manner that opinions purely philosophical, or directly contrary to superstition, have ever excited disturbances in the state. Tumults have generally arisen from theological notions, because both princes and people have always foolishly believed they ought to take a part in them. There is nothing so dangerous as that empty philosophy, which the theologians have combined with their systems. It is to philosophy, corrupted by priests, that it peculiarly belongs to blow up the embers of discord; to invite the people to rebellion; to drench the earth with human blood. There is, perhaps, no theological question, which has not been the source of immense mischief to man; whilst all the writings of those denominated atheists, whether ancient or modern, have never caused any evil but to their authors; whom dominant imposture has frequently immolated at his deceptive shrine.

The principles of atheism are not formed for the mass of the people, who are commonly under the tutelage of their priests; they are not calculated for those frivolous capacities, not suited to those dissipated minds, who fill society with their vices, who hourly afford evidence of their own inutility; they will not gratify the ambitious; neither are they adapted to intriguers, nor fitted for those restless beings who find their immediate interest in disturbing the harmony of the social compact: much less are they made for a great number of persons, who, enlightened in other respects, have not sufficient courage to divorce themselves from the received prejudices.

So many causes unite themselves to confirm man in those errors which he draws in with his mother's milk, that every step that removes him from these endeared fallacies, costs him uncommon pain. Those persons who are most enlightened, frequently cling on some side to the general prepossession. By giving up these revered ideas, we feel ourselves, as it were, isolated in society: whenever we stand alone in our opinions, we no longer seem to speak the language of our associates; we are apt to fancy ourselves placed on a barren, desert island, in sight of a populous, fruitful country, which we can never reach: it therefore requires great courage to adopt a mode of thinking that has but few approvers. In those countries where human knowledge has made some progress; where, besides, a certain freedom of thinking is enjoyed, may easily be found a great number of deicolists, theists, or incredulous beings, who, contented with having trampled under foot the grosser prejudices of the illiterate, have not dared to go back to the source—to cite the more subtle systems before the tribunal of reason. If these thinkers did not stop on the road, reflection would quickly prove to them that those systems which they have not the fortitude to examine, are equally injurious to sound ratiocination, fully as revolting to good sense, quite as repugnant to the evidence of experience, as any of those doctrines, mysteries, fables, or superstitious customs, of which they have already acknowledged the futility; they would feel, as we have already proved, that all these things are nothing more than the necessary consequences of those primitive errors which man has indulged for so many ages in succession; that in admitting these errors, they no longer have any rational cause to reject the deductions which the imagination has drawn from them. A little attention would distinctly shew them, that it is precisely these errors that are the true cause of all the evils of society; that those endless disputes, those sanguinary quarrels, to which superstition and the spirit of party every instant give birth, are the inevitable effects of the importance they attach to errors which possess all the means of distraction, that scarcely ever fail to put the mind of man into a state of combustion. In short, nothing is more easy than to convince ourselves that imaginary systems, not reducible to comprehension, which are always painted under terrific aspects, must act upon the imagination in a very lively manner, must sooner or later produce disputes—engender enthusiasm—give birth to fanaticism—end in delirium.

Many persons acknowledge, that the extravagances to which superstition lends activity, are real evils; many complain of the abuse of superstition, but there are very few who feel that this abuse, together with the evils, are the necessary consequences of the fundamental principles of all superstition; which are founded upon the most grievous notions, which rest themselves on the most tormenting opinions. We daily see persons undeceived upon superstitious ideas, who nevertheless pretend that this superstition "is salutary for the people;" that without its supernatural magic, they could not be kept within due bounds; in other words, could not be made the voluntary slaves of the priest. But, to reason thus, is it not to say, poison is beneficial to mankind, that therefore it is proper to poison them, to prevent them from making an improper use of their power? Is it not in fact to pretend it is advantageous to render them absurd; that it is a profitable course to make them extravagant; wholesome to give them an irrational bias; that they have need of hobgoblins to blind them; require the most incomprehensible systems to make them giddy; that it is imperative to submit them either to impostors or to fanatics, who will avail themselves of their follies to disturb the repose of the world? Again, is it an ascertained fact, does experience warrant the conclusion, that superstition has a useful influence over the morals of the people? It appears much more evident, is much better borne out by observation, falls more in with the evidence of the senses, that it enslaves them without rendering them better; that it constitutes an herd of ignorant beings, whom panic terrors keep under the yoke of their task-masters; whom their useless fears render the wretched instruments of towering ambition—of rapacious tyrants; of the subtle craft of designing priests: that it forms stupid slaves, who are acquainted with no other virtue, save a blind submission to the most futile customs, to which they attach a much more substantive value than to the actual virtues springing out of the duties of morality; or issuing from the social compact which has never been made known to them. If by any chance, superstition does restrain some few individuals, it has no effect on the greater number, who suffer themselves to be hurried along by the epidemical vices with which they are infected: they are placed by it upon the stream of corruption, and the tide either sweeps them away, or else, swelling the waters, breaks through its feeble mounds, and involves the whole in one undistinguished mass of ruin. It is in those countries where superstition has the greatest power, that will always be found the least morality. Virtue is incompatible with ignorance; it cannot coalesce with superstition; it cannot exist with slavery: slaves can only be kept in subordination by the fear of punishment; ignorant children are for a moment intimidated by imaginary terrors. But freemen, the children of truth, have no fears but of themselves; are neither to be lulled into submission by visionary duties, nor coerced by fanciful systems; they yield ready obedience to the evident demonstrations of virtue; are the faithful, the invulnerable supporters of solid systems; cling with ardour to the dictates of reason; form impenetrable ramparts round their legitimate sovereigns; and fix their thrones on an immoveable basis, unknown to the theologian; that cannot be touched with unhallowed hands; whose duration will be commensurate with the existence of time itself. To form freemen, however, to have virtuous citizens, it is necessary to enlighten them; it is incumbent to exhibit truth to them; it is imperative to reason with them; it is indispensable to make them feel their interests; it is paramount to learn them to respect themselves; they must be instructed to fear shame; they must be excited to have a just idea of honour; they must be made familiar with the value of virtue, they must be shewn substantive motives for following its lessons. How can these happy effects ever be expected from the polluted fountains of superstition, whose waters do nothing more than degrade mankind? Or how are they to be obtained from the ponderous, bulky yoke of tyranny, which proposes nothing more to itself, than to vanquish them by dividing them; to keep them in the most abject condition by means of lascivious vices, and the most detestable crimes?

The false idea, which so many persons have of the utility of superstition, which they, at least, judge to be calculated to restrain the licentiousness of the illiterate, arise from the fatal prejudice that it is a useful error; that truth may be dangerous. This principle has complete efficacy to eternize the sorrows of the earth: whoever shall have the requisite courage to examine these things, will without hesitation acknowledge, that all the miseries of the human race are to be ascribed to his errors; that of these, superstitious error must he the most prejudicial, from the importance which is usually attached to it; from the haughtiness with which it inspires sovereigns; from the worthless condition which it prescribes to subjects; from the phrenzy which it excites among the vulgar. We shall, therefore, be obliged to conclude, that the superstitious errors of man, rendered sacred by time, are exactly those which for the permanent interest of mankind, for the well-being of society, for the security of the monarch himself, demand the most complete destruction; that it is principally to their annihilation, the efforts of a sound philosophy ought to be directed. It is not to be feared, that this attempt will produce either disorders or revolutions: the more freedom shall accompany the voice of truth, the more convincing it will appear; although the more simple it shall be, the less it will influence men, who are only smitten with the marvellous; even those individuals who most sedulously seek after truth, who pursue it with the greatest ardour, have frequently an irresistible inclination, that urges them on, and incessantly disposes them to reconcile error with its antipode. That great master of the art of thinking, who holds forth to his disciples such able advice, says, with abundant reason, "that there is nothing but a good and solid philosophy, which can, like another

Hercules, exterminate those monsters called popular errors: it is that alone which can give freedom to the human mind."

Here is, unquestionably, the true reason why atheism, as it is called, of which hitherto the principles have not been sufficiently developed, appears to alarm even those persons who are the most destitute of prejudice. They find the interval too great between vulgar superstition and an absolute renunciation of it; they imagine they take a wise medium in compounding with error; they therefore reject the consequences, while they admit the principle; they preserve the shadow and throw away the substance, without foreseeing that, sooner or later, it must, by its obstetric art, usher into the world, one after another, the same follies which now fill the heads of bewildered human beings, lost in the labyrinths of incomprehensible systems. The major part of the incredulous, the greater number of reformers, do no more than prune a cankered tree, to whose root they dare not apply the axe; they do not perceive that this tree will in the end produce the same fruit. Theology, or superstition, will always be an heap of combustible matter: brooded in the imagination of mankind, it will always finish by causing the most terrible explosions. As long as the sacerdotal order shall have the privilege of infecting youth—of habituating their minds to tremble before unmeaning words—of alarming nations with the most terrific systems, so long will fanaticism be master of the human mind; imposture will, at its pleasure, cast the apple of discord among the members of the state. The most simple error, perpetually fed, unceasingly modified, continually exaggerated by the imagination of man, will by degrees assume a collossal figure, sufficiently powerful to upset every institution; amply competent to the overthrow of empires. Theism is a system at which the human mind cannot make a long sojourn; founded upon error, it will, sooner or later, degenerate into the most absurd, the most dangerous superstition.

Many incredulous beings, many theists, are to be met with in those countries where freedom of opinion reigns; that is to say, where the civil power has known how to balance superstition. But, above all, atheists as they are termed, will be found in those nations where, superstition, backed by the sovereign authority, most enforces the ponderosity of its yoke; most impresses the volume of its severity; imprudently abuses its unlimited power. Indeed, when in these kind of countries, science, talents, the seeds of reflection, are not entirely stifled, the greater part of the men who think, revolt at the crying abuses of superstition; are ashamed of its multifarious follies; are shocked at the corruption of its professors; scandalized at the tyranny of its priests: are struck with horror at those massive chains which it imposes on the credulous. Believing with great reason, that they can never remove themselves too far from its savage principles, the system that serves for the basis of such a creed, becomes as odious as the superstition itself; they feel that terrific systems can only be detailed by cruel ministers; these become detestable objects to every enlightened, to every honest mind, in which either the love of equity, or the sacred fire of freedom resides; to every one who is the advocate of humanity—the indignant spurner of tyranny. Oppression gives a spring to the soul; it obliges man to examine closely into the cause of his sorrows; misfortune is a powerful incentive, that turns the mind to the side of truth. How formidable a foe must not outraged reason be to falsehood? It at least throws it into confusion, when it tears away its mask; when it follows it into its last entrenchment; when it proves, beyond contradiction, that *nothing is so dastardly as delusion detected, or tyrannic power held at bay.*

CHAP. XIII.

Of the motives which lead to what is falsely called Atheism.—Can this System be dangerous?—Can it be embraced by the Illiterate?

The reflections, as well as the facts which have preceded, will furnish a reply to those who inquire what interest man has in not admitting unintelligible systems? The tyrannies, the persecutions, the numberless outrages committed under these systems; the stupidity, the slavery, into which their ministers almost every where plunge the people; the sanguinary disputes to which they give birth; the multitude of unhappy beings with which their fatal notions fill the world; are surely abundantly sufficient to create the most powerful, the most interesting motives, to determine all sensible men, who possess the faculty of thought, to examine into the authenticity of doctrines, which cause so many serious evils to the inhabitants of the earth.

A theist, very estimable for his talents, asks, "if there can be any other cause than an evil disposition, which can make men atheists?" I reply to him, yes, there are other causes. There is the desire, a very laudable one, of having a knowledge of interesting truths; there is the powerful interest of knowing what opinions we ought to hold upon the object which is announced to us as the most important; there is the fear of deceiving ourselves upon systems which are occupied with the opinions of mankind, which do not permit he should deceive himself respecting them with impunity. But when these motives, these causes, should not subsist, is not indignation, or if they will, an evil disposition, a legitimate cause, a good and powerful motive, for closely examining the pretensions, for searching into the rights of systems, in whose name so many crimes are perpetrated? Can any man who feels, who thinks, who has any elasticity in his soul, avoid being incensed against austere theories, which are visibly the pretext, undeniably the source, of all those evils, which on every side assail the human race? Are they not these fatal systems which are at once the cause and the ostensible reason of that iron yoke that oppresses mankind; of that wretched slavery in which he lives; of that blindness which hides from him his happiness; of that superstition, which disgraces him; of those irrational customs which torment him; of those sanguinary quarrels which divide him; of all the outrages which he experiences? Must not every breast in which humanity is not extinguished, irritate itself against that theoretical speculation, which in almost every country is made to speak the language of capricious, inhuman, irrational tyrants?

To motives so natural, so substantive, we shall join those which are still more urgent, more personal to every reflecting man: namely, that benumbing terror, that incommodious fear, which must be unceasingly nourished by the idea of capricious theories, which lay man open to the most severe penalties, even for secret thoughts, over which he himself has not any controul; that dreadful anxiety arising out of inexorable systems, against which he may sin without even his own knowledge; of morose doctrines, the measure of which he can never be certain of having fulfilled; which so far from being equitable, make all the obligations lay on one side; which with the most ample means of enforcing restraint, freely permit evil, although they hold out the most excruciating punishments for the delinquents? Does it not then, embrace the best interests of humanity, become of the highest importance to the welfare of mankind, of the greatest consequence to the quiet of his existence, to verify the correctness of these systems? Can any thing be more rational than to probe to the core these astounding theories? Is it possible that any thing can be more just, than to inquire rigorously into the rights, sedulously to examine the foundations, to try by every known test, the stability of doctrines, that involve in their operations, consequences of such colossal magnitude; that embrace, in their dictatory mandates, matters of such high behest; that implicate the eternal felicity of such countless millions in the vortex of their action? Would it not be the height of folly to wear such a tremendous yoke without inquiry; to let such overwhelming notions pass current unauthenticated; to permit the soi-disant ministers of these terrific systems to establish their power, without the most ample verification of their patents of mission? Would it, I repeat, be at all wonderful, if the frightful qualities of some of these systems, as exhibited by their official expounders, whom the accredited functionaries of similar systems, do not scruple, in the face of day, to brand as impostors, should induce rational beings to drive them entirely from their hearts; to shake off such an intolerable burden of misery; to even deny the existence of such appalling doctrines, of such petrifying systems, which the superstitious themselves, whilst paying them their homage, frequently curse from the very bottom of their hearts?

The theist, however, will not fail to tell the atheist, as he calls him, that these systems are not such as superstition paints them; that the colours are coarse, too glaring, ill assorted, the perspective out of all keeping; he will then exhibit his own picture, in which the tints are certainly blended with more mellowness, the colouring of a more pleasing hue, the whole more harmonious, but the distances equally indistinct: the atheist, in reply, will say, that superstition itself, with all the absurd prejudices, all the mischievous notions to which it gives birth, are only corollaries drawn from the fallacious ideas, from those obscure principles, which the deicolist himself indulges. That his own incomprehensible system authorizes the incomprehensible absurdities, the inconceivable mysteries, with which superstition abounds; that they flow consecutively from his own premises; that when once the mind of mortals is bewildered in the dark, inextricable mazes of an ill-directed imagination, it will incessantly multiply its chimeras. To assure the repose of mankind, fundamental errors must be annihilated; that he may understand his true relations, be acquainted with his imperative duties, primary delusions must be rectified; to procure him that serenity of soul, without which there can be no substantive happiness, original fallacies must be undermined. If the systems of the superstitious be revolting, if their theories be gloomy, if their dogmas are unintelligible, those of the theist will always be contradictory; will prove fatal, when he shall be disposed to meditate upon them; will become the source of illusions, with which, sooner or later, imposture will not omit to abuse his credulity. Nature alone, with the truths she discovers, is capable of lending to the human mind that firmness which falsehood will never be able to shake; to the human heart that self-possession, against which imposture will in vain direct its attacks.

Let us again reply to those who unceasingly repeat that the interest of the passions alone conduct man to what is termed atheism: that it is the dread of future punishment that determines corrupt individuals to make the most strenuous efforts to break up a system they have reason to dread. We shall, without hesitation, agree that it is the interest of man's passions which excites him to make inquiries; without interest, no man is tempted to seek; without passion, no man will seek vigorously. The question, then, to be examined, is, if the passions and interests, which determine some thinkers to dive into the stability or the systems held forth to their adoption, are or are not legitimate? These interests have, already been exposed, from which it has been proved, that every rational man finds in his inquietudes, in his fears, reasonable motives to ascertain, whether or not it be necessary to pass his life in perpetual dread; in never ceasing agonies? Will it be said, that an unhappy being, unjustly condemned to groan in chains, has not the right of being willing to render them asunder; to take some means to liberate himself from his prison; to adopt some plan to escape from those punishments, which every instant threaten him? Will it be pretended that his passion for liberty has no legitimate foundation, that he does an injury to the companions of his misery, in withdrawing himself from the shafts of tyrannical infliction; or in furnishing, them also with means to escape from its cruel strokes? Is, then, an incredulous man, any thing more than one who has taken flight from the general prison, in which despotic superstition detains nearly all mankind? Is not an atheist, as he is called, who writes, one who has broken his fetters, who supplies to those of his associates who have sufficient courage to follow him, the means of setting themselves free from the terrors that menace them? The priests unceasingly repeat that it is pride, vanity, the desire of distinguishing himself from the generality of mankind, that determines man to incredulity. In this they are like some of those wealthy mortals, who treat all those as insolent who refuse to cringe before them. Would not every rational man have a right to ask the priest, where is thy superiority in matters of reasoning? What motives can I have to submit my reason to thy delirium? On the other hand, way it not be said to the hierarchy, that it is interest which makes them priests; that it is interest which renders them theologians; that it is for the interest of their passions, to inflate their pride, to gratify their avarice, to minister to their ambition, &c. that they attach themselves to systems, of which they alone reap the benefits? Whatever it may be, the priesthood, contented with exercising their power over the illiterate, ought to permit those men who do think, to be excused from bending the knee before their vain, illusive idols.

We also agree, that frequently the corruption of morals, a life of debauchery, a licentiousness of conduct, even levity of mind, may conduct man to incredulity; but is it not possible to be a libertine, to be irreligious, to make a parade of incredulity, without being on that account an atheist? There is unquestionably a difference between those who are led to renounce belief in unintelligible systems by dint of reasoning, and those who reject or despise superstition, only because they look upon it as a melancholy object, or an incommodious restraint. Many persons, no doubt, renounce received prejudices, through vanity or upon hearsay; these pretended strong minds have not examined any thing for themselves; they act upon the authority of others, whom they suppose to have weighed things more maturely. This kind of incredulous beings, have not, then, any distinct ideas, any substantive opinions, and are but little capacitated to reason for themselves; they are indeed hardly in a state to follow the reasoning of others. They are irreligious in the same manner as the majority of mankind are superstitious, that is to say, by credulity like the people; or through interest like the priest. A voluptuary devoted to his appetites; a debaucheé drowned in drunkenness; an ambitious mortal given up to his own schemes of aggrandizement; an intriguer surrounded by his plots; a frivolous, dissipated mortal, absorbed by his gewgaws, addicted to his puerile pursuits, buried in his filthy enjoyments; a loose woman abandoned to her irregular desires; a choice spirit of the day: are these I say, personages, actually competent to form a sound judgment of superstition, which they have never examined? Are they in a condition to maturely weigh theories that require the utmost depth of thought? Have they the capabilities to feel the force of a subtle argument; to compass the whole of a system: to embrace the various ramifications of an extended doctrine? If some feeble scintillations occasionally break in upon the cimmerian darkness of their minds; if by any accident they discover some faint glimmerings of truth amidst the tumult of their passions; if occasionally a sudden calm, suspending, for a short season, the tempest of their contending vices, permits the bandeau of their unruly desires by which they are blinded, to drop for an instant from their hoodwinked eyes, these leave on them only evanescent traces; scarcely sooner received than obliterated. Corrupt men only attack the gods when they conceive them to be the enemies to their vile passions. Arrian says, "that when men imagine the gods are in opposition to their passions, they abuse them, and overturn their altars." The Chinese, I believe, do the same. The honest man makes war against systems which he finds are inimical to virtue—injurious to his own happiness—baneful to that of his fellow mortals—contradictory to the repose, fatal to the interests of the human species. The bolder, therefore, the sentiments of the honest atheist, the more strange his ideas, the more suspicious they appear to other men, the more strictly he ought to observe his own obligations; the more scrupulously he should perform his duties; especially if he be not desirous that his morals shall calumniate his system; which duly weighed, will make the necessity of sound ethics, the certitude of morality, felt in all its force; but which every species of superstition tends to render problematical, or to corrupt.

Whenever our will is moved by concealed and complicated motives, it is extremely difficult to decide what determines it; a wicked man may be conducted to incredulity or to scepticism by those motives which he dare not avow, even to himself; in believing he seeks after truth, he may form an illusion to his mind, only to follow the interest of his passions; the fear of an avenging system will perhaps determine him to deny their existence without examination; uniformly because he feels them incommodious. Nevertheless, the passions sometimes happen to be just; a great interest carries us on to examine things more minutely; it may frequently make a discovery of the truth, even to him who seeks after it the least, or who is only desirous to be lulled to sleep, who is only solicitous to deceive himself. It is the same with a perverse man who stumbles upon truth, as it is with him, who flying from an imaginary danger, should encounter in his road a dangerous serpent, which in his haste he should destroy; he does that by accident, without design, which a man, less disturbed in his mind, would have done with premeditated deliberation.

To judge properly of things, it is necessary to be disinterested; it is requisite to have an enlightened mind, to have connected ideas to compass a great system. It belongs, in fact, only to the honest man to examine the proofs of systems—to scrutinize the principles of superstition; it belongs only to the man acquainted with nature, conversant with her ways, to embrace with intelligence the cause of the SYSTEM OF NATURE. The wicked are incapable of judging with temper; the ignorant are inadequate to reason with accuracy; the honest, the virtuous, are alone competent judges in so weighty an affair. What do I say? Is not the virtuous man, from thence in a condition to ardently desire the existence of a system that remunerates the goodness of men? If he renounces those advantages, which his virtue confers upon him the right to hope, it is, undoubtedly, because he finds them imaginary. Indeed, every man who reflects will quickly perceive, that for one timid mortal, of whom these systems restrain the feeble passions, there are millions whose voice they cannot curb, of whom, on the contrary, they excite the fury; for one that they console, there are millions whom they affright, whom they afflict; whom they make unhappy: in short, he finds, that against one inconsistent enthusiast, which these systems, which are thought so excellent, render happy, they carry discord, carnage, wretchedness into vast countries; plunge whole nations into misery; deluge them with tears.

However this may be, do not let us inquire into motives which may determine a man to embrace a system; let us rather examine the system itself; let us convince ourselves of its rectitude; if we shall find that it is founded upon truth, we shall never, be able to esteem it dangerous. It is always falsehood that is injurious to man; if error be visibly the source of his sorrows, reason is the true remedy for them; this is the panacea that can alone carry consolation to his afflictions. Do not let us farther examine the conduct of a man who presents us with a system; his ideas, as we have already said, may be extremely sound, when even his actions are highly deserving of censure. If the system of atheism cannot make him perverse, who is not so by his temperament, it cannot render him good, who does not otherwise know the motives that should conduct him to virtue. At least we have proved, that the superstitious man, when he has strong passions, when he possesses a depraved heart, finds even in his creed a thousand pretexts more than the atheist, for injuring the human species. The atheist has not, at least, the mantle of zeal to cover his vengeance; he has not the command of his priest to palliate his transports; he has not the glory of his gods to countenance his fury; the atheist does not enjoy the faculty of expiating, at the expence of a sum of money, the transgressions of his life; of availing himself of certain ceremonies, by the aid of which he may atone for the outrages he may have committed against society; he has not the advantage of being able to reconcile himself with heaven, by some easy custom; to quiet the remorse of his disturbed conscience, by an attention to outward forms: if crime has not deadened every feeling of his heart, he is obliged continually to carry within himself an inexorable judge, who unceasingly reproaches him for his odious conduct; who forces him to blush for his own folly; who compels him to hate himself; who imperiously obliges him to fear examination, to dread the resentment of others. The superstitious man, if he be wicked, gives himself up to crime, which is followed by remorse; but his superstition quickly furnishes him with the means a getting rid of it; his life is generally no more than a long series of error and grief, of sin and expiation, following each other in alternate succession; still more, he frequently, as we have seen, perpetrates crimes of greater magnitude, in order to wash away the first. Destitute of any permanent ideas on morality, he accustoms himself to look upon nothing as criminal, but that which the ministers, the official expounders of his system, forbid him to commit: he considers actions of the blackest dye as virtues, or as the means of effacing those transgressions, which are frequently held out to him as faithfully executing the duties of his creed. It is thus we have seen fanatics expiate their adulteries by the most atrocious persecutions; cleanse their souls from infamy by the most unrelenting cruelty; make atonement for unjust wars by the foulest means; qualify their usurpations by outraging every principle of virtue; in order to wash away their iniquities, bathe themselves in the blood of those superstitious victims, whose infatuation made them martyrs.

An atheist, as he is falsely called, if he has reasoned justly, if he has consulted nature, hath principles more determinate, more humane, than the superstitious; his system, whether gloomy or enthusiastic, always conducts the latter either to folly or cruelty; the imagination of the former will never be intoxicated to that degree, to make him believe that violence, injustice, persecution, or assassination are either virtuous or legitimate actions. We every day see that superstition, or the cause of heaven, as it is called, hoodwinks even those persons who on every other occasion are humane, equitable, and rational; so much so, that they make it a paramount duty to treat with determined barbarity, those men who happen to step aside from their mode of thinking. An heretic, an incredulous being, ceases to be a man, in the eyes of the superstitious. Every society, infected with the venom of bigotry, offers innumerable examples of juridical assassination, which the tribunals commit without scruple, even without remorse. Judges who are equitable on every other occasion, are no longer so when there is a question of theological opinions; in steeping their hands in the blood of their victims, they believe, on the authority of the priests, they conform themselves to the views of the Divinity. Almost every where the laws are subordinate to superstition; make themselves accomplices in its fanatical fury; they legitimate those actions most opposed to the gentle voice of humanity; they even transform into imperative duties, the most barbarous cruelties. The president Grammont relates, with a satisfaction truly worthy of a cannibal, the particulars of the punishment of Vanini, who was burned at Thoulouse, although he had disavowed the opinions with which he was accused; this president carries his demoniac prejudices so far, as to find wickedness in the piercing cries, in the dreadful howlings, which torment wrested from this unhappy victim to superstitious vengeance. Are not all these avengers of the gods miserable men, blinded by their piety, who, under the impression of duty, wantonly immolate at the shrine of superstition, those wretched victims whom the priests deliver over to them? Are they not savage tyrants, who have the rank injustice to violate thought; who have the folly to believe they can enslave it? Are they not delirious fanatics, on whom the law, dictated by the most inhuman prejudices, imposes the necessity of acting like ferocious brutes? Are not all those sovereigns, who to gratify the vanity of the priesthood, torment and persecute their subjects, who sacrifice to their anthropophagite gods human victims, men whom superstitious zeal has converted into tygers? Are not those priests, so careful of the soul's health, who insolently break into the sacred sanctuary of man's mind, to the end that they may find in his opinions motives for doing him an injury, abominable knaves, disturbers of the public repose, whom superstition honours, but whom virtue detests? What villains are more odious in the eyes of humanity, what depredators more hateful to the eye of reason, than those infamous inquisitors, who by the blindness of princes, by the delirium of monarchs, enjoy the advantage of passing judgment on their own enemies; who ruthlessly commit them to the charity of the flames? Nevertheless, the fatuity of the people makes even these monsters respected; the favour of kings covers them with kindness; the mantle of superstitious opinion shields them from the effect of the just execration of every honest man. Do not a thousand examples prove, that superstition has every where produced the most frightful ravages: that it has continually justified the most unaccountable horrors? Has it not a thousand times armed its votaries with the dagger of the homicide; let loose passions much wore terrible than those which it pretended to restrain; broken up the most sacred bonds by which mortals are connected with each other? Has it not, under the pretext of duty, under the colour of faith, under the semblance of zeal, under the sacred name of piety, favoured cupidity, lent wings to ambition, countenanced cruelty, given a spring to tyranny? Has it not legitimatized murder; given a system to perfidy; organized rebellion; made a virtue of regicide? Have not those princes who have been foremost as the avengers of heaven, who have been the lictors of superstition, frequently themselves become its victims? In short, has it not been the signal for the most dismal follies, the most wicked outrages, the most horrible massacres? Has not its altars been drenched with human gore? Under whatever form it has been exhibited, has it not always been the ostensible cause of the most bare-faced violation—of the sacred rights of humanity?

Never will an atheist, as he is called, as called, as he enjoys his proper senses, persuade himself that similar actions can be justifiable; never will he believe that he who commits them can be an estimable man; there is no one but the superstitious, whose blindness makes him forget the most evident principles of morality, whose callous soul renders him deaf to the voice of nature, whose zeal causes him to overlook the dictates of reason, who can by any possibility imagine the most destructive crimes are the most prominent features of virtue. If the atheist be perverse, he, at least, knows that he acts wrong; neither these systems, nor their priests, will be able to persuade him that he does right: one thing, however, is certain, whatever crimes he may allow himself to commit, he will never be capable of exceeding those which superstition perpetrates without scruple; that it encourages in those whom it intoxicates with its fury; to whom it frequently holds forth wickedness itself, either as expiations for offences, or else as orthodox, meritorious actions.

Thus the atheist, however wicked he may be supposed, will at most be upon a level with the devotee, whose superstition encourages him to commit crimes, which it transforms into virtue. As to conduct, if he be debauched, voluptuous, intemperate, adulterous, the atheist in this differs in nothing from the most credulously superstitious, who frequently knows how to connect these vices with his credulity, to blend with his superstition certain atrocities, for which his priests, provided he renders due homage to their power, especially if he augments their exchequer, will always find means to pardon him. If he be in Hindoostan, his brahmins will wash him in the sacred waters of the Ganges, while reciting a prayer. If he be a Jew, upon making an offering, his sins will be effaced. If he be in Japan, he will be cleansed by performing a pilgrimage. If he be a Mahometan, he will be reputed a saint, for having visited the tomb of his prophet; the Roman pontiff himself will sell him indulgences; but none of them will ever censure him for those crimes he may have committed in the support of their several faiths.

We are constantly told, that the indecent behaviour of the official expounders of superstition, the criminal conduct of the priests, or of their sectaries, proves nothing against the goodness of their systems. Admitted: but wherefore do they not say the same thing of the conduct of those whom they call atheists, who, as we have already proved, way have a very substantive, a very correct system of morality, even while leading a very dissolute life? If it be necessary to judge the opinions of mankind according to their conduct, which is the theory that would bear the scrutiny? Let us, then, examine the opinion of the atheist, without approving his conduct; let us adopt his mode of thinking, if we find it marked by the truth; if it shall appear useful; if it shall be proved rational; but let us reject his mode of action, if that should be found blameable. At the sight of a work performed with truth, we do not embarrass ourselves with the morals of the workman: of what importance is it to the universe, whether the illustrious Newton was a sober, discreet citizen, or a debauched intemperate man? It only remains for us to examine his theory; we want nothing more than to know whether he has reasoned acutely; if his principles be steady; if the parts of his system are connected; if his work contains more demonstrable truths, than bold ideas? Let us judge in the same manner of the principles of the atheist; if they appear strange, if they are unusual, that is a solid reason for probing them more strictly; if he has spoken truth, if he has demonstrated his positions, let us yield to the weight of evidence; if he be deceived in some parts, let us distinguish the true from the false; but do not let us fall into the hacknied prejudice, which on account of one error in the detail, rejects a multitude of incontestible truisms. Doctor Johnson, I think, says in his preface to his Dictionary, "when a man shall have executed his task with all the accuracy possible, he will only be allowed to have done his duty; but if he commits the slightest error, a thousand snarlers are ready to point it out." The atheist, when he is deceived, has unquestionably as much right to throw his faults on the fragility of his nature, as the superstitious man. An atheist may have vices, may be defective, he may reason badly; but his errors will never have the consequences of superstitious novelties; they will not, like these, kindle up the fire of discord in the bosom of nations; the atheist will not justify his vices, defend his wanderings by superstition; he will not pretend to infallibility, like those self-conceited theologians who attach the Divine sanction to their follies; who initiate that heaven authorizes those sophisms, gives currency to those falsehoods, approves those errors, which they believe themselves warranted to distribute over the face of the earth.

It will perhaps be said, that the refusal to believe in these systems, will rend asunder one of the most powerful bonds of society, by making the sacredness of an oath vanish. I reply, that perjury is by no means rare, even in the most superstitious nations, nor even among the most religious, or among those who boast of being the most thoroughly convinced of the rectitude of their theories. Diagoras, superstitious as he was, and it was not well possible to be more so, it is said became an atheist, on seeing that the gods did not thunder their vengeance on a man who had taken them as evidence to a falsity. Upon this principle, how many atheists ought there to be? From the systems that have made invisible unknown beings the depositaries of man's engagements, we do not always see it result that they are better observed; or that the most solemn contracts have acquired a greater solidity. If history was consulted, it would now and then be in evidence, that even the conductors of nations, those who have said they were the images of the Divinity, who have declared that they held their right of governing immediately from his hands, have sometimes taken the Deity as the witness to their oaths, have made him the guarantee of their treaties, without its having had all the effect that might have been expected, when very trifling interests have intervened; it would appear, unless historians are incorrect, that they did not always religiously observe those sacred engagements they made with their allies, much less with their subjects. To form a judgment from these historic documents, we should be inclined to say, there have been those who had much superstition, joined with very little probity; who made a mockery both of gods and men; who perhaps blushed when they reviewed their own conduct: nor can this be at all surprising, when it not unfrequently happened that superstition itself absolved them from their oaths. In fact, does not superstition sometimes inculcate perfidy; prescribe violation of plighted faith? Above all, when there is a question of its own interests, does it not dispense with engagements, however solemn, made with those whom it condemns? It is, I believe, a maxim in the Romish church, that *"no faith is to be held with heretics."* The general council of Constance decided thus, when, notwithstanding the emperor's passport, it decreed John Hus and Jerome of Prague to be burnt. The Roman pontiff has, it is well known, the right of relieving his sectaries from their oaths; of annulling their vows: this same pontiff has frequently arrogated to himself the right of deposing kings; of absolving their subjects from their oaths of fidelity. Indeed, it is rather extraordinary that oaths should be prescribed, by the laws of those nations which profess Christianity, seeing that Christ has expressly forbidden the use of them. If things were considered attentively, it would be obvious that under such management, superstition and politics are schools of perjury. They render it common: thus knaves of every description never recoil, when it is necessary to attest the name of the Divinity to the most manifest frauds, for the vilest interests. What end, then, do oaths answer? They are snares, in which simplicity alone can suffer itself to be caught: oaths, almost every where, are vain formalities, that impose nothing upon villains; nor do they add any thing to the sacredness of the engagements of honest men; who would neither have the temerity nor the wish to violate them; who would not think themselves less bound without an oath. A perfidious, perjured, superstitious being, has not any advantage over an atheist, who should fail in his promises: neither the one nor the other any longer deserves the confidence of their fellow citizens nor the esteem of good men; if one does not respect his gods, in whom he believes, the other neither respects his reason, his reputation, nor public opinion, in which all rational men cannot refuse to believe. Hobbes says, "an oath adds nothing to the obligation. For a covenant, if lawful, binds in the sight of God, without the oath, as much as with it: if unlawful, bindeth not at all: though it be confirmed with an oath." The heathen form was, "let Jupiter kill me else, as I kill this beast." Adjuration only augments, in the imagination of him who swears, the fear of violating an engagement, which he would have been obliged to keep, even without the ceremony of an oath.

It has frequently been asked, if there ever was a nation that had no idea of the Divinity: and if a people, uniformly composed of atheists, would be able to subsist? Whatever some speculators may say, it does not appear likely that there ever has been upon our globe, a numerous people who have not had an idea of some invisible power, to whom they have shewn marks of respect and submission: it has been sometimes believed that the Chinese were atheists: but this is an error, due to the Christian missionaries, who are accustomed to treat all those as atheists, who do not hold opinions similar with their own upon Divinity. It always appears that the Chinese are a people extremely addicted to superstition, but that they are governed by chiefs who are not so, without however their being atheists for that reason. If the empire of China be as flourishing as it is said to be, it at least furnishes a very forcible proof that those who govern have no occasion to be themselves superstitious, in order to govern with propriety a people who are so. It is pretended that the Greenlanders have no idea of the Divinity. Nevertheless, it is difficult to believe it of a nation so savage. Man, inasmuch as he is a fearful, ignorant animal, necessarily becomes superstitious in his misfortunes: either he forms gods for himself, or he admits the gods which others are disposed to give him; it does not then appear, that we can rationally suppose there may have been, or that there actually is, a people on the earth a total stranger to some Divinity. One will shew us the sun, the moon, or the stars; the other will shew us the sea, the lakes, the rivers, which furnish him his subsistence, the trees which afford him an asylum against the inclemency of the weather; another will shew us a rock of an odd form; a lofty mountain; or a volcano that frequently astonishes him by its emission of lava; another will present you with his crocodile, whose malignity he fears; his dangerous serpent, the reptile to which he attributes his good or bad fortune. In short, each individual will make you behold his phantasm or his tutelary or domestic gods with respect.

But from the existence of his gods, the savage does not draw the same inductions as the civilized, polished man: the savage does not believe it a duty to reason continually upon their qualities; he does not imagine that they ought to influence his morals, nor entirely occupy his thoughts: content with a gross, simple, exterior worship, he does not believe that these invisible powers trouble themselves with his conduct towards his fellow creatures; in short, he does not connect his morality with his superstition. This morality is coarse, as must be that of all ignorant people; it is proportioned to his wants, which are few; it is frequently irrational, because it is the fruit of ignorance; of inexperience; of the passions of men but slightly restrained, or to say thus, in their infancy. It is only numerous, stationary, civilized societies, where man's wants are multiplied, where his interests clash, that he is obliged to have recourse to government, to laws, to public worship, in order to maintain concord. It is then, that men approximating, reason together, combine their ideas, refine their notions, subtilize their theories; it is then also, that those who govern them avail themselves of invisible powers, to keep them within bounds, to render them docile, to enforce their obedience, to oblige them to live peaceably. It was thus, that by degrees, morals and politics found themselves associated with superstitious systems. The chiefs of nations, frequently, themselves, the children of superstition, but little enlightened upon their actual interests; slenderly versed in sound morality; with an extreme exilty of knowledge on the actuating motives of the human heart; believed they had effected every thing requisite for the stability of their own authority; as well as achieved all that could guarantee the repose of society, that could consolidate the happiness of the people, in rendering their subjects superstitious like themselves; by menacing them with the wrath of invisible powers; in treating them like infants who are appeased with fables, like children who are terrified by shadows. By the assistance of these marvellous inventions, to which even the chiefs, the conductors of nations, are themselves frequently the dupes; which are transmitted as heirlooms from race to race; sovereigns were dispensed from the trouble of instructing themselves in their duties; they in consequence neglected the laws, enervated themselves in luxurious ease, rusted in sloth; followed nothing but their caprice: the care of restraining their subjects was reposed in their deities; the instruction of the people was confided to their priests, who were commissioned to train them to obedience, to make them submissive, to render them devout, to teach them at an early age to tremble under the yoke of both the visible and invisible gods.

It was thus that nations, kept by their tutors in a perpetual state of infancy, were only restrained by vain, chimerical theories. It was thus that politics, jurisprudence, education, morality, were almost every where infected with superstition; that man no longer knew any duties, save those which grew out of its precepts: the ideas of virtue were thus falsely associated with those of imaginary systems, to which imposture generally gave that language which was most conducive to its own immediate interests: mankind thus fully persuaded, that without these marvellous systems, there could not exist any sound morality, princes, as well as subjects, equally blind to their actual interests, to the duties of nature, to their reciprocal rights, habituated themselves to consider superstition as necessary to mortals—as indispensibly requisite to govern men—as the most effectual method of preserving power—as the most certain means of attaining happiness.

It is from these dispositions, of which we have so frequently demonstrated the fallacy, that so many persons, otherwise extremely enlightened, look upon it as an impossibility that a society formed of atheists, as they are termed, could subsist for any length of time. It does not admit a question, that a numerous society, who should neither have religion, morality, government, laws, education, nor principles, could not maintain itself; that it would simply congregate beings disposed to injure each other, or children who would follow nothing but the blindest impulse; but then is it not a lamentable fact, that with all the superstition that floats in the world, the greater number of human societies are nearly in this state? Are not the sovereigns of almost every country in a continual state of warfare with their subjects? Are not the people, in despite of their superstition, not withstanding the terrific notions which it holds forth, unceasingly occupied with reciprocally injuring each other; with rendering themselves mutually unhappy? Does not superstition itself, with its supernatural notions, unremittingly flatter the vanity of monarchs, unbridle the passions of princes, throw oil into the fire of discord, which it kindles between those citizens who are divided in their opinion? Could those infernal powers, who are supposed to be ever on the alert to mischief mankind, be capable of inflicting greater evils upon the human race than spring from fanaticism, than arise out of the fury to which theology gives birth? Could atheists, however irrational they may be supposed, if assembled together in society, conduct themselves in a more criminal manner? In short, is it possible they could act worse than the superstitious, who, saturated with the most pernicious vices, guided by the most extravagant systems, during so many successive ages, have done nothing more than torment themselves with the most cruel inflictions; savagely cut each other's throats, without a shadow of reason; make a merit of mutual extermination? It cannot be pretended they would. On the contrary, we boldly assert, that a community of atheists, as the theologian calls them, because they cannot fall in with his mysteries, destitute of all superstition, governed by wholesome laws, formed by a salutary education, invited to the practice of virtue by instantaneous recompences, deterred from crime by immediate punishments, disentangled from illusive theories, unsophisticated by falsehood, would be decidedly more honest, incalculably more virtuous, than those superstitious societies, in which every thing contributes to intoxicate the mind; where every thing conspires to corrupt the heart.

When we shall be disposed usefully to occupy ourselves with the happiness of mankind, it is with superstition that the reform must commence; it is by abstracting these imaginary theories, destined to affright the ignorant, who are completely in a state of infancy, that we shall be able to promise ourselves the desirable harvest of conducting man to a state of maturity. It cannot be too often repeated, there can be no morality without consulting the nature of man, without studying his actual relations with the beings of his own species; there can be no fixed principle for man's conduct, while it is regulated upon unjust theories; upon capricious doctrines; upon corrupt systems; there can be no sound politics without attending to human temperament, without contemplating him as a being associated for the purpose of satisfying his wants, consolidating his happiness, and assuring its enjoyment. No wise government can found itself upon despotic systems; they will always make tyrants of their representatives. No laws can be wholesome, that do not bottom themselves upon the strictest equity; which have not for their object the great end of human society. No jurisprudence can be advantageous for nations, if its administration be regulated by capricious systems, or by human passions deified. No education can be salutary, unless it be founded upon reason; to be efficacious to its proposed end, it must neither be construed upon chimerical theories, nor upon received prejudices. In short, there can be no probity, no talents, no virtue, either under corrupt masters, or under the conduct of those priests who render man the enemy to himself—the determined foe to others; who seek to stifle in his bosom the germ of reason; who endeavour to smother science, or who try to damp his courage.

It will, perhaps, be asked, if we can reasonably flatter ourselves with ever reaching the point to make a whole people entirely forget their superstitious opinions; or abandon the ideas which they have of their gods? I reply, that the thing appears utterly impossible; that this is not the end we can propose to ourselves. These ideas, inculcated from the earliest ages, do not appear of a nature to admit eradication from the mind of the majority of mankind: it would, perhaps be equally arduous to give them to those persons, who, arrived at a certain time of life, should never have heard them spoken of, as to banish them from the minds of those, who have been imbued with them from their tenderest infancy. Thus, it cannot be reckoned possible to make a whole nation pass from the abyss of superstition, that is to say, from the bosom of ignorance, from the ravings of delirium, into absolute naturalism, or as the priests of superstition would denominate it, into atheism; which supposes reflection—requires intense study—demands extensive knowledge—exacts a long series of experience—includes the habit of contemplating nature—the faculty of observing her laws; which, in short, embraces the expansive science of the causes producing her various phenomena; her multiplied combinations, together with the diversified actions of the beings she contains, as well as their numerous properties. In order to be an atheist, or to be assured of the capabilities of nature, it is imperative to have meditated her profoundly: a superficial glance of the eye will not bring man acquainted with her resources; optics but little practised on her powers, will unceasingly be deceived; the ignorance of actual causes will always induce the supposition of those which are imaginary; credulity will, thus re-conduct the natural philosopher himself to the feet of superstitious phantoms, in which either his limited vision, or his habitual sloth, will make him believe he shall find the solution to every difficulty.

Atheism, then, as well as philosophy, like all profound abstruse sciences, is not calculated for the vulgar; neither is it suitable to the great mass of mankind. There are, in all populous, civilized nations, persons whose circumstances enable them to devote their time to meditation, whose easy finances afford them leisure to make deep researches into the nature of things, who frequently make useful discoveries, which, sooner or later, after they have been submitted to the infallible test of experience, when they have passed the fiery ordeal of truth, extend widely their salutary effects, become extremely beneficial to society, highly advantageous to individuals. The geometrician, the chemist, the mechanic, the natural philosopher, the civilian, the artizan himself, are industriously employed, either in their closets, or in their workshops, seeking the means to serve society, each in his sphere: nevertheless, not one of their sciences or professions are familiar to the illiterate; not one of the arts with which they are respectively occupied, are known to the uninitiated: these, however, do not fail, in the long run, to profit by them, to reap substantive advantages from those labours, of which they themselves have no idea. It is for the mariner, that the astronomer explores his arduous science; it is for him the geometrician calculates; for his use the mechanic plies his craft: it is for the mason, for the carpenter, for the labourer, that the skilful architect studies his orders, lays down well-proportioned elaborate plans. Whatever may be the pretended utility of Pneumatology, whatever may be the vaunted advantages of superstitious opinions, the wrangling polemic, the subtle theologian, cannot boast either of toiling, of writing, or of disputing for the advantage of the people, whom, notwithstanding, he contrives to tax, very exorbitantly, for those systems they can never understand; from whom he levies the most oppressive contributions, as a remuneration for the detail of those mysteries, which under any possible circumstances, cannot, at any time whatever, be of the slightest benefit to them. It is not, then, for the multitude that a philosopher should propose to himself, either to write or to meditate: the Code of Nature, or the principles of atheism, as the priest calls it, are not, as we have shewn, even calculated for the meridian of a great number of persons, who are frequently too much prepossessed in favour of the received prejudices, although extremely enlightened on other points. It is extremely rare to find men, who, to an enlarged mind, extensive knowledge, great talents, join either a well regulated imagination, or the courage necessary to successfully oppugn habitual errors; triumphantly to attack those chimerical systems, with which the brain has been inoculated from the first hour of its birth. A secret bias, an invincible inclination, frequently, in despite of all reasoning, re-conducts the most comprehensive, the best fortified, the most liberal minds, to those prejudices which have a wide-spreading establishment; of which they have themselves taken copious draughts during the early stages of life. Nevertheless, those principles, which at first appear strange, which by their boldness seem revolting, from which timidity flies with trepidation, when they have the sanction of truth, gradually insinuate themselves into the human mind, become familiar to its exercise, extend their happy influence on every side, and finally produce the most substantive advantages to society. In time, men habituate themselves to ideas which originally they looked upon as absurd; which on a superficial glance they contemplated as either noxious or irrational: at least, they cease to consider those as odious, who profess opinions upon subjects on which experience makes it evident they may be permitted to have doubts, without imminent danger to public tranquillity.

Then the diffusion of ideas among mankind is not an event to be dreaded: if they are truths, they will of necessity be useful: by degrees they will fructify. The man who writes, must neither fix his eyes upon the time in which he lives, upon his actual fellow citizens, nor upon the country he inhabits. He must speak to the human race; he must instruct future generations; he must extend his views into the bosom of futurity; in vain he will expect the eulogies of his contemporaries; in vain will he flatter himself with seeing his reasoning adopted; in vain he will soothe himself with the pleasing reflection, that his precocious principles will be received with kindness; if he has exhibited truisms, the ages that shall follow will do justice to his efforts; unborn nations shall applaud his exertions; his future countrymen shall crown his sturdy attempts with those laurels, which interested prejudice withholds from him in his own days; it must therefore be from posterity, he is to expect the need of applause due to his services; the present race is hermetically sealed against him: meantime let him content himself with having done well; with the secret suffrages of those few friends to veracity who are so thinly spread over the surface of the earth. It is after his death, that the trusty reasoner, the faithful writer, the promulgator of sterling principles, the child of simplicity, triumphs; it is then that the stings of hatred, the shafts of envy, the arrows of malice, either exhausted or blunted, enable mankind to judge with impartiality; to yield to conviction; to establish eternal truth upon its own imperishable altars, which from its essence must survive all the error of the earth. It is then that calumny, crushed like the devouring snail by the careful gardener, ceases to besmear the character of an honest man, while its venomous slime, glazed by the sun, enables the observant spectator to trace the filthy progress it had made.

It is a problem with many people, *if truth may not be injurious?* The best intentioned persons are frequently in great doubt upon this important point. The fact is, *it never injures any but those who deceive mankind*: this has, however, the greatest interest in being undeceived. Truth may be injurious to the individual who announces it, but it can never by any possibility harm the human species; never can it be too distinctly presented to beings, always either little disposed to listen to its dictates, or too slothful to comprehend its efficacy. If all those who write to publish important truths, which, of all others, are ever considered the most dangerous, were sufficiently ardent for the public welfare to speak freely, even at the risk of displeasing their readers, the human race would be much more enlightened, much happier than it now is. To write in ambiguous terms, is very frequently to write to nobody. The human mind is idle; we must spare it, as much as possible, the trouble of reflection; we must relieve it from the embarrassment of intense thinking. What time does it not consume, what study does it not require, at the present day, to unravel the amphibological oracles of the ancient philosophers, whose actual sentiments are almost entirely lost to the present race of men? If truth be useful to human beings, it is an injustice to deprive them of its advantages; if truth ought to be admitted, we must admit its consequences, which are also truths. Man, taken generally, is fond of truth, but its consequences often inspire him with so much dread, so alarm his imbecility, that, frequently, he prefers remaining in error, of which a confirmed habit prevents him from feeling the deplorable effects. Besides, we shall say with Hobbes, "that we cannot do men any harm by proposing truth to them; the worst mode is to leave them in doubt, to let them remain in dispute." If an author who writes be deceived, it is because he may have reasoned badly. Has he laid down false principles? It remains to examine them. Is his system fallacious? Is it ridiculous? It will serve to make truth appear with the greatest splendor: his work will fall into contempt; the writer, if he be witness to its fall, will be sufficiently punished for his temerity; if he be defunct, the living cannot disturb his ashes. No man writes with a design to injure his fellow creatures; he always proposes to himself to merit their suffrages, either by amusing them, by exciting their curiosity, or by communicating to them discoveries, which he believes useful. Above all, no work can be really dangerous, if it contains truth. It would not be so, even if it contained principles evidently contrary to experience—opposed to good sense. Indeed, what would result from a work that should now tell us the sun is not luminous; that parricide is legitimate; that robbery is allowable; that adultery is not a crime? The smallest reflection would make us feet the falsity of these principles; the whole human race would protest against them. Men would laugh at the folly of the author; presently his book, together with his name, would be known only by its ridiculous extravagancies. There is nothing but superstitious follies that are pernicious to mortals; and wherefore? It is because authority always pretends to establish them by violence; to make them pass for substantive virtues; rigorously punishes those who shall be disposed to smile at their inconsistency, or examine into their pretensions. If man was more rational, he would examine superstitious opinions as he examines every thing else; he would look upon theological theories with the same eyes that he contemplates systems of natural philosophy, or problems in geometry: the latter never disturbs the repose of society, although they sometimes excite very warm disputes in the learned world. Theological quarrels would never be attended with any evil consequences, if man could gain the desirable point of making those who exercise power, feel that the disputes of persons, who do not themselves understand the marvellous questions upon which they never cease wrangling, ought not to give birth to any other sensations than those of indifference; to rouse no other passion than that of contempt.

It is, at least, this indifference not speculative theories, so just, so rational, so advantageous for states, that sound philosophy may propose to introduce, gradually, upon the earth. Would not the human race be much happier—if the sovereigns of the world, occupied with the welfare of their subjects, leaving to superstitious theologians their futile contests, making their various systems yield to healthy politics; obliged these haughty ministers to become citizens; carefully prevented their disputes from interrupting the public tranquillity? What advantage might there not result to science; what a start would be given to the progress of the human mind, to the cause of sound morality, to the advancement of equitable jurisprudence, to the improvement of legislation, to the diffusion of education, from an unlimited freedom of thought? At present, genius every where finds trammels; superstition invariably opposes itself to its course; man, straitened with bandages, scarcely enjoys the free use of any one of his faculties; his mind itself is cramped; it appears continually wrapped up in the swaddling clothes of infancy. The civil power, leagued with spiritual domination, appears only disposed to rule over brutalized slaves, shut up in a dark prison, where they reciprocally goad each other with the efferverscence of their mutual ill humour. Sovereigns, in general, detest liberty of thought, because they fear truth; this appears formidable to them, because it would condemn their excesses; these irregularities are dear to them, because they do not, better than their subjects, understand their true interests; properly considered, these ought to blend themselves into one uniform mass.

Let not the courage of the philosopher, however, be abated by so many united obstacles, which would appear for ever to exclude truth from its proper dominion; to banish reason from the mind of man; to spoil nature of her imprescriptible rights. The thousandth part of those cares which are bestowed to infect the human mind, would be amply sufficient to make it whole. Let us not, then, despair of the case: do not let us do man the injury to believe that truth is not made for him; his mind seeks after it incessantly; his heart desires it faithfully; his happiness demands it with an imperious voice; he only either fears it, or mistakes it, because superstition, which has thrown all his ideas into confusion, perpetually keeps the bandeau of delusion fast bound over his eyes; strives, with an almost irresistible force, to render him an entire stranger to virtue.

Maugre the prodigious exertions that are made to drive truth from the earth; in spite of the extraordinary pains used to exile reason—of the uninterrupted efforts to expel true science from the residence of mortals; time, assisted by the progressive knowledge of ages, may one day be able to enlighten even those princes who are the most outrageous in their opposition to the illumination of the human mind; who appear such decided enemies to justice, so very determined against the liberties of mankind. Destiny will, perhaps, when least expected, conduct these wandering outcasts to the throne of some enlightened, equitable, courageous, generous, benevolent sovereign, who, smitten with the charms of virtue, shall throw aside duplicity, frankly acknowledge the true source of human misery, and apply to it those remedies with which wisdom has furnished him: perhaps he may feel, that those systems, from whence it is pretended he derives his power, are the true scourges of his people; the actual cause of his own weakness: that the official expounders of these systems are his most substantial enemies—his most formidable rivals; he may find that superstition, which he has been taught to look upon as the main support to his authority, in point of fact only enfeebles it—renders it tottering: that superstitious morality, false in its principles, is only calculated to pervert his subjects; to break down their intrepidity; to render them perfidious; in short, to give them the vices of slaves, in lieu of the virtues of citizens. A prince thus disentangled from prejudice, will perhaps behold, in superstitious errors, the fruitful source of human sorrows, and commiserations, the condition of his race, it may be, will generously declare, that they are incompatible with every equitable administration.

Until this epoch, so desirable for humanity, shall arrive, the principles of naturalism will be adopted only by a small number of liberal-minded men, who shall dive below the surface; these cannot flatter themselves either with making proselytes, or having a great number of approvers: on the contrary, they will meet with zealous adversaries, with ardent contemners, even in those persons who upon every other subject discover the most acute minds; display the most consummate knowledge. Those men who possess the greatest share of ability, as we have already observed, cannot always resolve to divorce themselves completely from their superstitious ideas; imagination, so necessary to splendid talents, frequently forms in them an insurmountable obstacle to the total extinction of prejudice; this depends much more upon the judgment than upon the mind. To this disposition, already so prompt to form illusions to them, is also to be joined the force of habit; to a great number of men, it would he wresting from them a portion of themselves to take away their superstitious notions; it would be depriving them of an accustomed aliment; plunging them into a dreadful vacuum: obliging their distempered minds to perish for want of exercise. Menage remarks, "that history speaks of very few incredulous women, or female atheists:" this is not surprising; their organization renders them fearful; their nervous system undergoes periodical variations; the education they receive disposes them to credulity. Those among them who have a sound constitution, who have a well ordered imagination, have occasion for chimeras suitable to occupy their leisure; above all, when the world abandons them, then superstitious devotion, with its attractive ceremonies, becomes either a business or an amusement.

Let us not be surprised, if very intelligent, extremely learned men, either obstinately shut their eyes, or run counter to their ordinary sagacity, every time there is a question respecting an object which they have not the courage to examine with that attention they lend to many others. Lord Chancellor Bacon pretends, "that a little philosophy disposes men to atheism, but that great depth re-conducts them to religion." If we analyze this proposition, we shall find it signifies, that even moderate, indifferent thinkers, are quickly enabled to perceive the gross absurdities of superstition; but that very little accustomed to meditate, or else destitute of those fixed principles which could serve them for a guide, their imagination presently replaces them in the theological labyrinth, from whence reason, too weak for the purpose, appeared disposed to withdraw them: these timid souls, who fear to take courage, with minds disciplined to be satisfied with theological solutions, no longer see in nature any thing but an inexplicable enigma; an abyss which it is impossible for them to fathom: these, habituated to fix their eyes upon an ideal, mathematical point, which they have made the centre of every thing, whenever they lose sight of it, find the universe becomes an unintelligible jumble to them; then the confusion in which they feel themselves involved, makes them rather prefer returning to the prejudices of their infancy, which appear to explain every thing, than to float in the vacuum, or quit a foundation which they judge to be immoveable. Thus the proposition of Bacon should seem, to indicate nothing, except it be that the most experienced persons cannot at all times defend themselves against the illusions of their imagination; the impetuosity of which resists the strongest reasoning.

Nevertheless, a deliberate study of nature is sufficient to undeceive every man who will calmly consider things: he will discover that the phenomena of the world is connected by links, invisible to superficial notice, equally concealed from the too impetuous observer, but extremely intelligible to him who views her with serenity. He will find that the most unusual, the most marvellous, as well as the most trifling, or ordinary effects, are equally inexplicable, but that they all equally flow from natural causes; that supernatural causes, under whatever name they way be designated, with whatever qualities they may be decorated, will never do more than increase difficulties; will only make chimeras multiply. The simplest observation will incontestibly prove to him that every thing is necessary; that all the effects he perceives are material; that they can only originate in causes of the same nature, when he even shall not be able to recur to them by the assistance of his senses. Thus his mind, properly directed, every where show him nothing but matter, sometimes acting in a manner which his organs permit him to follow, at others in a mode imperceptible by the faculties he possesses: he will see that all beings follow constant invariable laws, by which all combinations are united and destroyed; he will find that all forms change, but that, nevertheless, the great whole ever remains the same. Thus, cured of the idle notions with which he was imbued, undeceived in those erroneous ideas, which from habit be attached to imaginary systems, he will cheerfully consent to be ignorant of whatever his organs do not enable him to compass; he will know that obscure terms, devoid of sense, are not calculated to explain difficulties; guided by reason, he will throw aside all hypothesis of the imagination; the champion of rectitude, he will attach himself to realities, which are confirmed by experience, which are evidenced by truth.

The greater number of those who study nature, frequently do not consider, that prejudiced eyes will never discover more than that which they have previously determined to find: as soon as they perceive facts contrary to their own ideas, they quickly turn aside, and believe their visual organs have deceived them; if they return to the task, it is in hopes to find means by which they may reconcile the facts to the notions with which their own mind is previously tinctured. Thus we find enthusiastic philosophers, whose determined prepossession shews them what they denominate incontestible evidences of the systems with which they are pre-occupied, even in those things, that most openly contradict their hypothesis: hence those pretended demonstrations of the existence of theories, which are drawn from final causes—from the order of nature—from the kindness evinced to man, &c. Do these same enthusiasts perceive disorder, witness calamities? They induct new proofs of the wisdom, fresh evidence of the intelligence, additional testimony to the bounty of their system, whilst all these occurrences as visibly contradict these qualities, as the first seem to confirm or to establish them. These prejudiced observers are in an ecstacy at the sight of the periodical motions of the planets; at the order of the stars; at the various productions of the earth; at the astonishing harmony in the component parts of animals: in that moment, however, they forget the laws of motion; the powers of gravitation; the force of attraction and repulsion;

they assign all these striking phenomena to unknown causes, of which they have no one substantive idea. In short, in the fervor of their imagination they place man in the centre of nature; they believe him to be the object, the end, of all that exists; that it is for his convenience every thing is made; that it is to rejoice his mind, to pleasure his senses, that the whole was created; whilst they do not perceive, that very frequently the entire of nature appears to be loosed against his weakness; that the elements themselves overwhelm him with calamity; that destiny obstinately persists in rendering him the most miserable of beings. The progress of sound philosophy will always be fatal to superstition, whose notions will be continually contradicted by nature.

Astronomy has caused judiciary astrology to vanish; experimental philosophy, the study of natural history and chemistry, have rendered it impossible for jugglers, priests or sorcerers, any longer to perform miracles. Nature, profoundly studied, must necessarily cause the overthrow of those chimerical theories, which ignorance has substituted to her powers.

Atheism, as it is termed, is only so rare, because every thing conspires to intoxicate man with a dazzling enthusiasm, from his most tender age; to inflate him from his earliest infancy, with systematic error, with organized ignorance, which of all others is the most difficult to vanquish, the most arduous to root out. Theology is nothing more than a science of words, which by dint of repetition we accustom ourselves to substitute for things: as soon as we feel disposed to analyze them, we are astonished to find they do not present us with any actual sense. There are, in the whole world, very few men who think deeply: who render to themselves a faithful account of their own ideas; who have keen penetrating minds. Justness of intellect is one of the rarest gifts which nature bestows on the human species. It is not, however, to be understood by this, that nature has any choice in the formation of her beings; it is merely to be considered, that the circumstances very rarely occur which enable the junction of a certain quantity of those atoms or parts, necessary to form the human machine in such due proportions, that one disposition shall not overbalance the others; and thus render the judgment erroneous, by giving it a particular bias. We know the general process of making gunpowder; nevertheless, it will sometimes happen that the ingredients have been so happily blended, that this destructive article is of a superior quality to the general produce of the manufactory, without, however, the chemist being on that account entitled to any particular commendation; circumstances have been decidedly favorable, and these seldom occur. Too lively an imagination, an over eager curiosity, are as powerful obstacles to the discovery of truth, as too much phlegm, a slow conception, indolence of mind, or the want of a thinking habit: all men have more or less imagination, curiosity, phlegm, bile, indolence, activity: it is from the happy equilibrium which nature has observed in their organization, that depends that invaluable blessing, correctness of mind. Nevertheless, as we have heretofore said, the organic structure of man is subject to change; the accuracy of his mind varies with the mutations of his machine: from hence may be traced those almost perpetual revolutions that take place in the ideas of mortals; above all when there is a question concerning those objects, upon which experience does not furnish any fixed basis whereon to rest their merits.

To search after right, to discover truth, requires a keen, penetrating, just, active mind; because every thing strives to conceal from us its beauties: it needs an upright heart, one in good faith with itself, joined to an imagination tempered with reason, because our habitual fears make us frequently dread its radiance, sometimes bursting like a meteor on our darkened faculties; besides, it not unfrequently happens, that we are actually the accomplices of those who lead us astray, by an inclination we too often manifest to dissimilate with ourselves on this important measure. Truth never reveals itself either to the enthusiast smitten with his own reveries; to the fellifluous fanatic enslaved by his prejudices; to the vain glorious mortal puffed up with his own presumptuous ignorance; to the voluptuary devoted to his pleasures; or to the wily reasoner, who, disingenuous with himself, has a peculiar spontaneity to form illusions to his mind. Blessed, however, with a heart, gifted with a mind such as described, man will surely discover this *rara avis:* thus constituted, the attentive philosopher, the geometrician, the moralist, the politician, the theologian himself, when he shall sincerely seek truth, will find that the corner-stone which serves for the foundation of all superstitious systems, is evidently rested upon fiction. The philosopher will discover in matter a sufficient cause for its existence; he will perceive that its motion, its combination, its modes of acting, are always regulated by general laws, incapable of variation. The geometrician, without quiting nature, will calculate the active force of matter; it will then become obvious to him, that to explain its phenomena, it is by no means necessary to have recourse to that which is incommensurable with all known powers. The politician, instructed in the true spring which can act upon the mind of nations, will feel distinctly, that it is not imperative to recur to imaginary theories, whilst there are actual motives to give play to the volition of the citizens; to induce them to labour efficaciously to the maintenance of their association; he will readily acknowledge that fictitious systems are calculated either to slaken the exertions, or to disturb the motion of so complicated a machine an human society. He who shall more honor truth than the vain subtilities of theology, will quickly perceive that this pompous science is nothing more than an unintelligible jumble of false hypothesis; that it continually begs its principles; is full of sophisms; contains only vitiated circles; embraces the most subdolous distinctions; is ushered to mankind by the most disingenuous arguments, from which it is not possible, under any given circumstances, there should result any thing but puerilities—the most endless disputes. In short, all men who have sound ideas of morality, whose notions of virtue are correct, who understand what is useful to the human being in society, whether it be to conserve himself individually, or the body of which he is a member, will acknowledge, that in order to discover his relations, to ascertain his duties, he has only to consult his own nature; that he ought to be particularly careful neither to found them upon discrepant systems, nor to borrow them from models that never can do more than disturb his mind; that will only render his conduct fluctuating; that will leave him for ever uncertain of its proper character.

Thus, every rational thinker, who renounces his prejudices, will be enabled to feel the inutility, to comprehend the fallacy of so many abstract systems; he will perceive that they have hitherto answered no other purpose than to confound the notions of mankind; to render doubtful the clearest truths. In quitting the regions of the empyreum, where his mind can only bewilder itself, in re-entering his proper sphere, in consulting reason, man will discover that of which he needs the knowledge; he will be able to undeceive himself upon those chimerical theories, which enthusiasm has substituted for actual natural causes; to detect those figments, by which imposture has almost every where superseded the real motives that can give activity in nature; out of which the human mind never rambles, without going woefully astray; without laying the foundation of future misery.

The Deicolists, as well as the theologians, continually reproach their adversaries with their taste for paradoxes—with their attachment to systems; whilst they themselves found all their reasoning upon imaginary hypothesis—upon visionary theories; make a principle of submitting their understanding to the yoke of authority; of renouncing experience; of setting down as nothing the evidence of their senses. Would it not be justifiable in the disciples of nature, to say to these men, who thus despise her, "We only assure ourselves of that which we see; we yield to nothing but evidence; if we have a system, it is one founded upon facts; we perceive in ourselves, we behold every where else, nothing but matter; we therefore conclude from it that matter can both feel and think: we see that the motion of the universe is operated after mechanical laws; that the whole results from the properties, is the effect of the combination, the immediate consequence of the modification of matter; thus, we are content, we seek no other explication of the phenomena which nature presents. We conceive only an unique world, in which every thing is connected; where each effect is linked to a natural cause, either known or unknown, which it produces according to necessary laws; we affirm nothing that is not demonstrable; nothing that you are not obliged to admit as well as ourselves: the principles we lay down are distinct: they are self-evident: they are facts. If we find some things unintelligible, if causes frequently become arduous, we ingenuously agree to their obscurity; that is to say, to the limits of our own knowledge. But in order to explain these effects, we do not imagine an hypothesis; we either consent to be for ever ignorant of them, or else we wait patiently until time, experience, with the progress of the human mind, shall throw them into light: is not, then, our manner of philosophizing consistent with truth? Indeed, in whatever we advance upon the subject of nature, we proceed precisely in the same manner as our opponents themselves pursue in all the other sciences, such as natural history, experimental philosophy, mathematics, chemistry, &c. We scrupulously confine ourselves to what comes to our knowledge through the medium of our senses; the only instruments with which nature has furnished us to discover truth. What is the conduct of our adversaries? In order to expound things of which they are ignorant, they imagine theories still more incomprehensible than what they are desirous to explain; theories of which they themselves are obliged to acknowledge they have not the most slender notion. Thus they invert the true principles of logic, which require we should proceed gradually from that which is most known, to that with which we are least acquainted. Again, upon what do they found the existence of these theories, by whose aid they pretend to solve all difficulties? It is upon the universal ignorance of mankind; upon the inexperience of man; upon his fears; upon his disordered imagination; upon a pretended *intimate sense*, which in reality is nothing more than the effect of vulgar prejudice; the result of dread; the consequence of the want of a reflecting habit, which induces them to crouch to the opinions of others; to be guided by the mandates of authority, rather than take the trouble to examine for their own information. Such, O theologians! are the ruinous foundations upon which you erect the superstructure of your doctrine. Accordingly, you find it impossible to form to yourselves any distinct idea of those theories which serve for the basis of your systems; you are unable to comprehend either their attributes, their existence, the nature of their localities, or their mode of action. Thus, even by your own confession, ye are in a state of profound ignorance, on the primary elements of that which ye constitute the cause of all that exists: of which, according to your own account, it is imperative to have a correct knowledge. Under whatever point of view, therefore, ye are contemplated, it must be admitted ye are the founders of aerial systems; of fanciful theories: of all systematizers, ye are consequently the most absurd; because in challenging your imagination to create a cause, this cause, at least, ought to diffuse light over the whole; it would be upon this condition alone that its incomprehensibility could be pardonable; but to speak ingenuously, does this cause serve to explain any thing? Does it make us conceive more clearly the origin of the world; bring us more distinctly acquainted with the actual nature of man; does it more intelligibly elucidate the faculties of the soul; or point out with more perspicuity the source of good and evil? No! unquestionably: these subtle theories explain nothing, although they multiply to infinity their own difficulties; they, in fact, embarrass elucidation, by plunging into greater obscurity those matters in which they are interposed. Whatever may be the question agitated, it becomes complicated: as soon as these theories are introduced, they envelope the most demonstrable sciences with a thick, impenetrable mist; render the most simple notions complex; give opacity to the most diaphanous ideas; turn the most evident opinions into insolvable enigmas. What exposition of morality does the theories, upon which ye found all the virtue, present to man? Do not all your oracles breathe inconsistency? Does not your doctrines embrace every gradation of character, however discrepant: every known property, however opposed. All your ingenious systems, all your mysteries, all the subtilties which ye have invented, are they capable of reconciling that discordant assemblage of amiable and unamiable qualities, with which ye have dressed up your figments? In short, is it not by these theories that ye disturb the harmony of the universe; is it not in their name ye follow up your barbarous proscriptions; in their support, that ye so inhumanly exterminate all who refuse to subscribe to your organized reveries; who withhold assent to those efforts of the imagination which ye have collectively decorated with the pompous name of religion; but which, individually, ye brand as superstition, always excepting that to which ye lend yourselves. Agree, then, O Theologians! Acknowledge, then, ye subtle metaphysicians! Consent, then, ye organizers of fanciful theories! that not only are ye systematically absurd, but also that ye finish by being atrocious; because whenever ye obtain the ascendancy one over the other, your unfortunate pre-eminence is distinguished by the most malevolent persecution; your domination is ushered in with cruelty; your career is described with blood: from the importance which your own interest attaches to your ruinous dogmas; from the pride with which ye tumble down the less fortunate systems of those who started with you for the prize of plunder; *from that savage ferocity, under which ye equally overwhelm human reason, the happiness of the individual, and the felicity of nations.*"

CHAP. XIV.

A Summary of the Code of Nature.

Truth is the only object worthy the research of every wise man; since that which is false cannot be useful to him: whatever constantly injures him cannot be founded upon truth; consequently, ought to be for ever proscribed. It is, then, to assist the human mind, truly to labour for his happiness, to point out to him the clew by which he may extricate himself from those frightful labyrinths in which his imagination wanders; from those sinuosities whose devious course makes him err, without ever finding a termination to his incertitude. Nature alone, known through experience, can furnish him with this desirable thread; her eternal energies can alone supply the means of attacking the Minotaur; of exterminating the figments of hypocrisy; of destroying those monsters, who during so many ages, have devoured the unhappy victims, which the tyranny of the ministers of Moloch have exacted as a cruel tribute from affrighted mortals. By steadily grasping this inestimable clew, rendered still more precious by the beauty of the donor, man can never be led astray—will never ramble out of his course; but if, careless of its invaluable properties, for a single instant he suffers it to drop from his hand; if, like another Theseus, ungrateful for the favour, he abandons the fair bestower, he will infallibly fall again into his ancient wanderings; most assuredly become the prey to the cannibal offspring of the White Bull. In vain shall he carry his views above his head, to find resources which are at his feet; so long as man, infatuated with his superstitious notions, shall seek in an imaginary world the rule of his earthly conduct, he will be without principles; while he shall pertinaciously contemplate the regions of a distempered fancy, so long he will grope in those where he actually finds himself; his uncertain steps will never encounter the welfare he desires; never lead him to that repose after which he so ardently sighs, nor conduct him to that surety which is so decidedly requisite to consolidate his happiness.

But man, blinded by his prejudices; rendered obstinate in injuring his fellow, by his enthusiasm; ranges himself in hostility even against those who are sincerely desirous of procuring for him the most substantive benefits. Accustomed to be deceived, he is in a state of continual suspicion; habituated to mistrust himself, to view his reason with diffidence, to look upon truth as dangerous, he treats as enemies even those who most eagerly strive to encourage him; forewarned in early life against delusion, by the subtilty of imposture, he believes himself imperatively called upon to guard with the most sedulous activity the bandeau with which they have hoodwinked him; he thinks his eternal welfare involved in keeping it for ever over his eyes; he therefore wrestles with all those who attempt to tear it from his obscured optics. If his visual organs, accustomed to darkness, are for a moment opened, the light offends them; he is distressed by its effulgence; he thinks it criminal to be enlightened; he darts with fury upon those who hold the flambeau by which he is dazzled. In consequence, the atheist, as the arch rogue from whom he differs ludicrously calls him, is looked upon as a malignant pest, as a public poison, which like another Upas, destroys every thing within the vortex of its influence; he who dares to arouse mortals from the lethargic habit which the narcotic doses administered by the theologians have induced passes for a perturbator; he who attempts to calm their frantic transports, to moderate the fury of their maniacal paroxysms, is himself viewed as a madman, who ought to be closely chained down in the dungeons appropriated to lunatics; he who invites his associates to rend their chains asunder, to break their galling fetters, appears only like an irrational, inconsiderate being, even to the wretched captives themselves: who have been taught to believe that nature formed them for no other purpose than to tremble: only called them into existence that they might be loaded with shackles. In consequence of these fatal prepossessions, the *Disciple of Nature* is generally treated as an assassin; is commonly received by his fellow citizens in the same manner as the feathered race receive the doleful bird of night, which as soon as it quits its retreat, all the other birds follow with a common hatred, uttering a variety of doleful cries.

No, mortals blended by terror! The friend of nature is not your enemy; its interpreter is not the minister of falsehood; the destroyer of your vain phantoms is not the devastator of those truths necessary to your happiness; the disciple of reason is not an irrational being, who either seeks to poison you, or to infect you with a dangerous delirium. If he is desirous to wrest the thunder from those terrible theories that affright ye, it is that ye way discontinue your march, in the midst of storms, over roads that ye can only distinguish by the sudden, but evanescent glimmerings of the electric fluid. If he breaks those idols, which fear has served with myrrh and frankencense—which superstition has surrounded by gloomy despondency—which fanaticism has imbrued with blood; it is to substitute in their place those consoling truths that are calculated to heal the desperate wounds ye have received; that are suitable to inspire you with courage, sturdily to oppose yourselves to such dangerous errors; that have power to enable you to resist such formidable enemies. If he throws down the temples, overturns the altars, so frequently bathed with the bitter tears of the unfortunate, blackened by the most cruel sacrifices, smoked with servile incense, it is that he may erect a fane sacred to peace, a hall dedicated to reason; a durable monument to virtue, in which ye may at all times find an asylum against your own phrenzy; a refuge from your own ungovernable passions; a sanctuary against those powerful dogmatists, by whom ye are oppressed. If he attacks the haughty pretensions of deified tyrants, who crush ye with an iron sceptre, it is that ye may enjoy the rights of your nature; it is to the end that ye may be substantively freemen, in mind as well as in body; that ye may not be slaves, eternally chained to the oar of misery; it is that ye may at length be governed by men who are citizens, who may cherish their own semblances, who way protect mortals like themselves, who may actually consult the interests of those from whom they hold their power. If he battles with imposture, it is to re-establish truth in those rights which have been so long usurped by fiction. If he undermines the base of that unsteady, fanatical morality, which has hitherto done nothing more than perplex your minds, without correcting your hearts; it is to give to ethics an immovable basis, a solid foundation, secured upon your own nature; upon the reciprocity of those wants which are continually regenerating in sensible beings: dare, then, to listen to his voice; you will find it much more intelligible than those ambiguous oracles, which are announced to you as the offspring of capricious theories; as imperious decrees that are unceasingly at variance with themselves. Listen then to nature, she never contradicts her own eternal laws.

"O thou!" cries this nature to man, "who, following the impulse I have given you, during your whole existence, incessantly tend towards happiness, do not strive to resist my sovereign law. Labour to your own felicity; partake without fear of the banquet which is spread before you, with the most hearty welcome; you will find the means legibly written on your own heart. Vainly dost thou, O superstitious being! seek after thine happiness beyond the limits of the universe, in which my hand hath placed thee: vainly shalt thou search it in those inexorable theories, which thine imagination, ever prone to wander, would establish upon my eternal throne: vainly dost thou expect it in those fanciful regions, to which thine own delirium hath given a locality and a shame: vainly dost thou reckon upon capricious systems, with whose advantages thou art in such ecstasies; whilst they only fill thine abode with calamity—thine heart with dread—thy mind with illusions—thy bosom with groans. Know that when thou neglectest my counsels, the gods will refuse their aid. Dare, then, to affranchise thyself from the trammels of superstition, my self-conceited, pragmatic rival, who mistakes my rights; renounce those empty theories, which are usurpers of my privileges; return under the dominion of my laws, which, however severe, are mild in comparison with those of bigotry. It is in my empire alone that true liberty reigns. Tyranny is unknown to its soil; equity unceasingly watches over the rights of all my subjects, maintains them in the possession of their just claims; benevolence, grafted upon humanity, connects them by amicable bonds; truth enlightens them; never can imposture blind them with his obscuring mists. Return, then, my child, to thy fostering mother's arms! Deserter, trace back thy wandering steps to nature! She will console thee for thine evils; she will drive from thine heart those appalling fears which overwhelm thee; those inquietudes that distract thee; those transports which agitate thee; those hatreds that separate thee from thy fellow man, whom thou shouldst love as thyself. Return to nature, to humanity, to thyself! Strew flowers over the road of life: cease to contemplate the future; live to thine own happiness; exist for thy fellow creatures; retire into thyself, examine thine own heart, then consider the sensitive beings by whom thou art surrounded: leave to their inventors those systems which can effect nothing towards thy felicity. Enjoy thyself, and cause others also to enjoy, those comforts which I have placed with a liberal hand, for all the children of the earth; who all equally emanate from my bosom: assist them to support the sorrows to which necessity has submitted them in common with thyself. Know, that I approve thy pleasures, when without injuring thyself, they are not fatal to thy brethren, whom I have rendered indispensably necessary to thine own individual happiness. These pleasures are freely permitted thee, if thou indulgest them with moderation; with that discretion which I myself have fixed. Be happy, then, O man! Nature invites thee to participate in it; but always remember, thou canst not be so alone; because I invite all mortals to happiness as well as thyself; thou will find it is only in securing their felicity that thou canst consolidate thine own. Such is the decree of thy destiny: if thou shalt attempt to withdraw thyself from its operation, recollect that hatred will pursue thee; vengeance overtake thy steps; and remorse be ever ready at hand to punish the infractions of its irrevocable mandates.

"Follow then, O man! in whatever station thou findest thyself, the routine I have described for thee, to obtain that happiness to which thou hast an indispensable right to challenge pretension. Let the sensations of humanity interest thee for the condition of other men, who are thy fellow creatures; let thine heart have commisseration for their misfortunes: let thy generous hand spontaneously stretch forth to lend succour to the unhappy mortal who is overwhelmed by his destiny; always bearing in thy recollection, that it may fall heavy upon thyself, as it now does upon him. Acknowledge, then, without guile, that every unfortunate has an inalienable right to thy kindness. Above all, wipe from the eyes of oppressed innocence the trickling crystals of agonized feeling; let the tears of virtue in distress, fall upon thy sympathizing bosom; let the genial glow of sincere friendship animate thine honest heart; let the fond attachment of a mate, cherished by thy warmest affection, make thee forget the sorrows of life: be faithful to her love, responsible to her tenderness, that she may reward thee by a reciprocity of feeling; that under the eyes of parents united in virtuous esteem, thy offspring may learn to set a proper value on practical virtue; that after having occupied thy riper years, they may comfort thy declining age, gild with content thy setting sun, cheer the evening of thine existence, by a dutiful return of that care which thou shalt have bestowed on their imbecile infancy.

"Be just, because equity is the support of human society! Be good, because goodness connects all hearts in adamantine bonds! Be indulgent, because feeble thyself, thou livest with beings who partake of thy weakness! Be gentle, because mildness attracts attention! Be thankful, because gratitude feeds benevolence, nourishes generosity! Be modest, because haughtiness is disgusting to beings at all times well with themselves. Forgive injuries, because revenge perpetuates hatred! Do good to him who injureth thee, in order to shew thyself more noble than he is; to make a friend of him, who was once thine enemy! Be reserved in thy demeanor, temperate in thine enjoyment, chaste in thy pleasures, because voluptuousness begets weariness, intemperance engenders disease; forward manners are revolting: excess at all times relaxes the springs of thy machine, will ultimately destroy thy being, and render thee hateful to thyself, contemptible to others.

"Be a faithful citizen; because the community is necessary to thine own security; to the enjoyment of thine own existence; to the furtherance of thine own happiness. Be loyal, but be brave; submit to legitimate authority; because it is requisite to the maintenance of that society which is necessary to thyself. Be obedient to the laws; because they *are*, or *ought to be*, the expression of the public will, to which thine own particular will ought ever to be subordinate. Defend thy country with zeal; because it is that which renders thee happy, which contains thy property, as well as those beings dearest to thine heart: do not permit this common parent of thyself, as well as of thy fellow citizens, to fall under the shackles of tyranny; because from thence it will be no more than thy common prison. If thy country, deaf to the equity of thy claims, refuses thee happiness—if, submitted to an unjust power, it suffers thee to be oppressed, withdraw thyself from its bosom in silence, but never disturb its peace.

"In short, be a man; be a sensible, rational being; be a faithful husband; a tender father; an equitable master; a zealous citizen; labour to serve thy country by thy prowess; by thy talents; by thine industry; above all, by thy virtues. Participate with thine associates those gifts which nature has bestowed upon thee; diffuse happiness, among thy fellow mortals; inspire thy fellow citizens with content; spread joy over all those who approach thee, that the sphere of thine actions, enlivened by thy kindness, illumined by thy benevolence, may re-act upon thyself; be assured that the man who makes others happy cannot himself be miserable. In thus conducting thyself, whatever may be the injustice of others, whatever may be the blindness of those beings with whom it is thy destiny to live, thou wilt never be totally bereft of the recompense which is thy due; no power on earth be able to ravish from thee that never failing source of the purest felicity, inward content; at each moment thou wilt fall back with pleasure upon thyself; thou wilt neither feel the rankling of shame, the terror of internal alarm, nor find thy heart corroded by remorse. Thou wilt esteem thyself; thou wilt be cherished by the virtuous, applauded and loved by all good men, whose suffrages are much more valuable than those of the bewildered multitude. Nevertheless, if externals occupy thy contemplation, smiling countenances will greet thy presence; happy faces will express the interest they have in thy welfare; jocund beings will make thee participate in their placid feelings. A life so spent, will each moment be marked by the serenity of thine own soul, by the affection of the beings who environ thee; will be made cheerful by the friendship of thy fellows; will enable thee to rise a contented, satisfied guest from the general feast; conduct thee gently down the declivity of life, lead thee peaceably to the period of thy days; for die thou must: but already thou wilt survive thyself in thought; thou wilt always live in the remembrance of thy friends; in the grateful recollection of those beings whose comforts have been augmented by thy friendly attentions; thy virtues will, beforehand have erected to thy fame an imperishable monument: if heaven occupies itself with thee, it will feel satisfied with thy conduct, when it shall thus have contented the earth.

"Beware, then, how thou complainest of thy condition; be just, be kind, be virtuous, and thou canst never be wholly destitute of felicity. Take heed how thou enviest the transient pleasure of seductive crime; the deceitful power of victorious tyranny; the specious tranquillity of interested imposture; the plausible manners of venal justice; the shewy, ostentatious parade of hardened opulence. Never be tempted to increase the number of sycophants to an ambitious despot; to swell the catalogue of slaves to an unjust tyrant; never suffer thyself to be allured to infamy, to the practice of extortion, to the commission of outrage, by the fatal privilege of oppressing thy fellows; always recollect it will be at the expence of the most bitter remorse thou wilt acquire this baneful advantage. Never be the mercenary accomplice of the spoilers of thy country; they are obliged to blush secretly whenever they meet the public eye.

"For, do not deceive thyself, it is I who punish, with an unerring hand, all the crimes of the earth; the wicked may escape the laws of man, but they never escape mine. It is I who have formed the hearts, as well an the bodies of mortals; it is I who have fixed the laws which govern them. If thou deliverest thyself up to voluptuous enjoyment, the companions of thy debaucheries may applaud thee; but I shall punish thee with the most cruel infirmities; these will terminate a life of shame with deserved contempt. If thou givest, thyself up to intemperate indulgences, human laws may not correct thee, but I shall castigate thee severely by abridging thy days. If thou art vicious, thy fatal habits will recoil on thine own head. Princes, those terrestrial divinities, whose power places them above the laws of mankind, are nevertheless obliged to tremble under the silent operation of my decrees. It is I who chastise them; it is I who fill their breasts with suspicion; it is I who inspire them with terror; it is I who make them writhe under inquietude; it is I who make them shudder with horror, at the very name of august truth; it is I who, amidst the crowd of nobles who surround them, make them feel the inward workings of shame; the keen anguish of guilt; the poisoned arrows of regret; the cruel stings of remorse; it is I who, when they abuse my bounty, diffuse weariness over their benumbed souls; it is I who follow uncreated, eternal justice; it is I who, without distinction of persons, know how to make the balance even; to adjust the chastisement to the fault; to make the misery bear its due proportion to the depravity; to inflict punishment commensurate with the crime. The laws of man are just, only when they are in conformity with mine; his judgements are rational, only when I have dictated them: my laws alone are immutable, universal, irrefragable; formed to regulate the condition of the human race, in all ages, in all places, under all circumstances.

"If thou doubtest mine authority, if thou questionest the irresistible power I possess over mortals, contemplate the vengeance I wreak on all those who resist my decrees. Dive into the recesses of the hearts of those various criminals, whose countenances, assuming a forced smile, cover souls torn with anguish. Dost thou not behold ambition tormented day and night, with an ardour which nothing can extinguish? Dost not thou see the mighty conquerer become the lord of devastated solitudes; his victorious career, marked by a blasted cultivation, reign sorrowfully over smoking ruins; govern unhappy wretches who curse him in their hearts; while his soul, gnawed by remorse, sickens at the gloomy aspect of his own triumphs? Dost thou believe that the tyrant, encircled with his flatterers, who stun him with their praise, is unconscious of the hatred which his oppression excites; of the contempt which his vices draw upon him; of the sneers which his inutility call forth; of the scorn which his debaucheries entail upon his name? Dost thou think that the haughty courtier does not inwardly blush at the galling insults he brooks; despise, from the bottom of his soul, those meannesses by which he is compelled to purchase favours; feel at his heart's core the wretched dependence in which his cupidity places him.

"Contemplate the indolent child of wealth, behold him a prey to the lassitude of unmeasured enjoyment, corroded by the satiety which always follows his exhausted pleasures. View the miser with an emaciated countenance, the consequence of his own penurious disposition, whose callous heart is inaccessible to the calls of misery, groaning over the accumulating load of useless treasure, which at the expense of himself, he has laboured to amass. Behold the gay voluptuary, the smiling debaucheé, secretly lament the health they have so inconsiderately damaged so prodigally thrown away: see disdain, joined to hatred, reign between those adulterous married couples, who have reciprocally violated the sacred vows they mutually pledged at the altar of Hymen; whose appetencies have rendered them the scorn of the world; the jest of their acquaintance; polluted tributaries to the surgeon. See the liar deprived of all confidence; the knave stript of all trust; the hypocrite fearfully avoiding the penetrating looks of his inquisitive neighbour; the impostor trembling at the very name of formidable truth. Bring under your review the heart of the envious, uselessly dishonored; that withers at the sight of his neighbour's prosperity. Cast your eyes on the frozen soul of the ungrateful wretch, whom no kindness can warm, no benevolence thaw, no beneficence convert into a genial fluid. Survey the iron feelings of that monster whom the sighs of the unfortunate cannot mollify. Behold the revengeful being nourished with venemous gall, whose very thoughts are serpents; who in his rage consumes himself. Envy, if thou canst, the waking slumbers of the homicide; the startings of the iniquitous judge; the restlessness of the oppressor of innocence; the fearful visions of the extortioner; whose couches are infested with the torches of the furies. Thou tremblest without doubt at the sight of that distraction which, amidst their splendid luxuries, agitates those farmers of the revenue, who fatten upon public calamnity—who devour the substance of the orphan—who consume the means of the widow—who grind the hard earnings of the poor: thou shudderest at witnessing the remorse which rends the souls of those reverend criminals, whom the uninformed believe to be happy, whilst the contempt which they have for themselves, the unerring shafts of secret upbraidings, are incessantly revenging an outraged nation. Thou seest, that content is for ever banished the heart; quiet for ever driven from the habitations of those miserable wretches on whose minds I have indelibly engraved the scorn, the infamy, the chastisement which they deserve. But, no! thine eyes cannot sustain the tragic spectacle of my vengeance. Humanity obliges thee to partake of their merited sufferings; thou art moved to pity for these unhappy people, to whom consecrated errors renders vice necessary; whose fatal habits make them familiar with crime. Yes; thou shunnest them without hating them; thou wouldst succour them, if their contumacious perversity had left thee the means. When thou comparest thine own condition, when thou examinest thine own soul, thou wilt have just cause to felicitate thyself, if thou shalt find that peace has taken up her abode with thee; that contentment dwells at the bottom of thine own heart. In short, thou seest accomplished upon them, as well as, upon thyself, the unalterable decrees of destiny, which imperiously demand, that crime shall punish itself, that virtue never shall be destitute Of remuneration."

Such is the sum of those truths which are contained in the *Code of Nature*; such are the doctrines, which its disciples can announce. They are unquestionably preferable to that supernatural superstition which never does any thing but mischief to the human species. Such is the worship that is taught by that sacred reason, which is the object of contempt with the theologian; which meets the insult of the fanatic; who only estimates that which man can neither conceive nor practise; who make his morality consist in fictitious duties; his virtue in actions generally useless, frequently pernicious to the welfare of society; who for want of being acquainted with nature, which is before their eyes, believe themselves obliged to seek in ideal worlds imaginary motives, of which every thing proves the inefficacy. The motive which the morality of nature employs, is the self-evident interest of each individual, of each community, of the whole human species, in all times, in every country, under all circumstances. Its worship is the sacrifice of vice, the practise of real virtues; its object is the conservation of the human race, the happiness of the individual, the peace of mankind; its recompences are affection, esteem, and glory; or in their default, contentment of mind, with merited self-esteem, of which no power will ever be able to deprive virtuous mortals; its punishments, are hatred, contempt, and indignation; which society always reserves for those who outrage its interests; from which even the most powerful can never effectually shield themselves.

Those nations who shall be disposed to practise a morality so wise, who shall inculcate it in infancy, whose laws shall unceasingly confirm it, will neither have occasion for superstition, nor for chimeras. Those who shall obstinately prefer figments to their dearest interests, will certainly march forward to ruin. If they maintain themselves for a season, it is because the power of nature sometimes drives them back to reason, in despite of those prejudices which appear to lead them on to certain destruction. Superstition, leagued with tyranny, for the waste of the human species, are themselves frequently obliged to implore the assistance of a reason which they contemn; of a nature which they disdain; which they debase; which they endeavour to crush under the ponderous bulk of artificial theories. Superstition, in all times so fatal to mortals, when attacked by reason, assumes the sacred mantle of public utility; rests its importance on false grounds, founds its rights upon the indissoluble alliance which it pretends subsists between morality and itself; notwithstanding it never ceases for a single instant to wage against it the most cruel hostility. It is, unquestionably, by this artifice, that it has seduced so many sages. In the honesty of their hearts, they believe it useful to politics; necessary to restrain the ungovernable fury of the passions; thus hypocritical superstition, in order to mask to superficial observers, its own hideous character, like the ass with the lion's skin, always knows how to cover itself with the sacred armour of utility; to buckle on the invulnerable shield of virtue; it has therefore, been believed imperative to respect it, notwithstanding it felt awkward under these incumbrances; it consequently has become a duty to favor imposture, because it has artfully entrenched itself behind the altars of truth; its ears, however, discover its worthlessness; its natural cowardice betrays itself; it is from this intrenchment we ought to drive it; it should be dragged forth to public view; stripped of its surreptitious panoply; exposed in its native deformity; in order that the human race may become acquainted with its dissimulation; that mankind may have a knowledge of its crimes; that the universe may behold its sacrilegious hands, armed with homicidal poniards, stained with the blood of nations, whom it either intoxicates with its fury, or immolates without pity to the violence of its passions.

The MORALITY OF NATURE is the only creed which her interpreter offers to his fellow citizens; to nations; to the human species; to future races, weaned from those prejudices which have so frequently disturbed the felicity of their ancestors. The friend of mankind cannot be the friend of delusion, which at all times has been a real scourge to the earth. The APOSTLE OF NATURE will not be the instrument of deceitful chimeras, by which this world is made only an abode of illusions; the adorer of truth will not compromise with falsehood; he will make no covenant with error; conscious it must always be fatal to mortals. He knows that the happiness of the human race imperiously exacts that the dark unsteady edifice of superstition should be razed to its foundations; in order to elevate on its ruins a temple suitable to peace—a fane sacred to virtue. He feels it is only by extirpating, even to the most slender fibres, the poisonous tree, that during so many ages has overshadowed the universe, that the inhabitants of this world will be able to use their own optics—to bear with steadiness that light which is competent to illumine their understanding—to guide their wayward steps—to give the necessary ardency to their souls. If his efforts should be vain; if he cannot inspire with courage, beings too much accustomed to tremble; he will, at least, applaud himself for having dared the attempt. Nevertheless, he will not judge his exertions fruitless, if he has only been enabled to make a single mortal happy: if his principles have calmed the conflicting transports of one honest soul; if his reasonings have cheered up some few virtuous hearts. At least he will have the advantage of having banished from his own mind the importunate terror of superstition; of having expelled from his own heart the gall which exasperates zeal; of having trodden under foot those chimeras with which the uninformed are tormented. Thus, escaped from the peril of the storm, he will calmly contemplate from the summit of his rock, those tremendous hurricanes which superstition excites; he will hold forth a succouring hand to those who shall be willing to accept it; he will encourage them with his voice; he will second them with his best exertions, and in the warmth of his own compassionate heart, he will exclaim:

O NATURE; sovereign of all beings! and ye, her adorable daughters, VIRTUE, REASON, and TRUTH! remain for ever our revered protectors: it is to you that belong the praises of the human race; to you appertains the homage of the earth. Shew, us then, O NATURE! that which man ought to do, in order to obtain the happiness which thou makest him desire. VIRTUE! Animate him with thy beneficent fire. REASON! Conduct his uncertain steps through the paths of life. TRUTH! Let thy torch illumine his intellect, dissipate the darkness of his road. Unite, O assisting deities! your powers, in order to submit the hearts of mankind to your dominion. Banish error from our mind; wickedness from our hearts; confusion from our footsteps; cause knowledge to extend its salubrious reign; goodness to occupy our souls; serenity to dwell in our bosoms. Let imposture, confounded, never again dare to shew its head. Let our eyes, so long, either dazzled or blindfolded, be at length fixed upon those objects we ought to seek. Dispel for ever those mists of ignorance, those hideous phantoms, together with those seducing chimeras, which only serve to lead us astray. Extricate us from that dark abyss into which we are plunged by superstition; overthrow the fatal empire of delusion; crumble the throne of falsehood; wrest from their polluted hands the power they have usurped. Command men, without sharing your authority with mortals: break the chains that bind them down in slavery: tear away the bandeau by which they are hoodwinked; allay the fury that intoxicates them; break in the hands of sanguinary, lawless tyrants, that iron sceptre with which they are crushed to exile; the imaginary regions, from whence fear has imported them, those theories by which they are afflicted. Inspire the intelligent being with courage; infuse energy into his system, that, at length, he may feel his own dignity; that he may dare to love himself; to esteem his own actions when they are worthy; that a slave only to your eternal laws, he may no longer fear to enfranchise himself from all other trammels; that blest with freedom, he may have the wisdom to cherish his fellow creature; and become happy by learning to perfection his own condition; instruct him in the great lesson, that the high road to felicity, is prudently to partake himself, and also to cause others to enjoy, the rich banquet which thou, O Nature! hast so bountifully set before him.

Console thy children for those sorrows to which their destiny submits them, by those pleasures which wisdom allows them to partake; teach them to be contented with their condition; to banish envy from their mind; to yield silently to necessity. Conduct them without alarm to that period which all beings must find; *let them learn that time changes all things, that consequently they are made neither to avoid its scythe nor to fear its arrival.*

[TRANSLATOR'S APPENDIX]

A BRIEF SKETCH

OF THE

LIFE AND WRITINGS

OF

M. DE. MIRABAUD.

At a time when we are on the eve of an important change in our political affairs, which must evidently lead either to the recovery and re-establishment of our liberties, or to a military despotism, those who are connected with the press ought to use every exertion to enlighten their fellow-citizens, and to assert their right of canvassing, in the most free and unrestrained manner, every subject connected with the happiness of man.

The priesthood have ever been convenient tools in the hands of tyrants, to keep the bulk of the people in a degraded servility. By the superstitious and slavish doctrines which they infuse into their minds, they prevent them from thinking for themselves and asserting their own independence. At a moment when national schools are erecting in every quarter of the country, not with a sincere desire of enlightening the rising generation, but with the insidious design of instilling into their minds the doctrines of "Church and King," in order to bolster up a little longer the present rotten, tottering, and corrupt system: at a moment, too, when thousands of fanatic preachers are traversing the country, with a view to subjugate the human mind to the baleful empire of visonary enthusiasm and sectarian bigotry to the utter extinction of every noble, manly, liberal, and pilantropic principle;—at such a moment as this, we thought that the "SYSTEM OF NATURE" could not fail to render essential service to the cause both of civil and religious liberty. No work, ancient or modern, has surpassed it, in the eloquence and sublimity of its language, or in the facility with which it treats the most abtruse and difficult subjects. It is, without exception, the boldest effort the human mind has yet produced, in the investigation of morals and theology—in the destruction of priestcraft and superstition—and in developing the sources of all those passions and prejudices which have proved so fatal to the tranquillity of the world.

The republic of letters has never produced an author whose pen was so well calculated to emancipate mankind from all those trammels with which the nurse, the schoolmaster and the priest have successively locked up their noblest faculties, before they were capable of reasoning and judging for themselves. The frightful apprehensions of the gloomy bigot, and all the appalling terrors of superstition, are here utterly annihilated, to the complete satisfaction of every unbiassed and impartial person.—These we considered as necessary observations to make, previous to any attempt at the biography of the author.

Biography may be reckoned among the most interesting of literary productions. Its intrinsic value is such, that, though capable of extraordinary embellishment from the hand of genius, yet no inferiority of execution can so degrade it, as to deprive it of utility. Whatever relates even to man in general, considered only as an aggregate of active and intelligent beings, has a strong claim upon our notice; but that which relates to our author, as distinguished from the rest of his species, moving in a more exalted sphere, and towering above them by the resplendent excellencies of his mind, seems to me to be peculiarly calculated for our contemplation, and ought to form the highest pleasure of our lives. There is a principle of curiosity implanted in us, which leads us, in an especial manner, to investigate our fellow creatures; the eager inquisitiveness with which the mechanic seeks to know the history of his fellow-workmen and the ardour with which the philosopher, the poet, or the historian hunts for details that may familiarize him with, a Descartes or a Newton, with a Milton, a Hume, or a Gibbon—spring from the same source. Their object, however, may perhaps vary; for, in the former, it may be for the sake of detraction, invidious cavil, or malice; in the latter, it is a sweet homage paid by the human heart to the memory of departed genius.

It has been repeatedly observed that the life of a scholar affords few materials for biography. This is only negatively true;—could every scholar have a Boswell, the remark would vanish; or were every scholar a Rousseau, a Gibbon, or a Cumberland it would be equally nugatory. What can present higher objects of contemplation—what can claim more forcibly our attention—where can we seek for subjects of a more precious nature, than in the elucidation of the operations of mind, the acquisition of knowledge, the gradual expansion of genius; its application, its felicities, its sorrows, its wreaths of fame, its cold, undeserved neglect? Such scenes, painted by, the artist himself, are a rich bequest to mankind: even when traced by the hand of friendship or the pencil of admiration, they possess a permanent interest in our hearts. I cannot conceive a life more worthy of public notice, more important, more interesting to human nature, than the life of a literary man, were it executed according to the ideas I have formed of it: did it exhibit a faithful delineation of the progress of intellect, from the cradle upwards; did it portray, in accurate colors, the production of what we call genius: by what accident it was first awakened; what were its first tendencies; how directed to a particular object; by what means it was nourished and unfolded; the gradual progress of its operation in the production of a work; its hopes and fears; its delights; its miseries; its inspirations; and all the thousand fleeting joys that so often invest its path but for a moment, and then fade like the dews of the morning. Let it contain too a transcript of the many nameless transports that float round the heart, that dance in the gay circle before the ardent gazing eye, when the first conception of some future effort strikes the mind; how it pictures undefined delights of fame and popular applause; how it anticipates the bright moments of invention, and dwells with prophetic ecstasy on the felicitous execution of particular parts, that already start into existence by the magic touch of a heated imagination. Let it depict the tender feelings of solitude, the breathings of midnight silence, the scenes of mimic life, of imaged trial, that often occupy the musing mind; let it be such a work, so drawn, so coloured, and who shall pronounce it inferior? Who rather will not confess that it presents a picture of human nature, where every heart may find some corresponding harmony? When, therefore, it is said, that the life of a scholar is barren, it is so only because it has never been properly delineated; because those parts only have been selected which are common, and fail to distinguish him from the common man; because we have never penetrated into his closet, or into his heart; because we have drawn him only as an outward figure, and left unnoticed that internal structure that would delight, astonish, and improve. And then, when we compare the life of such a man with the more active one of a soldier, a statesman, or a lawyer, we pronounce it insipid, uninteresting. True;—the man of study has not fought for hire—he has not slaughtered at the command of a master: he would disdain to do so. Though unaccompanied with the glaring actions of public men, which confound and dazzle by their publicity, but shrink from the estimation of moral truth, it would present a far nobler picture; yes, and a more instructive one:—the calm disciple of reason meditates in silence; he walks his road with innoxious humility; he is poor, but his mind is his treasure; he cultivates his reason, and she lifts him to the pinnacle of truth; he learns to tear away the veil of self-love, folly, pride, and prejudice, and bares the human heart to his inspection; he corrects and amends; he repairs the breaches made by passion; the proud man passes him by, and looks upon him with scorn; but he feels his own worth, that ennobling consciousness which swells in every vein, and inspires him with true pride—with manly independence: to such a man I could sooner bow in reverence, than to the haughtiest, most successful candidate for the world's ambition. But of such men, for the reason I have already mentioned, our information is scanty. While of others, who have commanded a greater share of public notoriety, venal or mistaken admiration has given more than we wished to know. Among these respected individuals of human nature, may be placed Mirabaud. Had Mirabaud been an Englishman, who doubts but that we should have possessed at least ample details of the usual subjects of biographical notice; while all that has been collected among his own countrymen, is a scanty memoir in a common dictionary. That we are doomed to remain ignorant of the life of such men, speaks a loud disgrace.—I lament it.

JOHN BAPTISTE MIRABAUD, was born at Paris in the year 1674. He prosecuted his infantile studies under the direction of his parents, and was afterwards entered a member of the *Congregation of the Priests of the Oratory*, where he passed several years, and produced some very bold writings, which were never intended for publication.

He was subsequently appointed tutor to the princesses of the House of Orleans, and then took the resolution of destroying the greater part of the manuscripts that he produced while a member of the *Congregation*; but the treachery of some of his friends, to whom he had confided his manuscripts, rendered this precaution useless, for some of his works were published during the time he remained the preceptor to his royal pupils; among which number may be reckoned his "New Liberties of Thought," a work but little calculated for gaining him friends in the purlieus of the Court of Orleans. The "Origin and Antiquity of the World," in three parts, was also published at this period, and from the publication of this work, may be dated the resolution of M. de Mirabaud to quit his office of preceptor, which he relinquished, having become more independent; he now gave himself up entirely to his philosophical studies, and produced the "System of Nature," with which he was assisted by Diderot, D'Alembert, Baron D'Olbac, and others.

The profound metaphysical knowledge displayed throughout the System of Nature, and the doctrines which are therein advanced, warrants the conclusion, that it is at once the most decisive, boldest, and most extraordinary work, that the human understanding ever had the courage to produce. The study of metaphysics his generally been considered the most terrific to the indolent mind; but the clear and perspicuous reasoning of a Mirabaud, who has united the most profound argument, with the most fascinating eloquence, charm and instruct us at the same time. But it was not, to be expected that such doctrines as are contained in the System of Nature, would be advanced without meeting with some opposition from the superficial and bigoted metaphysicians, who feel an interest in upholding a system of delusion and superstition. No! certainly not, Their interest was threatened, and their *craft* in danger, and the consequence was, that the *Atheist* or *Disciple of Nature*, has been abused with every scurrilous epithet, "full of sound and fury, signifying nothing."

Atheism is stigmatized with having "opened a wide door for libertinism, destroying the social and moral compact; and striking a deadly blow at religion. It is asserted that the atheist, who by his opinions has deprived himself of the hope and consolation of a future life, has no motive for the practise of virtue, or to contribute to the well being of society. Deprived of a chimera which religion every where presents him, he wanders through the cheerless gloom of scepticism, regardless of the consequences of an abandoned life. Without a God, he acknowledges no benefactor; without divine laws, he knows no rule for the conduct of life, and submits to no law but his passions. An enemy to all social order, he spurns at human laws, and breaks through every barrier opposed to his wickedness." Under such colours is an atheist painted: a short digression must be suffered to examine this picture, and to disprove the assertions so sweepingly made.

I admit that atheism strikes a deadly blow at religion; because under the cloak of religion, mankind have been oppressed in all ages; but that it encourages libertinism, or destroys the "social and moral compact," I have yet to learn. In all organized governments, men are restrained from crime and compelled to submission by laws supposed to be made for the general benefit. These laws are the effect of the first formation of society for mutual preservation. Here then is a sufficient motive for the one as well as the other, to contribute to the well-being of society. The laws of Nature are the same in effect on the atheist and the religionist. If man be led captive by his passions, and gives himself to debauchery and voluptuousness, nature will punish him with bodily infirmities and a debilitated mind. If he be intemperate, she will shorten his days and bring him to the grave with the most poignant remorse. The fatal effects of his vicious propensities will fall upon his own head. A disturber of social order will live in continual fear of the vengeance of society, and that very fear is a more dreadful punishment than the just vengeance which perhaps he escapes. It renders life burdensome, and makes a man hateful to himself. Can men have stronger motives for the practise of virtue? The atheist is in full possession of these motives, and the religionist is most completely swayed by them, whatever may be his pretensions to others derived from religion. But we are assured he has other motives; more powerful incentives, in the promise of future rewards and punishments. This, like all other chimerical doctrines, cannot be maintained if we look at the general practise of mankind. Let us trace the effects of this doctrine, or rather let us examine the actions, conduct, and character of men professing it, and we shall see how little influence it has over them. The bulk of society believe they shall answer in a future life for the deeds done in the present. Nay, I hardly think one in a hundred thousand will say they doubt it. What then is its effect? With this dreadful sentence, *"Thou shalt go into everlasting punishment,"* continually sounded in their ears, do we not daily see the greatest enormities committed? Are not the most horrid crimes perpetrated in all parts of the world? The most vicious propensities and the most extravagant follies are almost indiscriminately gratified. Is not vice frequently triumphant, and virtue compelled to seek her own reward in retirement? The laws of society are broken by the most flagrant injustice, and the laws of nature outraged by the most shocking depravity. All this evil exists in nations believing themselves to be accountable beings after death. Where then are the beneficial effects arising, to mankind from the promulgation of this doctrine? Men who cannot be restrained from doing evil by human laws, have no dread of any other. Their whole lives and conduct confirm this. Others who live in submission to the laws of society, give themselves up to those vicious habits, (without fear of divine laws) which the law does not take cognizance of. Men, not wholly depraved, or not without the pale of society, generally respect the laws, and fear the bad opinion of others. Hence we observe, when interest or passion leads them into secret vices, they invariably play the hypocrite; and although they are aware of the denunciations of their God, whom they acknowledge is a witness to all their actions, while they preserve their fair fame they still persevere. In fact, they live as if they disbelieved in his existence; and yet the greatest criminal, the most depraved wretch, would shudder at being told there is no God. The atheist, as a man, is liable to commit the same crimes, and fall into the same vices as the believer; but because he is an atheist, is he a worse criminal than the other? In one respect, I conceive he is not so bad. He only acts in defiance of *human* laws,—he only offends men; the other infringes *both divine* and *human*;—he defies both God and man. Both are injurious to society and themselves, and both are actuated by the came motives.

Again we are told, that the well disposed part of mankind are rendered more virtuous, and the vicious less vicious by this doctrine. How are we to know that? If the virtuous man acts uprightly, does good to his fellow creatures, restrains his passions, and returns good for evil, experience teaches him it is his interest so to do. Those who are viciously disposed are only deterred from crime by penal laws. Societies cannot long exist, where evil has the ascendency. Without social laws, this would really be the case, notwithstanding the threats of an avenging God. If men were told they would not be answerable for the evil committed in this life to human laws, but that God would punish them after death, it is evident the human race would soon be exterminated. On the other hand, tell them their crimes will never be punished by God, or, in other words, there is no other God than NATURE, but that the laws of men will avenge the offences against society; so long as those laws are administered with justice and impartiality, so long will such society continue to improve. Hence it is evident that the system which will maintain order in society by itself, must be the best and most rational. A good government without religion would be more solid and lasting, and tend more to the preservation of mankind, than all the theocratical or ecclesiastical governments that ever the world was subject to.—Thus much for the opponents of atheism.

It has been asserted with a perverse obstinacy, by the advocates for the existence of a deity, that the SYSTEM OF NATURE was never written by the author whose name it bears.—It is granted that it was not published during his life: but that circumstance forms no reason why such a conclusion should be drawn. The persecutions which the atheists have endured, were a sufficient excuse for the work not appearing in any form during the life time of its venerable author. The Athenians sought to try Diagoras the Melian, for atheism; but he fled from Athens, and a price was offered for his head. Protagoras was banished from Athens, and his books burnt, because he ventured to assert, that he knew nothing of the gods. Stephen Dolet was burnt at Paris for atheism. Giordano Bruno was burnt by the Inquisitors in Italy. Lucilio Vanini was burnt at Thoulouse, through the kind offices of an Attorney-General. Bayle was under the necessity of fleeing to Holland. Casimio Liszynski was executed at Grodno;—and Akenhead at Edinborough. And the body of the eloquent and erudite Hume, was obliged to be watched many nights by his friends, lest it should be taken up by the fanatics, who considered him one of the greatest monsters of iniquity, because he did not happen to believe as they believed.—With these pictures of Christian persecution before his eyes, is it surprising that M. de Mirabaud should adopt the resolution of suffering the SYSTEM OF NATURE to appear as a posthumous work? That the same fate would have attended him, the most devout Christian will not undertake to deny.

However the sentiments of M. de Mirabaud may be condemned by the fanatics, all those who knew him bear the most brilliant testimony of his integrity, candour, and the soundness of his understanding; in a word, to his social virtues, and the innocence of his manners. He died universally regretted, at Paris, the twenty-fourth of June, 1760, in the eighty-sixth year of his age.

The following works, written by him at different periods, were never published:—*The Life of Jesus Christ. Impartial Reflections on the Gospel. The Morality of Nature. An Abridged History of the Priesthood; Ancient and Modern. The Opinions of the Ancients concerning the Jews.* A wretched mutilated edition of this last work was published at Amsterdam, in 1740, in two small volumes, under the title of *Miscellaneous Dissertations.*